Architecture After
Deleuze and Guattari

Deleuze and Guattari Encounters

Series Editor: Ian Buchanan, Director of the Institute for Social Transformation Research, University of Wollongong, Australia

Titles available in the series:

Cinema After Deleuze
Richard Rushton

Philosophy After Deleuze
Joe Hughes

Political Theory After Deleuze
Nathan Widder

Theology After Deleuze
Kristien Justaert

Music After Deleuze
Edward Campbell

Space After Deleuze
Arun Saldanha

Anarchism After Deleuze and Guattari
Chantelle Gray

Architecture After Deleuze and Guattari
Chris L. Smith

Architecture After Deleuze and Guattari

Chris L. Smith

BLOOMSBURY ACADEMIC
LONDON • NEW YORK • OXFORD • NEW DELHI • SYDNEY

BLOOMSBURY ACADEMIC
Bloomsbury Publishing Plc
50 Bedford Square, London, WC1B 3DP, UK
1385 Broadway, New York, NY 10018, USA
29 Earlsfort Terrace, Dublin 2, Ireland

BLOOMSBURY, BLOOMSBURY ACADEMIC and the Diana logo
are trademarks of Bloomsbury Publishing Plc

First published in Great Britain 2023
This paperback edition published in 2024

Copyright © Chris L. Smith, 2023

Chris L. Smith has asserted his right under the Copyright,
Designs and Patents Act, 1988, to be identified as Author of this work.

For legal purposes the Acknowledgements on p. xiv constitute
an extension of this copyright page.

Cover image: Jonathan Walker, 'Thirsty Wall',
The Bladders (2010). Courtesy of Jonathan Walker.

All rights reserved. No part of this publication may be reproduced or transmitted
in any form or by any means, electronic or mechanical, including photocopying,
recording, or any information storage or retrieval system, without prior
permission in writing from the publishers.

Bloomsbury Publishing Plc does not have any control over, or responsibility for,
any third-party websites referred to or in this book. All internet addresses given in this
book were correct at the time of going to press. The author and publisher regret any
inconvenience caused if addresses have changed or sites have ceased to exist,
but can accept no responsibility for any such changes.

A catalogue record for this book is available from the British Library.

A catalog record for this book is available from the Library of Congress.
Library of Congress Control Number: 2023939091.

ISBN: HB: 978-1-3501-6849-7
       PB: 978-1-3503-8058-5
       ePDF: 978-1-3501-6850-3
       eBook: 978-1-3501-6851-0

Series: Deleuze and Guattari Encounters

Typeset by Integra Software Services Pvt. Ltd.

To find out more about our authors and books visit www.bloomsbury.com
and sign up for our newsletters.

To Frida Etta.

Contents

List of figures	xi
Foreword	xiii
Acknowledgements	xiv
Preamble	1
Defenestration	1
Entwining	2
Schizo-culture	3
Milieu from within	5
In the wake	7
Part 1 'Sympathies'	
1 Folds	13
Relation	13
Concrescence	14
Perplication	16
Prehension	18
Embryologic Houses	19
Provocation	22
2 Geophilosophy	25
Oedipus	25
Anti-Oedipus	26
Earth	27
Territory	28
Colonization	29
Deterritorialization	30
Blue Slabs	31
3 Sense	37
Chaodyssey	37
Representation	38
A Logic of Sense	40
Frame	43

4	Assemblages	47
	Other spaces	47
	Sympathies	48
	Flagrant Délit	51
	Identification and distance	54
	Desire	55

Part 2 'Exploration'

5	Constructivism	59
	Proust	59
	The machine	60
	Engendering subjects	62
	Architectural machines	62
6	Transversality	67
	To eat and be eaten	67
	Transference and transversality	68
	Anti-oedipal transversality	70
	Veronese stone	71
	Intermingling	74
7	Schizoanalysis	77
	Landing a legion	77
	Delirium	78
	Schizoanalysis walks	79
	Dogs on leashes	81
	Blur	83
8	Transcendental empiricism	87
	Tokyo Paris	87
	Looming nightmares	88
	Transcendental empiricism	89
	Palais de Tokyo	92
	Erewhon	94

Part 3 'Experimentation'

9	Islands	97
	Invagination	97
	Desert islands	100

		One Man Sauna	101
		Paralogism of displacement	103
10	Micropolitics		107
		Politics	107
		Molarity	107
		Molecularity	110
		Cruising Pavilion	112
		Macropolitics	113
		Micropolics	115
		Cruising Labyrinth	116
11	War machines		121
		Hangar 12	121
		Political philosophy	122
		The State	123
		The war machine	124
		Zeitz Museum of Contemporary Art Africa	126
12	Ethico-aesthetics		131
		Lesbos and London	131
		Strange contraptions	132
		Chaosmosis	133
		Grafting	135
		Killing Architects	137

Part 4   'Minor architectures'

13	Syntheses		143
		Sub-representational	143
		Three syntheses	144
		Graphic arts	146
		Communicating Vessels	148
		Longhouse Roof Garden	148
14	Cosmic artisans		153
		Lightning Ridge	153
		Crystals	154
		Cosmic artisans	156
		Palacio de Congressos	158

15	New materialism	161
	Meat	161
	Matters of fact	163
	Hylomorphism	164
	Becoming-animal	166
	Becoming-architecture	167
16	Affect	171
	Dark precursors	171
	Affect	172
	Lightning Farm	176
	Wakes	177

Notes	179
Selected bibliography	217
Index	225

List of figures

0.0 *Cover image*
Jonathan Walker, 'Thirsty Wall', *The Bladders* (2010). Image courtesy of Jonathan Walker

0.1 Poster for 'schizo culture', a symposium organized by Sylvère Lotringer and John Rajchman for *Semiotext(e)* and held at Columbia University in New York, 13–16 November 1975. Image courtesy of Semiotext(e) — 9

1.1 'The Baroque House (an allegory)' from Gilles Deleuze, *Le Pli: Leibniz et le Baroque*, (Paris: Les Editions Minuit, 1988), 7. Image courtesy of Minuit — 18

1.2 Swarming Embryo-logics. Collage courtesy of Kieran Richards. Source image: Greg Lynn, Embryologic House, 1998. Courtesy of San Francisco Museum of Modern Art, Accessions Committee Fund, © Greg Lynn, photo: Don Ross — 23

2.1 Zaha Hadid, 'Blue Slabs' *The Peak* (1982–3). Image © Zaha Hadid Foundation — 35

3.1 Bernard Cache and Patrick Beaucé, Sans titre, *Objectile* (1998). Image courtesy of Bernard Cache — 45

4.1 Madelon Vriesendorp, *Flagrant Délit* (1975). Image courtesy of Madelon Vriesendorp — 56

5.1 Yaohua Wang, *Beijing House II* (2011). Image courtesy of Yaohua Wang, Preliminary Research Office — 65

6.1 Verona Arena, aerial panoramic view. Image © Andrey Khrobostov/Alamy Stock Photo — 75

7.1 Diller + Scofidio, *Blur Building* (2002). Photograph by Beat Widmer. Image courtesy of Diller Scofidio + Renfro — 86

8.1 Lacaton and Vassal, *Palais de Tokyo, site de creation contemporaine* (2012–14). Image © Philippe Ruault — 94

9.1 Justino Serralta and André Maisonnier, 'Modulor', from Le Corbusier, *Modulor 2: (Let the User Speak Next) Continuation of 'The Modulor' 1948*, (Basel: Birkhäuser, 2004 reprint), 53. Image courtesy of Birkhäuser — 99

9.2 Modulorbeat, *One Man Sauna* (2014). Image courtesy of Modulorbeat — 105

10.1	Mateos, Myrup, Perrault and Teyssou, *Cruising Pavilion* (2018). Image courtesy of James F. Lima	115
10.2	Andreas Angelidakis, 'Every Hole Is a Goal', Cruising Labyrinth, *Cruising Pavilion*. Image courtesy of Andreas Angelidakis	119
11.1	Heatherwick Studio, *Zeitz MOCAA*, (2017). Image © Iwan Baan	129
12.1	Megha Rajagopalan, Alison Killing, and Christo Buschek, Compound in the County of Shufu (25 August 2019), 'China Secretly Built a Vast New Infrastructure to Imprison Muslims', *BuzzFeed* news investigation part 1, 27 August 2020. Google Maps, 25 August 2019. Google Maps [online]. Accessed 27 May 2021	139
13.1	Vaughan Oliver's cover for Pixies, *Doolittle* (1989). Image © 4AD	147
13.2	Neil Spiller, Longhouse Roof Garden, *Communicating Vessels* (2021). Image courtesy of Neil Spiller	151
14.1	SelgasCano, *Palacio de Congressos*, Plasencia (2017). Image © Hiseo Suzuki	160
15.1	John Deakin, 'Portrait of Francis Bacon' (1952)	163
15.2	JR, '28 Millimeters: Women are Heroes', Action in Favela Morro da Providência, Rio de Janeiro, Brazil, 2008. Image courtesy of JR	169
16.1	Farah Aliza Badaruddin, *Lightning Farm* (2013). Image courtesy of Farah Aliza Badaruddin	178

Foreword

The impact of the philosophy of Gilles Deleuze and Félix Guattari on twenty-first-century architecture is substantive. In the discourses of renowned architecture schools, in the explorations of architectural theorists, and in the refrains of architects, concepts derived from the individual and collaborative work of Deleuze and Guattari are reiterated ad nauseam. This nexus of philosophy and architecture does not however have the character of nausea; it operates more like a productive delirium. It is a delirium that fosters the critique and creation of cities, urban environments, buildings, public places, incursions, installations and landscapes. And it is a delirium that unleashes the practice and processes of architecture itself.

The four parts of *Architecture After Deleuze and Guattari* trace the entwining of the philosophy with contemporary architecture and explore how the relation between the two generates that which is new. Part One 'Sympathies' considers the key concepts that fostered early connections between Deleuze and Guattari's philosophy and communities of architects and architectural theorists. Part Two 'Exploration' focuses on how the 'regimes of thought' deployed by Deleuze and Guattari, their modus operandi, come to operate in architectural theory and design. Part Three 'Experimentation' considers the political philosophy of Deleuze and Guattari and the architectural experiments such thought might foster. And Part Four 'Minor Architectures' focuses on how the discipline of architecture continues to transform in the wake of Deleuze and Guattari. Each of the four parts is configured of four chapters. The sixteen chapters that constitute this book introduce the reader to key conceptual investments of the philosopher and the psychoanalyst and each negotiates this conceptual territory via a work of architecture. Though this organization was helpful in constructing the book, each chapter that constitutes *Architecture After Deleuze and Guattari* might be read singularly, sequentially or in any order – fast on a train or slow on a riverbank. The aim is not to exhaust all the points of connection between the philosophy and architecture but rather to focus on the production and experimentation that constitutes an architecture now inextricable from the conceptual territories of Deleuze and Guattari.

Acknowledgements

Sincere thanks to Ross Anderson for listening to the embryonic ideas of each chapter over the course of a pandemic and across a table of decent wine. And thanks, as ever, to Andrew Ballantyne who continues to demonstrate the closest of attention to the architectural pleasures of Deleuze and Guattari.

Thanks to Ian Buchanan for his ongoing support of a community of scholars exploring the shared territories of architecture and philosophy. To Liza Thompson, Lisa Goodrum, and Suzie Nash, my editors at Bloomsbury, for your enthusiasm for the work and for never letting a deadline pass unnoticed.

This book owes a debt to the many people who have read and commented on sections of this work or whose insights have helped frame my thinking: To Simone Brott for input on the early intersections. To Jason Dibbs for helping to affirm a queer phylum in architecture's pre-modernity. To Charlie Drozynski and Laurence Kimmel for introducing me to some intense dark places. To Hélène Frichot for prompting considerable thought on the ecologies of architecture and for productively challenging my more phenomenological of affections. To Farzaneh Haghighi and Nikolina Bobic for helping me think about architecture and micropolitics with greater clarity. To Melinda Gaughwin for prompting thought on post-Foucault digital futures. To Matthew Gill on all matters military, at the edge of a war machine. To Shervin Jivani for insights into the complexities of Guattari's metamodels. To Marko Jobst for thoughts on islands and for introductions. To Matthew Mindrup and Lilian Chee for raising questions of proximity and intensity in assemblages. To Michael Mossman, for a walk in a park with cygnets that helped me think about the colonizations of thought and the question of Country in the place I think of as home. To André Radman and Robert A. Gorny for encouraging a focused exploration of architecture's technologies and Bernard Steigler's forethoughts and legacy. To Kieran Richards for introducing me to all things cosmic and for assistance with all things graphic. To Alfredo Ramos for help with the sites of Rio and the bodies thereof. To Suely Rolnik for insights into Guattari, schizoanalysis, ecology and the throat as the 'nest of the word/soul'. To Neil Spiller for prompting consideration of the most joyously wayward architectural processes.

Heartfelt thanks to those who endured the pandemic lockdown not only with me but also with this manuscript. Thanks, and love to Jana Scheffler, Lynda Smith, Shirley Scanes, Byron Smith, Terence Triantafyllou, Liam Smith, Theo Triantafyllou and Luke Kirchner-Scheffler. It's hard to feel isolated in the company of so many adorable others.

Preamble

Defenestration

Let's commence at an end of a kind. On 4 November 1995 Gilles Deleuze would take flight by passing through a third-floor window of his apartment on Avenue Niel, Paris. The story is commonly recounted in geo-historic terms: the fixing of a date and a pinpointing of a location. Many recounts also engage a term that directly implicates architecture: *defenestration*.[1] When Deleuze took to a window, his collaborator Félix Guattari had already departed. Guattari had died of a heart attack on 29 August 1992 at La Borde, the psychiatric clinic in which he spent most of his working life. Though 'departed' is not how Deleuze framed the event. Deleuze would suggest someone never completely departs, and of Guattari's passing he notes 'gestures and glances that still reach us, that still come to us'.[2] It is these gestures and glances, of both Deleuze and Guattari, that I wish to explore. In the decades that followed Deleuze's defenestration and Guattari's heart failure, the relation between architecture and Deleuze and Guattari has become an internalized rhythm to which architecture itself swoons.[3] This book will explore the entanglements of the philosophy of Deleuze and Guattari with the discipline of architecture, introducing some of the most prominent intersections, some of the subversive deployments and some of the subtle incursions. This book will also note Deleuze and Guattari's own intense and fleeting engagements with architecture. This is not so difficult a task. Despite referring to architecture as 'the first of the arts' Deleuze and Guattari would only rarely address it directly.[4] Architecture was always there across Deleuze's oeuvre, but it never quite received the same focused attention he directed towards painting, cinema and literature. This focus would accord with Deleuze's lifestyle. He rarely ventured beyond his apartment and the neighbouring arrondissement, and one imagines this accounts for his preference for the arts which he could access without having to travel.[5] Guattari, on the other hand, ventured further across the planet and spent longer on the topic of architecture. Guattari had founded *Le Centre d'Études, de Recherchés et de Formation Institutionnelles* (CERFI), with a number of urbanists and philosophers of the city/state, and would later explore the *favelas* of Brazil and the 'machinic eros' of Japanese architecture.[6] For Deleuze, however, travel could be either in *extensity* or in *intensity* and he notes even 'flights can happen on the spot'.[7] I imagine this phrase summates Deleuze's engagement with architecture and might also gesture to a definition of defenestration.

Entwining

The key proposition – or provocation – of this book is that twenty-first-century architecture is DeleuzoGuattarian. Such a proposition will come as no shock to those who have noticed that when architects today speak of *assemblage* they speak of something quite different to what it was prior to Deleuze and Guattari. And the 'machine' architects once spoke of too is now very different. More *machinic* than machine. Today 'function' is less utilitarian and has become a question of *what something does*, and what it does is never merely instrumental. Our conceptions of the bodies we house too are now substantially altered, as is our sense of architecture's own subjectivities. And the way we speak of form and matter and the logical ordering of one and the other has turned. Our materialisms are now new. Our politics has become both macro and micro, and the word 'ethics' is now spoken of as intimate to aesthetics. The *affective* dimension of architecture is now so often discussed as to imply it was ever operative, and the *ecologies* of mental landscapes and the *decolonization* of thought occur to us today as architectural projects. All these changes owe a debt to the philosopher and the psychoanalyst. But how is it that philosophical ideas and modes of operation have come to configure our conception of architecture, modify architectural processes and transform the worlds we construct and that construct us?

In a crowded and smoky seminar room at the Université de Paris 8 in Vincennes early in 1978, Deleuze would note, '[I]t is less we who have the ideas than the ideas which are affirmed in us.'[8] I am interested in the question of what ideas are affirmed in twenty-first-century architecture, and how architecture operates in the wake of Deleuze and Guattari. But I want to start simply. I want to start with a brief recount of a few of the early key conduits between Deleuze, Guattari and architecture. It's a tentative start. It is tentative because the infusion of the concepts and assemblages that can be regarded as having passed through; having been reinvigorated; or having emerged within the discourses of Deleuze, Guattari and the collaborations of Deleuze and Guattari, are impossible to quantify. The depth of the infusion, that is, the fusions of the concepts with architectural logics and processes, is equally difficult to summate. It is easy to trace direct references to Deleuze and Guattari in the writing that accompanies the graphic, textual and built outputs of architecture. But references can serve many purposes: sometimes opportunistic, sometimes obfuscatory, sometimes elaborative and productive. Sometimes a mixture or all these things; and between the text and the built manifestation of architecture runs a complex and chaotic tensor. Though it is an almost achievable task to trace specific readers of the discourse of Deleuze and Guattari, reading neither implies impact nor specifies understanding and thus this task would also seem trivial. The literary critic Gillian Beer summarized the issue when exploring the influence of the work of Charles Darwin upon nineteenth-century fiction, by making the point: 'Who had read what does not fix limits.'[9] I imagine 'who has written what', 'who has spoken what' and 'who has built what' whilst citing Deleuze and Guattari might also fail to fix limits. But with this caveat in mind, I precede tentatively in this 'Preamble' with what is perhaps the most fleeting summary ever generated to document the *pre* to the architecture *after* Deleuze and Guattari.

Schizo-culture

Architectural audiences were introduced to the work of Deleuze and then the collaborations of Deleuze and Guattari in multiple ways, but it is also the case that architects introduced Deleuze and Guattari. Sanford Kwinter told Simone Brott, 'The American reception was essentially driven by architects.'[10] In a paper titled 'Deleuze and "The Intercessors"' (2010) Brott details the earliest points of contact in the late 1970s.[11] The account focuses on *Anti-Oedipus* (1972), the New York–based art scene, the journals *Semiotext(e)* and *October*, and the publication series *Zone*. John Rajchman and Sylvère Lotringer are singled out as protagonists. Rajchman and Lotringer were the founding editors of *Semiotext(e)* and published some of the earliest English translations of Deleuze. Rajchman recounts, he 'was really interested in Deleuze as a philosopher and also as an interesting way of doing philosophy in an academic context and so I wanted to extract for my own purposes a model and architecture happened to provide an opportunity to do this'.[12] Whilst the first issues of *Semiotext(e)* were focused on semiotics, in November 1975 the journal would run a symposium at Columbia University on 'schizo-culture' (Figure 0.1). Deleuze would present a paper on *rhizomes* that would later become the first chapter of *Milles Plateaux* (1980), and Guattari would present on the politics of signification.[13] *Semiotext(e)* released their *Anti-Oedipus* edition in 1977 and schizoanalysis would again become the focus of a 1978 issue.[14] Lotringer's Columbia seminar students included Michel Feher, Rajchman, Kwinter, Hal Foster and Manuel De Landa. These five would become art and architectural theorists. Foster would publish *The Anti-Aesthetic: Essays on Postmodern Culture* (1983) fixated on the complex relation between postmodernity and capitalism and later would come to edit *October*. De Landa would emerge as an *enfant terrible* and self-styled street philosopher of DeleuzoGuattarian thought within the architecture department at Columbia.

On the other side of the Atlantic there was at least one architect amongst the crowd and in the smoke of Deleuze's Vincennes seminars: Bernard Cache.[15] Cache's *Terre meuble* (1983) manuscript would be the first extensive work of architectural theory that located Deleuze's philosophy as central to architectural concerns. In turn, Deleuze would write in a footnote to *The Fold: Leibniz and the Baroque* (1988) that Cache's unpublished 'book seems essential to any theory of the fold'[16] and suggest Cache's notion of 'inflection' relates to what Gottfried Wilhelm Leibniz called an 'ambiguous sign' and what Deleuze himself would call 'an intrinsic singularity'.[17] Deleuze would also draw on Cache in defining an *objectile* as a contemporary conception of the technical object,[18] and in describing the moment where stretching becomes the tearing of matter under force.[19] The *Terre meuble* manuscript would be taken up by MIT Press, edited by Michael A. Speaks and published in 1995 as *Earth Moves: The Furnishing of Territories*. Cache's book would be dedicated to Deleuze and would form part of the 'Writing Architecture' series concerned with architectural theory and its relation to (primarily) post-linguistic-turn philosophy. The title page of the book would suggest the work was '[a] project of the Anyone Corporation' and here marks an important moment, where the work of the philosopher and psychoanalyst intersects again with the North American architectural theory machine.

It was Lotringer's Columbia university students that would form the publishing company *Zone*. The first output of *Zone (1/2)* turned to the question of *The Contemporary City* (1986). *Zone 1/2* thrust architecture and DeleuzoGuattarian thought into proximity. The city of *Zone 1/2* is a city that emerges in concert with materials, its people and stone, and 'a specific *power to affect*'.[20] A power that was 'the very fabric of the city's consistency'. Feher and Kwinter's introduction to the issue is also an introduction to Deleuze and Guattari.[21] They commence the book with the image of a carp formed in intimate connection with the reeds and rocks and water of its pond.[22] The image recalls Deleuze and Guattari's wasp and orchid description of the 'double-becoming' of bodies and worlds.[23] Feher and Kwinter discuss a 'power' outside the cause/effect logic, and indeed outside any dualistic divisions, and deferrals are made to 'affect', 'diagram', 'milieu', and that which was 'at once abstract and pragmatic' and 'both history and geography'. The book included chapters by Paul Virilio, Kwinter, Eric Alliez, Jonathon Crary, De Landa, Anne Querrien (with whom Guattari had founded CERFI), and the architect and design theorist Christopher Alexander.[24] Deleuze and Guattari offer a chapter 'City/State' focused on the 'reciprocal presupposition' of the city and the State. The work was drawn from the *Mille Plateaux* manuscript and was translated by Brian Massumi for the forthcoming University of Minnesota Press English edition.[25] The final sections of *Zone 1/2* were given over to a 'Zone Questionnaire' of only three questions related to mutations in the structure and operations of the 'new' city.[26] Artists, theorists and architects were involved. Guattari responded with a short piece asserting, 'The main function of the city as a node is the production of subjectivity.'[27] Many of the respondents to the questionnaire however seemed not to appreciate the philosophical shift that was occurring. When Kenneth Frampton was asked: 'what are the new "lines of force" of this new (postmodern, postindustrial, etc.) city?', he could only muster a reference to Michel Foucault: 'As to our "lines of force," what can one say? As far as I am concerned, it would be better to speak of boundaries of resistance or perhaps the hope embodied in them.'[28] But at least he addressed the question. Peter Cook, Raimund Abraham and Rosemarie Haag Bletter had little to say, and Daniel Libeskind offered aphorisms. Peter Eisenman would defer to an attack on anthropocentrism. In his tag line Eisenman is described as 'presently collaborating with the French philosopher Jacques Derrida to design a segment of Bernard Tschumi's Parc La Villette', but in 1986 the relationship was souring.[29] It was clear that as Eisenman's problems with Derrida were peaking, Deleuze and Guattari would offer a radical alternative for architecture. What was less clear was whether or not architecture was ready for it. Rem Koolhaas responded to the questionnaire with a curious series of musings on New York, Rome, Berlin, Nevada and clowns. He notes a nostalgia for 'that whole histrionic branch of the profession that leapt like clowns, pathetic yet courageous, from one cliff to the next, flapping with inadequate wings but enjoying at least the free fall of speculation'.[30]

Koolhaas's nostalgia for speculative leaps may have found some satiety in the formation of the Anyone Corporation, a New York–based architecture 'think-tank' formed by some of architecture's most 'in' crowd. Cynthia Davidson would front the organization. Where Eisenman had long explored structures that bound linguistics and architecture, introduced figures such as Noam Chomsky and Derrida to architectural audiences, and been key to the relation between philosophical and architectural deconstruction; Davidson would do much to introduce post-structuralism to an emerging avant-garde of architecturally inclined intellectuals. (Or where they intellectually inclined architects?) A series of conferences and publications commenced with the prefix 'Any'. The annual conference began in 1991 with *Anyone* and was followed by *Anywhere, Anyway, Anyplace, Anywise, Anybody, Anyhow, Anytime, Anymore* and *Anything*. The conferences would bring together philosophers, art, architectural and cultural theorists such as Sylviane Agacinski, Beatriz Colomina, Hubert Damisch, Derrida, Elizabeth Grosz, Fredric Jameson, Kojin Karatani, Rosalind Krauss, Massumi and Anthony Vidler; with architects such as Ben van Berkel, Caroline Bos, Elizabeth Diller, Eisenman, Zaha Hadid, Jacques Herzog, Tao Ho, Steven Holl, Osamu Ishiyama, Arata Isozaki, Romi Khosla, Koolhaas, Libeskind, Greg Lynn, Rafael Moneo, Enrique Norten, Jean Nouvel, Wolf Prix, Hani Rashid, Ignasi de Solà-Morales, Tschumi and Alejandro Zaera-Polo.

Milieu from within

In France, architects did seem to wonder what all the fuss was about. But they weren't alone. When Deleuze and Guattari published their last collaborative work, *What Is Philosophy?* (1991), it would make the bestseller lists, largely because people thought the book might answer the question the title posed. The philosopher Jean-Jacques Lecercle would recount a story of a métro ride observing middle-class pin-striped workers reading the book on their way to the office, looking quizzical.[31]

If *Zone* and the Anyone Corporation had brought the philosophy of Deleuze and Guattari into proximity with architecture, the 1992 book *Semiotext(e)/Architecture* edited and designed by Hraztan Zeitlian would be a deployment of the logics in graphic form. This was an important moment of aesthetic collusion. We are told early in the book, 'These projects are not based on the notion of singular, hierarchical ordering ideas, but on the interaction of multiple organizing systems.'[32] The same can be said for the book overall. This huge book is a subversion of conventions and systems of organization and operates as a fractious clanging of typography, image and information in a manner that was both perplexing and seductive. Even the page numbering system challenges the hierarchy of numeric orders. Guattari's contribution 'Deterritorialized' commences on page 122G5 and finishes on 121G4. The book featured projects by Asymptote, Maria Brooke Dammkoehler, Neil Denari, Diller and Scofidio, Catherine Ingraham, Eve Laure Moros and Margo Chase, Morphosis, Bob Somol and Linda Polla, and Lebbeus Woods; and a conversation between Jesse Reiser and Libeskind that makes *Finnegan's Wake* seem an easy read. Brott would note, for the discipline of architecture of the early 1990s, concepts such as rhizome, fold, the smooth and the striated 'should not be viewed so much as having been "appropriated" by architects, but as elements that enabled the transformation of the milieu from within'.[33] *Semiotext(e)/Architecture* is a raw and frenetic glimpse of a discipline somewhere between flux and reflux.

Deleuze's book most closely concerned with architecture emerged shortly after the English edition of *A Thousand Plateaus* (1987 [1980]) and would be translated into English as *The Fold: Leibniz and the Baroque* (1993 [1988]). Special issues of the UK journal *AD* would focus on themes drawn from this well. Greg Lynn's 1993 *AD* editorial to the edition *Folding in Architecture* proposed that an architecture would be a subject of its environment and formed by forces at once Baroque and piercingly contemporary.[34] A new avant-garde of digitally savvy architects was forming on the philosophical edge of a DeleuzoGuattarian wave. The fluidities of the digital and the collapse of representation in alignments of computer-aided design and manufacturing processes made the alliance seem a very smooth move. Almost as soon as it rose however the *formal* implications of an architecture that was aligning itself with a philosophy that questioned the privileging of form came to look suspicious. Rajchman would introduce a piece by Paul Virilio in *Art Forum* in 1995 calling for novel practices of urbanism with the words: 'ONCE THERE WAS AN "AVANT-GARDE." It started in Europe, and came to the United States; some say it got "stolen."'[35] It was obviously an era where the titles of journal papers tended to say it all. In 1998 Speaks noted the same tension in a paper titled 'It's Out There ... The Formal Limits of the American Avant-Garde'.[36] Lynn had failed sneak in prior to the limit being reached, publishing his book *Animate Form* in 1999.

By the end of the 1990s *Any* magazine under Davidson's lead had published two issues which explicitly engaged with DeleuzoGuattarian concepts: *The Virtual House* (1997), guest-edited by Rajchman, and *Diagram Work* (1998), guest-edited by van Berkel. Davidson was also on the editorial board of the MIT Press series *Writing Architecture* that, following Cache's *Earth Moves*, would publish three of the earliest texts introducing the work of Deleuze and Guattari to non-philosophers in a manner that sought not to convert the concepts into architectural form but rather to explicate and experiment: Rajchman's *Constructions* (1998) and *The Deleuze Connections* (2000), and Elizabeth Grosz's *Architecture from the Outside* (2001). These books were fundamental in taking Deleuze and Guattari's work outside philosophy, prompting a critical engagement whilst fostering the architectural impulse for exploration and experimentation. Significant in this respect too was the journal *Assemblage* edited by K. Michael Hays and Alicia Kennedy. This journal operated from 1986 to 2000 and would bathe in the milieu of architectural theory and post-structural philosophy over forty-one issues. Looking back through editions is a little like watching tides turn. The advisory and editorial board of *Assemblage* would overlap with the contributor list of *Any* and *Zone*, and the journal would likewise be published by MIT Press. The shift from deconstruction towards Deleuze and Guattari coincided with Robert McAnulty's appointment to the editorial board for volumes 17–41. The end of the decade was, however, demarcated by editorials reading more like familial disputes than either architectural or philosophical encounters.

These were heady days for architectural theory. The turn of the twenty-first century saw philosophers offering Deleuze and Guattari c/o architecture and architects and architectural theorists offering Deleuze and Guattari c/o philosophy. The cover of the final issue of *Assemblage* (41,2000) featured an image of characters reading the journal on the New York subway, looking less quizzical than they should have been.[37]

In the wake

In *What Is Philosophy?* we are told a 'spider's web contains "a very subtle portrait of the fly," which serves as its counterpoint'.³⁸ The relation between architecture and philosophy in the twenty-first century is similarly poised. One shadows the other in complex ways. Architecture is sometimes entwined with philosophy, sometimes entranced, sometimes prey. Likewise, philosophy feeds off architecture, weaves its structures, and choreographs its movements. And in the wake of Deleuze and Guattari architecture offers philosophy something well worth savouring. Though the early decades of the twenty-first century are harder to see with the same sort of clarity with which we see the later decades of the twentieth, one can discern a 'subtle portrait' in the intermingling of the philosophy of Deleuze and Guattari and architecture.

In recent decades a few key texts arrived to further elucidate the relation. Andrew Ballantyne's engaging *Deleuze and Guattari for Architects* (2007) ran with the 'experimentalist side of their thinking' and brought both a range of concepts and a sense of the mode of operation of Deleuze and Guattari to architectural audiences.³⁹ Brott's *Architecture for a Free Subjectivity: Deleuze and Guattari at the Horizon of the Real* (2011) is a sober and exacting exploration of the idea of subjectivity that concerns both philosophers and architects alike. Jill Stoner's *Toward a Minor Architecture* (2012) draws directly from the literary engagements of Deleuze and Guattari to critique some of the most prevalent habits of architectural thought. There has of late also been those who have turned a critical eye to the *use* of Deleuze and Guattari in architecture, turning heads towards the manner by which the philosophy might be engaged for purposes at odds with the philosophical privileging. Douglas Spencer's *The Architecture of Neoliberalism* (2016) would be an example of this type of analysis. Edited books too have traced the logics of Deleuze and Guattari with a variety of inflections: Lecercle and Franciose Kral's *Architecture and Philosophy: New Perspectives on the Work of Arakawa and Madeline Gins* (2010) turned to the work of the Japanese architect and the North American beat-poet with a DeleuzoGuattarian gaze. Ballantyne and my *Architecture in the Space Flows* (2012) sought to reinvigorate the idea of flow and flux under the impetus of Deleuze and Guattari. Hélène Frichot and Stephen Loo's *Deleuze and Architecture* (2013), Graham Livesey's three volume set *Deleuze and Guattari on Architecture* (2015), Andrej Radman and Heidi Sohn's *Critical and Clinical Cartographies* (2017), Constantin V. Boundas and Vana Tentokali's *Architectural and Urban Reflections after Deleuze and Guattari* (2018), and Marko Jobst and Frichot's *Architectural Affects after Deleuze and Guattari* (2020) together chart a rich web of explorations between philosophy, architectural theory and critique. Though these works often focus on key concepts drawn from the philosophy, collectively they constitute less a singular project than a rhizome of investments that continue to proliferate and launch forth to the extent that 'what persists is an ethos which perhaps no longer even needs to be signed by Deleuze', as Frichot and Loo note.⁴⁰ The rise of *new materialism* and the *affective turn* to which architecture is central can be traced through these collective works, signed or not. We can trace, too, the growing recognition of Guattari's independent scholarship. Works such as Peg Rawes's *Relational Architectural Ecologies* (2013), my own *Bare Architecture: A schizoanalysis* (2017), Hélène Frichot's *Creative Ecologies: Theorizing the Practice of Architecture* (2018) and Radman's recent *Ecologies of Architecture: Essays on Territorialisation* (2022) owe a particular debt to the activism and ecological impulses of Guattari and are early explorations of the political relation between the territories of architecture, the colonizations of thought and architecture's capacity to decolonize.

Journals of architecture and architectural theory continue to proliferate references to the work of Deleuze and Guattari and more importantly express the philosophy in the modus operandi of the architects and authors they feature. The long-standing UK journal *AD* continues a tradition of finding the thought of the philosopher and psychoanalyst at architecture's contemporary edges. *Architecture and Culture, arq: Architecture Research Quarterly, Architectural Theory Review, Places, Grey Room, Log,* and *Architecture Philosophy* and online offerings like *The Charnel-House* have become outlets where both explicit and implicit references flutter in novel associations. I tend to think of *Footprint*, the journal of TU Delft, as the staider offspring of *Assemblage*. It is notable for its rigorous pursuit of intersections between philosophy and the contemporary techniques and technologies of architecture, and remains overtly mindful of the DeleuzoGuattarian legacy. Though charting their own territories, all these journals are also attempts to make less subtle the relation between architecture and philosophy, giving footnotes so much of the thought that vibrates quietly through the architecture of the twenty-first century.

Architecture, for its part, continues to thread between the abstractions of thought and the no-less-abstract concrete of the geo-historic real. In this regard it operates like the spider that scurries through Deleuze and Guattari's oeuvre, a constructor of 'subtle portraits' and weaver of traits. Sometimes architecture intersects directly with the philosophy that flies about it, sometimes it strains to find connection and sometimes it tears in the wake of the philosophy it ensnares. 'From the virtual it actualizes it draws a potential that it appropriates', as Deleuze and Guattari note of the relation between a *state of affairs* and a *thing*, suggesting that even '[t]he most closed system still has a thread that rises toward the virtual, and down which the spider descends'.[41] This book, *Architecture After Deleuze and Guattari*, is a sort of *flyderspy* web, a mutant manifestation of both the philosophy of Deleuze and Guattari and contemporary architecture. Sometimes noting connections, sometimes announcing them, sometimes stitching them, sometimes sliding along them. The intent is not to pin down a singular line of logic as to how an architect might engage with the philosophy of Deleuze and Guattari, nor is the intent to summate the value of the philosophy to architecture as a discipline. Rather, the aim is to activate the 'subtle portraits' of one discipline in the other and to encourage an exploration and experimentation that might continue to disrupt disciplinary habits and norms.

Figure 0.1 Poster for 'schizo culture', a symposium organized by Sylvère Lotringer and John Rajchman for *Semiotext(e)* and held at Columbia University in New York, 13–16 November 1975. Image courtesy of Semiotext(e).

Part One

'Sympathies'

Part One focuses on early moments of concurrency between Gilles Deleuze and Félix Guattari's philosophy and late twentieth-century architecture. For Deleuze the effective transformation of a given field, a discipline or a regime of thought requires the connection of deterritorialized elements in mutually supportive and productive ways, a 'sympathy'.[1] The following four chapters explore four concepts that come to constitute the cosmos of Deleuze and Guattari: territories, universes, fluxes and phyla. It is not coincidental that these concepts operated as entrance points or *sympathies* by which architecture would quickly (and at times brazenly) access the philosophy of Deleuze and Guattari and establish resonance.

1

Folds

Relation

The relation between philosophy and architecture is complex. The migration of ideas from one discipline to another is rarely a simple matter of uni-directional appropriation, and it is equally rare that a concept that emerges in one discipline is adopted seamlessly by another. Gilles Deleuze's concept of *the fold* is an example of the complexities of conceptual migration. The concept was derived from a late sixteenth-century architectural invention that accorded with a contemporaneous philosophical intervention and found itself (re)deployed in late twentieth-century architecture under the aegis of a reclamation. The story of the fold is a story of interwoven conceptual and concrete sympathies over centuries. The moment I am particularly interested in is the 1990s where the conceptual and expressive capacities of the fold reached a particular zenith. Soon after the initial French publication of Deleuze's *Le pli: Leibniz et le baroque* (1988) came a series of architectural explications: In 1991 Judy Geib and Sabu Kohso's edited text *Unfolding Frankfurt* emerged, under the auspices of Peter Eisenman and Cynthia Davidson, and was seen to mark a shift in architecture's philosophical focus from the deconstruction of Jacques Derrida to the post-structuralism of Deleuze and Guattari. John Rajchman's contribution to the book, a chapter titled 'Perplications' focused on 'cross-foldings'. In 1993 Eisenman's former employee Greg Lynn edited a special issue of the journal *AD (Architectural Design)* titled *Folding in Architecture*. It contained Lynn's essay 'Architectural Curvilinearity: The Folded, the Pliant and the Supple'. This essay was republished in Lynn's *Folds, Bodies & Blobs: Collected Essays* (1998), where the subtitle for the paper became the title proper. It was a mild change, but it marked a shift of a kind. By 1996, when *ANY Magazine* published Lynn's essay 'Blobs, or Why Tectonics is Square and Topology is Groovy', the fold had started to serve a different purpose, and by 1997 Lynn had embarked on his *Embryologic Houses©* project. In the closing year of the decade, indeed the closing year of the twentieth century, Lynn's book *Animate FORM* (1999) focused squarely on the use of animation and motion graphic software for design. The fold was liberated from Baroque architecture, enfolded into philosophy and then at once *perplicated* and *parametricised* into the architecture of the emerging digital era.

In order to explain the dynamic relation between architecture and the philosophy of Deleuze and Félix Guattari in the early 1990s, it may be helpful to turn to one of the key concerns of Deleuze's text, *The Fold*. The concern is how elements – both thoughts and things – might find themselves interwoven. This focus on the manner by which the rich complexity of 'thoughts', 'things', indeed 'anythings' come into relation was an oeuvre-long pursuit of Deleuze. He had for many years been hopping onto the back of his predecessor philosophers and 'delivering their monstrous offspring' in an act that was itself a folding of a kind.[1] In *The Fold* Deleuze would mount the Franco-German philosopher of the Enlightenment Gottfried Wilhelm Leibniz. Leibniz was both a philosopher and a mathematician, of folds, pleats, curves and the undulations of surfaces. And in recent times might even be thought of as a 'philosopher of habitat and ecology'.[2] *The Fold* is an explication of Leibniz that concerns itself in diagrammatic ways with the architecture of the Baroque. Deleuze would deliver the concept of 'the fold' as an offspring that at once owes a debt to Leibniz and the Baroque but also to a long line of philosophers. This offspring would also bear the characteristics of Deleuze's own conceptual progeny and the thoughts that had populated his collaborative work with Guattari. The fold was thus a monstrous offspring, and yet its Baroque architectural roots made it familiar to architectural theorists. There is always an intimate relation between antecedents and progeny that which comes before and that which comes after, but the very idea of the fold reminds us, temporality is a complex matter. *The Fold* was published in 1988, 8 years after *A Thousand Plateaus* (1980). There is thus a definite sense by which architecture's early engagement with the philosophy of Deleuze was itself 'after Deleuze and Guattari'.

Concrescence

On the question of how something comes into being, Deleuze would turn to what he identifies as a 'secret society' of philosophers of which Leibniz and Alfred North Whitehead, the British twentieth-century philosopher and mathematician, were prominent. For Deleuze, Leibniz and Whitehead would concur (if two can concur two centuries apart) on the idea of the individual as 'a "concrescence" of elements'.[3] The term 'concrescence' was drawn from Whitehead's magnum opus *Process and Reality: An Essay in Cosmology* (1927–8) but it might just as easily have come from Leibniz's *La Monadologie* (1714), for the term refers to processes by which an entity might manifest from existing elements that themselves might be without form.[4] Leibniz's *Monadologie* is an account of a type of base unit – an indivisible 'simple substance' from which all things and thoughts might pertain. He calls this simple substance the *monad*. Leibniz's monad might be thought of as the common denominator of all that has drive, and life, and thought – a type of pre-programmed substance 'endowed with perception and appetite' that acts in resonance with the cosmos.[5] *La Monadologie* would resolve the old rationalisms of order with the dynamisms of the universe itself. In disposing of Cartesian axioms Leibniz arrives at a complex but comprehensive account of god, the universe, substance and matter. The monad compacts the dualism of mind and body into a singular substance that is at once both. It is both, but it is also unitary, connected and relational. Leibniz notes, the monad is an 'inter-communication of things' whereby 'every body feels the effect of all that takes place in the universe'.[6] The soul would be a dominant monad, god another (even more dominant, and the only monad without a body). In reference to the soul Leibniz refers to a folding. It is the only direct reference to a fold in his *Monadologie*. He suggests the soul 'cannot all at once unroll everything that is enfolded in it, for its complexity is infinite'.[7] Whilst the soul might constitute a single endless pleating every other 'portion of matter' of which the cosmos of *Monadologie* is composed might be thought of in terms of multiplicities best summated in terms that serve as collective pronouns: gardens, branches, ponds, masses and swarms. For Leibniz,

> §67. Each portion of matter may be conceived as like a garden full of plants and like a pond full of fishes. But each branch of every plant, each member of every animal, each drop of its liquid parts is also some such garden or pond.
>
> §68. And though the earth and the air which are between the plants of the garden, or the water which is between the fish of the pond, be neither plant nor fish; yet they also contain plants and fishes, but mostly so minute as to be imperceptible to us.
>
> §69. Thus there is nothing fallow, nothing sterile, nothing dead in the universe, no chaos, no confusion save in appearance, somewhat as it might appear to be in a pond at a distance, in which one would see a confused movement and, as it were, a swarming of fish in the pond, without separately distinguishing the fish themselves.

It may have been this image that led Voltaire to ask, 'Can you really believe that a drop of urine is an infinity of monads, and that each of these has ideas, however obscure, of the universe as a whole?'[8] I imagine Deleuze would answer 'yes', as he would come to define an element as 'everything that has parts and is a part'.[9] Bertrand Russell was gentler than Voltaire in his critique of Leibniz, describing the monadology as 'a kind of fantastic fairy tale, coherent perhaps, but wholly arbitrary'.[10] Deleuze however had a penchant for such cosmologies. It is also what drew him to the work of Antonin Artaud, Wilhelm Reich and Whitehead and led him to describe both organic and inorganic life as a 'fish-hatchery'.[11]

Whitehead would note, '[M]onads are best conceived as generalizations of contemporary notions of mentality' and qualify the statement in suggesting, 'contemporary notions of physical bodies only enter into his [Leibniz's] philosophy subordinately and derivatively'.[12] Of this I'm not so certain. Whilst Whitehead is accurate in suggesting that for Leibniz the image of fish and pond might serve analogical purposes allowing him to conceive of the relation between gods, thought and things, I suspect the animals swarming in *La Monadologie* are not only analogical. These animals swarm as the *corps vivant* that animates Leibniz's thought, they are a mobile concrete real, and just because the fish and the pond might at times stand in place of concepts in thought, it is only because the fish and the concept, and the pond and thought, share characteristics: a sympathy, as Deleuze might call it.[13] It would be the concurrence of the conceptual and the concrete that would draw Deleuze to

Leibniz. The relation between the swarming organic and inorganic masses outside of ourselves, along with the swarming of organic and inorganic that we rally to conceive of ourselves, comes to be a key point of concrescence in *The Fold*. For Deleuze, 'two kinds of force, two kinds of folds – masses and organisms – are strictly coextensive'.[14] Deleuze would wrangle Leibniz's animals into a post-Darwinian ecology collapsing the centuries that interceded *La Monadologie* and *The Fold*:

> The first fly contains the seeds of all flies to come, each being called in its turn to unfold its own parts at the right time. And when an organism dies, it does not really vanish, but folds in upon itself, abruptly involuting into the again newly dormant seed by skipping all intermediate stages. The simplest way of stating the point is by saying that to unfold is to increase, to grow; whereas to fold is to diminish, to reduce, 'to withdraw into the recesses of a world.'[15]

Deleuze quotes Leibniz's correspondence with Antoine Arnauld, the French theologian, mathematician and philosopher, when referring to 'the recesses of the world' and the correspondence makes it clear such 'recesses' are the inorganic materials of the earth that also possess soul.[16] The fold thus comes to be thought of as *the ever-manifesting relation of selves and worlds*. But selves here should not be thought of as singular. They too are swarms. We too are swarms – swarms within swarms. The swarming selves that unfold a sense of themselves into the world, and the swarm beyond selves that might be enfolded in a withdraw from the outside. The art of living thus becomes something like the complex concrescence of a fluid context with a viscous self. The art theorist Simon O'Sullivan states it clearly in noting, 'subjectivity for Deleuze-Leibniz is a question of mastery – a kind of Nietzschean mastery – over the swarm of one's being'.[17] (And three can concur two or three centuries apart.)

Perplication

Baroque architecture helped Deleuze express the idea of concrescence, in both diagrammatic and affective forms. In a diagrammatic way a simple line drawing of 'The Baroque House (an allegory) would assist[18] (see Figure 1.1). The simple image conveys a structure of two levels. The base is a horizontally oriented occupied space, of rooms and windows, a door and some odd, rounded entrance steps. The upper unoccupied chamber is enclosed by a '"diversified by folds" as if it were a living dermis'.[19] We know this not from the drawing but because Deleuze tells us so. The drawing itself just has some vague wavy lines rising in the upper space. Between the lower and upper level there are five openings that might correspond with the five senses of those bodies that might occupy the lower level. This is to emphasize the idea that though the upper level cannot be physically accessed, it can be perceived. The image is basic and far from a detailed architectural section. A better image for the affective qualities of the Baroque, and a far more evocative image for an architectural reader, might be Borromini's San Carlo alle Quattro Fontane (1641).[20] Though the lower level here is without openings, when we stand in the church and gaze into the deep and complex coffering of arches and ovals soaring above, there is a clear sense that what we are incurring is a pulse, a palpitation of a kind, between an intense and joyous space we cannot physically access and the cold of the marble alter we hold to steady ourselves as we peer upwards. There is also a sense that we might be able to occupy the upper level, and if we did, we might be able to look down upon the spaces, pews and people of the level below, as if peering into a pond teeming with life. We have here ideas of connection and interpenetration between realms and the sense of existence itself stretching between what Deleuze refers to as 'the pleats of matter and the folds in the soul'.[21]

But this easy slide from seventeenth-century architecture to the conceptual matter of *The Fold* comes with a caution or two. Deleuze was not turning to the Baroque in the manner an architectural historian might. His passing references to architecture are invoked without much explication of form, structure or construction, nor what architects might imagine to be defining stylistic characteristics. The translator of the English edition of *The Fold*, Tom Conley, would note Deleuze's 'Baroque thus does not comprise what we associate with Bernini, Borromini, or Le Brun'.[22] However, for the same reasons I suspected the animals swarming in *La Monadologie* were not only analogical, I suspect the architecture populating *The Fold* is not only allegorical. Deleuze invokes the architecture not to embed a story or a moral, but rather in order to define the mechanisms, the outcomes and affects of Baroque thought. This is because the architecture makes what Leibniz calls the 'inter-communication of things' both operable and palpable. And Deleuze starts *The Fold* with the simple assertion: 'The Baroque refers not to an essence but to an operative function, to a trait.'[23] It is the intense modulations of thoughts and things, the organic and inorganic, and the body and soul, that lead Deleuze to refer to the Baroque as 'l'art informel par excellence'[24] and he suggests, 'The new status of the object no longer refers its condition to a spatial mould – in other words, to a relation of form-matter – but to a temporal modulation that implies as much the beginnings of a continuous variation of matter as a continuous development of form.'[25] In this sense the pulse of San Carlo has both frequency and wavelength; it is a temporal modulation from which the space and material of the church unfold. And this leads to a second caution for the architectural reader: The 'concrete' of architecture Deleuze evokes is neither as hard, nor fixed, nor stable as we might imagine. For Deleuze the Baroque is mobile, sweeping and surging, and the matter of the Baroque itself is 'porous' and 'spongy' and even the veins of marble ripple like 'a lake that teems with fish'.[26] In *The Fold* movements in materiality became an image for motions in thought. No, this is not correct. A better way of saying it would be: *Movement as the continuous variation of matter becomes the operation of both concrete materiality* and *thought*. In this regard, it was not Leibniz's monad, in and of itself, to which Deleuze's attention is drawn, but rather the movement of the monad – or more particularly, the fold as the *nomadology* of a monadology:

> [I]n the Baroque the soul entertains a complex relation with the body. Forever indissociable from the body, it discovers a vertiginous animality that gets it tangled in the pleats of matter, but also an organic or cerebral humanity (the degree of development) that allows it to rise up, and that will make it ascend over all other folds.[27]

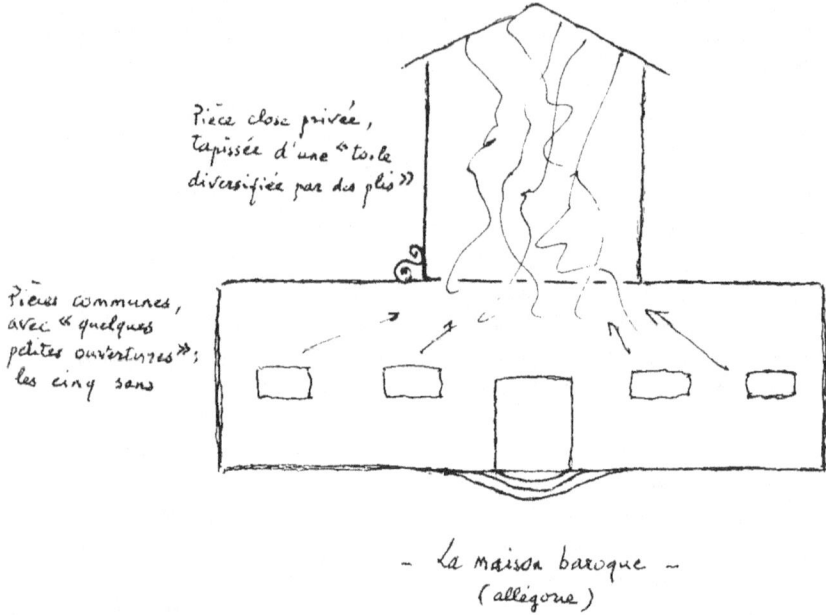

Figure 1.1 'The Baroque House (an allegory)' from Gilles Deleuze, *Le Pli: Leibniz et le Baroque*, (Paris: Les Editions Minuit, 1988), 7. Image courtesy of Minuit.

Prehension

In *The Fold* the fish of Leibniz's pond become the fish of evolutionary time, a continuous material evolution in ecological concert with the pond itself. It would be Whitehead who would offer Deleuze a concept for the relations between the fish and the swarm and the plants and the pond that would negate the need for any central organizer or necessary hierarchy of impulses, whilst still imagining forms of organization and relation.[28] For Whitehead was a cosmologist for whom elements do not just haphazardly come together (connect) or collide (conjugate): instead, they *prehend*. The word 'prehend' shares a base (or datum) with words such as 'apprehend' and 'comprehend', words which suggest the concurrency of a physical holding and an intellectual grasping. The point being, there is little need to unpick the 'forever indissociable' manner we might hold or grasp that which is formed and that which is unformed. The tail of a monkey prehends the branch when it encircles it, just as I prehend the back of the pew in front, in those rare moments when I rise in a church and just as I prehend the movement of the monkey when my thoughts brachiate between San Carlo's branching pendentives and the foliage of the coffered dome above. Prehension is thus a concept equally applicable to things and thoughts – *anythings*, including the swarm we might think of as our-self. Deleuze would reiterate Whitehead's own definition of prehension when in *The Fold* he writes:[29]

Prehension is individual unity. Everything prehends its antecedents and its concomitants and, by degrees, prehends a world. The eye is a prehension of light. Living beings prehend water, soil, carbon, and salts. At a given moment the pyramid prehends Napoleon's soldiers (forty centuries are contemplating us), and inversely.[30]

Thus, one might say Baroque architecture prehended Leibniz, Whitehead, Deleuze and the secret society of philosophers, and the Baroque prehended the monad and the fold, that was in turn prehended again at a given moment in late twentieth-century architecture. There is in *The Fold* a concurrence of thought on the concrescence of selves across a multiplicity of disciplines centuries apart. In the case of the fold, four centuries are contemplating us, and inversely.

Embryologic Houses

An event such as the enfolding of the fold back into architecture would involve what Whitehead calls a 'nexus of actual entities' and what Deleuze refers to as a 'nexus of prehensions'.[31] Architecture in the early 1990s was an interweaving of conceptual and digital entities in an aesthetic concurrency. The theorists of architecture at this time were well prepared to grasp the conceptual content of Deleuze's fold. Sylvère Lotringer's Columbia university students had formed *Zone* and the first output was the volume dedicated to *The Contemporary City* (1986). *Zone 1/2* brought architecture and DeleuzoGuattarian thought into proximity, and the key ground for the sympathy was forming. The city of *Zone 1/2* is a city that emerges in concert with materials, its people and stone, and 'a specific *power to affect*'.[32] Architecture had long cast itself in the relation between body and world and yet the simplistic causalities of a logic that suggests *either* we make architecture *or* it makes us were due for an overhaul. Michel Feher and Sanford Kwinter commence the book with the image of a carp that is formed in intimate connection with the reeds and rocks and water of its pond: 'a carp that must be *apprehended* as a certain power to affect and be affected by the world'.[33] The image was referenced back to Chinese art, but this carp could just as easily have leapt from Leibniz's pond.

Architecture in the early 1990s was also grappling with, if not grasping, the smoother relations that digital technology was beginning to foster. The clunky disconnect between a modern architect (who designs) and a builder (who builds) was becoming a smoother relation as technology started to incorporate material parameters into the design process, and designers and fabricators would come to concur in shared software. This processual smoothness found an aesthetic correlate in slicker geometries. The jarring and disjunctive forms of deconstruction were seen to have run their course, and more immediate material connections and spatial fluidities were called for. Even architects well known for their clashing elements were celebrating the potential of digital technologies to smooth relations. In an interview with Frank Gehry, Lynn asked when he had started using computers. Gehry replies, 'The first thing we did was the Fish in Barcelona.' The shimmering gold fish high above the beach was completed in 1992. Gehry notes, 'My initial design was a wave, and then, pretty soon it became a fish.'³⁴ Just as emerging digital technologies made the relation between design and construction a simpler translation, so too would it be a simpler matter for a pond to become a fish and inversely a fish a pond.

To explore the enfolding of the concept of the fold into architecture in more detail, it might be helpful to turn to the hatching of the logics in Lynn's *Embryologic Houses*© project (1997–2001) (Figure 1.2). This project is less the 'vertigenous animality' Deleuze had ascribed to the Baroque than the eggs of an obese frog, but it is an animality, nevertheless. Lynn had been a prolific contributor to the discourse that introduced architects to Deleuze and Guattari's work, and the *Embryologic Houses*© project was a significant deployment of the philosophy. But it wasn't just that. It was also a significant cross-folding of conceptual and technological content in the frame of late capitalism. That is to say, Lynn attempted both to enfold the philosophy of Deleuze and Guattari into the technological field of architecture and simultaneously to unfold the architecture into a commercial marketplace. Lynn introduces the project:

> *The Embryologic Houses*© can be described as a strategy for the invention of domestic space that engages contemporary issues of brand identity and variation, customisation and continuity, flexible manufacturing and assembly and, most importantly, an unapologetic aesthetics of undulating surfaces rendered vividly in iridescent and opalescent colours.³⁵

Though the *Embryologic Houses*© may be like the eggs of a frog, this animal was thoroughly house-trained, domesticated into the logic of late capitalism: branded, patented, copyrighted. How much of this is tongue-in-cheek is hard to say, but it does make one imagine the project operates as both capitalism and schizophrenia – the capitalism of 'brand identity', 'customisation' and 'manufacturing'; the schizophrenia of 'variation', the 'flexible' and 'undulating'. And one can only assume that to unapologetically render 'vividly in iridescent and opalescent colours' must be to go completely *rococo*. The description of the *Embryologic Houses*© is, however, not nearly as foreign to the philosophy of the fold as we might imagine. In his paper 'Architectural Curvilinearity' (1993) Lynn notes, 'If there is a single effect produced in architecture by folding, it will be the ability to integrate unrelated elements within a continuous mixture.'³⁶ The *Embryologic Houses*© would become an example of how such a folding might operate in a digital era, enfolding forces from contexts and deforming, contorting, and adapting in response. Each house would have 'a unique shape and size while conforming to a fixed number of components and fabrication operations'.³⁷ Each house was composed of six 'house system components': an 'egg matrix', a 'voltaic surface treatment', a 'shred surface treatment', a structural matrix, a 'glass base' and a 'site plan' in the form of a responsive garden. Each system related to one another, and much like a monad, Lynn tells us 'a change in any individual panel or strut is transmitted throughout every element in the whole'.³⁸ Whilst such a description of the relation between components of a building would describe almost *every* building, what Lynn is spruiking is a smoother relation that taps into the evolving capacity of architecture to transmit that which was being generated via computer-aided design into computer-aided manufacturing. Here components had certain homogenous capacities; these components were part of a system that itself had a range of capacities, systems related one to the other algorithmically, and as we might push one element all others heterogeneously flex. This is to say, as Deleuze does, 'an element is the given, the "datum" of another element that prehends it'.³⁹

The *Embryologic Houses*© would demonstrate what Lynn had called a few years earlier the quality of a folded mixture. He suggests, 'A folded mixture is neither homogenous, like whipped cream, nor fragmented, liked chopped nuts, but smooth and heterogenous.'⁴⁰ This architecture represented a move thus from a type of tectonic construction of fixed components towards an architecture which might be a material *whole* responsive to both contexts and its own componentry. It would be the architect's role to establish the preconditions and parameters of response, shifting emphasis from the form of the architecture towards the parameters that might generate it, change it, deform it. Like the Baroque, it would thus be more *l'informe* than form. And when form comes to be less dominant in the equation, other parameters come to be expressed. Deleuze had noted, 'Matter that reveals its texture becomes raw material, just as form that reveals its folds becomes force. In the Baroque the coupling of material-force is what replaces matter and form.'⁴¹ For Lynn too, force comes to replace form as a generative logic. He came to herald an architecture that might better be thought as the material implication of forces and a design process that might fixate upon 'variable deformation', 'discontinuous development' and the 'internalisation of heretofore external forces'.⁴² His terminology was a direct import from the work of Deleuze and Guattari, and Deleuze's concept of the fold would be a particularly valuable tool. For Lynn, a philosopher who might find in architecture's own history a smoother relation between body and world was a gift. *The Fold offered architecture an image of the connection between thoughts and things, between selves and masses, and particularly the organic and inorganic world.* The architecture would adopt logics more often associated with animality, vertiginous or not.

But the fold also offered an aesthetic: an undulating surface that was as much about philosophical production as it was about architectural technologies. Lynn was pursuing a fluid geometry that allowed a 'curving away from deconstructivism'.⁴³ The supple, pliant geometries deployed in the *Embryologic Houses*© derive from the mathematics of Leibniz. Calculus would be 'part and parcel of the shift from whole number and fractional dimensions to formal and material sensibilities of the infinitesimal' and an 'intensive whole'.⁴⁴ Whilst calculus becomes a simple matter in digital operations, material parameters and the interplay between geometry and materiality were also important for Lynn. He derives inspiration from the offspring of Leibniz's mathematics: the shifting surfaces and flexible grids of the early twentieth-century biologist D'Arcy Wentworth Thompson, and the undulating topologies and morphogenetic landscapes of the mid twentieth-century mathematician René Thom. Both provided evidence for the physical and material possibilities (and impediments) for species transformations. Thompson would demonstrate what Lynn calls 'variable deformation' and 'discontinuous development' and illustrates the potential by transforming one type of fish into another by shifts in a grid.⁴⁵ Lynn appropriates the deformable geometry of Thompson as the best expression of the flow of force upon matter.⁴⁶ Lynn's forces, like those of Thompson and Thom, are *anexact*: unencumbered by immutable conditions of formal relation and pragmatic in their effect. The fluid geometry of the *Embryologic Houses*© has the ability to register particular localized transformations. This is what

Lynn calls the 'internalisation of heretofore external forces'[47] and the 'blob space' developed by Lynn is an attempt to enfold forces of dynamic urban contexts onto and into architectural objects.[48] Each of the *Embryologic Houses©* operates its own internal characteristics, whilst flexing to the masses of force that might impact upon it from the outside. Thompson's remark that a form is 'a diagram of forces' might be a hallmark of Lynn's *Embryologic Houses©* project and to all architectural *blobs* that come thereafter.[49] The idea is particularly Baroque: that matter may be organized into a body by the action of forces that are themselves without form.

Provocation

Lynn's depiction of the manner by which architecture might fold would be similar to the image we have of the enfolding of philosophy into architecture. For Rajchman, speaking in reference to *The Fold*, 'it wasn't so much that Deleuze was good at architecture or that there was some connection between the two but that architecture appeared as its own development in which they could absorb Deleuze in their own interesting way'.[50] The relation operates much like a folded mixture, 'smooth and heterogenous', somewhere between cream and crushed nuts. *The Fold* was enfolded first as a logic for architectural interdisciplinarity, and the near boundless movement of thought into and out of architecture in the late twentieth century. Second, as an image for the new digital technology that allowed the fluid and supple surface to be apprehended, manipulated and ultimately fabricated. The fold also became an image for a temporal collapse. Just as the pyramids prehended Napoleon, the Baroque prehended the digital turn in architecture. And that very image of the Baroque as a relation between the unformed and the formed became an image for architectural design processes. A type of scaffold that runs between the concrete materiality of architecture (the lower level of San Carlo) and its transformative capacities (up into the dome). But there remains more to the fold that might yet be exercised.

Deleuze's reminder that 'masses and organisms – are strictly coextensive' is for contemporary architecture, a provocation.[51] It is a provocation for architecture in the wake of Deleuze and Guattari to confront that question of the art of living. The capacities of architecture to mediate the swarm beyond selves, to enfold and withdraw from the outside 'into the recesses of the world', is realized in Lynn's *Embryologic Houses©*. Lynn develops a system whereby the inorganic forces of architecture and a dynamic urban context deform and distort, bending like reeds in a pond. However, the *Embryologic Houses©*, like much of the architecture that emerges in the parametric era, remains a little like a fish-hatchery without fish. That is, it's all mass and no organism. That the capacities of architecture to unfold a swarm of selves and to deform the sense selves have of themselves is yet to be explored. That is – in simple terms – it would seem that whilst we have endowed architecture with a type of vitality, we have simultaneously neglected to construct inhabitants. For the living things, the humans and other domesticated animals that might move about, through and occupy architecture are also a swarm, a continuously varying and a deformable material. What Deleuze had apprehended in the Baroque is yet to be prehended in the architecture of parametricism and The *Embryologic Houses©* are yet to truly spawn. This unmined intensity, in the wake of Deleuze and Guattari, is noted by Deleuze in the early pages of *The Fold*:

> Here the figure of the lake or pond acquires a new meaning, since the pond – and the marble tile – no longer refer to elastic waves that swim through them like inorganic folds, but to fish that inhabit them like organic folds. And in life itself the inner sites contained are even more hatcheries full of other fish: a 'swarm'. Inorganic folds of sites move between two organic folds. For Leibniz, as for the Baroque the principles of reason are veritable cries: Not everything is fish, but fish are teeming everywhere …[52]

Figure 1.2 Swarming Embryo-logics. Collage courtesy of Kieran Richards. Source image: Greg Lynn, Embryologic House, 1998. Courtesy of San Francisco Museum of Modern Art, Accessions Committee Fund, © Greg Lynn, photo: Don Ross.

2

Geophilosophy

Oedipus

Placing architecture in an oedipal frame is a habit for the discipline. Each generation of architects, each successive movement, is cast as killing off one portion of its past whilst making love to another. It was a habit invoked by the architectural historian and theorist Beatriz Colomina in an editorial published in the journal *Assemblage* in 1996.[1] 'Much of the history of architecture is a family history', she writes, 'with its rival generations, incestuous relationships, long-kept secrets, inheritances, resentments, jealousies, and a multitude of deep-set pathologies.'[2] The journal *Assemblage* was itself born from two 'role models', *Oppositions* and *October*, and operated from 1986 till 2000, which I think makes it *generation y*.[3] The journal was a serious investment in the architectural theory that had blossomed in that period and had been an important site seeding the shift from deconstruction to DeleuzoGuattarian post-structuralism. But the journal also sprouted psychoanalysis and Colomina's editorial would cast the architect Greg Lynn as a young Oedipus and note the shame that should befall those who seek to kill off forefathers. The editorial was provocatively titled 'At Home with His Parents'. Colomina writes of Lynn:

> Indeed, he never left home. A protege of [Peter] Eisenman, he lightly pretends to criticize him but dutifully submitted his review to Eisenman for approval before sending it to *Assemblage*. It reminds me of that new generation of Italian and Spanish men who are staying at home with their parents into their twenties and even thirties. If you never leave home, you only ever criticize your parents while clinging to them and eating their pasta.[4]

Whilst no elaboration is made about the habits of Italian and Spanish men of 'that new generation', Colomina is unrestrained in charting the many faults of Lynn. The critique comes in the wake of Lynn's 'pseudoreview', published in the preceding edition of *Assemblage*.[5] Lynn's review focused on the Columbia University colloquium *Origins of the Avant-Garde in America* (1996) and the Museum of Modern Art's *Light Construction* exhibition (1996).[6] At stake was a position on architectural history, the question of how much respect should be shown to architecture's avant-garde and, more pointedly, what Lynn saw as the questionable habit of 'revising the history of modernism as source material for the present'.[7] Whilst Lynn is concerned that the major figures of modernism were being opportunistically rebirthed into contemporary discourse, he was not immune to conflating the history of architecture with pre-modern psychoanalytic tropes. He would divide the 'preeminent architectural theorists of the United States'[8] who attended the colloquium into 'generations' in order to demonstrate what he called the 'institutional paternity' at stake.[9] Lynn summates an exchange between the architect Phillip Johnson and the theorist Jeffrey Kipnis with the phrase 'Hey Dad, can I borrow the car?'[10] Colomina, along with K. Michael Hays, a founding editor of *Assemblage*, was described as representative of a 'middle generation' with tendencies 'to gravitate toward canonical modern heroes' and 'to recover radical and critical cultural practices out of the failed strategies of modernism'.[11] It is no wonder that Colomina responded to the critique. In many respects, however, the bigger issue here has less to do with a commitment to a modernist avant-garde than the commitment to a pre-modern discursive and critical strategy that reduces cultural complexity to crude psychoanalytic accounts of daddies, mummies and an Oedipus or two. In this regard, both Colomina and Lynn seem to be at home on the same couch.

Anti-Oedipus

Early in their first collaborative text *Anti-Oedipus: Capitalism and Schizophrenia* (1972) Gilles Deleuze and Félix Guattari suggest, 'A schizophrenic out for a walk is a better model than a neurotic lying on the analyst's couch. A breath of fresh air, a relationship with the outside world.'[12] But *Anti-Oedipus* is not only an attack on the traditions of psychoanalysis and the centrality of oedipal theory. The book is an attack on structures, laws and habits of all kinds. It is *anti-oedipal* in the sense that the text is against, is *anti* to, all unquestioned habits of thought that regulate the flows of desire and which reinforce any singular form of subjectivity.[13] Oedipal theory is seen as a particularly noxious example of a habit of thought by which a subject came to be entrapped and by which abhorrent desires and associated subjectivities were pathologized. 'It is the fate of all of us, perhaps, to direct our first sexual impulse towards our mother and our first hatred and our first murderous wish against our father,' Sigmund Freud wrote (obviously with more than Italian and Spanish men in mind).[14] For Freud the myth of Oedipus became a law of primordial longings to which all people were subject and the base from which he would construct elaborate theories aimed at understanding our inner world. The word 'understanding' though may be as problematic as the word 'perhaps'. Understanding may have been Freud's aim, but the outcome and effect of the theory was a comprehensive system of shame and judgement cast over the desires, behaviours and thoughts of 'all of us, perhaps'. Deleuze and Guattari were to describe oedipal theory as a 'grotesque error' that channelled desire into closed narratives of loss and anxiety and that came with a capacity to generate 'internal suffering'.[15]

Earth

The incitement of *Anti-Oedipus* is to leave habitual codifications and simplistic narratives that might be used to organize the complexities of life and instead to enter the intense and intimate outside world. This is framed by Deleuze and Guattari as 'the schizo's own way of rediscovering the earth'.[16] Posing an 'outside world' as an antidote to 'internal suffering' is to suggest geography is in direct relation to subjectivity. In *Anti-Oedipus* the earth, territory and landscape become intimately bound with systems of logic and thought itself. To put it simply, the idea is that *where we are* cannot be dissociated from *who we are*. Someone on an analyst's couch is an analysand bound to any number of diagnostic labels; they are a narcissist, a fetishist, a masochist, an Oedipus, an Electra. That same someone wandering the street is a pedestrian; when they wander the countryside, they are a rambler, and when they wander across landscapes, a wayfarer. A subject can be many things in many places. Such an idea comes as no shock to architects. It is a much-repeated refrain in architecture that architects construct not only alternate worlds but in doing so, also the people that occupy them. The nexus of geo-historic realism – the concrete of our buildings, cities, and landscapes – alongside the construction of subjectivities has always been a fundamental concern of architectural theory.[17] This concern made an early adoption of Deleuze and Guattari's collaborative project a simpler matter. The interweaving of interior senses of self and an exterior that is no less intimate underpins their *geophilosophy*. This shared fixation was the subject of Deleuze and Guattari's first collaborative text, *Anti-Oedipus*, and it flowed through all that were to come.

One of the key reasons the outside world offers opportunities for a productive merge with the internal is that the two are already connected and attuned. For Deleuze and Guattari both are a landscape. In *What Is Philosophy?* (1991) they write, 'Mental landscapes do not change haphazardly through the ages: a mountain had to rise here or a river to flow by there again recently for the ground, now dry and flat, to have a particular appearance and texture.'[18] At a first glance one might imagine that such an idea is metaphorical. It's not. *It is not that the territories of geography and the texture of thought are brought together by Deleuze and Guattari, but rather that these things already are.* The slow rumble of a mountain, the surge of waves, the pulsing of tides, the flow of rivers through seasons and across time were not only about the ever-flowing field of the exterior but were also a quality of thought itself. An unanswered question rumbles, a good idea pulses and the calmest thought trickles: *Panta Rhei* as Heraclitus observed.[19] When Deleuze and Guattari refer to 'the schizo's own way of rediscovering the earth' they are referring to the capacity to engage with an earth that is already replete – a full, throbbing, spinning, drifting, material intensity where everything is already connected as a geography of things and thoughts. They suggest, 'The earth is not one element among others but rather brings together all the elements within a single embrace.'[20]

Deleuze and Guattari offer this earth as a remedy to primordial longings and fears. When you go out for a walk, passing your weight from foot to foot at about 5 kilometres per hour, the earth under your feet swivels about a shifting axis anywhere between

0 and 460 metres per second, depending where on the planet you ramble. The sun doesn't rise or set; the earth itself turns. In this hemisphere, on this autumn day, the sun is set low, and clouds are forming. But it's fast becoming winter, and this earth orbits the sun at about 30 kilometres per second. There's little that is circular about the revolution. The centre is, as the philosopher of science Michel Serres says, 'itself adrift'.[21] The sun about which this earth orbits is one of an estimated 100,000 million stars that dance through a universe of an estimated 100,000 million galaxies. It is less the case that we wander *on* the earth, but rather that we wander *with* it through a cosmos without centre. It is hard to be neurotic in such an embrace. None of this earth revolves around you and it has zero to do with a celestial mummy or daddy. Take a breath.

Territory

For Deleuze and Guattari, '[s]ubject and object give a poor approximation of thought. Thinking is neither a line drawn between subject and object nor a revolving of one around the other. Rather, thinking takes place in the relationship of territory and the earth'.[22] The suggestion is that thought itself circulates between the heaving, drifting intensity of the earth and the codification systems, the *territory*, extracted from it. We can think of this idea of territory quite simply by thinking about human history. Over the earth (*terre*) that 'is itself adrift' we commenced a programme of classification that extracts territory (*territoire*) from it. Human histories demarcate borders and boundaries, continents, countries, nations, realms, empires and eras. Such demarcations have been extracted from the chaos of the earth. A tectonic shift, a mountain range or a violent ocean might be invoked to demarcate an edge of a continent. The ever-changing course of a river might become a property border, a left bank and a right. From the flow of time an era might be extracted to be thought of as a period of planetary existence. Thought itself relies on similarly codified systems. Language is such a system. From the raw intensity of sound, we extract words and phrasing in order to speak of the earth, to communicate with others and to order thoughts. A language is a territory of sound, just as a border is a territory of earth. There is no necessary problem with territory; with thinking about borders and boundaries, nations, realms, empires, and eras; or with the territories of language, except when we start to imagine that there is a grand or god-given truth behind such systems of order. As was the case with oedipal theory, the real problem for thought is when we allow the codifications (the classifications, generalizations, demarcations) to 'rise' and become unquestioned habits of thought. Deleuze and Guattari remind us that we configure and speak of the world in certain ways not because there is any big truth to these ways, but 'because it's nice to talk like everybody else, to say the sun rises, when everybody knows it's only a manner of speaking'.[23]

When a system of codification is allowed to *transcend* and comes to denote all the possibilities for what a people or a place must be, or may do, we make a gross logical error.[24] The tides about Hong Kong Island rose and fell long before the Sui Seung Yan people came to occupy the banks.[25] Their very name suggests as much, translating as 'those born of water'. And the waters of this harbour and sea shifted long before the historians of the Han Dynasty first recorded the early incursions that demarcated this land a homeland. The mountainous island itself barely flinched when the opportunistic British 'secured' the territory under an opium haze. And the stars above shone no less brightly as capitalism made love to lingering local deities, and Feng-shui principles found themselves lodged deep in skyscrapers. The island has been framed as a territory, a colony, a new territory, a special administrative region, and a system in a one-country-two-system bind and is currently being tightly embraced by a fatherland. The waters which gave birth to it all continue to rise and fall despite the territorial status of the island. But it is easy to forget that which comes first: the earth that precedes territory. For Deleuze and Guattari, when systems of territory are mistaken for eternal truths, suffering ensues. Borders and boundaries, nations, realms, empires, and eras that come to imagine themselves fixed and stable and connected to immovable logics and the order of the universe routinely enact cruelties. And there's little crueller than the embrace of a fatherland and laws written in a mother tongue. Even those born of water now live in the shadow of skyscrapers and Beijing. 'There or here, it's the same thing.' Deleuze and Guattari write, 'Oedipus is always colonization pursued by other means, it is the interior colony, and we shall see that even here at home, where we Europeans are concerned, it is our intimate colonial education.'[26]

Colonization

When Deleuze and Guattari come to refer to colonial education as 'intimate' it is because it is *internalized* as unquestioned habit. Our school libraries are riddled with accounts of the earth that reduce material intensity and cultural complexity to crude colonial summaries, and we took such accounts to be truths. We came to place ourselves in these stories: as inheritors of conquering civilizations; as the offspring of empires; as colonists, pilgrims and patriots; or as survivors of incursion; as displaced; as refugee. It was as if we found ourselves on these library shelves, Dewey decimalized. Such histories and their demarcations became part of how we ourselves identified, how our very identities were formed. *The colonizations of the earth are intimately contiguous with the colonization of thought and the construction of subjectivities.* (The 900 of History almost imperceptibly becomes the 910 of geography and the 920 of biography on a library shelf.) *As we extract territory from the chaos of the Earth, so too are we territorialized.* The term 'territorialization' is derived from Lacanian psychoanalysis to refer to the imprint of maternal nurture and nourishment on the libido of the infant, formed by organ-orifice connections.[27] For Jacques Lacan this process extracts the infant from the material immediacy of what he called 'the Real'. The Real might be thought of as the stage where the infant makes no differentiation between themselves, their parents, bedding and nursery walls. At this moment, all and everything is connected as unmediated material intensity. From this moment, however, the infant commences a project of demarcation and classification. I am *x*, not *y*. These are my lips; those are your nipples. This is the territory of me; this is the territory of my room. This system of division and differentiation is subject-formation or what Lacan called 'territorialization'. Again, the problem is not that psychoanalysis formulated readings for the manners by which we come into being; it is that such readings transcended and become axioms for infants to fulfil, measures to be met, percentiles to be delivered. An 'A' for your history report on this or that British colony. A 'C+' for Mandarin. Territorialization equals colonization.

According to Eugène Holland, for Deleuze and Guattari the notion of territorialization functions as 'a kind of hinge term to connect Marx and Freud, to articulate the concepts of libido and labour-power'.[28] But the concept also functions as a hinge between land and thought – what would come to be referred to as *geophilosophy*. Holland maintains that Deleuze and Guattari 'rewrite the process Marx called "primitive accumulation" in terms of territorialization'.[29] Put simply, for Karl Marx the idea of primitive accumulation was the fallacy that wealth, property and power were held by those who had been witty enough to accumulate it. Marx suggests that 'primitive accumulation plays in political economy about the same part as original sin in theology. [...] preached to us in the defence of property'.[30] Both political economy and theology serve to instate a political order as if it were pre-given – as if the order were fixed, eternal and connected to capital 'T' truths. As if the order preceded (or pre-seeded) the earth. Such an order serves conservative purposes in perpetuating the idea that there is some cosmological or god-given reason as to why some have (land, homes, wealth, real-estate in heaven) and some have not. Colonialism comes to be the imposition of an order over those David Harvey refers to as the 'landless proletariat' – those that are framed as being without.[31] Such systems of order seek to disempower subjects and pathologize societies. For Deleuze and Guattari thoughts and desires are colonized as much as the earth is. And thus, in the same breath, we can speak of the terror of territories and territorialization. Or, likewise, we can choose to retreat into our libraries, theologies, economies and political orders: 'Such is neurosis, the displacement of the limit, in order to create a little colonial world of one's own.'[32]

Deterritorialization

Anti-Oedipus offers a means of escape, not surprisingly called *deterritorialization*. This escape is both a departure and a return. Deterritorialization is a departure from the codes and classifications, regimes of thought and over-bearing logics that have colonized our thinking. It is to depart the couch and the colony and take '[a] breath of fresh air'.[33] But deterritorialization is also a return. It is a return to the earth and to unmediated material intensities. In this regard Deleuze and Guattari's engagements with both Marx and Freud are joyously opportunistic. When they turn to the accounts of labour-power and the libido they are not completely terrified but rather fascinated by what is liberated in such accounts. Marx gives an account of labour that heaves with the capacity to revolt. Freud gives us an account of the libido that is wild and roaming. Deleuze and Guattari's idea of deterritorialization owes both a debt. It is the idea that that which is territorialized might be liberated from habitual classifications and returned to more fluid possibilities. A labourer might join a free association of producers. A libido might come to lodge itself in acts of ecological care. It is deterritorialization that is enacted when elements that are habitually classified in one manner escape the classification: to down tools, to get off the couch. This is a departure. And it is deterritorialization that occurs when elements which were once considered the domains of separate territories come back together: labour power and the libido, Marx and Freud, land and thought, a revolution. This is a return. And indeed, why Deleuze and Guattari summate, 'The earth is the primitive, savage unity of desire and production.'[34]

For Deleuze and Guattari it is geography that 'wrests history from the cult of necessity in order to stress the irreducibility of contingency'.[35] This is to say that it is geography that has the capacity to deterritorialize human histories. We should be clear to note here that the geography of which Deleuze and Guattari speak is not the geography of high-school atlases, where identifying the distinctions between deserts and savannahs and locating capital cities was at stake. For Deleuze and Guattari, '[g]eography is not confined to providing historical form with a substance and variable places. It is not merely physical and human but mental, like the landscape.'[36] History's constructions of truth and fixations on origins and classifications, borders and boundaries, tends to be undermined when one considers the mobilities, material intensities and contingencies of geography. Whilst geography comes to address the particularities and specificities of *anywhere in particular*, geophilosophy extends the concern to the cultures, thinking and regimes of thought that are concurrent with that embrace. Deleuze and Guattari pose a geophilosophy against the colonial ideal that a land doesn't exist until we account for it by our maps, speak of it in our languages and firmly lodge it in our history books. Whilst geography pushed atlases off the library shelf, geophilosophy uses them as kindling to set the full embossed set of the *Encyclopaedia Britannica* alight. *Deterritorialization is a liberation from habitual codes in order that new connections might be forged and new worlds constructed, that new peoples might come to occupy, afresh.* Here is 'the new earth, and the machine that hums, around which the schizos revolve, planets for a new sun'.[37]

Blue Slabs

Such an articulation of desire and production that hums between earth and territory hums loudly in the early paintings and drawings of the architect Zaha Hadid. I will turn particularly to her graphic construction of the colonially contested Hong Kong. Hadid's engagements with the island over many decades (1982–2016) were intermittent but near boundless, ranging in scale from complete urban reimagining that blurred architecture and topography, through to the detailing of balustrades and ramps. Her first internationally acclaimed project, *The Peak* (1982–3) was for a private leisure club in the hills of Kowloon. The club would sit high in the hills as sweeping horizontal slabs, above the vertical city. The project was described by Hadid as 'a building that was to be based on the landscape, and intended as a new man-made geology or ecology'.[38] She would win the competition, but the project was never built. 'When Margaret Thatcher went to Hong Kong, that was the end of that project,' Hadid quipped in an interview.[39] Thatcher visited Hong Kong in 1982 before proceeding to Beijing to discuss the colony's return to Chinese *sovereignty*. That the architectural project did not proceed did not however stop Hadid's paintings and drawings changing the way Hong Kong was conceived.

The 'Blue Slabs' painting is one of the most compelling images of *The Peak* project (Figure 2.1). At just over 2.5 metres tall and 1.5 metres wide, you can almost step within, or likewise, it almost spills out. The image frames Hong Kong, askew and poised. A harbour of sapphire blue sits deep and flat in the lower right section of the image and a mountain of sky blue and light grey tones rises high above. The mountain has a folded and textured geological quality. The soft sky is likewise in blue hues but with a pink tinge. This sky sits in the upper left section of the painting. It appears as if the sun has just passed over the mountain. (Or is it that the mountain has just turned its back to the sun?) Over the folded surface of the mountain, sleek orthogonal volumes have sprung up as a field of skyscrapers with surfaces that either reflect the shades of the mountain or take on orange and pink tones. Their relationship with the earth is eccentric, abstract, and relates perhaps to Hadid's overall summations of an architecture of 'floating pieces' that might be 'suspended like planets'.[40] These abstract skyscraper forms are dense over the lower portion of the mountain and become sparser in the steeper upper sections. Some, but only some, cast long shadows over the harbour front and waters. The proposed building itself, *The Peak*, is subdued in this image. It sits high in the mountain and is more horizontal than the skyscrapers. It is distinguishable from the topography but less so than the vertical structures. But it is perhaps wrong to speak of horizontal and vertical here. It is very difficult to find anything that aligns itself with the edge, the frame, of the image. Even the most orthogonal of forms – the skyscrapers – seem to lean in one direction or another. The mountain too isn't just sitting there; it's coming towards us. This is a world poised and askew.

What Hadid is doing in such a painting would seem to be twofold. On the one hand Hadid is negotiating the territories of Hong Kong, an urban structure laid over a topography that was itself laid over a geology. We can note what are likely buildings, streets, wharves and docks, and shadows cast. We have a clear sense of a sky, a skyline, a mountain and a harbour. There is here an ordering system that demarcates the sky as depth and atmosphere, the mountain as more crystalline, a city as more rectilinear, and a water that is flatter and deeper. *This is recognizably Hong Kong*. It's the Hong Kong that we fly onto. A Hong Kong from a plane that ducks sharply into the mountains to land. On the other hand, Hadid generates a sense of the force and thrust of this part of the earth. The geological force of the mountain. The fold and slide of a topography. The ascent of a city. The gravity of water. And these forces all have directionality. It is clear in which direction the mountain leans, the topography slides and the architecture rises; which I guess makes it a vectoral system. And overall, the image pivots about a shifting axis. The whole might tip into the harbour, the waters from which it was born. *This is intensely Hong Kong*. It's the Hong Kong that we fly *into*. A Hong Kong that surges towards us and causes us to gasp as the land rises sharply to meet our plane.

When this work, poised between territory and earth, comes to be spoken of however, it is to the well-trodden paths of art and architectural histories and the territories of representation to which our attention is turned. Hadid herself practised the habit of locating her early drawings and paintings in art-historical terms. This 'man-made geology' would also be spoken of as 'a Supremacist geology' and tied to a lineage of Russian constructivisms.[41] Hadid's collaborators at Zaha Hadid Architects (ZHA) bind the images to the broader oeuvre of the office and what they consider to be their role in 'the incomplete project of modernism'.[42] Art and architectural historians repeat the refrain of historically situating the work but look to more fine-grained codifications. The work has been discussed in terms of constructivism, Russian supremacism, cubism, futurism, futurist architecture, German functionalism, expressionist architecture, German expressionism, folding and free-space architecture. Perhaps the oddest attempt to wrangle the work into the frame of art historical demarcations was when 'Blue Slabs' would come to feature in MoMA's *Deconstructivist Architecture* exhibition in 1988, co-organized by Philip Johnson (the man with the keys to the car). In a 1989 addition of the journal *Assemblage*, Mary McLeod would note 'the categorisation "deconstructivists" itself presents numerous problems, not the least of which is that many of the participants in the recent MoMA exhibition [...] themselves reject the label'.[43] Hadid was amongst them. This was only 'perhaps' the oddest attempt to pin the work down because more recently Woody Yao, a director at ZHA, suggested that Hadid's 'paintings for the Peak were also partly inspired by traditional Chinese watercolour landscapes'.[44] One assumes this ambitious art historical (re)codification is merely coincidental to the recent influx of projects from China, and China's forceful colonization of the island. This framing of the early drawings and paintings of Hadid, like all art-historical processes, operates much like genetic testing, or in this case paternity-testing, fixated on identifying the forefathers and fatherlands of the work.

When not tied to art historical lineages, the paintings and drawings came to be tied to biographic accounts. Aaron Betsky described such images as 'Hadidworld'.[45] What is suggested by such a descriptor is that this work is an idiosyncratic expression of the self. Such a biographic position raises the question *who the architect is*, over *where the architecture is*, and restricts us from exploring the geographic world that these images excite. This position also inadvertently plays into the pained cult of personality that encircled Hadid and the clammy hands of limp critics such as Harry Francis Mount, who described Hadid as 'one of architecture's greatest narcissists'.[46] Incidentally Mount's father, Sir William Robert Ferdinand Mount, 3rd Baronet, was in charge of the 'Number 10 Policy Unit' when Thatcher visited Hong Kong and then Beijing in 1982. It is likely the younger Mount knows much of narcissism having never left that little colonial world of his own.

The tension present in an image like 'Blue Slabs' is not one between Hadid and the world, but rather between the habitual codification of place and the seething force of the earth itself. Fortunately, there are attempts to think about the early drawings and paintings that also note the forces that *precede* the impulse to codify and colonize. Though no elaboration is made, Patrik Schumacher, Hadid's long-term collaborator suggests that via these drawings and paintings 'Hadid reconstitutes the functions of territorialization'.[47] I imagine that another way of saying this is to say, the images deterritorialize. The manner by which a place habitually or traditionally is captured by architects is departed from in such work. The images are not maps, aerial views, plans, elevations or sections. They are not even perspectives constructed as perspectives were traditionally or are habitually. Hadid departs from the habits by which a place might come to be framed and instead operates an image as a device which coheres the landscape of thought and the lands with which we build. This is a considerable achievement. Deleuze and Guattari note that 'it is not easy to de-oedipalize even nature, even landscapes'.[48]

That 'Blue Slabs' operates as a departure point does not however preclude it from also being a return. The painting liberates Hong Kong to be thought afresh by articulating or amplifying the forces that are already there. I think this may be what Hal Foster is suggesting when he notes of Hadid: '[T]he primary motive of her architecture seems to be the release of forces detected in a given project or site, out of which unforeseen structures, spaces, and functions might then be developed.'[49] Elements are deterritorialized from habitual frames in order that they might reconnect with the outside and on occasions settle afresh into new forms: a reterritorialization. Hadid's 'Blue Slabs' is a reconfiguring of Hong Kong that at once unpacks the habits of thought applied to this place and fosters the construction of the new. In *What Is Philosophy?* Deleuze and Guattari note deterritorialization 'does not preclude reterritorialization but posits it as the creation of a future new earth'.[50] This new earth is what Foster might have been referring to as the 'unforeseen structures' of Hadid's work, what Betsky calls the 'constellation of possible compositions' and what Frank Gehry refers to as Hadid's 'new idea, a new world'.[51] The construction of the new had been a long-held ambition for Hadid. When asked about the origins of her paintings and drawings, Hadid turned her attention to her time as a student of architecture during the Thatcher era: 'I think the dire economic situation in the West in those years fostered in us similar ambitions to those of early 20th-century Russian artists: we thought to apply radical new ideas to regenerate society.'[52] This act was neither art historical nor biographic. It was revolutionary. The outcome is the generation of a new earth, a new Hong Kong, which new architectures might yet come to populate.[53] Hadid drew a collective breath of fresh air.

Figure 2.1 Zaha Hadid, 'Blue Slabs' *The Peak* (1982–3). Image © Zaha Hadid Foundation.

3

Sense

Chaodyssey

The Finnish architect Alvar Aalto suggested to his students, 'When you are designing a window, imagine your lover sitting inside looking out.'[1] The appeal was for design processes that embraced intensities and for fecund fenestration. A window for the attentive architecture student would not be just a mark on a piece of paper, nor a frame that holds glass, but rather an erotic moment, a moment of pleasure. I imagine I'm outside a house and looking through a courtyard towards the window in which your lover sits. They are holding a weighty book, but not reading. They are looking out over a landscape, towards approaching clouds and waiting for me to pass on an autumn day's walk. This is not any generalized window in any universal house in any possible landscape. It is a very particular window that frames a body known intimately. The window takes a proportion that relates to that body. It involves a sill that becomes a seat on which your lover sits, a frame against which they recline a little, an orientation towards a view into which they turn. This portion of that body is demarcated, that portion hidden, this bend in the knee constructed, that curve to the spine articulated. The window is a component of a wall that is part of an envelope of a house that carefully holds the frame as it gently holds the body. There is a clear sense here that the architecture student is constructing the territories of the earth (the window, the wall, the building, the landscape) and also populating them, making of them a home. In the second text of their *Capitalism and Schizophrenia* series, *A Thousand Plateaus* (1980), Gilles Deleuze and Félix Guattari note:

> Now we are at home. But home does not preexist: it was necessary to draw a circle around that uncertain and fragile center, to organize a limited space. Many, very diverse, components have a part in this, landmarks and marks of all kinds, now the components are used for organizing a space. [...] The forces of chaos are kept outside as much as possible, and the interior space protects the germinal forces of a task to fulfil or a deed to do.[2]

From an exterior, the window frames an enticing internal world of 'germinal forces' and 'deeds to do'. The window is a glimpse inside. Sigmund Freud suggested as much when he wrote of dreams that related to the custom of *fensterln*, the tradition of wooing lovers at windows.[3] His focus, of course, was not what the windows revealed of the interiors of homes, but rather what the windows revealed of the interior of the dreamer. Aalto's attentive students however were not just dreamers. They didn't merely imagine a lover; rather they harnessed them to mediate between a drawing and a window that 'does not preexist'. If to fantasize is, as Freud suggests, 'one species of thought activity [that] was split off [...] kept free from reality-testing' then the student of architecture is less a fantasist than a pervert.[4] They don't just dream; they enact the fantasy, they draw it, model it, construct it and then look up towards the window which frames their lover. Freud himself noted, an artist 'finds the way back to reality [...] by making use of special gifts to mould his [sic] phantasies into truths of a new kind', transforming fantasies into material creations instead of symptoms.[5] But the 'truths of a new kind' that architecture constructs are likely both fantasy and symptom.

From an interior, the window frames the chaos of the earth, 'the forces of chaos are kept outside'. The lover, in an interior space, looks out through the glass to landmarks, landscapes and lingering figures. Menacing clouds and beckoning skies, the torrents of an approaching storm and the wild of sex and strangers are all on the other side. The window protects the lover from the chaos of exteriors, keeping the chaos outside. Outside, yes; but a window doesn't seek to erase chaos. Instead, it frames it. The lover can see the approaching storm and the window celebrates the turmoil. In this way, architecture is always harbouring both the remedy and the malady, the fantasy and the symptom. When your lover, sitting inside looking out, sees someone lingering, they might smile knowingly, lower the book, open the adjacent door and let the storm surge in.

Architecture, what Deleuze and Guattari refer to as 'the first of the arts', would accord with their definition of all art as 'not chaos but a composition of chaos, that yields the vision or sensation, so that it constitutes, as [James] Joyce says, a chaosmos'.[6] Joyce uses the word 'chaosmos' early in *Finnegans Wake* (1939) to account for the fluidity of 'every person, place and thing in the chaosmos of Alle'.[7] Alle is a world of difference that fails to settle into fixed identity. It would seem to be both a place and *all* places in Joyce's weighty book. In his early work, *The Logic of Sense* (1969), Deleuze had described the negotiations and experiments of art in terms of Joyce's chaosmos and would adapt the word into the affirmative task of 'chaodyssey'.[8] If a chaosmos is best thought of as the relative ordering of chaos, then a chaodyssey is a quest 'to make chaos an object of affirmation instead of positing it as something to be denied'.[9] And far from fearing chaos, the philosophy of Deleuze and the collaborative work of Deleuze and Guattari would celebrate it, affirm it. This affirmation would be a core point of concurrency, a sympathy, shared with architecture. The architecture student sitting around the table in the Helsinki studio isn't just sketching a window; they're constructing a relative ordering of chaotic skies, climates and clouds, and a relative ordering of the chaos of eros. The creation of every window in which a lover might sit is an intense chaodyssey.

Representation

The window of which Aalto spoke isn't a window yet. It 'does not pre-exist'. On paper, in the architecture studio, the window is both de facto and a priori. It is de facto in the sense that a drawing, a sketch or a model stands in place of an actuality, an actual window, wall and building. It is a priori in the sense that this drawing is a thousand swirling options, a thousand possible refinements that may come to settle temporarily in pencil and paper, well before it might settle into a wall. So much architecture occurs in this de facto and a priori realm that we call *representation*. Most of the maps, sketches, drawings and models of architecture seek to pin down an image that might stand in place of a yet-to-be actuality. This is to say, much architectural practice is a quest to *represent* that which might find itself concurrent with the event of building. And not surprisingly much time, in every architecture school and studio, is dedicated to developing skills and refining techniques of representation. The endgame here is the development of a perfect set of images, or a perfect model, that might perfectly pre-empt the actuality of just this one window in just this one building.

The history of philosophy too, according to Jacques Derrida, has been a quest to find perfect representations. In this case, not drawings, but rather *words* that would exactly connect with *things*. And in this case more de facto than a priori, in that these words seek to stand in place of that which exists more often than the yet-to-be. Derrida diagnoses this goal of a direct correspondence between words and things within *Of Grammatology* (1967) and would call it 'logocentrism'. The word derives from the Greek *logos* which translates as the direct relation between 'words' and 'things' (or the 'world'). The history of philosophy according to Derrida – from Plato, through Aristotle, Kant, Hegel, right up to Wittgenstein and Heidegger – has been a logocentric quest. Logocentrism desires a perfectly rational language that perfectly represents the real world. The seductive endgame here is that words would be truth. Such a language of Reason would guarantee the presence of the world. The essence of all that is in the world would be transparently (re)present(ed) to an observing subject who could speak of it with certainty. Both architecture and philosophy find something seductively reasonable about representation.

And herein lies the problem of representation: its reasonability, its self-consistent coherence, its common-sensical character. The deconstruction of Derrida and the post-structuralism of Deleuze would concur on the point. In *Of Grammatology* Derrida suggests the conviction to Reason is a habit that is only maintained by repressing or excluding that which is uncertain, that which does not fit in, that which is different. In *Difference and Repetition* (1968) Deleuze turns to the very question of the way a 'dogmatic image of thought' such as representation might consume all the possibilities for that which is different to be liberated from measures and judgements.[10] The question was a difficult one to formulate. Like Derrida, Deleuze would find the history of philosophy itself to be implicated in the validation of representation, noting 'the history of philosophy plays a patently repressive role in philosophy, it's philosophy's own version of the Oedipus complex'.[11] Deleuze suggests that since Aristotle representation formulates all measures of difference as *difference 'to' or 'from' something*.[12] This is to say, any assertion of difference comes to be thought of as difference *to* or *from* a standard, a standard bearer, or what is referred to as a 'predicate'. A predicate is the base from which difference is measured. Deleuze notes that '[t]he dogmatic image of thought supports itself with psychologically puerile and socially reactionary examples', and thus I'll offer one to help explain how representation suppresses difference.[13] The example is how the identity of Oedipus predicates Electra. For Freud, the masculine figure comes first from which the feminine is then measured. Her difference is framed not as difference 'in and of itself' but rather as a difference *to* or *from* him. She becomes 'the feminine Oedipus attitude' or the 'negative Oedipus complex', subsumed by the masculine measure.[14] And for Freud this order is then unfolded in elaborate systems of logic. Penis envy henceforth would always be predicated on castration anxiety, despite the obvious perversity of the position. Electra was subject to an early form of what today is referred to as 'cock-blocking'. Deleuze would describe such relations enshrined in representation as 'subordinating difference to instances of the Same, the Similar, the Analogous and the Opposed'.[15] That is, to 'identity'; wherein the 'primacy of identity' of a predicate is reinforced, as the difference of an *other* is subsumed.[16]

We notice that all acts of representation tend to involve two things: the standard bearer and that which is measured from it; the original and the copy; the predicate and that which is predicated. And *the dualism, the two-ness is not pragmatic, but rather a brutal political ordering: a distinct subjugation of one mode of existence under another.* Predication indeed is predatory. For Deleuze judgement always appeals to the infinite and the absolute.[17] It is the measurement of the degree of perfection of a term's self-resemblance in relation to a supreme standard. That is, there is always *something* against which we judge. This might be a law, an ideal, an actuality, a type of perfection. The lover judges against the ideal of perfect love, the priest judges against the notion of a perfect god, the map is judged against the actual place. The very endeavour of representation is to be submitted to a system of condemnation. No architecture student, not even those he took as lovers, got Aalto's windows just right. That which was seductively noble, coherent and reasonable about representation comes to be highly problematic. Representation as Deleuze suggests 'remains only a dead letter confronting that which it represents, and stupid in its representiveness'.[18]

A Logic of Sense

There is a phrase that Deleuze engages in *Difference and Repetition* that was a rehearsal for a line in his book *The Logic of Sense* (1969). The sentence 'With eternal return chao-errancy is opposed to the coherence of representation' becomes 'To the coherence of representation, the eternal return substitutes something else entirely, its own chaodyssey (*chao-errance*)'.[19] There is much shared between Deleuze's logic of sense, Nietzsche's idea of that which returns eternally and Joyce's chaosmos: All refer to the temporal and contingent coherency to a thought or a thing that is not reliant on the repetitions, measures and judgements of representation. Deleuze's logic of sense is posited against the 'logic of predication and truth' upon which representation is based.[20] For him there are no grand and great capital 'T' truths. All truths are constructed, much as one might construct a home. Like a home, truth 'does not pre-exist'; it is 'fragile and uncertain' and functions only in 'a limited space'. Against the image of a fixed and eternal truth, Deleuze's logic of sense involves a multiplicity of small 't' truths that operate in specific and particular ways. They are *chao-errant* rather than coherent, and contingent rather than fixed and eternal. There are truths that wander, jump fences, run, and stop and run again in different places at different times. *This mobility of truths means that meaning itself wavers.* Joyce would be a prime example of a composer of small 't' truths, a master of sense who made meaning mobile, a waverer of words. In the Norwegian Captain's episode of *Finnegan's Wake,* a tailor's daughter *might* be engaging in *fensterln* and *might* be responding to an approaching storm when 'titting out through her droemer window for the flyend of a touchman over the wishtas of English Strand'.[21] Meaning here is mobile, multiplied and decodified and Joyce distils from the chaos of sound an almost-language, an almost English, a strand of English. We cannot state with surety as to what any singular meaning to such a sentence is because there isn't one. A logic of sense counters the reasonability, coherence and common-sensical character of reason. There is no standard bearer here – no predicates that might justify the type of judgements that extend from them. *A logic of sense places multiplicity as the counter of judgement.* What we access from Joyce's work is a *sense* of the multiplicitous implications that resist any simplistic explication. The '*chao-errance*' that Joyce shares with Nietzsche is the unfolding of a living logic as opposed to the burial of a dead letter.

There are two key texts in which Deleuze explicates his logic of sense. *Nietzsche and Philosophy* (1962) was the first, and herein Deleuze's interest was a genealogy of sense, that is, sense as 'de facto and de jure'.[22] For Nietzsche there were 'no facts, only interpretations' and 'truths are illusions about which one has forgotten that this is what they are'.[23] The question then becomes how sense (including what we regard as good or common sense) comes into being. Reflecting on Nietzsche, Deleuze notes, 'We will never find the sense of something (of a human, a biological or even a physical phenomenon) if we do not know the force which appropriates the thing, which exploits it, which takes possession of it or is expressed in it.'[24] The suggestion here is that we should always consider in what system or 'regime of thought', something *makes* sense. In the drawing of a window for example, Cartesian geometry is assumed; translations of scale and a correspondence of dimensionality are assumed. An external viewpoint is assumed, the object-ness of something drawn is assumed, as is a functionality, its use. These *assumed* things are 'forces of appropriation', the unseen and silent assumptions that allow the marks on the page to stand in place of (to be de facto to) an actual window. Without these assumptions, and off the inclined table of the architecture studio, the drawing is something radically different. And just as a window might exist in one sense, so can it in another.

The window of the experimental summerhouse Aalto built on Muuratsalo island for his former student and lover can be approached from many directions. I could draw you a map. But that map will do little to capture the sense of the denuded birch trees that lined the cool stillness of the lake and the anxious clouds that were gathering that autumn's day. Indeed, there is little about my map, or any map for that matter, that has the sense of that day. Likewise, the collection of drawings of the summerhouse and its window bears little actual relation to the many diverse components that have a part in this particular place. It is not that my map and these drawings are without sense. It is that all the maps, plans, sections and words assigned to this summerhouse have a radically different sense than the sense of that day's approach. 'Sense', Deleuze notes in his book on Nietzsche, is 'a complex notion; there is always a plurality of senses, a constellation, a complex of successions but also of coexistences which make interpretation an art'.[25]

If the referential (representational or signifying) aspects of maps, plans, sections and words convey 'meaning', Deleuze comes to describe the combined referential-performative aspects as 'sense' in his second book that turns to the topic.[26] In *The Logic of Sense*, sense is presented as being 'a posteriori and a priori', prior to a judgement or the law about which a judgement of meaning may be made.[27] Deleuze speaks of a sense prior to meaning, propositions, predicates and references, which is nonetheless requisite to thought or thinking itself.[28] We can think of *sense as the chaoerrence of an event before that event comes to be classified, organized, and falls into a regime of thought or any codified system*. It is an autumn day's walk, an encounter with a building, a window and a lover, prior to it being constructed in words and refigured in text. As sense is prior to codifications that attempt to tie an event to a fixed meaning or truth, sense thus has *an intimate relationship with nonsense*. Indeed, for Deleuze '[s]ense is produced by nonsense and its perpetual displacement'.[29] Deleuze isolates such displacements in the nonsense of Lewis Carroll's fiction, where logocentrism becomes more like a *logodecentring*. In the work of Carroll, the connection between words and things, bodies and propositions, the corporeal and incorporeal, is displaced from the habitual.[30] A bigger Alice is figured as a smaller world, and even the simplest of words chortle in a referential-performative play. This form of play is one architects engage too. The Swiss historian Sigfried Giedion describes Aalto's work as a 'dare to leap from the rational – functional to the irrational – organic' and he places Aalto alongside Joyce, as an artist capable of embracing life by displacing the habits and rationalisms of modernism.[31] For Giedion, Aalto's step away from the mechanistic logics that had consumed architecture of the period gave him access to that which was prior. Giedion described Aalto's work as a Baroque revival and as a means 'to re-establish a union between life and architecture'.[32] There is much that remains enticingly vague in Aalto's work and if not incoherent, then at least chao-errent. 'Aalto is restless,' Giedion says.[33]

The move from *Nietzsche and Philosophy* to *The Logic of Sense* is important in charting sense in two ways, or rather as a restless play in two directions. In the first, sense is de facto as a genealogical or genetic character, as something behind expressions or the eternal return behind any actualization. In the second, we have an idea of sense as a priori, that is, sense as a starting point. It is this dual directionality that led Deleuze to describe sense as like 'a pervert' prior to medical or legal diagnoses and as a 'bastard concept' somewhere between the corporeal and incorporeal.[34] We should note, however, that just because sense plays in two directions does not mean that sense is configured as *either* de facto *or* a priori. Sense embraces both. It is corporeal and incorporeal, actual and virtual, of both mobile bodies and the textuality of thought. Sense holds maps *and* passes still lakes *and* jumps fences *and* lingers at windows *and* occurs between the lover held *and* the one of which we speak or of which we write. In *The Logic of Sense*, 'sense is presented both as that which happens to bodies and that which insists in propositions'.[35] The word used is 'insists' [*insiste*] rather than subsists [*subsiste*].[36] Sense comes to be not an underlying system of logic that is mobilized but rather that which in mobilization is constructed. It insists. *Sense therefore should not be conceived of as the depth behind a drawing or indeed being behind anything. Rather sense should be thought of as the surface from which things are drawn*. In architecture the highly codified practices of drawing and modelling that seek to pin down or determine outcomes also involve the vagueness and incoherence necessary for the production of serendipitous events and novel encounters, irreducible to any drawing or model. Sense is a little like the paper on the table that the student of architecture faces – ripe with possibility. Deleuze suggests, 'Sense appears and is played out at the surface (at least if one knows how to mix it properly) in such a way that it forms letters of dust. It is like a fogged-up windowpane on which one can write with one's finger.'[37]

Frame

When considering what to call the 'new philosophical operation' of sense, Deleuze suggests, 'Perhaps we can call it "perversion," which at least befits the system of provocations of this new type of philosopher – if it is true that perversion implies an extraordinary art of surfaces.'[38] The architectural implications of such a thought would not have been lost on at least one attentive student. Bernard Cache wavered between the architecture studio of Vittorio Gregotti and the smoke-filled seminar rooms of Deleuze. Cache would reflect on Gregotti's fascination for the geographical and complete his doctorate under Deleuze, publishing the work as *Earth Moves: The Furnishing of Territories* in 1995. The work would challenge many of the habits of thought that were dominating architecture at the time, and the dualisms that related directly to representation were specifically targeted. Cache fears that '[w]e have gotten into the habit of classifying images in our inside while leaving things outside of ourselves'.[39] His point is that the habitual assumptions of subject/object, interior/exterior, image/actuality distinctions, operate much as any 'dogmatic image of thought' in repressing alternate conceptions of architecture. And for Cache the dominance of 'model and imitation, figuration and abstraction'[40] inherent to a logic of representation leads to acritical and mechanical conclusions.[41]

By way of example Cache turns to the much-repeated idea in architecture: that a window frames a landscape, and to this idea offers an alternate: 'The window frames the landscape as much as the landscape encompasses the frame.'[42] A logic such as this makes a meal of predication: prompting a predicate to be consumed by that which it might otherwise have subsumed. Against the dualisms of representation and fixations with interior and exterior codifications, Cache comes to define architecture instead as 'the art of the frame'.[43] The frame is posed as a logic by which something coheres without relying on the orders of predication, and the standards and judgements of representation. The frame is described thus as 'an art whose rules are never determined but are always determinable',[44] and in a similar vein Cache suggests the frame 'belongs to a register of autonomous forms whose principle must still be defined'.[45] This is to say, the frame is not the product of, or bound to, any singular logic and not measured *to* or *from* any standard but rather is determinable and definable *in and of itself*. And a frame isn't a singular entity, a one-liner or an essentialized ideal, but rather a multiplicity that remains ever open to its outside. For Cache, '[o]ne simple frame could structure several continua, but, conversely, one continuum could become individuated through different structures'.[46] The frame is thus much like the surface of sense, 'a condensation of coexistences and a simultaneity of events', as Deleuze had defined it.[47]

When Cache states, '[o]ne simple frame could structure several continua', it is to suggest a singular frame might negotiate a multiplicity of modes or what he refers to as 'continua'. Cache offers 'the sexual continuum, the affective continuum, the sound continuum, the action continuum' as examples.[48] A simple frame, a window for instance, comes to structure all these continua alongside the continua of enclosure, sunlight, ventilation, etc. Likewise, every drawing of a window is a frame, structuring a continua of a thousand swirling options, a thousand possible refinements, alongside those of the sexual, affective, sound, action, etc. Where the endgame of representation was the development of a perfect set of images, or a perfect model, which perfectly pre-empts the actuality of just this one window in just this one building, the frame is a game that distils its own rules, its own small 't' truths. Cache frees what drawing is or does in the same way Joyce frees a word from dictionaries and the restraints of grammar. It is not that a drawing or an object is without coherence; it is that its *choerrancy* is distinct from overarching or dogmatic logics. *A drawing of a window is its own frame of reference, operating in and of itself as a conduit for the continua that surge through.* 'All we need to do,' states Cache, 'is to leave images where we see them, which is to say in things themselves.'[49]

When Cache states, 'conversely, one continuum could become individuated through different structures' we are invited to think of the frame as an unfolding.[50] For example, a continuum of an enclosure might become structured as interior and exterior. A continuum of opening might be structured as wall or window or door. What was said of a logic of sense can equally be said of Cache's frame. Deleuze noted, 'Even the frontier is not a separation, but rather the element of an articulation.'[51] The key architectural significance of this idea in the mid-1990s most piquantly relates to the continuum Cache called '[f]rom conception to fabrication'. Just as the continua of enclosure might be structured as inside, outside, wall, window or door, so too might the continua of conception 'become individuated' in a drawing of a window and a home. Against the 'primacy of identity', we get the idea of the 'individuated', a temporal collapse of the genetic forces that bring something into being in a de facto sense and the multiplying expressions of the a priori. For Cache, 'a field of surfaces thus governs the object that has now become the set of possibilities of their intersection'.[52] The idea was one that wavered between the seminar room of philosophy and the studio of architecture. Cache was the first to intersect parametric design software with robotic manufacturing.[53] This would be an architecture of interface, an architecture of code that pulses through both design and manufacturing, 'to script and program rather than model and draw', as Greg Lynn said of Cache's method.[54] The move was a radical shift for architecture. Its very reliance upon representation faded at the moment when to draw a window was to construct a window. *The architect would no longer be the figure who arrives at a drawing that might stand in place of the yet-to-be, but rather the architect creates the code that served as a continuum from which both drawing and actuality unfold.* The figure that articulates an impulse. The pervert rather than the fantasist, '(at least if one knows how to mix it properly)'.

We are led to an architecture that is what Cache calls '*objectile*' rather than object, an architecture of continual variation or, as Mario Carpo says, an architecture that has moved 'from identicality to variability', where the thousand marks on the paper and the thousand refinements fail to settle into this or that window, this or that object, but remain ever mobile.[55] But Cache is more precise: 'We will call variable objects created from surfaces "subjectiles," and variable objects created from volumes "objectiles."'[56] Henceforth the two-dimensionality of the architectural representation is an enfolding of three and four dimensions. The architectural objectile also enfolds subjects, like lovers in windows. For Deleuze, 'the pervert is not someone who desires, but someone who introduces desire into an entirely different system and makes it play',[57] and Cache played between architecture and philosophy, and helped both take flight from representation. Deleuze would note the debt to Cache in *The Fold*, and Cache's book *Earth Moves* would be dedicated to Deleuze. It is architecture that likely gets more out of the relation. Architecture would no longer be that which subsists (an architect that lingers in the background of every construction) but instead that which insists (the architect that opens windows and doors in every act). And the aspiration is that the frame of architecture itself might come to operate like the frame of a painting Cache describes in *Earth Moves*, 'no longer like a window, but rather like a kite'.[58]

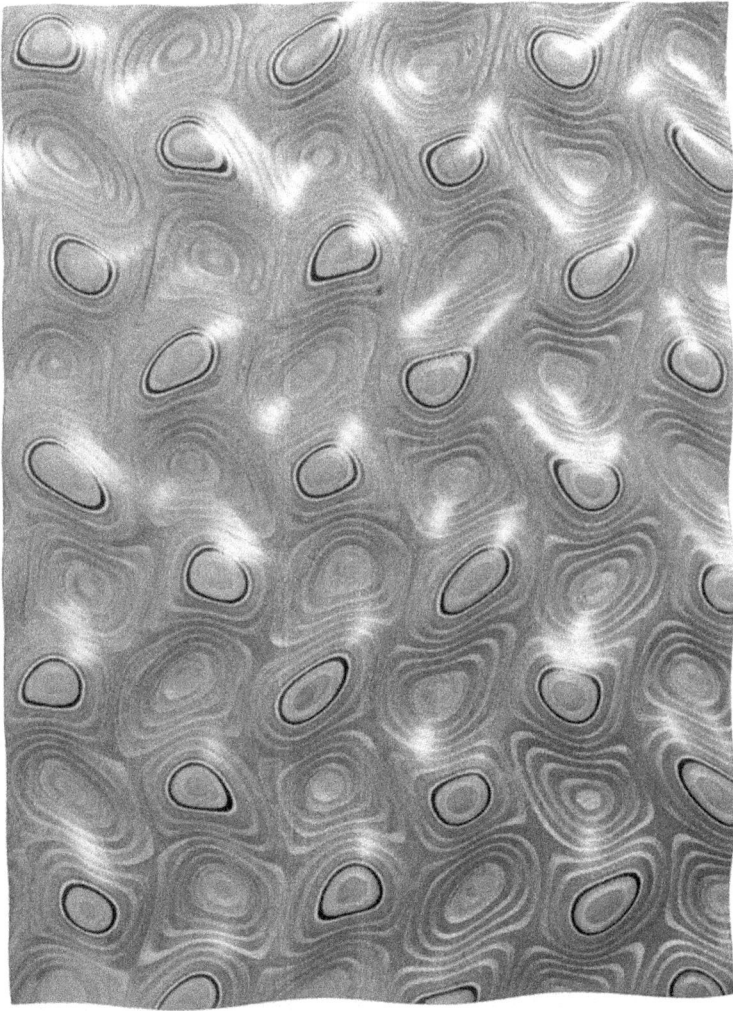

Figure 3.1 Bernard Cache and Patrick Beaucé, Sans titre, *Objectile* (1998). Image courtesy of Bernard Cache.

4

Assemblages

Other spaces

Michel Foucault starts his short paper 'Of Other Spaces: Utopias and Heterotopias' (1967) with the suggestion that 'history' has been the great nineteenth-century 'obsession' and then characterizes history as being fixated on the 'themes of development and of suspension, of crisis, and cycle, themes of the ever-accumulating past, with its great preponderance of dead men and the menacing glaciation of the world'.[1] What we see in such a descriptor is the deferral to time as the key organizing principle: evolution, entropy and the reversibility of the progressionists. The role of the historian is to glaciate, to try to fix the world into stable demarcations and enduring truths, in an attempt to construct a *true and proper* understanding of our past. To this past Foucault would offer a present that architects well recognize, a present he would call 'the epoch of space'.[2] The epoch of space, Foucault suggests, is one where the logics of space itself come to dominate. But this is not space as a complete Cartesian field, but rather space that seems to adopt the characteristics of montage, collage, bricolage – where multiple spaces co-exist and have a mobility. For Foucault, '[w]e are in the epoch of simultaneity: we are in the epoch of juxtaposition, the epoch of the near and far, of the side-by-side, of the dispersed'.[3] In this sense the present itself is about proximity and the assembling of elements that bring something into proximity and that might equally cast something afar. The logic isn't complex. It is that the simultaneity of the present, the collapse of slow accumulative, glacial time, into the instantaneity of events and moments means that instead of time being the key measure, space is. In such an epoch proximity and remoteness are no longer a type of measure of the time it would take to move between things, but rather the relations between.

I was noting this, whilst working on a bed with a laptop on my knees. The ever-advancing digitizations of archives accessible at a click make stories about travel and dusty days spent in basements of far-flung libraries seem nostalgic. These sites now seem to belong to a group of spaces that Foucault would refer to as 'celestial places' out of the frame of habitual practices.[4] It is common now, or more than common, it is habitual now, to trace threads of research across the ever-present but exhausting rhizomes of the internet rather than in moving one's body slowly across geographies and through architectures. In so many ways, *onsite* has been replaced by *website*. And even within a book, time is now compressed. The book that previously took time to locate, to get to, to occupy and to read becomes near-instantaneous. A Google search away. And lines of text can be traversed at an equally concerning rate. PDFs allow singular words to be found instantaneously, and auto-narrators read a text for you at variable speeds. And yet the time-consuming search that comes to be set *on*-site or *in* an archive or book, that reaches its pinnacle with the exclamation: 'There it is!', still seems more magical than the story that ends with 'and then I clicked it!'. Foucault would note, 'Today the site has been substituted for extension which itself had replaced emplacement. The site is defined by relations of proximity between points or elements; formally, we can describe these relations as series, trees, or grids.'[5] But on this point, I too am collapsing time in making Foucault a diagnostician of the cybernetic age. The 'today' of which Foucault was writing was the today of 1967.

Foucault would note of his time: 'Our epoch is one in which space takes for us the form of relations among sites.'[6] And his concern is not (what he refers to as) the 'internal' space of psychology but rather for an 'external space'.[7] That is to say, Foucault is not focused on the 'you' or the 'I' and the way we collate images, stories and events in a type of phenomenological or autoethnographic process, but rather the space that 'draw us out of ourselves' or as Foucault also puts it, 'the space that claws and gnaws at us'.[8] He identifies sites not by type or typology or property lines or geo-coordinates as an architect might, but by the 'set of relations' that define a given site. An example would be relations of transportation that come to configure streets and trains; parenthetically Foucault notes, '[A] train is an extraordinary bundle of relations because it is something through which one goes, it is also something by means of which one can go from one point to another, and then it is also something that goes by.'[9] He also describes sites of temporary relaxation (cinemas, cafes and the beach) and what he refers to as 'the closed or semi-closed sites of rest – the house, the bedroom, the bed etcetera'.[10] But, as the much-repeated story goes, Foucault is interested in *other spaces* that have 'the curious property of being in relation with all the other sites, but in such a way as to suspend, neutralize, or invert the set of relations that they happen to designate, mirror, or reflect' and these are utopias and what Foucault would refer to as heterotopias.[11] I will avoid retracing the account of utopias and heterotopias. What I am more interested in is the idea Foucault gives us of *space as a relation among sites*. It is an image of elements that are in proximity or brought into proximity – and defined by their relations or what he calls a 'set of relations': relations of movement, of rest, of suspension, of neutralization, of inversion. Foucault, in this sense, is operating much like a pre-GIS surveyor. That is, he's identifying space as something like the logic by which a series of occurrences or elements might be brought into proximity, made proximate. But the question of proximity is not always framed in relations of connection. At its edge, proximity is also about making something remote: It is about the 'near *or* the far', and even the 'dispersed' is part of this story.

Sympathies

One critic suggested that the relationship between Foucault and Gilles Deleuze might be summarized as the sending of flowers.[12] Were this so, then the concept of *assemblage* is a letter attached to a bouquet. The concept would explore the manners by which different things, often considered incompossible or without a clear common denominator, might be brought together. The concept fluttered between Foucault and Deleuze and it is also a concept that blossomed in architecture, a discipline that brings the most disparate of things into proximity: cities, populations, rooms, streets, beds, bodies, love and hate, subjects, and senses of self. These elements do not necessarily have a common denominator that allows them to simply intertwine, and yet they do.

Whilst Foucault may have been diagnostic in laying out the turn from time to space and in generating tools by which we might explore the production of spaces, Deleuze is operative and across his oeuvre negotiates the forces and desires, that might forge the relations, that might bring disparate elements into proximity. Such forces are what, across *Anti-Oedipus* (1972), Deleuze and Félix Guattari would refer to as 'desiring-production'.[13] For present purposes though, I want to briefly extol the idea via Claire Parnet and Deleuze's *Dialogues* of 1977 where Deleuze, in discussion, in dialogue with the journalist, would address the question of the assembled nature of things and the manners by which different types of bodies interact. 'The minimum real unit is not the word, the idea, the concept or the signifier, but the assemblage,' Deleuze tells Parnet.[14] The logic is that elements don't tend to have any value or sense on their own, and it is only in connection that anything operates. A postcard might serve as an example. It does nothing in and of itself. Without a stamp, a sender, a postal system, and a receiver – without all those things with which it is assembled – it fails to operate. Likewise, this postcard is assembled. An assembling of card, geometry, an image of New York on one side, a space for writing and a stamp on the other. These heterogenous elements come to be collectively known as 'postcard', and the postcard itself operates as a heterogenous element in a relation between friends, givers and receivers. 'Structures are linked to conditions of homogeneity, but assemblages are not,' Deleuze notes.[15] *What makes an assemblage is not the structural demarcation of a part within a system, but rather a 'deepest sympathy' between that which is heterogenous.*[16] 'The assemblage is cofunctioning, it is "sympathy", symbiosis.'[17]

For Deleuze the effective transformation of a body, a discipline, or a regime of thought requires the connection of elements in manners that are supportive and productive, a 'sympathy'.[18] From this perspective, neither time nor space is a necessary precondition for a sympathy. In a bed with a laptop on my knees I cannot but help feel connected to a loved body that once occupied and passed from this same mattress. They were of a time that is not now, and are now at an insurmountable distance, and yet remain core to how I compose of myself. For Deleuze, what makes something either proximate or at the edge of proximity – remote – has little to do with loss, or absence, or lack, but rather with assemblage. An assemblage might be thought of in terms of production: the production of an utterance, a pleasure, a grief, of connections made, of couplings maintained. The 'sympathy' of which Deleuze speaks is not a bland type of mutuality or nostalgic feeling. In conversation with Parnet he suggests that sympathy is 'not a vague feeling of respect' but rather as 'bodies who love or hate each other, each time with populations in play, in these bodies or on these bodies'.[19]

Sympathy thus might be thought of as the impulse that organizes the assemblage, the near and far, the side by side, the dispersal. The closest Foucault gets to suggesting some form of impulse or force that might generate proximity is perhaps where he refers to 'the space that claws and gnaws at us' in 'Of Other Spaces', or decades later when he turned to the work of Maurice Blanchot and finds in Blanchot's writing, spaces 'in which approach and distance – the approach of forgetting, the distance of the wait – draw near to one another and unendingly move apart'.[20] Here we have a sense of the complexity of space as a measure of anything. A spatial logic seems inept at dealing with that which both draws near and moves apart, and yet it is a sense which one can understand. For Deleuze, the force that might produce the proximate (the drawn together) and the remote (the moved apart) does not exist between entities or elements or as the 'relation among sites' as Foucault had defined space itself. The force is best thought of as a mode of operation: sympathy *operates* to make proximate, to produce the remote, and it operates via 'collective agents and bodily passions'.[21] If sympathy had a conceptual persona I imagine it would be a joyous 'polymorphous pervert' in an eternal love-fest (to misuse the Freudian term). Swept up, loved, and loving all manner of subject and object, present and absent, now and then, playing and played 'with populations in play'. *There is an unmediated immediacy to sympathy that sweeps everything up, prehending the subjects and objects it carries away.* This may be why Deleuze comes to identify 'distance and identification' as a 'trap'. Deleuze notes in regard to the work of Henry Miller and D.H. Lawrence:

> We are trying to extract from love all possession, all identification to become capable of loving. We are trying to extract from madness the life which it contains, while hating the lunatics who constantly kill life, turn it against itself. We are trying to extract from alcohol the life which it contains, without drinking: the great scene of drunkenness on pure water in Henry Miller. Becoming is loving without alcohol, drugs and madness, becoming-sober for a life which is richer and richer. This is sympathy, assembling. Making one's bed, the opposite of making a career, being neither simulator of identifications nor the frigid doctor of distances. You will get into your bed as you made it, no one will come to tuck you in. Too many people want to be tucked in by a huge identifying mother, or by the social medical officer of distances. Yes, lunatics, madmen, neurotics, alcoholics and drug addicts, the infectious ones, let them get out of it as best they can: our very sympathy is that it should be none of our business. Each one of us has to make his own way. But being capable of it is sometimes difficult.[22]

In this account there is a desire for the life of which affirmation is but one mode of operation. In this account the love of *this* or the love of *that* are merely assemblages through which love itself throbs. And love too is a matter of proximity but not a proximity of time (as a historian might have it), nor a proximity of space (as Foucault might have it), but rather the ever-proximate intensity. And we all know that we can be swept up and away *in intensity* when we think of the love we make – the love to which we are proximate. And this is equally the case with the love of a lover we can no longer access – the love from which we are remote. In a text published around the time of the dialogues with Parnet, Deleuze and Guattari would note the deterritorialization of love in the love letter, and the 'Kafkaesque love' of the person whom one can never visit.[23] The drive (again to misuse a Freudian term) that is at stake in Deleuze's idea tends towards an unmediated assembling – a sympathy – rather than a relation of substitution (alcohol for love) or relations of measure (an evocation of quantities over qualities). Those that seek to codify the proximity and remoteness of sympathy, to mediate relations or measure distance, are what Deleuze is referring to as 'the simulator of identifications' and 'the frigid doctor of distances', respectively. The point to note here is that there is a creative power Deleuze associates with sympathy, and Deleuze and Guattari collectively came to use another, perhaps more intense word to describe the intensity.[24] The philosopher and the psychoanalyst would come to speak of 'passion', the 'passional', the 'passional sphere' and 'passional regimes'.[25] In the twelfth plateau of *A Thousand Plateaus* (1980), '1227: Treatise on Nomadology – The War Machine' Deleuze and Guattari note, all '[a]ssemblages are passional, they are compositions of desire. Desire has nothing to do with a natural or spontaneous determination; there is no desire but assembling, assembled, desire.'[26] In this case proximity and remoteness are both matters of making one's bed.

Flagrant Délit

The assembling of cities, populations, rooms, streets, beds, bodies, love and hate, and the passions of buildings and the city itself are the concern of Madelon Vriesendorp's *Flagrant Délit* (1975) image (Figure 4.1). Vriesendorp is a London-based Dutch artist (painter and sculptor) and art collector. She co-founded the Office of Metropolitan Architecture (OMA) in the 1970s with Rem Koolhaas and Elia and Zoe Zenghelis. *Flagrant Délit* came into being in 1974/5 as one of a collection of paintings that shared the title 'Manhattan'. The image is of aquarelle and gauche. It is just a little larger than the size of a vinyl record-cover and a little less square. The image became known to architectural audiences largely by its location on, and then in, Rem Koolhaas's *Delirious New York: A Retroactive Manifesto for Manhattan*. That is, it was located *on* the 1978 Oxford University Press edition, and *within* the 1994 Monacelli Press edition.[27] However, the image was not produced *for* either edition.

We have in such descriptions, as the above paragraph, a series of times, dates and orderings that are used to bring elements into proximity and equally to make them remote. The core deferrals here are historical timings and fixations on origins that become important to much of the discourse around the *Flagrant Délit* image: first the painting (1974 or 1975) and then the book cover (1978). The dating of the founding of OMA is more difficult to define and the laptop on my knees suggests the early 1970s, 1975 and 1978, which might speak to the complexity of forces that bring anything into being. The publication dates of an edition of a book are easier to define, but the work that comes to compose of a book is of course far harder to pin down in so simple a demarcation. All these times and dates form of logic that constitutes the 'great preponderance of dead men', as Foucault would call it. We also have in such descriptions, as the above paragraph, a demarcating of 'sites' that are used to bring elements into proximity: Vriesendorp *in* OMA, Koolhaas *in* OMA, Vriesendorp *from* the Netherlands *in* London, *Flagrant Délit on* a book, *Flagrant Délit in* a book, Manhattan *as* a backdrop. These spaces might operate as a logic by which proximities are habitually established in a form that constitutes any site as a 'set of relations', as Foucault suggests. Beyond these deferrals to time and space, there is also something quite fluid that occurs in such descriptions as the above paragraph. To describe Vriesendorp as a painter and sculptor is to generate a proximity to disciplines and artistic investments, and yet in a book ostensibly concerned with architecture these same descriptions may simultaneously construct Vriesendorp as remote from architecture itself, drawing together and moving apart, simultaneously. Likewise, defining the size of *Flagrant Délit* in respect to a vinyl record cover speaks of both the time and the space of the image in a less categorical manner that nevertheless sweeps both up and generates a sympathy of a kind.

Vriesendorp's image *Flagrant Délit* depicts the Empire State and Chrysler buildings in a room, a bedroom, on a bed. The image brings into proximity a series of things that already were proximate. By this I mean the oddity here is not that we have cities, populations, rooms, streets, beds, bodies, love and hate in a singular image. The oddity is that in *Flagrant Délit* they're not quite as we're used to seeing them – they're not quite as we habitually think of them. The title of the image suggests as much. *In flagrante delicto* (flagrant délit en droit français) refers to the idea of being caught in a criminal act or misdeed. It's a legal term, but colloquially it tends to refer to being caught in a sexual act. In Vriesendorp's image it is buildings that appear to have caught and been caught. The image is a depiction of a 'site of rest' (as Foucault refers to a bedroom), but one assumes that love is also involved. Both the Empire State and Chrysler appear to be relaxed, in that they rest horizontally and have adopted the curvatures of bodies – adjusted to the contours of a mattress and pillows. (The *lit* of *Flagrant Délit*.) The Empire State appears to be on its back (if a building such as this had a back) and it's 20W 34th St facade faces upwards. There is something masculine about it. The Empire State building, so large as to have its own zip code, is solid and with the characteristic geometry and volumetric, of art deco. The Chrysler curves more and the radial circularity of its crown and spire rests on a pillow. The Chrysler seems to be on its side facing the Empire State. Strangely its angular crystalline Lexington Avenue entrance has become rounded in the image and is barely covered by the sheet that has gathered at the base of the bed. Deleuze and Guattari note, 'Passions are effectuations of desire that differ according to the assemblage' and what this means is that just because buildings don't copulate as we do doesn't mean they don't.[28] It is the RCA building that is catching the Empire State and Chrysler in the wake of the act. The RCA, also known as 30 Rockefeller Plaza, is also art deco but, completed a decade after the Empire State and Chrysler, it begins to take on forms of expression more associated with modernism. It's a great hulking structure that barely fits through the door. A spotlight or torch shines from its top onto the couple on the bed. Likewise, the city itself is watching on. The buildings that compose the city beyond the window have human heads. Also, beyond the window is a sullen Statue of Liberty cum Venus de Milo, the flame-bearing arm of which sits on bedside drawers. Beyond the suggestion of the title what makes this site of rest clearly post-coital-passional is the Goodyear blimp-like prophylactic that droops deflated over the edge of the bed and over the carpet map of New York. The blimp is likely a reference to the blimp docking station proposed for the Empire State building. The blimp never got to dock. *Float-us interruptus.*

Vriesendorp's own 2016 account of the image is thus:

> It was the early 1970s. Rem [Koolhaas] was very interested in the future, and I was interested in the past, what the past was like. That divided our collections very much: his postcards of New York and my souvenirs of Americana. I had already made one painting of Lady Liberty [from the Statue of Liberty] falling backwards onto New York while we lived in Ithaca, Upstate New York. In Manhattan, I started the paintings of the buildings in bed together. In the 1930s, the Empire State and Chrysler Buildings were being built and were sort of competing: which was going to be the tallest? Both were important in Rem's story of the beginning of the skyscraper. It struck me that the Empire State was masculine, and the Chrysler Building was sort of dressed up with lots of jewelry [sic] and little details that were very feminine. There is a phenomenon where people fall in love with inanimate objects called 'Object Affection'. For example, a woman fell in love with the Berlin Wall. If this was possible, then, inanimate objects should be able to fall in love with each other too. I did lots of little sketches with the Empire State and the Chrysler in bed with one another, then, Rem said, 'Modernity has to come in.' So he forced me to put the Rockefeller Center into the scene, catching the other two in the act. It's about relationships.[29]

This is more than a description. It's a recollection, a collecting together of the disparate and dispersed elements in the *graphia* of a biographic moment, a relation. Vriesendorp offers a vague timing: the past, the present, the 1970s, the 1930s, 'while we lived in Ithaca'. And the vagaries of space: 'postcards of New York and my souvenirs of Americana', 'falling backwards onto New York', Empire State, Chrysler, Rockefeller Center, and an amorous Berlin Wall. Beyond the timings and spacings of Vriesendorp's account is a simple strategy that suggests why the elements of the story come to be located in the narrative. The strategy seems to be to couple elements of concern. That is to say, Vriesendorp's description operates as a coupling. The couples configured in the text are Vriesendorp and Koolhaas; postcards and souvenirs; the Chrysler and Empire State; the feminine and masculine; a woman and the Berlin wall. If one is to follow the route of Deleuze in accounting for the force that collects these elements together, the sympathies that surge here are clear. The sympathy that flows through these couples would seem to be love, and in that, an intimacy, and a distancing. Vriesendorp moves towards Koolhaaas in the use of 'Rem' and then moves from him in establishing differences (my postcards, his souvenirs, 'sort of competing') and then further and more definitively in the very force of the use of the word 'forced'. One wonders whether the title *Flagrant Délit* came before or after the Rockefeller Centre was forced into the room. And there are moments in Vriesendorp's account that occur as instances when sympathies that play between couplings sweep the couples away: Vriesendorp and Koolhaas; postcards and souvenirs; the Chrysler and Empire State; the feminine and masculine; a woman and the Berlin wall, come to drift into a sentence or two. Vriesendorp notes: 'In Manhattan, I started the paintings of the buildings in bed together.' So easily this sentence could have been 'In Manhattan, I started the paintings of the buildings, in bed together.' And I imagine either might be accurate, both likely are. ('It was the early 70s.')

Identification and distance

Vriesendorp's sympathies might be contrasted with the more habitual accounts of the image, and the analysis in architectural discourse that proceeds from such accounts. The Fonds Régional d'Art Contemporain (FRAC) Centre-Val de Loire that holds the work in its collection poses this as its catalogue description:

> Flagrant délit, drawn in 1975 by Madelon Vriesendorp, with another version made in 1978 used for the cover of the 'retroactive manifesto' Delirious New York, borrows its dreamlike imagination not only from the Surrealist legacy, but also from Pop Art, which consummates the loss of the original object. In this nighttime scene, two skyscrapers are surprised in a bed. *The work is a reminiscence of architecture, which proceeds by conglomerates of local and disjunctive memories, echoing the blocks which, joined together, form the urban archipelago. The illustrative quality of Flagrant délit subscribes to the Freudian mechanisms of the dream which operate through displacement and condensation.* Flagrant délit is above all the transcription of the 'Manhattanism' and the 'culture of congestion' described by Rem Koolhaas, where fantastic narratives exist side by side with fragments of reality, where the body is a mutant and symbiotic body, where the city yields up its *mechanistic unconscious,* and where skyscrapers are so many *'desiring machines'*.[30]

The description is worthy of analysis – not much, just a little. This description is careful on some points and fascinatingly perplexing on others. Other scholars have noted and repeated cautions related to the complex origins entailed in the authorship of the image and its precedence, chronologically fixing it in a timeline that reminds us that what Foucault called the 'great nineteenth century obsession' with history is alive and well.[31] What is fascinating about the FRAC catalogue description is the idea that 'the work is a reminiscence of architecture'. I like that idea. It's not reminiscent of sex. Not reminiscent of post-coital regrets or the sense of voyeurism; no, it's reminiscent of architecture. And why? Because it 'proceeds by conglomerates of local and disjunctive memories'. The descriptor conflates Freudian and DeleuzoGuattarian terms as if interchangeable. Phrases such as 'consummates the loss of the original object' and the 'Freudian mechanism of the dream' are parsed alongside ideas of a 'mechanistic unconscious' and in inverted commas 'desiring machines'. The problem here is that the intensities of the image are mediated. Highly mediated. Excruciatingly mediated. The love and hate of sex, the 'bodies who love or hate each other, each time with populations in play, in these bodies or on these bodies', isn't dealt with at all and instead we get the *isms* of Freud, Deleuze and Guattari, and indeed the *isms* of Koolhaas ('Manhattanisms' if you will) and are left with only 'a vague feeling of respect'.

It is a problem that architectural theorists also indulge in – often more interested in structural substitutions than sympathies. In the book *The World of Madelon Vriesendorp* (2008) we see this in exaggerated form. A type of proximity or a making proximate of the work of Vriesendorp that seeks not to deal with the work at all, but rather to turn down architecture's sheets and to diagnose remoteness as repression. If we remember Deleuze's discussion with Parnet he names the two figures which, instead of just letting you get into bed, come not to love but to 'tuck you in'. The first was what he calls 'the simulator of identifications'. He also calls this figure the 'huge identifying mother'. It is a figure that wants to locate repressions, subjugations, lack and loss. And in accounts of Vriesendorp's image we recognize this figure in statements and comments that seek to wrangle the passion from the image into classificatory readings. Beatriz Colomina asks Vriesendorp, 'In the architectural world you are best known for your painting *Flagrant Délit*, which appeared on the cover of *Delirious New York*, and it is part of a long series. Would you say that the series is about the sexual and psychological life of buildings?'[32] It was a leading question, but it's not surprising, *Flagrant Délit* is a legal term. Vriesendorp however responds clearly: 'Yes the sexual or the romantic life'. Colomina has a second shot; she's not prepared to let the opportunity to simulate an identification go and prompts, 'But also the psychological', to which Vriesendorp concedes, 'Yes'. And at this moment we are tucked tightly into the Freudian theatre of representation. From this point the image, its intensities, elements and couplings now come to be merely stand-ins or characters in a psychoanalytic drama. The 'simulator of identifications' grants a means to read, to frame, to draw conclusions that relate to frames of reference that the image itself fails to construct.[33] It's an easy (far too easy of a) read. We notice now that the *Flagrant Délit* image on the front cover of Koolhaas's *Delirious New York* (Oxford University Press edition) has been cropped, and surely such cropping is synonymous with castration. The *Flagrant Délit* image would then fall completely inside the cover (or under the covers) of the later Monicelli Press edition.[34]

The second figure to which Deleuze refers is what he called 'the frigid doctor of distances' and this figure is also referred to as 'the social medical officer of distances'. Though a doctor, this figure has no bedside manner and is equally averse to dealing with sympathy and passion. Charles Jencks writes that Vriesendorp 'played a significant role in forming the image of his [Rem Koolhaas'] early work, and continues to bring architecture the fresh perspective of an outsider'.[35] Consider the distance created in such a statement. Architecture, it turns out, has an inside and the co-founder of OMA is not there. But the doctor of distances is also about arranging elements in logical systems. Jencks, referring to Vriesendorp's early collections, suggests they are ordered according to a 'new logic' and notes that 'the world can always be reordered according to heterogeneous classes, and Vriesendorp following Koolhaas following Salvador Dalí is interested in heterodoxies, not orthodoxies'.[36] Seriously. Vriesendorp *following* Koolhaas *following* Dalí. He need only have added Freud to this list. The distancing that is engaged here is a benevolent bropriation. The doctor means well, but his incapacity to deal with the space that, as Foucault puts it, 'claws and gnaws at us', nor the passional regimes at stake, means he is left sticking cold thermometers in warm places.

Desire

Deleuze and Guattari would note, '[A]ll desiring-production is, in and of itself, immediately consumption and consummation, and therefore, "sensual pleasure."'[37] They go on to say, '[W]hen the theoretician reduces desiring-production to a production of fantasy, he is content to exploit to the fullest the idealist principle that defines desire as a lack, rather than a process of production, of "industrial" production.'[38] I am perhaps being cruel to the theorists though – Jencks gets it right on one important point: He notes that Vriesendorp 'sees behind the perverse and generic a simple force of desire others may wish to hide'.[39] The populations at play in Vriesendorp's *Flagrant Délit*, the cities, rooms, streets, beds, bodies, love and hate, subjects and senses of self, do come to be assembled by a simple force of desire, a sympathy as Deleuze defined it. This would be Vriesendorp's own summation: 'It's about relationships.'

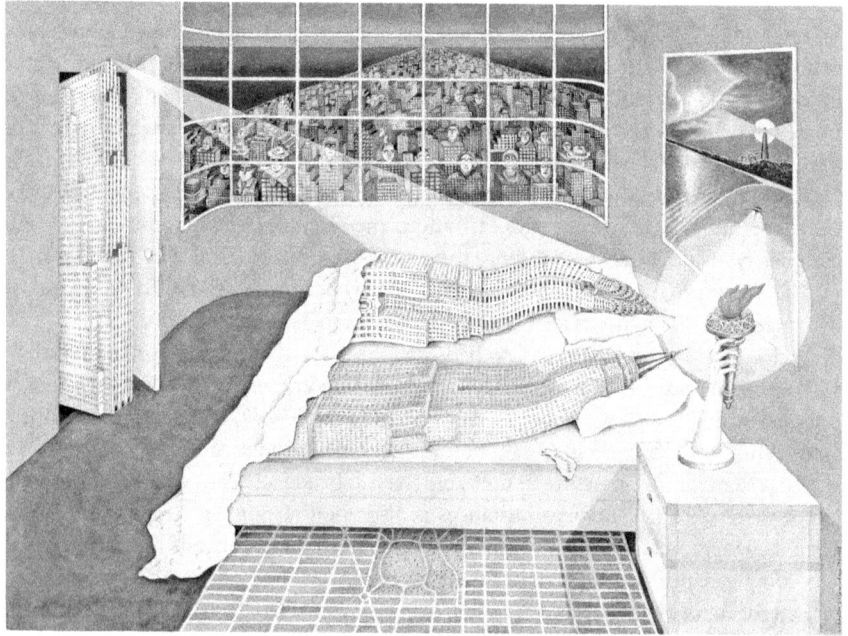

Figure 4.1 Madelon Vriesendorp, *Flagrant Délit* (1975). Image courtesy of Madelon Vriesendorp.

Part Two

'Exploration'

Part Two focuses on the critical capacities of Gilles Deleuze and Félix Guattari's philosophy and its impact upon contemporary architectural design and theory. Consideration is made of four key modes of operation deployed by Deleuze and Guattari and the way in which these modes of thought come to operate as a means of thinking about architecture: its history, its styles, its currencies. But such explorations are not entirely unidirectional. Just as the architecture of the Baroque gives us a vantage point for understanding Leibniz, so too may the architecture of the twenty-first century allow us to better understand the work of Deleuze and Guattari.

5

Constructivism

Proust

When considering the shared constructivism of Gilles Deleuze, Félix Guattari and architecture, one cannot help but delay the task and read Marcel Proust. It's not that Proust is a form of procrastination. It is that Proust offers a model for the construction of worlds that suspends habitual fixations, sweeps us up like a daydream and swallows us gently with Madeleine. To read Proust is to be better acquainted with a world in flux from which dreams, places, figures, thoughts and events are temporarily brought into focus before fading back into the air from which they were drawn. I turn to Proust's *À la recherché du temps perdu* (1913–27).[1] Proust's exhausting novel in seven volumes is translated under the titles *Remembrance of Things Past* or *In Search of Lost Time*. C.K. Scott Moncrieff's translation is the one I read, but it is D.J. Enright's more literal translation of the title *In Search of Lost Time* that better summates the experience of reading Proust. This is because the word 'search' seems more constructive than 'remembrance'. Indeed, it may be far better to refer to Proust's novel, as the French often do, simply as *The Search* [*La recherché*]. For there is no great sense of loss associated with 'lost time', just as there is no sense that something might be definitively found. Rather, Proust's search involves timely focus and a growing comfortability with that which fades. *The Search* is a nebular construction. Not a clunky building of blocks, but a swooning of inchoate material. The book becomes what Proust refers to in the third volume, *The Guermantes Way* (1920–1), as a 'new and perishable universe'.[2] The nature of this universe is elucidated by the Narrator in a reflection on women, streets, carriages, water, sky, forests, tapestry, the geological, and what it might be to paint or to write:

> Women pass in the street, different from what they used to be, because they are Renoirs, those Renoir types which we persistently refused to see as women. The carriages, too, are Renoirs, and the water, and the sky: we feel tempted to go for a walk in the forest which reminds us of that other which when we first saw it looked like anything in the world except a forest, like for instance a tapestry of innumerable shades but lacking precisely the shades proper to forests. Such is the new and perishable universe which has just been created. It will last until the next geological catastrophe is precipitated by a new painter or writer of original talent.[3]

The critical reception of the paintings of Pierre-Auguste Renoir was fraught. The light-suffused fleshy figures in landscapes, and landscapes of mobile unblended colour, seemed uncertain and ill-defined. Renoir's paintings were relegated to *Le salon des refusés*, the exhibition of works rejected from the official Paris *Salon*. Neo-classical representation had been the manner by which people were used to seeing the world in paint. It was, as Proust notes, 'a time at which people recognised things quite easily in pictures when it was [Eugène] Fromentin who had painted them'.[4] The imprecise gust of brush strokes of the *en plein-air* paintings was bound to confuse. In response to Renoir's early showing at the Société Anonyme on Rue Le Peletier in 1876 the critic Albert Wolff decried 'a woman's torso is not a mass of decomposing flesh',[5] and a few years later Émile Zola would accuse the impressionists of being 'too easily satisfied to deliver barely dry sketches'.[6] The critique was that the paintings had little to do with the hard reality of the world and the sense of incompletion could be mistaken for lethargy. Renoir's response was his 'Luncheon of the Boating Party' (1880). The paintings and the world they articulated would outlive the critique. The period of Renoir's work from 1883 to 1884 became known as the 'dry' period. And by the very fin-de-siècle Renoir's works were being purchased by the French state. This was not because Renoir better captured the essence of the world than the artists he succeeded, but because he constructed an alternate universe. Carriages, water and sky become Renoirs and forests became tapestries.

Proust's consideration of 'those Renoir types' draws attention to the way in which an artist might prise open new worlds that were previously unseen. Worlds, yes. But even a 'new and perishable universe' is populated. What Proust notes is that art produces audiences who were once otherwise. This may be what he means, when noting an artist 'reminds us of that other'. Art transforms dispositions, expressions, senses. It wasn't that the women of Paris were suddenly bathed in light and fleshy tones. It wasn't that bodies now occupied places, landscapes, in a manner that further reduced disparities between selves and geographies. It was that having seen Renoir's 'Bal du moulin de la Galette' (1876) it is hard not to then occupy it on a crowded Sunday afternoon in Montmartre. Proust suggests that the artist shouts 'Now Look!' [*Maintenant regardez*].[7] And having looked, we occupy that place accordingly. That which was once unseen, odd or abstracted from reality becomes the 'new and perishable universe' we ourselves populate.

The machine

In his early text *Proust and Signs* (1964) Gilles Deleuze suggests that *The Search* is 'not only an instrument, but a machine'.[8] Before describing the machine, it is worth noting as an instrument Proust's novel would be something specific; 'the Search is the telescope', Deleuze writes.[9] *The Search* is an optical device that brings elements in the universe into focus. Elements that, Proust himself notes, 'were situated at a great distance, and each of which constituted a world'.[10] This instrument thus operates differently to the telescope of an astronomer. The telescope of Proust does not discover and pinpoint celestial bodies in a pre-existent universe but rather invests in parts that constitute their own worlds. Dreams, places, figures, thoughts, and events that are the subject of focus at one moment are not fixed into position eternally, but rather fade or fall from focus as we turn away. The book is a lens onto which parts fall and fade. *The Search* thus is a work of literature that challenged the assumption that a book must be a whole (narrative or structure) which controls parts (fragments of a story, characters, points of reference), and Deleuze would rally Proust in a critique of any logic that seeks to totalize, solidify and unify. In Deleuze's analysis, *The Search* was an 'antilogos':

> To the *logos*, organ and organon whose meaning must be discovered in the whole to which it belongs, is opposed the antilogos, machine and machinery whose meaning (anything if you like) depends solely on its functioning, which, in turn, depends on its separate parts. The modern work of art has no problem of meaning, it has only a problem of use.[11]

Focusing on the 'problem of use' shifts concerns from what a work of art *means* towards what it *does*. This focus counters the fixed and non-contingent 'meaning' that is the object of modern and organic criticism, with the search for the small 't' truths produced in parts, partialized parts. This focus is also a shift from the idea that a book like *The Search* is an instrument, to the sense that it is a machine. And we should note of this literature machine, that there is nothing particularly *mechanical* about it. Whilst a mechanical machine like a wheelchair, a carriage or a car would not be excluded from the definition, a machine for Deleuze might simply be defined as *parts connected in order to produce*, and the point is production. Deleuze and Guattari would come to use the word *machinic*.[12] Instead of fixating on the symbolic or hidden meaning behind a work of art, the machinic is a performative analysis that poses the questions: What does it do? How does it do it? And the answers are sought in close consideration of the work of art itself. That is, the frame of reference is not the doxa of art history or axioms of art theory, but rather the work *in and of itself*. For the modern work of art, the 'problem of use' prompts a focus on the artwork's components, *its* connections and *its* multiplicities and implies a relationship between the art and *its* interpretation that can be located in these same connections and their articulations. This is an inversion of our traditional or habitual regard for art. It is an inversion of the idea that we produce art and instead states clearly: *art produces*. And for Deleuze, 'from the moment *it works*: the modern work of art is a machine and functions as such'.[13]

> Why a machine? Because the work of art, so understood, is essentially productive – productive of certain truths [...] that the truth is produced, that it is produced by orders of machines which function within us, that it is extracted from our impressions, hewn out of our life, delivered in a work.[14]

The work of art is a machine because it functions, and its function is the production of *truths*.[15] This is not the production of absolute truths but rather truth as the formulation of a particular and relative organization of the world. The machine does not allow us access to a sanctified *meaning* of that which exists but significantly provides the apparatus by which one may access the 'certain truths' it, itself, has produced. In

Proust and Signs Deleuze writes, '*It is the work of art which produces within itself its own effects, and is filled with them, and nourished by them*: the work of art is nourished by the truths it engenders.'[16]

Engendering subjects

We should be careful to note, in the literature machine, the painting machine, or indeed the architecture machine, the subject is but a part. That is, the subject (you, me, us, they, them) is not the object of art or what art is about, but rather the subject is bound to the art machine like condensation on the lens of a telescope. In a chapter titled 'The Three Machines', Deleuze quotes Proust: 'Women walk by in the street, different from women of the past, because they are Renoirs, those Renoirs in which we once refused to see women at all. The carriages too are Renoirs, and the water, and the sky.'[17] The subject is neither reified nor essentialized here. There is neither 'woman' nor collective 'women' in any essential form. The neoclassical women of Fromentin, the Renoirs, Odette and Albertine, were all swept along in brushstrokes and words, along with the landscape, tablecloths, men in top hats and straw hats, chairs and wine bottles. The seamstress, pink and fleshy, in 'Luncheon of the Boating Party' stitched a life beyond the painting, just as the actresses performed one. The painting brought parts of them into focus on a canvas, but only for a passing moment. Similarly, Deleuze notes of the characters Proust recalled in *The Search*, 'to remember is to create, is *to reach that point where the associative chain breaks, leaps over the constituted individual, is transferred to the birth of an individuating world*'.[18] The chain of representation that links *this figure* in that book or painting to *this or that* actual person is broken. A partialized individual is but a part of the world the work of art brings into being. The point is not this figure or that, that woman or this, but rather the universe that is constructed, of which that mode of life is a part. Renoir's women need not be thought of as the subject, but rather a part, of a bigger machine. Organs connected to pigments, carriages, sky and water, forests and tapestries become part of a universe. Proust too was swept up for a moment. In *Proust and Signs* Deleuze was not writing *about* Proust as such, but rather encountering parts of Proust as a means to explore and experiment philosophically. He was constructing, building, from what he had. Putting things together and finding what they did, what the connections produced. *This is constructivism*. Renoir is for Proust, much as Proust is for Deleuze: a constructor of that 'which substitutes for the individual in the world the viewpoint toward a world'.[19] Now look!

Architectural machines

The constructivism of Deleuze that finds itself elaborated in his collaborations with Guattari takes the term 'machinic', and their philosophy takes a form that architects may well recognize. Deleuze and Guattari conceive of philosophy as the assembling of concepts and encounters to produce outcomes and effects that are never entirely foreseen. It is a topic that they take up in *What Is Philosophy?* (1991) in suggesting, 'philosophy is the art of forming, inventing, and fabricating concepts'.[20] The constructivism of their philosophy means that it operates much like the machines to which they turn across their work; machines that are not mechanical and that negate the representational in favour of the performative. In architecture too, the machine has moved on from its mechanical origins. The house may still be 'a machine for living in' as Le Corbusier declared in 1923, but the machine of the twenty-first century is barely recognizable.[21] The contemporary machine is one whose boundaries shift, whose connections are multiplicitous and for whom the body is at once a component and a construct.

I turn to Yaohua Wang's *Beijing House II* of 2011 to explore what the machine has become and to chart the constructivism that Deleuze, Guattari and architecture share[22] (Figure 5.1). *Beijing House II* is an architecture that occupies the less than *plein-airspace* above Beijing. It is a single dwelling, an independent house, in a place where independent houses are now extremely rare. The machine configures three sleeping spaces, a green room and a studio. It connects to the adjacent walls of a non-descript apartment or commercial building. It also connects to the plumbing systems below, the air around and a small family within. There is a steel-framed bracing system, an earthquake resistance system, a mechanical ventilation system, a hydraulic system and an envelope system. Each system is particularly heterogenous. That is, each is expressed clearly and is just what it is. The bracing system that holds *Beijing House II* to the adjacent building is just that, a functional system whose job it is to triangulate structure and to cleave. The earthquake mitigation system is equally pronounced, a system of pistons that might absorb a shock. The plumbing system is also just that – clearly articulated pipes fall to the earth as the mechanics of plumbing (hydrology and gravity) might demand. The fluid geometry of the enveloping shell serves to cover the mechanical systems and the spaces in which the operations of a house might occur, but only when and where necessary.[23] Each system of *Beijing House II* has its own logic, geometry and a form of expression that is tied to the pragmatic operation of the system. A pipe bends in a manner that such a pipe that shifts liquids might and different to how a trussed frame shifts forces. This is not to say *Beijing House II* doesn't have an image of its own, but rather to suggest the overall image is a production reliant upon the separate parts. This architecture operates similarly to Proust's novel. It is 'a production of partial objects' as Deleuze suggests of *The Search*, 'fragments without totality, disintegrated parts, vessels without communication, partitioned scenes'.[24]

However, it may be overstatement to suggest *Beijing House II* is a machine whose parts are 'without communication'. Rather, this is a machine where systems speak their own dialects but remain in adjacency. The architect Wang describes the digital geometric repertoire of contemporary architecture as a 'secret technology' that operates 'like an interpreter', and it is the expressive capacity of that technology which becomes the awkward Esperanto of the parts.[25] This productive technology, so often unseen, is a vital part of the contemporary architectural machine. It functions like the aluminium paint tubes that proliferated early in the twentieth century, without which 'there would have been no Cézanne, no Monet, no Sisley or Pissarro, nothing of what the journalists were to call Impressionism', as Renoir noted.[26] The hardware of the aluminium paint tube, unseen in the paintings, was nevertheless vital to the world *en plein-air*. The paint tube was no less a machine than the software of complex geometry from which contemporary architecture is squeezed. If it is 'like an interpreter' as Wang suggests, it is far more Moncrieff than Enright – an interpreter that has its own effects on that which it translates. Even the author or architect need not be reified when one considers the complex and fluid machines that bring a work of art into existence. They are, like all the parts of the machine, partialized. Partly this and partly that and resistant to any totalizing impulse. This part is taken up into this system when needed, that part left aside till it is required. When our attention is turned to the whole of *Beijing House II*, we tend not to notice the parts. We fail to notice the adjacent structures, the technologies that foster the production, the architects, engineers and the builders, but likewise when we turn our attention to a piston that might pump to mitigate an earthquake, the fluidity of the envelope and the bend of pipes seem less pronounced. If a 'structure' is thought of as an overarching organization to which parts concede – or a law which all parts abide by – then the architecture of *Beijing House II* is *post-structural*. The philosopher Jean-Jacques Lecercle defines what Deleuze and Guattari mean by machine and how it is differentiated from structure:

> What, then, is a machine? First, what it is in daily life: a machine is a machine is a machine; it produces effects. Second, it is also defined by contrast with what it is not, in spite of the logic of unification (everything, especially the human body, is a machine–the old opposition between machine and man disappears); a machine is not a structure. [...] If a structure produces anything, it is the idea of totality and the idea of a subject, who appropriates and masters the totality. The point of view of machines, on the other hand, is predictably–one of production; and what they produce is not the subject.[27]

Just as *Beijing House II* is a machine, so too is it a part. If our focus zooms out to the mobility of materials, forms, forces and the flow of aesthetic impulses over time, the singular architectural object that we may have mistaken for a totality fades.[28] In this regard, *Beijing House II* might become a small passing phrase in the very long book of architectural machines that commences with Vitruvius's interest in the machines that might mount the walls of cities. The chapter that mentions *Beijing House II* might commence post–Second World War when the modernist machine began to scream with the same sounds as an abattoir, as Siegfried Giedion noted in his 'anonymous history' *Mechanization Takes Command* (1948).[29] The modernist machine would be dismantled, but later in the century the parts came to assemble architectures as diverse as Archigram's Walking City (1966), Richard Rogers and Renzo Piano's Centre Pompidou (1977), Coop Himmelb(l)au's Falkestrasse rooftop (1983), Daniel Liebeskind's Venice Biennale installation of 1985, Wes Jones's Tract House (1987), Shin Takamatsu's post-industrial gothic Origins (1981–6) and Ark (1983); Neil Denari's hulking Prototype Architecture School No.5 (1992), and would cling to war-torn walls again in Lebbeus Woods' parasitic structures (1992–3). Parts of these machines, material parts, forms, forces and the flow of aesthetic impulses would come to pulse through *Beijing House II*.

In this way, any singular piece of architecture is like a place in *The Search* 'only a thin slice among contiguous impressions which formed our life at that time'.[30] And as Proust had noted of a place, so too of a people: a singular excursion was seen as 'an excerpt from the innumerable flight of passing women'.[31] One of the key consequences of the constructivism shared by Deleuze, Guattari and architecture is that the question of where to draw the line to mark out an entity is pragmatic and derives from the kind of description that we find it helpful to make in order to deal with the situation in which we have to act. Even the boundaries of the self dissolve into the things we engage with – people, places, streets, carriages, cities, water, sky, forests, tapestry, earthquakes and other geological catastrophes: all machines. *Beijing House II* is a machine and a part. A part of a long story in architecture and a part of what Louis Mumford might have called the 'megamachine' of Beijing.[32] This is not metaphor. These are real machines. Machines within machines, constructed with what we have. The crowded apartment residents in the buildings onto which *Beijing House II* cleaves – those apartments that had faded into the background of this new architecture – might yet tap into its plumbing.

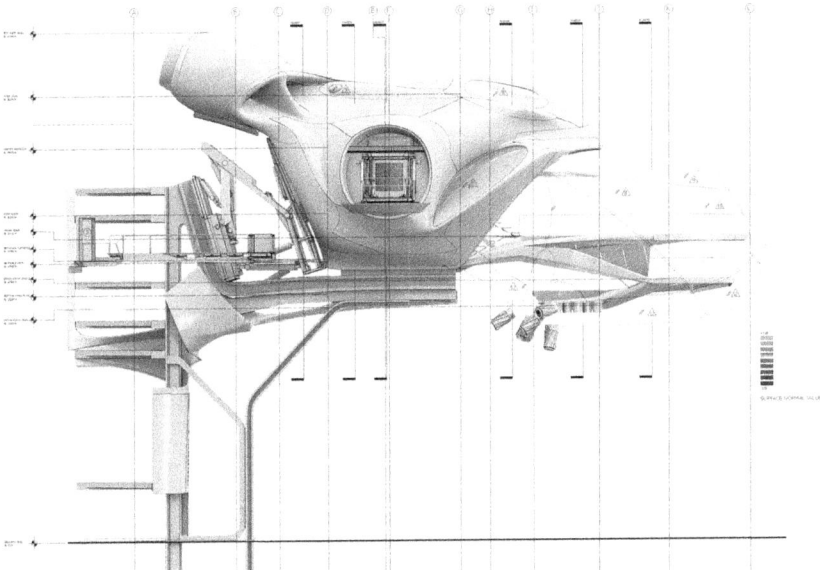

Figure 5.1 Yaohua Wang, *Beijing House II* (2011). Image courtesy of Yaohua Wang, Preliminary Research Office.

6

Transversality

To eat and be eaten

When John Ruskin, the pre-eminent English art and architectural critic of the nineteenth century, wrote to his father of an encounter with Verona he could not help but place it in his mouth. He writes: 'I should like to draw all St. Mark's and all this Verona stone by stone, to eat it all up into my mind, touch by touch.'[1] It is not the taste of Verona that Ruskin wants (nor wants to send to his father). Nor is it the touch. Nor the drawing thereof. What Ruskin wants is 'all this Verona'. That is, an unmediated engagement with all stones and all buildings. But he doesn't necessarily need it all at once. He's happy to have it 'stone by stone', which is fortunate because more than a stone at a time would play havoc with any Victorian's digestive tract. It's a nonsense, of course, and at the same time a very real desire: to consume all, to put all of it inside yourself, bit by bit.

In *The Logic of Sense* (1969), Gilles Deleuze suggests, 'To eat and to be eaten – this is the operational model of bodies, the type of their mixture in depth, their action and passion, and the way in which they coexist with each other.'[2] What is fascinating about the idea is the use of the word 'and'. It is not to eat *or* be eaten, as in Goethe's advice 'be the anvil or the hammer', but rather to eat *and* be eaten.[3] It is an operation that is, as Deleuze notes, a 'mixture', an 'action *and* passion'. Ruskin's phrase 'to eat it all up' may at first glance seem an odd deferral to have placed in a sentence about stone and warm places, that comes to constitute a paragraph about desire and passion, in a letter that is sent home to a cold and judgemental father. But Ruskin had a capacity to roll sentences through this *and* that and to connect things that were previously dislocated. Indeed, he rolled thoughts through multiple letters to his father during his trip to Venice and Verona in 1852 across topics as broad as taxation, property, suffrage, education, political economy, the design of the British Houses of Parliament, and fawning requests for funds to purchase a Turner or two. All these things coexisted in the context of Ruskin's travels and the frame of the places that exercised his thoughts.

At the time of his 'to eat it all up' letter, on 2 June, Ruskin was scouring Verona for what he referred to as 'touchstones'.[4] These would be exemplar fragments of architecture that would come to occupy the second and third volumes of his *Stones of Venice* (1851–3). These touchstones would serve as centres of gravity for all that was profound in architecture. The idea was that in the accumulation of singular instances – bit by bit, stone by stone – Ruskin might locate and then transfer the qualities that were exquisite, wild and strange. Decades later in a lecture titled 'Verona and Its Rivers' (1870) he called these qualities 'the inner heart of it'.[5] So much of what is placed in letters and sent when travelling is of this 'inner' quality. Strange titbits of our internal sensibilities, our emotional states, our passions and pains are mixed with unusual places and unhomely spaces in letters, on postcards, and now in the emoji-laden image captions of social media. Our engagements with places often incite self-reflection and internalization.[6] But Ruskin did not only want to locate 'the inner heart of it'; he also wanted to send it elsewhere. Ruskin puts Verona in his mouth not only to swallow it but also to spit it out – in this instant via post – to his father. And it is also the case that our relationship with places incites the desire to exteriorize. To send on a sensibility or a sensation, to transfer it to others, in letters across the English Channel or in chapters of a second or third volume. Travel clears a space between a sender and a receiver and activates the desire to share that which is often considered to be part of a body's interior and its depths. And in many ways, it is easier to speak of the beautiful and odd places we visit than the pleasures and oddities of ourselves.[7] In this letter cast from Verona towards his father, Ruskin spoke of himself as the product of the dual impulse 'to eat and to be eaten', to enfold and to expel. He would describe his instinct to externalize, 'to draw and describe the things I love' as a desire that might only be fulfilled in consumption 'a sort of instinct like that for eating and drinking'.[8] What is transferred in such phrases is the sense that we are consumed as we consume.

Transference and transversality

The way in which we swallow and are swallowed by worlds was the topic of a report Félix Guattari delivered to the International Psycho-Drama Congress in Paris in 1964. The report would be published in the *Revue de psychothérapie institutionnelle* (1965) and then in his book *Psychoanalyse et transversalité* (1972).[9] The report would come to be simply titled 'Transversality'. For Guattari, transversality would account for the psyche of individuals as constructed in concert with a constellation of contexts. It is the breadth and plurality of contexts that would set transversality in opposition to the Freudian concept of *transference*.

For Sigmund Freud transference was the process whereby feelings associated with one figure are redirected to another.[10] This was the oft problematic transference of feelings for fathers and mothers onto authority figures or 'surrogates' that come to stand in place of the oedipal relation: mummy, daddy and me. Ruskin's letters are replete with examples that a Freudian would read as transference. He wrote to his friend and confidante Lady Pauline Trevelyan of his vexed relation with his father: 'he hates all my friends (except you)'.[11] Ruskin transfers a feeling for his father into a parenthetical expression of friendship. Transference for Freud was thought of in terms of substitution. Whether it is a friend, confidante, lover, or a therapist, or the relation we have with places, transference will frame all as substitutes for overbearing fathers or over-caring mothers.

As transference is rooted in oedipal theory, so too is it thought of in terms of castration anxiety. Its logic relies on the idea that an individual is an internal affair; that is, that our psyche is of our inside and cut off from exteriors in some manner. This form of isolation is reinforced in the institutions of the *psy* sciences. In the 'Transversality' paper Guattari notes the manner by which traditional, habitual, psychoanalysis and its institutions enact a 'segregation' of 'the world of the mad and the rest of society'.[12] Guattari framed this as a type of social castration.[13] Transversality would oppose both the *vertical* hierarchies of an institution (medical directors above clinicians above patients) that might repeat the pattern of oedipal relations, and the *horizontal* formation of divided sections, units, wards or compartments that come with the anxieties of castration. (It was a simple matter for an institution to cut off an underperforming unit.) Though in the 'Transversality' paper Guattari makes no direct reference to architecture, his description of the vertical and horizontal organization of the institution may as well be an architectural brief, and he would note elsewhere, '[A]rchitecture has always occupied a major place in the making of the territories of power, in the fixing of its emblems, in the proclamation of its eternity'.[14] For Guattari, the habitual hierarchical manner by which authority was constructed and fixed in stone reinforced the relations of transference with its 'imaginary reference to the master/slave relationship'.[15] Doctors, nurses and hospital administrators having come to occupy the institution encode its implicit social relation in all manner of diagnosis, 'interiorizing bourgeois repression by the repetitive, archaic and artificial re-emergence of the phenomena of caste'.[16]

Guattari's transversality may have had a psychoanalytic heritage in a reaction against transference, but where one is framed in terms of pathology, the other becomes a positive therapeutic act. Transversality departs the psychoanalytic bind that might have tethered all relations to an oedipal fixation and opens itself to a broader social field.[17] Guattari focuses on the individual as an external concern, as constituted by the group, organization, society and its institutions. This involved returning the individual to the world and simultaneously extending diagnostic capacities beyond the individual and beyond the walls of the asylum. What Guattari called 'transversality', his colleague, and the founder of the La Borde clinic Jean Oury, called the 'transferential constellation'.[18] The idea was that if a mental illness is socially constructed, the broader constellation that comes to constitute what we regard as an individual psyche must be engaged in any therapy. The 'group' thus seemed like the appropriate forum for dealing with the multiplicity of ecologies in which the psyche was formed. Again, in a description which seems as architectural as it is clinical, Guattari notes:

[C]learing a space, keeping room for a first plane of reference for this group desire to be identified, will immediately place the whole statement of the problem beyond chance relationships, will throw an entirely new light on 'problems of organization,' and to that extent obscure attempts at form and apparently rational description. In other words, it is the trial run for any attempt at group analysis.[19]

This would be a very different institution. An anti-oedipal institution. An institution that would not threaten to cut one off from the world. Guattari wants for the discipline of *institutional therapeutics*[20] both a technical-level expertise and an awareness at the 'widest possible social level'.[21] Such an awareness would be of the social, cultural, national, political forces that impact directly on individuals and their construction. The departure from the Freudian tradition of psychological pathology and therapy fixated on the interior state of the individual would mean that a practitioner of transversality would have to 'rid oneself of all preconceptions – psychological, sociological, pedagogical or even therapeutic'.[22] Everything about traditional *psy* institutions was to be contested, starting with the demarcation of analyst and analysand. For Guattari, '[t]ransversality in the group is a dimension opposite and complementary to the structures that generate pyramidal hierarchization and sterile ways of transmitting messages'.[23] Transversality would transform the therapeutic relation via reciprocal and interchangeable roles. The medical superintendent would be swallowed into the transversal institution as a member of the group and all involved would be clinician *and* patient.[24] It's a nonsense, of course, and at the same time it's an opportunity to externalize all that we considered to be interior. To lick a letter and not just the stamp. To stamp feet on institutions. For Guattari transversality would come to excite creativity, that same creativity that 'is strangled at birth by its complete rejection of nonsense'.[25] The Guattari scholar and cultural theorist, Gary Genosko, perhaps states it in the clearest terms: 'Transversality does nothing less than schizophrenize the transference.'[26]

Anti-oedipal transversality

The logic of transversality would clearly lend itself to political critique. Guattari met Gilles Deleuze in the tumult of 1968, and Deleuze would shortly after adopt the term 'transversal' in the second edition of *Proust and Signs* (1970) to describe the manner by which the author travelled from one 'sequestered event' to another paying little heed to the boundaries that traditionally excluded such different occurrences and phenomena from a singular narrative.[27] The concept would become a key logical operation in the collaborative work that consumed the two. The term 'transversality' would come to describe an intermingling that complicates all those things that habitually were thought of in terms of dualistic or binary constructs: fathers and sons, mouths and stone, to eat and be eaten.

Transversality negotiates dualisms in two key manners: Firstly, it operates to *intermingle* terms that often existed in opposition or barely related one to the other. It is transversality that is in operation when Deleuze and Guattari come to speak of a 'geology of morals', or of an 'ethico-aesthetics', or of 'desiring machines', and it is transversality that allows us now to speak of 'capitalism and schizophrenia' in the same panting breath. Deleuze and Guattari would give the very example of that intermingling I commenced with, when in consideration of Samuel Beckett's *Malone Dies* (1951) and the figure Molloy who sucked stones, one at a time. They note the arbitrary boundaries that may be drawn around individuals or characters and ask whether 'the mouth, too, plays a role as a stone-sucking machine?'[28] The shift here is from the habitual focus on the isolated individual, towards the object-organ, in this case a stone-sucking mouth. A Freudian reading of Beckett would find the stone to be a stand-in for the nipple of a rigid mother, and the mouth a needy suckling infant. But for Deleuze and Guattari, neither the mouth nor the stone is a 'surrogate' here, but rather in connection forms a machine that produces its own effects. *That which might have been fixed in transference is mobilized by transversality.* When Ruskin wrote to Lady Trevelyan, 'he hates all my friends (except you)', Ruskin, his father and Lady Trevelyan are beside the point when one considers the transversality of the statement. They are a residue for the social orders and passions of Victorian life.[29] We have in such statements what Deleuze and Guattari write of parenthetically '(Transversals between the two, since social symbolism can become a sexual material, and sexuality, a ritual of social aggregation.)'[30] This is the transversality of the social and sex, of what Michel Foucault refers to in the Preface to *Anti-Oedipus* (1972) as 'Marx and Freud in the same incandescent light'.[31] The philosopher and psychoanalyst (Deleuze and Guattari) operate transversally when they find sex in the social field and the social field in acts of sex, when they speak of '[t]he primacy of the social field as the terminus of the investment of desire'.[32] Or likewise, when they find 'sexuality is everywhere [...] the way the bourgeoisie fucks the proletariat; and so on'.[33] *In transversality there is an intense intermingling of terms that are ordinarily related via dualistic or binary constructs.*

Secondly, and perhaps most importantly, tranversality operates by affirming that which moves between any binary construct by prioritizing or privileging the line that passes through the terms of any dualism. In geometry, the word 'transversal' tends to refer to a line which cuts two other lines. Often the lines that are *transversed* are parallel and have no point of concurrence; that is, they operate like two sides of a dualism – running alongside each other without ever really meeting. The transversal line cuts through these two parallel lines. Whilst in geometry a transversal might be abstract and defined by the two lines it passes through, in the work of Deleuze and Guattari *all that is abstract is operative and the transversal takes precedence*. What is affirmed in transversality is not the two parallel lines, but that which runs between. The logic is easy enough to explain. And can be done in reference to all manner of geometric, geographic, cultural or social formation including architecture, our cities and landscapes. It works a little like this: we can take any dualism we habitually (traditionally) tend to engage – the left and right banks of a river for example. We can imagine that the left and right banks come first and that these two sides (this dualism) make the river. For Deleuze and Guattari operating in this way is odd. The left bank and the right bank of a river do not make the river. It is the river that generates the left and the right bank. The dualism here, of left and right, is constructed in the very act of the passing, of the flow of the river. It is the river which generates the two sides – and not vice versa. For Deleuze and Guattari, *it is the transversal, that which passes between, that generates the binary.*

Veronese stone

When Guattari suggests 'architecture has always occupied a major place in the making of the territories of power, in the fixing of its emblems, in the proclamation of its eternity', he is only partially right.[34] It is true that architecture has a long history of fawning to the powers-that-be in symbolic proclamation, constructing all manner of hierarchy, and enacting all manner of castration.[35] But this is a partial truth. The material actuality of architecture is far more *particular*, and by 'particular' I mean of parts, particles and particularities. *Architecture is born from the world stone by stone and engaged bit by bit.* And architecture is far more transversal, the product of that which passes through it. Ruskin's 'touchstones' were just that.[36] Parts and partial objects touched in a moment of time, fragments that might come to build something else, elsewhere. Even his most complete work, *The Stones of Venice*, was a constellation of fragments. It was full of stones engaged one at a time, never tending to generate any totalizing image. These stones were not always architecture and not entirely Venetian. He would start the first volume with a chapter on 'The Quarry' where labour and iron intersected with stone; and at the other end of a spectrum (deep in another volume) he stands in St Mark's square and notes the red stone of Verona woven into the intricate polychrome patterns of the Ducal Palace.[37] Venice had been dining on Verona for centuries before Ruskin came 'to eat it all up'. Though the sense of consumption fills all of Ruskin's work, there is one lecture, in particular, where Ruskin is swept away along a transversal that runs through architecture. It was a lecture delivered at the Royal Institution on 4 February 1870, titled 'Verona and Its Rivers'. Here Ruskin would transverse territories, disavow the emblematic and engage in the contingencies and temporalities of geologies and cultures alike. He foregrounds ecological sensibilities and identifies a refreshingly minor place for architecture 'among the Stones of Verona, instead of Venice'.[38]

As Ruskin's *Stones of Venice* commences in a quarry, so too does his lecture on Verona. He would note of the trip he'd made shortly prior, 'this last time of my stay at Verona I was quite seriously impeded in my examinations of sculpture [...] by involuntary misgivings whether the churches were real churches, or only museums of practical geology in connexion with that of Jermyn Street'.[39] Ruskin starts his lecture by placing himself on a ridge past the eastern gate of Verona parenthetically '(on the way to the station for Venice)' and references the Museum of Practical Geology, on Jermyn street, London.[40] It is geology that connects the three places: Verona, Venice and London. Though Ruskin frames the idea as 'whether the churches were real churches, *or* only museums of practical geology', the overarching logic of the lecture is that what he faces in Verona is a mobility of stone that is sculpture *and* church *and* geology. Verona's sculpture, streets, architecture and landscape are hewn out of Paleogene sedimentary rock formed in the wake of the Adige River. The river runs from the Alps in the north to the Adriatic Sea in the east and its curvature around Verona is so acute that we cannot speak of a left or right bank here. The waters formed the stone in concert with life itself. Veronese stone is both geological and petrographic. Fish fossils can still be found within it and the nearby Bolca quarry was known as the *Pesciara* (the fishbowl). It is the presence of the minerals iron and manganese that ran through fish as it runs through stone that give Veronese sculpture, streets and architecture, indeed 'all this Verona', its wonderous pinkish glow. Here we have a transversal image that brings together elements that might be habitually kept apart, fish and stone, geology and churches, rivers of colour. The title of Ruskin's lecture makes the point clearly. He uses the plural: 'Verona and its Rivers'. There is, in one sense, only one river to

Verona: the Adige. But for Ruskin Verona was the residue of a multiplicity of flows. He would count the river Po of Dante, and the Dora, and the Ticino. And he includes the flow of geologies that made it all the way to Venice, the Royal Institution and Jermyn street, the words of Shakespeare, and the paint of John Bellini, Mantegna, and Vettor Carpaccio. And for Ruskin the very mouths of Venetians were formed in the wake of the rivers of Verona: 'for at least six hundred years', he notes, 'the Venetians have been contending with those great rivers – at their mouths'.[41]

Though there is something accumulative in the 'and' of all that Ruskin connects in his account of 'Verona and its Rivers', he does not seek to totalize the city. He does not organize Verona via plan nor section nor map,[42] but rather walks us in bit by bit via paths that lead from the quarries of 'the peach-blossom marble, of which Verona is chiefly built'.[43] The quarried stone came to generate arched bridges that traversed the river and fortifications that at once secured the land from the waters and (temporarily) from Teutonic hordes. And it would be carried along paths that would become streets and arranged as architecture that would house armies and now museums that now hold the sculpture also of the stone. The fortifications, Castelvecchio and what remains of the Roman walls were at once outcomes to the flow of material as much as they came to articulate material flows. These walls fostered art, by securing this place for long periods from the tumult of war. The stone that formed walls formed art, and the iron that flows through the stone also flows as exquisite, sculptured grilles of Verona's Romanesque, Gothic, Medieval, and Renaissance churches. It is a city of the fluid, dynamic, and at times grotesque. Many pedestrian streets are today lined with the stone, and the water that collects after rain flows through the centre of these streets in drains carefully cupped from the rock before returning to the river. There is little more joyous than the sun hitting these streets after a summer shower. The whole place glows yellow-pink. The streets are lined with buildings that carry the colour too. The pigment which flowed as iron through limestone now flows more often in paint pots and plaster washes over facades. Most buildings are engaged not as a succession of objects but rather an unfolding of facades out of the street. The shape of the buildings of the old town is the alimentary tract of the streets. They were formed more in the wake of the movement of the horse, labourers, carts and stone than by any geometric or formal system of organization. The diameter of the cartwheel that bore the weight of the stone had a bigger impact than any architect's compass here. This city reminds us *architecture is geographically and historically secondary to the movements that precede it*. This is part of architecture's inherent transversality.

The immense elliptical colosseum of double arches that stands today at the heart of Verona was once just beyond the city walls and has been falling apart now for just short of 2000 years. Ruskin would have had more to eat here if an earthquake hadn't robbed the coliseum of its outer ring and layers of stone a 1000 years ago. That white and pink limestone came to settle elsewhere. This architecture is a debris that remains from that which traverses it. The sweat of slaves in underground tunnels, the flicker of life and death in public executions and blood sports, an orgy under the direction of deities, wild animals gorging themselves before being engorged by gladiators, and all manner of *ludi* under the open sky. The word 'arena' means 'sand'

and the material held in this stone bowl was used to soak up the blood spilt. And since the renaissance, the arena has been shaped by the violence and passion of operatic performance. The architecture was configured in the wake of excessive pleasure and pain, a fishbowl for sex and the social. When Ruskin wanted to describe the play between the Roman and Gothic forces of Verona, he suggested it was 'not out of clay, but out of splendid wild beasts'.[44] These forces still play themselves out here, and there is something splendid about the place yet.[45]

The contemporary intervention related to this amphitheatre that gives me immense pleasure is simple but not simplistic (Figure 6.1). It is the way the seats at the base of the arena are set for opera performances across summer. The seats are ordered in the usual rational way, one by one, row by row, but they are blood red and an equally deep-red cushion can be rented to soften the blow of those sitting on stone. This colour does not come with the singular fixation of *this* equals *that* of transference but opens to the and … and … and of transversality. An opening to material histories and new thoughts, semiotic chains and symbolic linkages that pass in a colour. This intervention articulates passion as tonal and becomes a vibrant bridge to 'all this Verona'.

Intermingling

The outcome of transversality is explained in *Anti-Oedipus* in reference to the work of the writer Marcel Proust and an episode of a passenger on a train moving through a landscape that is only accessed one window at a time. Proust's Narrator notes, 'I was lamenting the loss of my strip of pink sky when I caught sight of it afresh, but red this time, in the opposite window which it left at a second bend in the line.'[46] Deleuze and Guattari write, 'Thus in the trip on the train in *In Search of Lost Time*, there is never a totality of what is seen nor a unity of the points of view, except along the transversal that the frantic passenger traces from one window to the other, "in order to draw together, in order to reweave intermittent and opposite fragments."'[47] And they go on to suggest '[t]his drawing together, this reweaving is what [James] Joyce called *re-embodying*'.[48] The transversal operates by building our worlds from partial objects (stone by stone) and mobile images (bit by bit), gathered as we might build *journeys* from the windows of a train. We are never able to see both sides at once, never able to look through all windows at once. Though the transversal may give me a 'total' of what I think of as *a* place or a journey, there is nothing totalizing about the perspective offered. In this regard it was inaccurate for Foucault to suggest *Anti-Oedipus* presents 'Marx and Freud in the same incandescent light'. What the transversal gives us is more like the flickering of candles or the dizzying twinkle of fairy lights or stars themselves overhead. The transversal does not take the 'opposite fragments' of any dualism and merely illuminates the two as one. Nor does the transversal generate or reinforce the identity of the elements it passes between.[49] Rather, *the transversal is the zone between indistinct entities that are formed in the very wake of the movement.*

On the way to the station for Venice Ruskin notes of Verona, 'I know nothing in architecture at once so exquisite, and so wild, and so strange, in the expression of self-conquest achieved almost in a dream.'⁵⁰ The transversality Ruskin engages is a tool – a touchstone – that architects might suck upon to foster such conquests elsewhere. Indeed, transversality might foster a self-conquest of architecture itself or at least a conquest of the discipline as we currently know it. What we arrive at (in departing from Verona) is a very different discipline. An anti-oedipal discipline. An architecture that would not threaten to cut itself off from the world and that might instead find itself in its very midst. An architecture that leaks passion and fish and rolls down streets. Like iron in stone.

Figure 6.1 Verona Arena, aerial panoramic view. Image © Andrey Khrobostov/Alamy Stock Photo.

7

Schizoanalysis

Landing a legion

There is much that is shared between a soldier on the march and a schizophrenic out for a walk. Elizabeth Diller and Ricardo Scofidio suggest as much in a work launched to mark the 50th anniversary of the D-Day Landing. Their publication, *Back to the Front: Tourisms of War* (1995), explores the shared territories of those forging 'a relationship with the outside world' through war and tourism and the sharp logistics and hazy blur of landings.[1] In the book, two of Diller and Scofidio's projects – 'suit Case Studies: The Production of a National Past' and 'Hostility into Hospital' – serve as provocative preamble and postscript to a series of essays in French and English from Jean-Louis Déotte, Thomas Keenan, Frédéric Migayrou, Lynne Tillman and Georges Van den Abbeele. The book thus plays between architectural practice and theorization as well as war and tourism, across the English Channel and the Atlantic. The question of how history and architecture come to constitute subjects (soldiers or tourists) is a concern that runs cover to cover. In Migayrou's chapter 'The Extended Body: Chronicle of a Day with No History' the architectural theorist explores 'strategies of historicization' surrounding D-Day, and in particular what he calls a 'strategy of inscription' that he defines as 'a normative system that helps organize and hierarchize and to establish a teleology and an orientation that permeates the whole "Modern" project'.[2] Migayrou would find this 'strategy of inscription' in tension with the actuality of the D-Day Landing which he would cast as 'the theoretical object'.[3] But this theoretical object is less an object per se than an objective. An objective to fixate on parts and details and their small 't' truths liberated from overarching inscriptions. For Migayrou the theoretical object 'reveals the workings of the different strategies of historicization, and the degrees of a process of restoration around an impossible factual truth'.[4] Migayrou frames history as a neurotic exercise fixated on uncovering an incontrovertible truth, and he frames the forays of theory as a two-fold process that first identifies the historicizing systems in play and then seeks to restore to the event – in this case the Landing – the immediacies and intensities that history has repressed. He notes of his process:

> I have reviewed all the articles and documents, and all the books with their eye-catching covers which retrace the occurrences of 6 June 1944, and which are accountable for its proper reinstatement within the polemics of historians, where

the illusory truth of history has turned into a strategy for constructing validity. In this entire literature, running to thousands of pages, it is, oddly, impossible to extract more than a handful of lines dealing with the actual moment of the Landings. In these lines, the language seems booby-trapped and stifled, caught up in a chaos which suspends the temporal continuum, and does away with any objectivizing distance.[5]

The point is one that has been reiterated ever since Hannah Arendt endured the Eichmann trials and is that which Migayrou suggests is permeating 'the whole "Modern" project'. It concerns the alignment of history with logistical quantifications, strategic objectifications and statistical generalizations, set clearly against theory's grappling with sheer irrational intensities, tactical constructions and the rawer-than-raw violence of war and life itself. Migayrou is explicit on this point, noting that theory is poised as 'the reverse of the extreme rationalization engendered by conflict'.[6] And yet there is an odd reversal of roles here: Migayrou constructs an image of a theorist soldiering on methodically through 'all the articles and documents, and all the books' and an 'entire literature' in order to locate accounts from *actual* soldiers 'caught up in a chaos'. The theorist spends months retracing the output of rationalist historians whilst the soldier, on the other hand, 'suspends the temporal continuum, and does away with any objectivizing distance', blurring that same day.[7] For Migayrou the 'handful of lines' that address the immediacy of the Landing resonate with Robert Capa's blurred and grainy photographs and Samuel Fuller's 'syncopated' images of the event. Black-and-white images of a legion surging, swarming, drifting, half swimming, half stumbling, here and there in geographic terms. The temporality of the accounts was equally adrift. Migayrou suggests that accounts of that day 'continually extend and elaborate it, to turn it into a longer day: the longest day'.[8] Migayrou's attempt to resist the pull towards normative histories via those same histories, in the restoration of that which is blurred, reminds us that to resist anything in particular – to be 'anti' something – comes with the risk of reinforcing that very thing we set ourselves against. This is theory *back-to-front*. Not a case of 'rationalization engendered by conflict' but rather of conflict engendered by rationalization. The soldier becomes the schizo constructor of new worlds, a legion of a thousand bodies confronting fascism, washed up at dawn and emerging from waters onto a land fast becoming otherwise, adrift in 'the longest day'.[9] The theorist becomes Arendt's anal manager of train timetables and surveyor of 'thousands of pages' confronting history emerging from books in archives geographically removed from Omaha Beach, Normandy, and 50 years away from 6 June 1944. Soldiering on in archives as a legion of schizos makes land.

Delirium

For Gilles Deleuze and Félix Guattari, *schizoanalysis* was a way of negotiating these two poles or what in *Anti-Oedipus* (1972) they refer to as two *deliriums:* one a neurotic (indeed paranoiac), reactionary, rational, consuming and colonial delirium. The other, a schizophrenic, flow and break flow (schizzes), revolutionary, irrational, blurred and syncopated delirium. Using the term 'delirium' to describe each makes it clear that the relation between the two was not one of dialectical opposition (which would likely have demarcated the rational as 'the real' and the irrational as 'delusion').[10] Where a dialectic seeks to establish opposition and at the same time establish a political order of one term over another, for Deleuze and Guattari, both the rational and the irrational are deliria, surging together.[11] Deleuze writes, 'Reason is always a region cut out of the irrational – not sheltered from the irrational at all, but a region traversed by the irrational and defined only by a certain type of relation between irrational factors. Underneath all reason lies delirium, drift.'[12] An image is generated of *the inherency of difference*: the irrational at once different to and at the core of rationality.[13] We might think of it in this way: Migayrou traverses accounts of soldiers related to a rational hour (the H-hour) and to a singular historically identifiable day (D-Day), but in these well-ordered chronologies he finds 'the longest day', a blurred and irrational temporality. The D-Day and 'the longest day' do not preclude each other; rather they are both deliria: one the delirium of historians furtively slotting life into finely tuned chronologies; the other the delirium of soldiers surging through waters. These different accounts circulate one through the other and make land together.

Schizoanalysis walks

Schizoanalysis operates in neither the affirmation of the rational over the irrational nor the affirmation of the irrational over the rational, but rather in the negation of both in order that a desire might be liberated from the 'habits of thought' to which it is subject. But it's a long story and even a coroner's report starts with a date and place of birth: schizoanalysis emerged in the first collaborative work of Deleuze and Guattari, *Anti-Oedipus*, but was conceived in Guattari's work at the La Borde clinic and would carry traces of the thirteenth series of Deleuze's *Logic of Sense* (1969), 'Of the Schizophrenic and the Little Girl', which plays between the different productive nonsenses of the author Lewis Carroll and the playwright Antonin Artaud.[14] In *Anti-Oedipus* schizoanalysis confronts the problem of dominant understandings, belief systems or what Deleuze and Guattari refer to as 'regimes of thought'.[15] The problem is not so much that we operate with understandings, beliefs or within regimes of thought; it is when such systems *transcend*. That is, when a system of logic extends its branches *ad infinitum*. Or when it enters the interior and is deemed essential. Or when it rises above in order that it appears as the overarching logic into which one fits. Or when it sinks below as if it were eternally there waiting to be discovered. What we have at such times is no longer just *this or that* system of logic, but rather an axiom, a law or a pervasive truth which seems to precede all that it organizes. *Anti-Oedipus* takes aim at two particularly noxious examples that take the names: Freud and Marx. Any psychoanalyst can hear any thought expressed by any one of us and can place that thought into a complex and proliferating series of classifications that have Oedipus as its trunk and neuroses as branches. Any Marxist can look at any social relation and dig down to find class struggle in our callouses or likewise look above to find ideology swirling about our sweaty brow. Again, the problem is not that psychoanalysis or Marxism has formulated readings for the events of life; it is that such readings transcended and become associated with 'the rational' and 'the real'.

Schizoanalysis unthreads the regimes of thought that had stitched up the world. And the psychopathy of schizophrenia seemed to be an ideal antidote for neurotic oedipal compulsions. Deleuze and Guattari tell us, 'Freud doesn't like schizophrenics. He doesn't like their resistance to being oedipalized.'[16] Where an oedipal (indeed paranoiac) logic might be 'how do I reconcile *x* with the overarching organization of the world?' schizophrenia subscribes to no overarching or foundational logic and instead, as Guattari notes, 'will work towards its complexification, its processual enrichment, towards the consistency of its virtual lines of bifurcation and differentiation, in short towards its ontological heterogeneity'.[17] It is a pouncing from one thought to another that resists being domiciled in any particular regime of thought and indeed that unthreads the most tightly woven systems of logic. This is, for Deleuze and Guattari, 'the pure schizophrenic process'.[18] It must be noted, however, that although the schizophrenic is invoked in *Anti-Oedipus* as a *conceptual persona*, schizoanalysis is less concerned with the clinical aspects of schizophrenia than the critical and conceptual possibilities for a mode of operation that might allow us to deal with the real and yet non-structured. Schizophrenia posed a mode of operation that connected that which was not yet organized, heard what was not yet audible and saw what was not yet configured in visibility. Across *Anti-Oedipus*, Deleuze and Guattari define schizoanalysis in terms that at once negate the psychoanalytical paradigms from which it departs and in terms that relate to its functioning in and of itself:

> There are no excavations to be undertaken, no archaeology, no statues in the unconscious: there are only stones to be sucked, a la Beckett, and other machinic elements belonging to deterritorialized constellations. The task of schizoanalysis is that of learning what a subject's desiring-machines are, how they work, with what syntheses, what bursts of energy in the machine, what constituent misfires, with what flows, what chains, and what becomings in each case.[19]

There was a set of clear rules to schizoanalysis. Deleuze and Guattari note four *theses* that sought to weave the social and the sexual (Marx and Freud)[20] 'to analyse the specific nature of the libidinal investments in the economic and political spheres'.[21] There were also four *functors* that set out to define the unconscious in terms of territories, universes, fluxes and phylums. And also, four *components* that demarcate the different manners by which the connections between semiotic, physical matters and matters of expression might be studied in their generative, transformational, diagrammatic and machinic modes. The logic of schizoanalysis does start to read like a flow diagram of unfolding demarcations that perhaps threaten to reinstitute a clinical model of the unconscious, albeit unlike the clinical models Deleuze and Guattari hoped to dispel. This complication, or rather implication, of psychoanalysis *in* schizoanalysis occurs also at the level of references Deleuze and Guattari invoke. A constellation of wayward psychoanalysts are drawn upon to at once establish the conceptual roots of schizoanalysis and simultaneously to liberate schizoanalysis from its psychoanalytic origins: Wilhelm Reich who found psychic repression based on social oppression and who would trace the blue energy of the orgone through the skies as much as through the orgasm; Bruno Bettelheim who would locate autism in fairy tales and mass behaviour in the air; and Gisela Pankow who would massage, bath and swath schizophrenics and have them spatialize their bodies in clay.

When it comes down to it though, schizoanalysis departs the psychoanalysis from which it emerges and becomes *critical* rather than *clinical*. It becomes far more a stone-sucking than a building of walls. Despite its *theses, functors* and *components*, the process of schizoanalysis might be summated as a simple two-step operation: We start with what seems to be a 'raw desire' – say the desire to make love with someone (that person you saw swimming at the lake, for example) or the desire to earn a decent income (as a builder, for example). For Deleuze and Guattari such desires are both sexual and social and at once neurotic *and* schizo in character – framed by logics and systems and yet wild and expressive. They are 'a mixture of forms of desire and of interest that are specifically reactionary and vaguely revolutionary'.[22] Schizoanalysis proceeds by way of the destruction of codifications to which something is habitually or traditionally subject. This is step one: 'Destroy, destroy. The task of schizoanalysis goes by way of destruction – a whole scouring of the unconscious, a complete curettage.'[23] This would be the destruction of sexual and gender classifications and the normative sexualities promulgated by Freud, from the desire felt at the lake that day. And the destruction of the class constitution, the ideo-economic imposition of Marx, from a drive to build.

Having destroyed the reactive regimes, schizoanalysis proceeds with the liberation of revolutionary desire or what might be thought of as a *rawer-than-raw* desire. This is step two. For Deleuze and Guattari, '[w]ith every structure dislodged, every memory abolished, every organism set aside, every link undone, they [desires] function as raw partial objects, dispersed working parts of a machine that is itself dispersed. In short, *partial objects are the molecular functions of the unconscious*'.[24] A desire is a 'partial object' in that the part pays no respect to the whole with which it was traditionally or habitually associated. In the text *Schizoanalytic Cartographies* (1989), Guattari notes that these rawer-than-raw objects of schizoanalysis 'are like crystals of singularization, points of bifurcation outside the dominant coordinates, on the basis of which mutant universes of reference can spring up'.[25] Schizoanalysis is thus simultaneously an act of departure and flight: a departure or destruction of the 'dominant coordinates' of thought – the thinking habitually imposed upon a subject. And a flight towards 'mutant universes' – alternate modes of critique and creation – generative of new subjects. To suck on a stone without choking on orality or the perverse pleasure of building a pontoon to make love on a lake. Schizoanalysis is described by Deleuze and Guattari as the 'little additional effort' that is necessary 'to overturn everything, and to lead us finally toward other far-off places'.[26]

Dogs on leashes

Exactly how far the flight of schizoanalysis might go, and how many 'far off places' might be arrived at, was a point of some contention. In his Preface to *Anti-Oedipus*, Michel Foucault identifies 'three adversaries' that the book would confront: The first was the 'political ascetics, the sad militants, the terrorists of theory'.[27] Largely those who find a Marxism in every kiss. The second would be what Foucault called 'the poor technicians of desire'.[28] Largely those who find a mommy or a daddy in every job advertisement. *Anti-Oedipus* would not force any event, thing or thought into a singular reading but instead find sex in the social, and the social in sex, placing 'Marx and Freud in the same incandescent light' as Foucault notes.[29] But it is the third 'adversary' to which Foucault draws our attention and which might constitute both the fundamental achievement of *Anti-Oedipus* and yet pose a challenge to schizoanalysis itself. Foucault writes:

> Last but not least, the major enemy, the strategic adversary is fascism (whereas *Anti-Oedipus*' opposition to the others is more of a tactical engagement). And not only historical fascism, the fascism of Hitler and Mussolini – which was able to mobilize and use the desire of the masses so effectively – but also the fascism in us all, in our heads and in our everyday behavior, the fascism that causes us to love power, to desire the very thing that dominates and exploits us.[30]

The reason such an adversary might operate as a challenge to schizoanalysis is the inherence of its link with that which it rallies against: the psychoanalysis *in* schizoanalysis. It may be that schizoanalysis involves the incorporation of difference, an incorporation of Oedipus in the schizo, a difference in itself, but where the Oedipus in *Anti-Oedipus* is denuded of its psychoanalytic function and swept up in critique of all manner of colonialism, of all hierarchies and of all regimes of thought and has us looking beyond them towards revolutionary expressions of desire; the psychoanalysis in schizoanalysis is less convincingly departed from. It comes to feel more like a resistance than a departure. More like a French resistance than a D-Day Landing. This critique is a little back-to-front and *back to the front*, but it is nevertheless a critique well established. It is the idea that in resistance we often reinstate that which we resist. William Shakespeare had put it this way: 'The lady doth protest too much, methinks.'[31] In arguing so vehemently against the accusations of Prince Hamlet, Queen Gertrude's resistance does little more than reinforce Hamlet's case. Foucault identified a similar logic in the first volume of his *History of Sexuality* (1976). He would call it 'the repressive hypothesis' and notes that the position against something, anti-something, is caught in a bind with that which it opposes.[32] His example would be the priest and the supposed repression of sex from the seventeenth to the mid-twentieth century – the priest in the confessional with his hand on his cock saying, 'Tell me more my son'. An overenthusiastic indulgence in that which one was meant to be departing from. Could this be the relation between schizoanalysis and the psychoanalysis to which it is opposed? It is possible to argue that the clinical aspects of schizophrenia constructed in psychoanalysis have too tight a hold over the revolutionary critical capacities of schizoanalysis. The threat is that schizoanalysis itself might come to be just another regime of thought 'in our heads and in our everyday behavior', replacing a Freudianism and a Marxism with a DeleuzoGuattarianism. Replacing two adversaries with an even more insidious fascism 'in us all'. And there were already in *Anti-Oedipus*, symptoms, signs, that schizoanalysis might house all too comfortably the very disease it sought to cure. Though Deleuze and Guattari commence the book with the image of 'a schizophrenic out for a walk', there is always a risk that a walk becomes a dogmatic march:

> We are all little dogs, we need circuits, and we need to be taken for walks. Even those best able to disconnect, to unplug themselves, enter into connections of desiring-machines that re-form little earths. Even Gisela Pankow's great deterritorialized subjects are led to discover the image of a family castle under the roots of the uprooted tree that crosses through their body without organs.[33]

On the one hand there is a sophistication to a schizoanalytic incorporation of Oedipus, and it should be accounted for if for no other reason than 'the disjointed fragments of Oedipus remain stuck to all the corners of the historical social field as a battlefield'.[34] In this regard, schizoanalysis inheres difference, enfolding different regimes of thought rather than seeking to repress them. And this logic plays itself out in many ways in *Anti-Oedipus* as the reason within the irrational, and 'the presence of antiproduction within production itself'.[35] But, on the other hand, how clearly schizoanalysis risks reproducing the Freudian state. Schizoanalysis invoked as the walk of the schizo and the need for fresh air threatens to become the walk of a dog on a leash. And the root of an upturned tree might look more like a family home for mummy, daddy and me than it did the puckering lips of a stone-sucking mouth, or the puckering of an anus, or a galaxy. One wonders how close schizoanalysis came to landing 'the very thing that dominates and exploits us'.

Blur

Despite the issues, Guattari would soldier on with schizoanalysis, writing that it 'was never conceived as a self-enclosed field'.[36] His point is that it was less a fixed 'model' than what he calls a 'metamodel' that had no orientation or teleological or clinical inclination. 'Schizoanalysis, I repeat, is not an alternative modelling. It is metamodeling,' Guattari doth protest.[37] Deleuze didn't want to talk about it. In a discussion published as 'Five Propositions on Psychoanalysis' (1973), Deleuze suggests schizoanalysis was fighting for air at the very moment it made land:

> [T]oday we're looking for the new mode of unification in which, for example, the schizophrenic discourse, the intoxicated discourse, the perverted discourse, the homosexual discourse, all the marginal discourses can subsist, so that all these escapes and discourses can graft themselves onto a war-machine that won't reproduce a State or Party Apparatus. For that very reason we no longer want to talk about schizoanalysis, because that would amount to protecting a particular type of escape, schizophrenic escape.[38]

The Deleuze scholar Ian Buchanan summates the position as 'the new medicine will have neither doctors nor patients, just cases and subjects at risk'.[39] It is also likely that the new medicine would depart clinics and those disciplines that have been the arbiters of good health and become far more critical than clinical. This language of a 'new medicine' resonates with Diller's account of architecture: 'Given the technological and political re-configurations of the contemporary body, spatial conventions may be called into question by architecture. Architecture can be used as a kind of surgical instrument to operate on itself (in small increments).'[40] Where nineteenth-century critique was all about taste, late-twentieth- and early-twenty-first-century architecture would pursue alternate senses of the body and probe organs historically repressed. The cover of Diller and Scofidio's book *Flesh: Architectural Probes* (1994) would feature buttocks, creased across the spine, and within, would house all manner of partial object. The body, its organs, productions and expressions have little to do with habitual engagements and become the site for Diller and Scofidio's architectural exploration. In a paper that served as an introduction to *Flesh* titled 'The Mutant Body of Architecture', Georges Teysott refers to the body that Diller and Scofidio incite as 'a pre-tensioned structure whose stresses are rendered visible'.[41] Migarou, in *Back to the Front*, repeated the refrain noting, 'The procedures of the technological field are an a priori domain that must be conceptualized without distance. Diller + Scofidio are architects, and their respective production abides by this definition of a body which, at any given moment, assumes the tension inherent in any relationship to context.'[42]

This 'pre-tensioned' tension is no more apparent than in Diller and Scofidio's Blur building, constructed for the Swiss Expo 2002 on a lake in Yverdon-les-Bains, Switzerland (Figure 7.1). In this case it is a tension with a lo-fi hum. The Blur building brings the operations of the body back to the front and performs as an architectural probe to flesh. It was constructed as a tensegrity structure, elliptical in plan about 90 metres wide by 60 deep, and in elevation took the form of a disc, just over 20 metres high. This skeletal disc stood in the lake on four columns sunk deep beneath the water. It was connected to the land via two bridges – one for entrance, the other for exit – that were approximately 120 metres long and of a pre-fabricated ribbed steel. Bodies would make their way in, and different bodies would make their way out, and the procession looked rather like workers might move into and out of a factory on a conveyor in a Jacques Tati film. Visitors wore clear plastic raincoats, fitted with tracking and location technologies. They were called 'braincoats', a sort of high-tech lo-fi organization of bodies. But these bridges of bodies – in and out – were less bridges than jetties. Where a bridge tends to connect two things, a jetty tends to connect one and just reach outward. From the bank of the lake what this jetty ran towards was indiscernible – a fog or a cloud. The intricate tensegrity skeleton held 35,000 high pressure nozzles operating at 924 PSI emitting a rich fog of droplets of .01 millimetre in diameter. The water was pumped from the lake, pressure regulated and filtered and then sprayed. The filtration of the water was necessary to deal with a legion of bacteria (*legionnaires*) that might have infected the bodies that swarmed to this place. Smart weather technology was incorporated which continuously adjusts the water pressure in relation to temperature, humidity, wind speed and direction to regulate the cloud. The result was a droning sound and a vapour that would encase the structure in a mobile cloud of mist. It was an encompassing 'white-out' in 'white noise', a humming tension between the most rational of technologies and irrational of atmospheres. For Diller and Scofidio, the 'objective is to weave together architecture and electronic technologies, yet exchange the properties of each for the other'.⁴³ For Deleuze and Guattari the rational technologies and the irrational atmosphere generated would likely have both been considered deliria, and as Deleuze says, 'we bathe in delirium'.⁴⁴

Step 1: Destroy, destroy. Scofidio notes that the Blur building was 'to produce a "technological sublime" parallel to the "natural sublime" experienced in the scaleless and unpredictable mass of fog'.⁴⁵ We have here the technology of tensegrity, water filtration and the numeracies of nozzles. And the immersive, haze of cloud formations drifting above a lake. But this is just a starting point. It was always the quality of the sublime that a division or quantification of this or that element (this or that place and placement) was not possible. The dialectic between the technology and the cloud and between the body and place becomes a site for an experiment of erasure and the Blur building enacts a type of deletion that makes one inherent to the other:

> Upon entering Blur, visual and acoustic references are erased. There is only an optical 'white-out' and the 'white-noise' of pulsing nozzles. Contrary to immersive environments that strive for visual fidelity in high-definition with ever-greater technical virtuosity, Blur is decidedly low-definition. In this exposition pavilion there is nothing to see but our dependence on vision itself.⁴⁶

Blur removes that which allows normal orientations, and it negates that which was *architectural* about this 'building'. Insides and outsides, structure and envelope, technologies and atmospheres, people and places would come to swarm one within the other as the dominant frames of reference were departed from. Teysott had described a similar character to the earlier work of Diller and Scofidio in noting 'the dis-embodiment of place and the dis-placement of body'.⁴⁷ The Blur building takes this inversion a step further, into negation. Diller would describe the building as 'featureless, depthless, scaleless, spaceless, massless, surface less, and context less', and it was temporally transient too. It was entered on 15 May and exited on 21 October that same year. And every hour of every day was different. There were moments during its operation where the fog of the building blended near seamlessly with the clouds beyond and other moments where the wind stripped the structure bare. The result was 'an exhibition pavilion with nothing on display' and even '[a]rchitecture would be absent'.⁴⁸

Step 2: Rouse the 'dispersed working parts of a machine that is itself dispersed'. In 2013 Diller was interviewed by the architectural historian Anthony Vidler for a publication, *Log 28*, of The Anyone Corporation. The issue was a self-declared 'Stocktaking' of the current state of architectural practice, pedagogy, theory and criticism. The interview took its title from a quote from Diller: 'Architecture is a technology that has not yet discovered its agency'.⁴⁹ The idea is a simple one and one that others had identified in the operations of Diller and Scofidio. Teysott had noted of their work that '[t]he incorporation of technology is not effected by "imagining" a new environment, but by reconfiguring the body itself, pushing outward to where its artificial extremities encounter "the world."'⁵⁰ When Blur stripped the body of its capacities, it was only first to neutralize the body and then second (with 'little additional effort') to articulate new affordances, in this case to allow one to see 'our dependence on vision itself'. The white light and white noise of Blur incited other organs than eyes and ears and set them in motion upon that lake. The mass entering and exiting the Blur building are only ever vaguely constituted and the blur itself operated as a condition under which difference overcomes identity. It is a mass just as likely to contain tourists, victims, civilians, the perverted, homosexual, marginal, neurotics and schizophrenics. A legion that at times moved in certain directions and at times constituted solid figures, a force of a single body, stepping in unison on jetties that run in one direction only, but likewise that fragments, fades and falls. It is less that this architecture 'has not yet discovered its agency' than it is *an architecture that affords capacities not yet interned in identity*. What Migayrou wrote in his *Back to the Front* essay, when writing of D-Day and 'the longest day' seems equally a description of the 'far-off places' Diller and Scofidio continue to take us:

> Landings here take on the form of an impossible inscription whereby the body sheds all incidental value in the mastery of the territory. The body finds in it this abandonment, an autonomy and a vacancy which in turn becomes a resource, a capacity to coherence of its multi-dimensional nature: the extended body, the body prostrate, an elementary point of exit from rational space.[51]

Figure 7.1 Diller + Scofidio, *Blur Building* (2002). Photograph by Beat Widmer. Image courtesy of Diller Scofidio + Renfro.

8

Transcendental empiricism

Tokyo Paris

In the Palais de Tokyo on a Tuesday evening in March 1987, Gilles Deleuze cautioned students: 'If you are trapped in the dream of others, you are fucked'.[1] The students who comprised the bulk of the audience that evening were studying cinema at the newly created film school 'La fémis' and Deleuze's lecture focused on what it is 'to have an idea', to create, in cinema and philosophy.[2] La fémis was inaugurated a few months earlier and joined the Cinémathèque française, the Institut National de Formation aux Métiers de l'Image et du Son and the Centre National de la Photographie, collectively under the auspices of the 'Palais de l'image'. The Palais de l'image occupied draughty spaces in the West wing of the Palais de Tokyo. The students of La fémis plied their trade that evening, filming Deleuze's lecture. The film took the title 'What Is the Creative Act?' [Qu'est-ce que l'acte de creation?]. Deleuze would parry the questions: '[W]hat exactly do you, who do cinema, do?' and 'What exactly do I do, when I do, or hope to do, philosophy?'.[3] He had recently published his second book on cinema but claimed no mastery of the art and instead was focused on the philosophy that the cinematic encounter might prompt. This positioning was important for one main reason that Deleuze would summarize that evening as '[i]deas must be treated as potentials as already engaged in this or that mode of expression and inseparable from it'.[4] What Deleuze was conveying was a sense of the *déjà là* – the already there – harboured in any idea and inextricable from the material upon which our disciplines focus. Deleuze suggests that different disciplines operate in different manners, take different objects, set different parameters, such that 'ideas in cinema can only be cinematographic'.[5]

This is not to suggest that between disciplines resonances might not be engaged, such as when a novel becomes a film, but rather to suggest what corresponds in such moments is the filmic idea that is encountered *in* the novel. That is, that communication between different disciplines, or what might be thought of as different regimes of logic, is indeed communication between that which is the *already there of one logic in another*. In his lecture Deleuze would refer to the Japanese director Akira Kurosawa and his film *Seven Samurai* (1954) as a case of a literary idea that 'corresponds' to a cinematographic work. In this case, a novel of Fyodor Dostoyevsky with which Kurosawa 'finds himself in familiarity'.[6] Kurosawa finds resonance with the agitation of characters 'taken by urgency' in Dostoyevsky's novel *Idiot* (1869). It is not that Kurosawa as a cinematographer takes Dostoyevsky as an author and adopts or adapts the literary Russian idiot into a cinematic samurai, but rather that there is an *encounter* with a common problem or concern. In this case, a problem that finds itself in an oval space drenched by rain and in a question given voice by one of Kurosawa's characters 'What is it to be a samurai?' A 'question deserving of the Idiot', Deleuze says.[7] A necessary question. To be a victim to other's dreams it seems is to be French, Russian, Japanese, to be a philosopher, a cinematographer, an idiot, a samurai, or an architect and to not ask 'What exactly do you, who do *x*, do?'

The filming of Deleuze's La fémis Tuesday talk involved cameras and lights focused on the bespectacled philosopher wearing a purple woollen pullover, pulled over a white collared shirt, a tall full bottle of water and a microphone to his left, an empty glass and a watch to his right, and a scattering of papers in between to which he rarely referred. The film relies on two main shots: one close, framed about the philosopher's shoulders and face, and another further out, that captured more of the blackened backdrop of the talk. The film students were communicating with the aspects of this space that mattered to them at that moment and removing that which did not. Deleuze too was in communication with that which mattered to him at that moment. Zooming in and focusing on a drift of thoughts and a line of logic, as a philosopher does. The students of cinema and the philosopher rendered the architecture in which the event occurred *indiscernible*. Neither were trapped in any architect's dream. For an architect though – for the architect in me, that does or hopes to do architecture – the philosophy and the cinema of this event are complot with an intense architectural pleasure: of Deleuze adrift in the Palais de Tokyo, Paris.

Looming nightmares

The building, darkened and out of focus, in which Deleuze spoke that evening is complex, odd and profound. Constructed for the 1937 *Exposition Internationale des Arts et Techniques dans la vie modern*, the building was the outcome of a competition. Le Corbusier, Georges Pingusson and Robert Mallet-Stevens were among the contenders who likely had the most pronounced idea of what a 'vie modern' might be, but the architects Jean-Claude Dondel, André Aubert, Paul Viard and Marcel Dastugue would win the competition to construct this Palais. The building was one of many of the 1937 exposition poised between nationalisms and styles. Albert Speer's Nazi pavilion and Boris Iofan's Soviet structure faced off across the Trocadero fountains. A towering eagle and swastika-laden square-columned monument leered at an art deco plinth complete with massive lunging social realist sculptures. On postcards produced for the event, French architects were listed as 'collaborateurs'. Even the mildest of pavilions would be swept into the looming nightmare. Alvar Aalto's Finnish timber pavilion titled 'Le bois est en marche' was described by the journal *Architecture d'Aujourd'hui* as a project of a nation that 'had only to build, and nothing to tear down'.[8] France, on the other hand, was demolition-ready.

The Palais de Tokyo, named after the street upon which it was constructed, rather than the river towards which it opened, would house the modern art collections of the French state and the City of Paris, previously housed in the Petit Palais, Jeu de Paume and Palais du Luxembourg. It was the discordance between the state and city that led the architects to design a twin building, with a symmetrical facade flanking a piazza that steps down towards the river. An *escalier d'honneur* and a raised peristyle were decorated with Alfred Janniot's bas reliefs depicting 'La Gloire des Arts', along with the legends of the earth of the sea, flanked by reclining nymphs. Despite these decorative flourishes, the building is a type of stripped classicism – its characteristics falling somewhere between a strained Italian fascism and a restrained French art deco. The exterior and its colonnades were stone-clad in travertine, marble and Comblanchien limestone, which convincingly hid a rawer concrete structure below.[9] Enormous windows on the north, east and south facades and glass rooves in all other galleries provided daylight, laterally for sculptures and overhead for paintings. Despite the editor of *Architecture d'Aujourd'hui*, André Bloc, cautioning '1937 should resist the triumph of mediocracy',[10] the architectural historian Andrew Ayers's description of the Palais de Tokyo seems appropriate. He calls it 'moderate modernism'.[11] The design sparked heated debate in the modernist architecture reviews of the time.[12] It's classicism was framed as the problem, not its fascism. The debate was a distraction in a discipline-stuck daydreaming, as war erupted. The Vichy regime would use the upper levels of the Palais de Tokyo as a museum, as the Nazis used the basements to hoard property stolen from Parisians sent en masse down the Seine to concentration camps.

By 1945 Avenue de Tokio was renamed Avenue de New-York, but the fascist sympathies persisted. Deleuze notes that 'peoples dreams are always devouring' and in architecture Le Corbusier's dreams are positively cannibalistic.[13] His own fascisms are still blacked out and made digestible in a discipline that distracts with style, form, light and the bourgeois niceties of a 'vie modern'.[14] Though Corbusier lost the competition to build the Palais de Tokyo, a room within would be dedicated to his work in the 1950s. Not all the 1950s, just up till 1956 when the glass ceiling fell in. I think of this less as a constructional deficiency than a moment where matter and thought coincide in an act of material ethics. The western half of the building was temporarily abandoned in 1976 when the Centre Pompidou moved to occupy its high-tech Richard Rogers, Renzo Piano and Gianfranco Franchini piped structure on the other side of Paris. Between 1978 and 1986 the west wing housed multiple arts organizations, organized under multiple titles – the 'Musée national d'art moderne' that became the 'Musée d'Art et d'Essais'; that became the 'Palais de l'image'; that would be proposed as, but not entirely become, a 'Palais de Cinéma', all within the Palais de Tokyo. La fémis, the French state film school opened here on a Tuesday late in November 1986. Deleuze spoke on a Tuesday the following March.

Transcendental empiricism

To escape the dreams of others is not just to exchange one dream for another, one name for another, one discipline for another, one regime of thought for another, but rather to escape via the material, the texture, the grain, of what it is that we do. For those who do *x*. It is to focus, 'beginning at a degree zero' as Deleuze and Guattari say, on the particularity and specificity of the materials with which we work.[15] And to raise thought in concert with this material. The call to escape the dreams of others is a call to tight investments in empirical phenomena. A call to a *transcendental empiricism*.

We should be careful to note, to focus on that which is *already there [déjà là]* in *what we do* should not read as a call to loyally embrace the conventions and habits of our disciplines. That is, it is not the role of anyone – a philosopher, a cinematographer, an architect – to merely hold and reinforce the overarching traditions of a discipline as commemorative or reactive exercises. Deleuze makes the point in noting the difference between the *history of philosophy* whose focus is the institutional organization of the discipline,[16] and the *practice of philosophy* as a creative act. For Deleuze, '[t]o do philosophy' is not an act of discovering ideas, or an uncovering of systems of thought and logic, because whilst an idea might be inextricable from the logics in which it is found, 'far from having as their milieu good sense or common sense, Ideas determine only the communication between disjointed faculties'.[17] For Deleuze the *already there* is a disjointed complex of thought and field. A complex resistant to the generalizations of history, but that instead incites practices of creation and construction. And in philosophy '[c]oncepts must be made'.[18] Similarly for cinema, Deleuze suggests, 'it is not a matter of invoking a story or of contesting one' and not a matter of communication (*á la* representation). But rather of inventing and constructing, in this case 'blocks of movement/duration'.[19] These ideas were one's Deleuze had been freshly negotiating at the time of his La fémis lecture. The talk coincided with the production of his last collaborative work with Félix Guattari, *What Is Philosophy?* (1991), but these ideas were also long-standing. They had emerged in his first monograph *Empiricism and Subjectivity* (1953) focused on the work of the classical empiricist David Hume, and his early work *Difference and Repetition* (1968) where the notion of *transcendental empiricism* arose to resist overbearing logics, the 'dreams of others'.

The very idea of *transcendental empiricism* is both a negation and an alignment: First, transcendental empiricism is a negation. It is a negation of the 'transcendental idealism' of Immanuel Kant which suggests that experience only makes sense when organized by intellectual foundational logics and forms of sensibility (space and time). Deleuze would invert this logic and draw on the work of Alfred North Whitehead in describing the empiricism with which he was concerned: 'the abstract does not explain, but must itself be explained; and the aim is not to rediscover the eternal or the universal, but to find the conditions under which something new is produced (creativeness)'.[20] This is to say, overbearing systems of logic, or regimes of thought, do not in themselves explain anything but rather we must focus tightly on empirical particularities if we are ever to understand anything, including ourselves. The *empirical* is personal and experienced, where the *transcendental* is impersonal and pre-individual. Transcendental empiricism will thus not generate a subject but explore the conditions by which that subject might emerge (albeit as a residue) like an orchid from a wasp or a samurai from an idiot. The architectural implications are clear: *The role of an architect is not to follow the logics of styles and the manifestoes of movements that might address problems but rather to fixate on the problems as instances, material conditions and particularities that themselves might help to explain aesthetic abstractions, stylistic mobilities and the force of manifestoes.*

Second, transcendental empiricism is an alignment. It is an alignment with the 'radical empiricism' of the philosopher and proto-psychologist William James. For James, empiricism concerns itself with the closest of studies of *what is*. His *Essays in Radical Empiricism* (1906) finds forms and logics in all material and in all its configurations. Systems of logic and regimes of thought *unfold* from the abstractions of concrete itself and not vice versa. This position resonates with that developed in *What Is Philosophy?*, where thoughts and concrete, content and expression, surge together 'ceaselessly being woven like a gigantic shuttle'.²¹ This is to say, for Deleuze and Guattari, a thought is not *in* a system of logic, nor is a material *in* a form, but rather they are inextricable, enfolded, woven.²² The outcome is that any explanation for something does not require what James calls 'extraneous trans-empirical connective support' because, as he goes on to say, a thing or a thought 'possesses in its own right a concatenated or continuous structure'.²³ Concatenated and continuous with its multiplicitous contexts. What James calls a 'transempirical entity' was what Fredrich Engels called 'the mysterious junk in which the old idealistic philosophy wrapped itself' or what Deleuze and Guattari would call an oedipal colony.²⁴ It is the habitual philosophical or theoretical frame, considered as the net into which phenomena might fit. Thus, the shared position of James, Engels, and Deleuze and Guattari can be summarized as: *close exploration and experimentation with the material world itself will reveal more than any deferral to habitual codes or traditional axioms.* And here the word 'material' is particular. Material is what we do and what we work with, and should not be understood as divorced from thought. A philosopher works with the material *thought*, as a cinematographer works with the material *blocks of movement/duration*, as an architect works with material *concrete in circulation*. This is *materialism*, as a compact of thought and matter. David Lapoujade states it clearly in his summation of Deleuze and Guattari's position: 'Material is neither Matter, nor Thought, though it is the fabric [tissue] of both.'²⁵ It is for this reason that Deleuze had told the film students of La fémis that '[i]deas must be treated as potentials as already engaged in this or that mode of expression and inseparable from it'.²⁶ Ideas are like the aggregate of concrete.

It is by way of the particularity and specificity of material encounters that transcendental empiricism liberates us from generalized and consuming nightmares, 'the dreams of others'. This attention to particularity and specificity is an attention to the geo-historic. We need not approach material – a book, a film, a building – with logics or stylistic overtures that are imposed from above (transcendent), but rather let the encounter itself (empiricism) unfold a logic directly from a material that is at once thought and matter (transcendental empiricism). There is a realism here, a type of geo-historic real that locates thought in the *already there* world that we encounter. It is already there both in the sense that it pre-exists us and in the sense that it comes first. 'Something in the world forces us to think,' Deleuze writes: 'This something is an object not of recognition but of a fundamental encounter'.²⁷

Palais de Tokyo

Both Deleuze and La fémis departed in 1995. Deleuze from a window, and La fémis from the Palais de Tokyo to a new site in Montmartre. A culture ministry project to place a cinema museum in the empty spaces of the west wing was abandoned by 1997, but only after the space had been 'gutted'. By 1999 a 'Centre for Contemporary Creation' was proposed. When the French architects Anne Lacaton and Jean-Phillippe Vassal approached the grand but long-abandoned spaces of the west wing, they were concerned with a simple question. It was the question of *what it is* – its concrete, its structure, its graffiti, its reclining nymphs. This was because, for them, '[t]he architecture was already there'.[28] It was a case of *déjà là*. This wasn't the *tabula rasa* approach that had excited modernist architects, but rather a geo-historic realist approach, a transcendental empiricism. This gutted, weakened shell was for Lacaton and Vassal a 'hidden structure, the modernity of the place. It was magnificent'.[29] A living modernity, as opposed to a moderate modernism.

By January 2002 the architectural work had prised open one (and a bit) level of space for the exhibition and performance of contemporary art (Figure 8.1). The miserly budget proposed for the initial work suited Lacaton and Vassal who do not consider budgets a restraint, but rather a prompt to restrain from the habitual impulses of the profession: 'It is our duty to start from scratch with each new Project,' Vassal writes. 'That can also mean fundamentally questioning our own profession – and with that the way in which architecture is practiced.'[30] These architects ask of themselves, what exactly do you do, who do architecture? Lacaton and Vassal are not stylistically bound or radicled to defined movements or preordained manifestoes. All of their projects start from scratch, the itch of an encounter with a space, and what they found here at the Palais de Tokyo was already 'striking because of the rightness of its architecture, its dimensioning, its balance of relationships'.[31] To start from scratch is not to start from nothing, but rather to start with the material traces and the dents of an extant architecture. To start by scratching.

The Palais de Tokyo would become an architecture of caravans as ticket booths and shower-curtain screens that might be pulled when overhead daylighting becomes too intense. A bookshop and cafe were demarcated by chicken-wire. It was an odd mix of some original lux surfaces and a rawer negotiation of necessity – the occasional smooth ceiling roundel and marble cladding adjacent to exposed concrete and flaking paint. The architects would access a full-sized art deco cinema in the otherwise Piranesi basement. And access is the word for it. It would be made accessible, but not much more than that. This cinema had never been used because the projection box failed to align with the screen.[32] It was the architectural in this cinema that was engaged, not the cinematographic. The building would remain a 'fragile shell' as Vassal called it.[33] Industrial steel ceiling trusses were added where the threat of another glass ceiling collapse was too great to bear. There were columns that had been weakened by the gutting process, which needed to be reinforced. The material of modernity, once sheafed in stone, now a point of communication in a gutted space. The columns gesture to the flow of force through the structure and bear the scars of both building and demolition processes. For Lacaton and Vassal each column was a stutter that might be liberated rather than attenuated. Steel plate was affixed to reinforce that which it is, rather than to efface or to hide. Lacaton and Vassal attend to actual existing conditions rather than ideological or stylistic imposition. As architects they collaborate with material rather than ideology. There's something joyful in this constructive, creative, particularized practice. What Lacaton and Vassal achieve here is to suggest that difference is not a prior identity but rather a transcendental principle that constitutes empirical diversity. There is no ground zero or shared ground here, but instead a proliferation of difference. Just this one column, reinforced in just this one way.

The success of the early interventions led to the Palais de Tokyo being extensively renovated in 2012 across four floors. It grew from 7,000 to a massive 22,000 square metres of accessible space. The approach was the same, grounded in material specificity and particularity. The logics by which Lacaton and Vassal approach a space are not imposed from above (they are not transcendent) nor does the approach come from the outside, but rather it unfolds from the object under examination that is at once thing and thought. Vassal notes that 'as an architect, you explore the concept of building. Building can be seen in very material and systematic terms because you build with bricks, concrete, steel, and windows. But in our view building means first and foremost thinking'.[34] This is not to say, Lacaton and Vassal are closed to outside influences or thoughts from elsewhere, but rather to say, these associations are established in relation to a common problem or concern that is already embedded in the Palais. The architects would find in other places familiarity. They found 'from the outside' relations with spaces as diverse as the Djemaa el-Fna square in Marrakesh and Alexanderplatz in Berlin. Here they found practises of non-hierarchical movement, open encounters and unscripted performative public space. There was no attempt to import the character of such spaces, but rather an acknowledgement of the common problems such spaces address.

For Lacaton and Vassal there was 'never any question' of taking 'an aesthetic position with respect to the unfinished, to the ruin'.[35] It is the encounter with the ruin that prompts a thought, even the thought to refrain from the disciplines most reified of impositions: style. Architecture's own Vichy syndrome. An oval conference hall, peeling and ruinous, abandoned in 1937 and left untouched, would remain so. It is open now but remains much as it was. The classifications of style, labels of aesthetic movements, and demarcations of motive and architectural intent do not explain this architecture but rather must be explained by the presence of the peeling paint, cracked plaster castings and sweeping stained concrete. The abstractions of concrete so rich, so complex, that our thinking, thought itself, can only but hope to meet it. Vassal notes that '[i]n architecture, the aesthetic is important but it's a consequence of the working process. It's an outcome. And if there exists an aesthetic in the Palais de Tokyo, it's certainly not that of the walls left in their natural state. It's rather the aesthetic that arises from the totality of the design work and now from its use'.[36] From what it exactly does, when it does, or hopes to do. Such a position is so radically different to that of hiding concrete behind stone veneer or hiding Nazi hoards in basements.

Erewhon

Deleuze suggests that '[e]mpiricism is by no means a reaction against concepts nor a simple appeal to lived experience. On the contrary, it undertakes the most insane creation of concepts ever seen or heard'.[37] He makes the point in *Difference and Repetition* (1968), in reference to Samuel Butler's novel *Erewhon* (1872). Butler's work was an exploration of a fictional place, the name of which was an almost-inversion of the word 'nowhere'. It was at once a negation and an alignment. At once a critique of the habits by which the world was traditionally thought and the social, political and logical structures upon which it was built, and an alignment with novel ways of operating and configuring life that was no less particular and specific. For Deleuze, 'Butler's *Erewhon* seems to us not only a disguised no-where but a rearranged now-here.'[38] The Palais de Tokyo is this. A novel engagement with a world afresh, a fictional Paris Tokyo, that operates as an object of 'an essential encounter rather than of recognition'.[39] Every mark made by the architects and construction teams remains visible in the concrete here. Every wall removed can be traced in the surfaces that once were connected, every scratching of the machines of demolition and construction consecrated, in and of the architecture. The Palais de Tokyo escapes the dreams of others as a creative celebration of the already there, here and now.

Figure 8.1 Lacaton and Vassal, *Palais de Tokyo, site de creation contemporaine* (2012–14). Image © Philippe Ruault.

Part Three

'Experimentation'

Part Three turns to the manner by which Gilles Deleuze and Félix Guattari's political philosophy comes to foster all manner of architectural experimentation. Architecture's complicity with conservative power structures and neoliberalism makes the political philosophy of Deleuze and Guattari a hard pill to swallow, but also a crucial corrective. These chapters seek not to deliver the monstrous offspring of Deleuze and Guattari, but rather to explore the capacity of their political philosophy to enrich and disrupt architectural critique and creation. In this regard the following chapters take as their motto the prompt of the philosopher and psychoanalyst:

> Stop! You're making me tired! Experiment, don't signify and interpret! Find your own places, territorialities, deterritorializations, regimes, lines of flight! Semiotize yourself instead of rooting around in your prefab childhood and Western semiology.[1]

9

Islands

Invagination

Rosalind Krauss would draw upon the work of Jacques Derrida in defining *invagination* as 'the folding of one story within another through the invention of a character who exactly repeats the opening of the first story'.[1] For the story of architectural modernism, Modulor was such a character. Le Corbusier's Modulor was an anthropomorphic scale of proportions based on the height of a man with a muscular raised arm and a rather large navel. The man, silhouetted, stands adjacent to two vertical measures: one red and another blue. The red is based on the figure's navel height (1.08 metres in the original version) and is segmented in a spiral graphic according to *phi*. The blue is based on the figure's overall height, including outreached arm, which is exactly two navel heights high (2.16 metres) and similarly segmented. Whilst establishing its trans-historic concurrency with a long lineage of occidental measurement systems – the cubit, the Fibonacci series, and the golden ratio – Modulor was also a character that would embody a contemporary conversion conundrum negotiating both imperial and metric measures and would promise future applications in the 'new order' of modernism. In the first of his two books dedicated to the Modulor, Corbusier notes:

> [T]he 'Modulor' is a measuring tool based on the human body and on mathematics. A man-with-arm-upraised provides, at the determining points of his occupation of space – foot, solar plexus, head, tips of fingers of the upraised arm – three intervals which give rise to a series of golden sections, called the Fibonacci series.[2]

The story into which this 'human body' (that just happens to be that of 'a man') was folded was one of measurement, rationalism and systems of logic largely tied to industrial and commercial expedience. For Corbusier architecture 'must be a thing of the body'[3] even when a house may have been 'a machine for living'.[4] The Modulor was a character that would repeat the story of both, being 'universally applicable to architecture and to mechanics'.[5] A universal masculine body in the long tradition of 'man as measure'.[6]

Modulor was the body as 'epiphoric object', as Alexander Tzonis and Liane Lefaivre define the term, an object that presents in a 'stenographic' way, a conceptual 'framework in use'.[7] And for Tzonis and Lefaivre, such an object operates to confirm that a given framework, the story into which it fits, is a *fait accompli*. Corbusier writes of Modulor, 'It had to be found, and found it was, by the grace of the Muses whose wings brushed the foreheads of two young men.'[8] The two young men to which he is referring were architects working in Corbusier's studio on the rue de Sevres, Justino Serralta a Uruguayan and André Maisonnier a Frenchman. They drew the definitive version of Modulor in 1951. This version was for Corbusier a 'liberating tool' which 'yielded intellectual and artistic satisfaction in full measure'.[9] It was shown at the 'Divina Proportione' Exhibition at the 1951 Milan Triennale, amongst other divine things. Corbusier tells us it was 'in the company of manuscripts or first editions of the works of Vitruvius, Villars de Honnecourt, Piero della Francesca, Durer, Leonardo da Vinci, Alberti, etc., etc.'[10] Corbusier casts the divinely proportioned Modulor as a fulfilled prophecy and casts Seralta and Maisonnier as boys graced by a winged mythological goddess – Seralta and Maisonnier a Romulus and a Remus at the teat of the modern age.

On the one hand invagination is an opening of the inside of a story to a character, an *other*, that might seem like an act of self-confirmation, a *fait accompli*, a tautology and a cosmology. On the other hand, invagination implies an unstable identity. This would be how Maurice Merleau-Ponty had used the term to describe the dynamic self-differentiation of the *flesh*[11] and how Derrida would use the term to denote a 'double bind at work on examples of all undecidable figures'.[12] It is a double bind in the sense that a figure such as Modulor is first bound *neutrally* to the story into which the character was cast as a bare and generalizable form, the empty mathematics of the so-called human body, and yet, second, was bound to its *specificity* – masculinity, muscularity, ability and featured orientation to the world. The double bind shudders in the incompatibility of the story of modernism and the flesh of Modulor. This was no more apparent than in one rupturing version of the drawing where Serralta had cast Modulor in female form – not with the eliding wings of a Muse but rather with breasts, rounded hips and vulva (Figure 9.1). If the figure was as neutral as the blind mathematics and measures might have suggested; if the figure was as bound to the machine as it was professed to be, this might not have caused a ripple. But it did. Corbusier's response to the drawing was far more Victorian than modern: 'Here is the drawing,' he tells readers of *Modulor 2*: 'Here is the drawing prepared by Serralta and Maisonnier: you take the square of the "Modulor man" of 1·83 m. (but, since Serralta has a soft spot for the ladies, his man is a woman 1·83 metres tall: Brrrh!).'[13] In all the measure, the calculation, the mathematics – in all the triumphal acclamations and heroic articulation of Corbusier – comes a parenthetical and inarticulate howl-breath (*cris-souffles*) that escapes more from the gut than the tongue or typewriter: Brrrh!

Islands 99

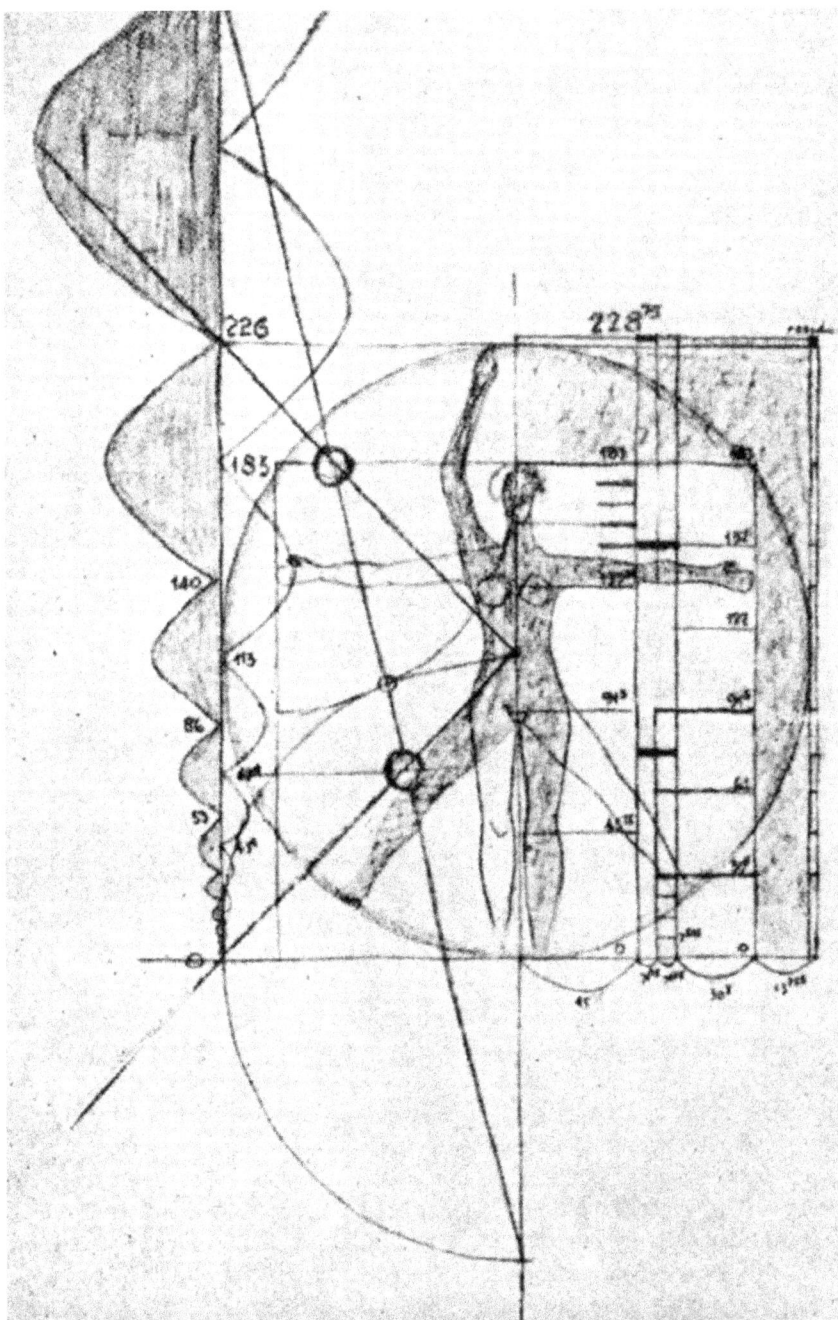

Figure 9.1 Justino Serralta and André Maisonnier, 'Modulor', from Le Corbusier, *Modulor 2: (Let the User Speak Next) Continuation of 'The Modulor'* 1948, (Basel: Birkhäuser, 2004 reprint), 53. Image courtesy of Birkhäuser.

Desert islands

The 'double bind' is a concern of Gilles Deleuze's first published essay 'Desert Islands' (1953)[14] and is a concept elaborated in *Nietzsche and Philosophy* (1983) when Deleuze explores its relation to 'the chaos in oneself'.[15] This double bind might be simply explained as the will to access otherness and outsides – phenomenologies beyond the generalized human (that which might be thought of as post-human, animal, alterior, ecological, etcetera) – with the sense that these things are only accessible by an all-too-human logic, an all-too-human brain.[16] In 'Desert Islands' the allure of escaping the bind is expressed as an island 'toward which one drifts'.[17] The essay originally carried the title 'Causes et raisons des îles désertes' and was intended for a special issue of the magazine *Nouveau fémina* devoted to islands.[18] *Nouveau fémina* was a magazine of the ilk of *La Vie Heureuse*, *Vogue* and *Elle*, a fashion and lifestyle magazine with an inclination towards public intellectuals, artists, designers, architects and writers of 1950s Paris.[19] (Though I can't imagine anyone less festive, Corbusier was featured in a 1955 edition dedicated to Christmas.)[20] Though Deleuze's essay did not end up in the magazine, there are moments in his 'Desert Islands' paper which might defer to *nouveau fémina*. Deleuze speaks of 'female communities' and 'mythological maternity' with a similar sense of elision that Corbusier had engaged in speaking of the Muses.[21] Though included in a bibliography that Deleuze assembled in 1989, the essay would only be published after his death.[22] It is thus both a first essay and posthumous.

The essay is a perplexing one, but it starts simply enough. Deleuze commences his account with the assertion that there are two kinds of island: oceanic and continental. Oceanic islands are islands that rose from the sea itself and are framed as 'originary, essential islands'.[23] Continental islands, on the other hand, are those which have been cleaved from continents, 'born of disarticulation, erosion and fracture'.[24] These two kinds of island lead Deleuze to suggest two different manners by which islands might be thought: 'Islands are either from before or from after humankind.'[25] Oceanic islands are prior to the human in the sense that they drift beyond our line of vision and are independent of any overbearing structure to/from which they might be measured. Continental islands, on the other hand, are after humankind. They are cleaved from our comprehension and drift in relation to continents, fatherlands and mother tongues. Like many dualisms invoked by Deleuze the point here is not the two terms of the dualism itself but rather the forces that bring a dualism into being and perpetuate it and that which flows between the two. The dualisms of oceanic/continental islands and of pre-/post-human are invoked in order to upset that more profound dualism of body/world. Deleuze's essay negotiates the shared territories between the geographic and the bodily, of islands and desire: 'The *elan* that draws humans toward islands extends the double movement that produces islands in themselves.'[26] It is this conjunction, or *doubling*, that concerns Deleuze – the manner by which geological formations come to be enfolded with human desires and the manner by which human desires generate islands. It may be a type of resonance that is at stake:

It is no longer the island that is separated from the continent, it is humans who find themselves separated from the world when on an island. It is no longer the island that is created from the bowels of the earth through the liquid depths, it is humans who create the world anew from the island on the waters.[27]

This account resonates well with Krauss's idea of 'the folding of one story within another', but Deleuze notes that islands present a case where the human doesn't exactly repeat 'the opening of the first story'.[28] It's thus not really a resonance that is at stake here, but rather a type of dissonance or a dynamic tension. Deleuze notes that in the creation of islands lies two (often simultaneous) 'radical and absolute' desires: the desire for 'pulling away. Of being already separate [...] lost and alone' and the desire of 'starting from scratch, recreating, beginning anew'.[29] These may be the two desires implied by the original title of the paper: *causes et raisons*, and are the fracture line, the irresolvable tension that constitutes islands. Whilst there is a human conception of a thing, an island, for example, it remains perpetually incompatible with geological concerns. Deleuze asserts, 'An island doesn't stop being deserted simply because it is inhabited. [...] Far from compromising it, humans bring the desertedness to its perfection and highest point.'[30] Whilst for Deleuze, the human conceives of the island and in doing so brings it into being in one sense (even as a desert island), the human implication is not the only concern. It is a double movement of at once defining a thing in respect to its alterity (even when that thing is 'lost and alone') and of that which operates its own logic (in and of itself) that is in play in Deleuze's essay. The logic of the essay, though, does not seek to negate one position for the sake of the other but rather to indulge in the rich (albeit unsettling) character of the paradox. Deleuze goes on to suggest the relation between the geographic formations and the formulations of desire is interwoven: 'The island would be only the dream of humans, and humans, the pure consciousness of the island.'[31]

One Man Sauna

The *One Man Sauna* (2014), designed by the architectural firm Modulorbeat, is an island of a kind (Figure 9.2). It is located in the grounds of an abandoned factory on the outskirts of Bochum, Germany – though 'located' is not really the right word. It's more that the *One Man Sauna* is displaced here. Bochum lies in the heart of the industrial Ruhr district. The region was historically the site of coal mines and steel mills and factories manufacturing vehicles. The mines and mills gradually closed, and in 2014 even the factories of the car manufacturer Opel ceased production. This was the first closure of a German auto-plant since 1945. The *One Man Sauna* was constructed for a one-year international city project and art festival titled 'Das Detroit-Projekt', which ran from 26 April till 5 July 2014.[32] The Detroit Project is an initiative of the Bochum theatre and the Urban Art Ruhr group which encourages local creatives to develop practical and artistic projects in response to the changing employment situations in one-time booming motor cities. The Detroit Project 'encouraged Bochum's inhabitants to see themselves not as victims, but active participants in industrial transformation'.³³

Modulorbeat is a small architectural practice working in 'the tension between city and landscape'.³⁴ They are based in Münster not far geographically but at some distance socio-economically from the industrial edge of Bochum. Modulorbeat's *One Man Sauna* project is a simple shaft projecting into the sky rather than into the earth. Cast concrete components were ordered from a catalogue of mining supplies. The dimension of the components meant that a stack of five would equate closely to the dimension of Corbusier's Modulor 'man-with-arm-upraised'. These concrete rectangular sections were stacked 7.3 metres high (roughly four Modulors high) to create a hollow structure that is separated into three distinct functional zones: a relaxation space with a view of the sky, a sauna on the medium level and a plunge pool below. The concrete units that were once used to keep water out are here used to keep water in. Vertical ladders link the three floors. This is an industrial type of architecture in its material components: ladders and metal grilles and mine shaft concrete, and its form is singular, erect, proud, and strong. It sits in its abandoned factory context like an oceanic island, enclosed and internally focused, an outpost from the pressures of the world beyond it. In and of itself there's something compelling here that relates to the desire for 'pulling away. Of being already separate [...] lost and alone'.³⁵ One of the Modulorbeat architects, Jan Kampshoff, was interviewed about the origins of the *One Man Sauna*: 'Our idea was to transform a former industrial site into a sauna, which is connected to the idea of doing nothing. [...] People working in the mines or the factories receive healthcare and leisure time so when these companies disappear they need other ways to look after themselves. That's why we made a sauna.'³⁶ The *One Man Sauna* is a place where an individual deserted by the society that they once occupied might find respite – a chance to start afresh in the warmth and moisture of a sauna, the 'mythological maternity' to which Deleuze refers.

This architectural island belongs to a long tradition of isolated spaces designed for the solitary male in architecture. These spaces are an archipelago of isolation and insulation for Vitruvian men and Modulors alike, and we might think of Martin Heidegger's hütte, Henry David Thoreau's cabin, Bernard Shaw's rotating shed, Corbusier's cabanon and Archigram's cushicle, as examples. These spaces occur today as odd attempts to deal with something that has long departed. But they keep reappearing as an odd tradition (a bind of a kind) preserving the solitary male as a means of dealing with a world that has already exceeded him. Elizabeth Grosz, writing about Merleau-Ponty's use of invagination, describes the 'impossible no-man's land of the excluded middle', and the phrase might just as easily have been describing the industrial landscape of Bochum.³⁷ Geographically, this sauna conceived as a particular point of resistance to neocapitalism is indeed firmly *in* the wasteland it generates. I imagine a former worker within the sauna not only relaxing but plotting to overthrow the system that crushed them. They have only to raise the roof panels of the sauna to remind them of the context in which they find themselves. Deleuze would refer to this dissonance of inside senses and outside worlds as 'doubling'.³⁸ It is the sense by which we at once know the world and understand it as an autonomous *outside* and yet know that we are unable to engage in any unmediated way with its rich concrete realities because of the particular mechanisms by which we conceive of it, our *inside* situation. In the 'Desert Islands' paper Deleuze describes subjectivity 'as if the relations of the outside folded back to create a doubling, allowing a relation to oneself to emerge, and constitute an inside which is hollowed out and develops its own unique dimension'.[39] For Deleuze a subject may lack something only in respect to an assemblage from which it is excluded and in this sense the man of the *One Man Sauna* lacks nothing and is contently invaginated.[40] But it is also true that for Deleuze a subject desires only because of its inclusion in an assemblage, and he would note inclusion in an assemblage may itself be in an 'association of banditry or revolt'.[41] The image at stake in the *One Man Sauna* seems to be that of a man against the world, in revolt against the world to which he is bound. This is indeed a world away from Isabelle Stengers's *cosmopolitics* and occurs as a retreat into architectural habits, but it might be a necessary retreat:[42] a retreat from 'the chaos in oneself'.

Modulorbeat's sauna on the weedy asphalt of a former workplace is conceived in a delirium that is difficult to conceive of. We cannot approach it without noticing that the warm intensions and high ideals of the project disappeared in the hardening of its concrete. The architectural historian and theorist Adrian Forty in a chapter titled 'Memory or Oblivion' in his book on concrete speaks of the oddity of the material in the use of memorials, given that 'concrete has, at the same time, been so often regarded as the material of oblivion, erasing and obliterating memory, cutting people off from their past. From themselves, from each other'.[43] The one-man sauna of Bochum does not pose the question of 'memory or oblivion' but rather gestures towards the productive conjunction 'memory and oblivion'. It is necessary to have both. It is the double bind necessary for re-beginning. There is a history of letting epiphoric objects speak of the *fait accompli* in Bochum. At the train station there is a Richard Serra sculpture simply called 'Terminal' (1977).[44]

Paralogism of displacement

This embodied and interwoven tension between the desire of 'starting from scratch, recreating, beginning anew' and a desire for 'pulling away. Of being already separate [...] lost and alone'[45] is one that would come to occupy much of Deleuze's oeuvre and his work with Félix Guattari.[46] In *Anti-Oedipus* (1972) it relates to one particular double bind, which Deleuze and Guattari would come to refer to as the 'paralogism of displacement'.[47] This is a particularly noxious double bind. The parologism of displacement is less 'the folding of one story within another through the invention of a character' and moreso the invention of a character via the rejection of a fiction. In *Anti-Oedipus* the parologism is described as where 'the law prohibits something that is perfectly fictitious in the order of desire of the "instincts," so as to persuade its subjects that they had the intention corresponding to this fiction'.[48] It's a complex concept but an important one. To put it simply, the paralogism of displacement proceeds by two key steps: First, a fiction is created. It is a fiction related to desire, our desires, our wants, our wishes. This fiction is presented as some form of universal or generalizable condition. Secondly, we are told that such desires are negative, and we should not pursue them. This is simple enough. However, prohibition itself generates desire – even when that desire was (at the outset) fictitious. For Deleuze and Guattari, the oedipal complex and the 'sham image' of Oedipus is a prime example of a paralogism:[49] The subject of psychoanalysis (reclined on a couch) is told that they want to kill their father and bed their mother – but that they are prohibited from doing so. The initial suggestion (the killing and bedding) is 'perfectly fictitious'. But one doesn't have to fight the fiction because it is fiction; what one has to do is avoid drifting into the fiction. The subject is then told oedipal desires need to be repressed, which seems to be an easy pill to swallow. So, swallow we do. We think we're repressing something. We think we're successfully dealing with something – until something goes wrong. And when it does go wrong the subject of psychoanalysis has a simple scapegoat named Oedipus. At this moment the earnest psychoanalyst has a case study to write up confirming the fiction.

The *One Man Sauna* might serve as another example. It is a concrete marker of an oft-recited fiction – a neo-liberal story of inevitability and the futility of resistance. The *One Man Sauna* may speak of 'active participants in industrial transformation', but it also screams of its absence. It screams of acts of architecture rather than acts of resistance. Art installations rather than activisms. Year-long festivals rather lifelong work. The *Modulorbeat* architect suggests, 'The organisation of the different areas [of the *One Man Sauna*] represents a methodical process, like working in a factory.'[50] And if there were any question as to whether this particular architect knew anything at all about factory work, he goes on to say, 'We thought the ritual of taking a sauna is connected to the idea of how work is organised.'[51] Bhhhr! This is the leaky logic of a particularly noxious double bind. A double bind is not merely the assertion of two contradictory statements but it relates to the inability for one to define the paradox itself. It's too complex. Too painful. Too unsettling. The fiction of Bochum's residents as 'active participants in industrial transformation' was a refrain rehearsed and polished over thousands of mine, mill and factory closures.[52] The fiction of a paralogism. Each of the Detroit Projekt initiatives restates something of the universal ideal at stake and is careful not to associate itself with the particularity of the humans involved, cleaved from the continent to which they once belonged. The Detroit Projekt is explicit on the point 'the closure of the plant, rather than its maintenance, is the premise for this project'.[53] It was up to the funded art installations and minor architectural interventions to deal with the individual. The subjects of Opel were convinced 'that they had the intention corresponding to this fiction'. If one is told enough times of *inevitable* closure one might be joyous to be offered a day out, a trip to a *One Man Sauna* as an escape from a neoliberal horror, but only one man at a time, and not a woman. The mid-twentieth-century project of peace and unification in mass social movement disappeared fast in this landscape. The *One Man Sauna* by Modulorbeat is the image of an end-of-world subjectivity, a subjectivity for an end of the world from which the subject as such has disappeared, no longer having anything left to grapple with. The subject is left bare-assed.

Figure 9.2 Modulorbeat, *One Man Sauna* (2014). Image courtesy of Modulorbeat.

10

Micropolitics

Politics

For Gilles Deleuze and Félix Guattari, 'everything is political, but every politics is simultaneously a *macropolitics* and a *micropolitics*'.[1] This distinction between *macro* and *micropolitical* frames is also referred to in terms of *molar* and *molecular* assemblages and is core to the political philosophy Deleuze and Guattari develop and deploy. Despite the lexical association, the distinctions between a macro and micropolitics, and molar and molecular assemblages, are not simply differences in scale but rather differences *in kind*. The distinctions between molar and molecular conditions are introduced in the first book of their *Capitalism and Schizophrenia* series, *Anti-Oedipus* (1972), as the difference between two modes of desire or two sides of any *assemblage*: one side faces the strata which make it a body, subject or complete entity of some kind; and the other faces what is referred to as the 'plane of immanence' on which the body tends to breakdown or is transformed into something else. It is a point reiterated in the second book of the series *A Thousand Plateaus* (1980) where they would note, 'every assemblage has two sides, the machining of bodies or objects, and group enunciation'.[2] In one case, politics is played out in conflicts between molar social entities such as social classes, races, sexes and nations. In the other, it is played out at the micro level in terms of those qualities of bodies that escape broad classification: affinities, forms of belonging, sexual proclivities, pains and pleasures, indeed desire itself.

Molarity

The molar might be thought of as the habits by which we conceive of ourselves and the world. The quickest way to identify a molar assemblage may be to ask someone, 'Who are you?' The responses you tend to receive are molar in character: I am an architect, 32 years old, a man, gay, of a Danish father and English mother, born in London, studied at The Bartlett, living in the south of France, agnostic, left-leaning, an amateur singer. These things are molar because they belong to the world of habits and traditions of classification and quantification. Molar assemblages tend to relate to demarcations that are socially assembled or what Deleuze and Guattari refer to as 'large aggregates functioning statistically'.[3] They are statistical in the sense the demarcations are like drawing thick boundaries around large portions of a population or a group. The appeal here is to fixities: biographic, geographic, historic, cultural pinpoints, related to a person imagined as a singular being of this nation or that, of this age or that, of this gender or that. These fixities are concerned with generalizations about both what someone or something is, and simultaneously about what someone or something is not.

Consistent with their broader politico-philosophical thrust, for Deleuze and Guattari the macropolitical is not only about the organizing of something into molar categories but is also concerned with the manners by which the categories themselves (and systems of categorization) construct their subjects and objects. It's not difficult to explain. The simplest and most repeated phrase in almost every language is: 'I am'. These two words tend to suggest the terms that follow are somehow set and defining. In stating 'I am' one imagines one is speaking of something essential to the self, or considered essential *of* the self, essential in the construction *of* self. The words that follow the phrase 'I am' tend to be nouns: common nouns, proper nouns, abstract nouns, collective nouns. These nouns operate as classifications we assign ourselves and are deferrals of a kind, repeated a*d nausea* on the forms we fill in (rental forms, taxation forms, passport and immigration applications, census forms, and every time we establish a social media account). I imagine such things are collectively referred to as 'forms' because through the repetition of descriptors we *form* a more and more solid sense of ourselves. Every tick in every box of every form reinforces an image of what one is, should be, must be. A tick for *this* or a cross for *that*. There is thus also something of the social contract associated with the molar – a type of bind that at once reinforces the idea we are essentially something, but that also places this something in systems of order and control. This tends to be the point of collective nouns, but indeed almost all the nouns that follow the phrase 'I am' tend to collectivize in one way or another, and it is these controls, orders and collectivizing forces that constitute a macropolitics.

Deleuze and Guattari would refer to the macropolitical in terms of the 'code' or the 'axiomatic' of 'the common social field' and the macro is thus like the rules of the game or the dominant logics that occur as a type of hard wiring of the socius.[4] The architect can vote in UK elections, because of his current citizenship status, and is very welcome to join the *Choeur Gay de Marseille* and develop his voice in resonance with others in a supportive environment. A Facebook algorithm put him in contact. Such a description makes the macropolitical sound pervasive but perhaps innocuous like the droning *base* behind the *superstructure* Karl Marx spoke of or the tut-tutting *superego* behind every *ego* Sigmund Freud elaborated. Such concepts operate as something like the background conditions that allow the relations and operations of a society to proceed. A macropolitics has a similar character to the formulations of Marx and Freud in that its focus is the conditioning or ground rules of the social; however, for Deleuze and Guattari the impact of the macropolitical is not necessarily mediated and does not belong to a background or backdrop. They refer to the macro social field 'as the terminus of the investment of desire' and go on to say it 'defines the cycle, and the states through which a subject passes'.[5] This is to say the macro might commence with supposedly 'open' questions related to 'Who are you?' but it is also forceful in demarcating 'Thus, what can you do?' and 'Thus, what should you desire?'. It is not a background condition, but rather a force that plays itself out directly on selves and worlds. The 'I am' of the macropolitical self becomes an 'I can' in terms of what actions are possible and also generates a common collective voice of 'We are' that belongs to the macro social field. But in doing so, the macro simultaneously generates what 'We are not' and the 'Thus, we should not' and the 'Thus, we can't', and operates as a force for the collective restraint of desire. A macropolitics has a similar character to the formulations of Marx and Freud for the mere fact so much of the habitual account of ourselves and our world is riddled with Marxian and Freudian conception. The architect, who is more than his labour, cannot vote in French elections, because of his current citizenship status (recently demarcated *migrant économique*), but is still very welcome to join the *Choeur Gay de Marseille* and develop his voice in resonance with others. He is, however, not welcome at the church in whose hall the choir operates and is wary about protesting the fact for fear of arrest and the prospect of deportation. He'd hate to have to move back to his fatherland or back into his mother's home.

The macropolitical is not only how we tend to speak of and organize ourselves but also how we tend to speak of and organize the world. In disciplines that fixate on the built world, like architecture, we tend to operate in systems that commence with classification and demarcation before we get to systems of variation. We speak of 'typologies' and 'types', 'functions' and 'uses', 'styles' and 'movements'. Such molar classifications allow us to order the built world, negotiate it with confidence and frame our investments. Such classifications, much like property lines and GPS coordinates, tend to be taken for granted and even the rich ways in which we interpret the built world come to be a matter of macropolitical demarcation. In his text of 1981, *The Political Unconscious: Narrative as a Socially Symbolic Act*, Fredric Jameson draws heavily on the collaboration of Deleuze and Guattari and refers to the 'structural limitations' of all systems of interpretation and exposes a few of the ways in which systems of interpretation constitute 'strategies of containment' and reinforce the illusion of 'authenticity' and 'coherence'.[6] Jameson's point is that frames of reference tend to be self-reinforcing and defensive, and though Jameson's focus is literature, I think the same can be said of architecture and its discourse. The term 'Modern' and its forms of 'modernism' and its architects 'modernists' would be a case in point. Much cited tomes that define, reinforce definitions, construct rules and logics thereof, and shelves of books that then identify variations, multiplied furiously across the second half of the twentieth century. Rarely do we examine the political baggage of architectural definitions, but such demarcations are clearly political, in part because they are contested, fraught and anxiously defended. And in part because they negate. That is to say, *architectural definitions, like all molar classifications, tend to operate their own immune systems, reducing, displacing and rejecting aberration.* Modernism was all too sensible, hygienic and logical for its father figure's fascism to be deemed as particularly relevant to histories of the movement, and Corbusier's perplexing penchant for placing toilets centrally in a room is rarely recounted.[7] The macropolitical structuring of architecture routinely overwrites *minor* infringements. Beatriz Colomina and Mark Wigley succinctly put it: '[A]rchitectural discourse is a deodorizer.'[8]

Molecularity

Molecular assemblages, on the other hand, might be thought of as those which escape demarcation, classification and control. This is to say, a molecular assemblage is not generalizable or classifiable in the sense that one can draw clear boundaries or statistically define it. The numeracy and measurability of molar assemblages do not apply to what Deleuze and Guattari call the 'pure multiplicity' of the molecular.[9] The multiplicity of the molecular has little to do with the 'multiplication' of mathematics and is defined in *Anti-Oedipus* as 'beyond both the One and the many, [and] beyond the predicative relation of the One and the many'.[10] Multiplicity thus might best be thought of in terms similar to the non-denumerability of *qualities*, those things that exist *in intensity* rather than in numeric measure. For example, whilst it is possible to say simply 'The architect has 1 mouth, 1 tongue and 31 teeth' and defer to the statistical aggregate that constitutes the mouth of a given architect,[11] it is impossible for me to define the coloration of the lips or the odd sense of shame felt when they are pursed against the teeth in anything like numeric terms. Such molecular assemblages (of colour, lip, teeth and tongue, pressure and shame) are hard to summate, and this is perhaps why Deleuze and Guattari also refer to the multiplicity of the molecular as that which is 'without unity or totality', a 'nonorganic and nonorganized multiplicity'.[12]

But we must be careful here for two reasons: First, it would be a mistake to imagine molecular assemblages were like subsets of organized molar categories. The molecular is without unit, unity or totality, but this does not mean it operates as a subset to the unity and totality of the molar. The molecular is not the fragments that add up to or constitute the molar-like hydrogen and oxygen atoms in valency might constitute water, or like the water, sand and cement that in ratio might constitute concrete. Whilst the molecular should not be considered a *part* of a molar whole, we need not over-value the elements that themselves form a molecular assemblage. The force of a molecular assemblage comes not from its parts but from their assembling. Deleuze and Guattari explain, molecular assemblages 'are not partial (*partiels*) in the sense of extensive parts, but rather partial ("*partiaux*")* like the intensities under which a unit of matter always fills space in varying degrees (the eye, the mouth, the anus as degrees of matter)'.[13] This is to say, *molecular assemblages are heterogenous; have their own ratios and valences, their own intensities, their own 'degrees of matter'; and need not be understood as part of some greater whole or as a summation of parts*. Second, it is not that the molecular assemblage is without order nor that it negates organic order, but rather that a molecular assemblage has its own order. By way of example, an eye, a mouth or an anus can be understood in the terms of the functionality of the organism and its place in/of the organism, and this would constitute the macropolitics of the organism, but those same organs can also be understood in terms their own structure and order *in and of themselves* and indeed can operate independently of the organism just as an organism might operate independently of an organ. This is a point I will return to later. The outcome is *the molecular operates in terms of its own specificity and particularity and pays little heed* to (or indeed operates in spite of) the unity, totality, or organization, of the broader social field. In spite of declarations of agnosticism the architect prayed earnestly when their father was ill; and though they studied at The Bartlett they have a secret (albeit unrequited) lust for the neoclassical. Molecular passions and desires pass irrespective of macropolitical organization. These qualities mean that molecular assemblages are difficult to pin down and that a micropolitics is constituted by the vague and the slippery, the liminal, the fleeting and mobile.

The molecular tends not to relate to statements that commence with the phrase 'I am' and the nouns that might follow and indeed tends not to relate to statements or pronouncements at all. The micropolitical is what something *does* and tends to find itself (when it finds itself) in verbs rather than nouns. The architect recurrently dreams of his father's last breath, purses his lips immediately prior to deceiving someone and pinches an ear lobe at the most intense moment of sex. When singing at a precise octave the vibration in his throat causes a tingle to pass over his left wrist that bears a tiny scar. These qualities are micropolitical in character. Piquant revolutions in intensity. They are no less real and no less forceful than the disputes and battles of a macropolitics but are more difficult to hold and articulate. Where the force of the macro might be *to form*, to give form to selves and societies, to classify and coagulate, the force of the micro is in connections that are particularized, partial and without codified meaning. That is, a micropolitics is not a politics of left and right or any of the broader political categories or banners under which a group assembles. Where the macro generates the large statistical groups with which we identify, the micro pays little respect to these categories.

A micropolitics is unconcerned with establishing fixed relations between assemblages, which is to say, a micropolitics is uncoded and does not generate meanings nor accord to pre-existent logical systems. The axiomatic logic of causality of the macro operated much like: 'I am w *therefore* I love x, I do y, I dream of z'; but the logic of the micro is: loving x this way just now; doing y at this moment; dreaming of z and biting my lip last night' ... and, and, and. It is not the case of I am *x* therefore I desire *y*, but rather that *y* is desired and what I am is beside the point. This may be why a molecular assemblage is a 'magical chain' as Deleuze and Guattari call it, that 'brings together plant life, pieces of organs, a shred of clothing, an image of daddy, formulas and words: we shall not ask what it means, but what kind of machine is assembled in this manner – what kind of flows and breaks in the flows, in relation to other breaks and other flows'.[14] Pursed lips that break a lie, pinched lobes that incite a joyous flow. Where a micropolitics brings things together it does so fleetingly, and though not spoken of openly, the molecular might come to be whispered between conspirators and lovers, and carried in cries, grunts, sighs and smells and moments of raw intimacy, eroticism and violence. Where the macro was considered the 'terminus of the investment of desire' the molecular assemblage doesn't tend to heed any tautology. And where a micropolitics is at stake it tends to be the subject which is terminated rather than desire. It is the micro that sweeps us away and transforms us. The architect forgets he's an architect as much as he forgets he is a 'he' when a vibration passes over a scarred wrist. The sensation carries them away.

Cruising Pavilion

The distinction between a macro and a micropolitics becomes piquant in architecture, a discipline which deals with the privatization and organization of space, alongside the moulding of materials that might prompt action and affection, construct affinities and propagate forms of belonging. And the distinction is particularly pronounced in the case of spaces that might accommodate the more revolutionary expressions of desire. The *Cruising Pavilion* of the 2018 Venice Architecture Biennale squirts joyously (Figure 10.1). Conceived by the curators Pierre-Alexandre Mateos and Charles Teyssou, the architect Octave Perrault, and the artist Rasmus Myrup, the *Cruising Pavilion* is an architecture of exhibition and exhibitionism, of identities and post-identitarian dissolutions, configured spaces and sexual positions, of hard walls and glory holes. This is a space of two sides, where the macropolitical categorization of bodies bangs hard against a fluid micropolitics.

The molar assembling of the *Cruising Pavilion* is easy to recount. It is defined as 'a curatorial project about the architecture of gay sex and cruising culture', conceived in Paris and sited at Spazio Punch on the Giudecca Island during the Biennale.[15] Spazio Punch describes itself as 'between institutional and underground' and though most arts organizations imagine themselves thus, Spazio Punch has pursued a suitably provocative curatorial agenda over the last decade.[16] The siting of the Cruising Pavilion was fleeting, from 24 May till 1 July 2018. The pavilion housed installations and included works by Andreas Angelidakis, Atelier Aziz Alqatami, Monica Bonvicini, Tom Burr, Etienne Descloux, Pascal Cribier & Louis Benech, Lili Reynaud Dewar, Diller Scofidio + Renfro, DYKE_ON, Pol Esteve & Marc Navarro, Andrés Jaque/Office for Political Innovation, Özgür Kar, Henrik Olesen, Hannah Quinlan & Rosie Hastings, Carlos Reyes, Prem Sahib, S H U Í (Jon Wang & Sean Roland), Studio Karhard, Studio Odile Decq, Alison Veit, Ian Wooldridge and Trevor Yeung.

The *Cruising Pavilion* was located within the 'Ex Birrerie' large concrete bunker in which beer and spirits were once stored on the island. The Birrerie lent the pavilion a raw aesthetic with very few openings and walls that bore the mark of long-term incidental occupation. There was little attempt to clean a surface or present the type of smooth white wall associated with so many of the exhibitions of the Biennale. The pavilion was set within the warehouse and replicates the architecture of sex club dark rooms.[17] The defining features are tightly restricted contact with the outside, an interior configured to promote encounter, dim red lighting, surfaces that are easily washed down, concrete floors that are often wet and occasionally scattered with condoms. The *Cruising Pavilion* was primarily composed of two timber structures that visitors climbed via simple stairs. It seemed like a construction site of timber and particle board platforms, within a warehouse of brick and raw concrete. The tower structures generated many spaces that were both defined and open; one had a sense of entering a series of spaces and yet also the sense of being exposed. Along with the dimensions of the configured spaces, a mildly contorted circulation system would encourage serendipitous encounters (or make it impossible not to brush up against others). The pavilion was at times a tool for voyeurism, at times an inciter of exposure, and at times a frottage machine, configuring proximities and processing bodies.

The installations of the pavilion were organized as odd instances, pinned to walls, on floors, or propped up, as a series of small perhaps incidental acts within the space, and only a few constituted spaces of their own. There were projects presented which had already had wide circulation, such as Diller and Scofidio's Blur building (2002), which found itself convincingly homoerotic. Screens glowed against the darkness much like those of porn cinemas or like the screens which titillate in the dark of our bedrooms at night. One critic of the Pavilion noted, '[T]oday, class, race, and gender might be as regulated by the erotic surface of the screen as the architecture of the city.'[18] Some installations abided by the disciplinary conventions of architecture involving the display of sketches, plans and sections and models, such as Alison Veit's drafts of spaces in which women might cruise, or Pol Esteve and Marc Navarro's 'Atlas of Plans', of Barcelona's dwindling collection of dark rooms. Others were less architecturally focused and would not have been out of place in a sex museum. There was a machine which squirted eucalyptus oil that might cover the smell of sex, but in doing so seemed to operate as a proof of Michel Foucault's *repressive hypothesis:* that acts which position themselves as counter sex are themselves sexual.[19] If true, architectural discourse might be both a 'deodorizer', as Colomina and Wigley suggest, and simultaneously a pheromone.

Macropolitics

The deferral of the press releases, interviews with the curators, and pithy pieces of art and architectural journalism related to the *Cruising Pavilion* are deferrals to a macropolitical narrative. The story the curators tell is of a statistical group in society, clearly demarcated segments of the city and the accommodation of expressions of desire that are consigned as subversive. The press release put out to mark the opening of the Pavilion states:

> Cruising usually describes the quest for sexual encounters between homosexual men in public spaces, but it cannot be reduced to neither men nor homos. This sexual practice generally takes place in public sites like parks, toilets, and parking lots, or in dedicated establishments like bathhouses and sex clubs. [...] the Cruising Pavilion looks at the conflictual architecture of cruising. Somewhere between anti-architecture and vernacular, the spatial and aesthetic logic of cruising is inseparable from the one of the proper metropolis. Cruising is the illegitimate child of hygienist morality. Relegated to the realm of depravity, it feeds off its most structuring disciplinary features.[20]

This story relies on molar assemblages: the first thing we might notice about the press release is that the *Cruising Pavilion* is defined in terms of what it is *inseparable* from and simultaneously *in conflict* with. That is to say, definitions of the *Cruising Pavilion* rely on both an establishment of the social field upon which cruising is seen to be at once in resonance with and yet conflicted against. The text might simply be broken down into phrases related to these two interpretive positions: on the one hand cruising is 'inseparable from the one of the proper metropolis', a 'child of hygienist morality', and 'feeds off its most structuring disciplinary features'. This phrasing infantilizes cruising as the metropolis' nurtured/ nurturing child. But on the other hand, cruising is of 'conflictual architecture', 'between anti-architecture and vernacular', and 'the illegitimate child', 'relegated to the realm of depravity'. Thus, what we arrive at is a molar demarcation with an equally molar qualification: I am x in this regard. I am not x in that regard.

With molar aggreges in place, this story then repeats the pattern of macropolitics: this is a story in resonance with traditional and habitual ideological political constructions. It is a story replete with deferrals to Marx and to Freud, and that likely owes a debt to the Frankfurt School's conjoining of both. And one might also note in this story a Foucauldian construction or two. This is, in summary, the repeated story of a repressed minority enacting a moment of resistance or, in common parlance, 'sticking it to the man'. The only real difference here is that 'the man' of this story is now 'the metropolis', but they share every characterization attributed to dominant social structures. We are told that cruising 'takes place in public sites like parks, toilets, and parking lots, or in dedicated establishments like bathhouses and sex clubs' and such spaces are commonplace in almost every metropolis. The serendipitous, anonymous, non-committal encounters of cruising culture are positioned as a subset of the social, just as the spaces in which these encounters occur are spoken of as a subset of the metropolis.[21] That is to say, text like this measures all moves as moves to or from an authority, habit or tradition (x). And regrettably the statements 'I am x' and 'I am not x' both tend to reinforce the political dominance of x.[22]

For Deleuze and Guattari it is not that the macro isn't important, but what they remind us of is the fact that such demarcations are not encompassing and need not be respected. For them the core problem is not that there are molar assemblages and that there is a macropolitics, but rather the assumption of the 'primacy of the social field'. And it is the odd assumption of 'primacy' that might lead one to imagine one is bound to it, and that it is 'the terminus of the investment of desire'.[23] Though the philosopher and the psychoanalyst track the problematic assumption back to psychoanalysis, *in the discipline of architecture the word 'city' can simply stand in place of the word 'father' when it comes to identifying macropolitical forces that are treated as the ever-looming backdrop or 'field' to which we submit or rebel*. And so much architecture frames itself as rebellion to/from the dominant forces of a city-social-field. For Deleuze and Guattari, even the framing 'against' this macro field is a reinforcement of it because it is to operate *within* the macropolitical. And even acts of resistance regrettably pay respect to that which is resisted. When the architect thinks 'I hate the way my father [add any verb here]', one invokes that same father. And Deleuze and Guattari caution that in doing so one 'invests the formation of central sovereignty; overinvests it by making it the final eternal cause' and in doing so 'disinvests in every free "figure" of desire'.[24]

Micropolitics 115

Figure 10.1 Mateos, Myrup, Perrault and Teyssou, *Cruising Pavilion* (2018). Image courtesy of James F. Lima.

Micropolics

I noted above that the *Cruising Pavilion* was sited at Spazio Punch 'during' the Biennale. It was during, but not a part of. The *Cruising Pavilion* was self-initiated and independent. The official 2018 Biennale was curated by Yvonne Farrell and Shelley McNamara of Grafton Architects. The biennale took the moniker 'Freespace' as its thematic. Farrell and McNamara defined 'freespace' as a 'generosity of spirit and a sense of humanity at the core of architecture's agenda'.[25] Optimism, delusion and ostentatious demonstrations of political naivety are so often core to hegemonic agendas, and the *Cruising Pavilion* curators took the opportunity to emphasize the point by configuring their own manifesto directly over that of the official version. They didn't go to too much effort. Their subversion involved simply crossing out words and over-writing. The text would come to illustrate the heteronormative assumptions at stake in the official version. The curators of the Pavilion appropriate the official text and suggest: 'CRUISING ~~FREESPACE~~ focuses on architecture's ability to provide free and additional spatial gifts to those who use it and on its ability to address the unspoken wishes of strangers'.[26] The 'generosity' that Farrell and McNamara had spoken of was not of the same intensity as 'the unspoken wishes of strangers' that the *Cruising Pavilion* was about to satisfy. The incommensurability of the official pronouncements of the biennale curators and the *unspoken* acts of the *Cruising Pavilion* are an index of the difference between the macro and micropolitical.

Because the molecular assemblage does not anchor in codification and meaning, the micropolitical tends not to find form in communication and representation. Tending to pass without being recorded, and more often than not passing without anchoring in discourse, its politics is not that of the speech, the flag, the banner or the manifesto, nor any of those signifiers of sovereignty that all tend to shout: 'Make Macropolitics Great Again'. A micropolitics, a politics of the molecular, is a politics bound loosely and fleetingly in glances and micro-gesture and allegiances unspoken. Indeed, *the micropolitical is less about engagement with a social contract than an escape from it*. The word choice here is particular; the word 'escape' is an important one for Deleuze and Guattari. They note macro-ideological politics has tended to root itself in dualistic binds, a politics of 'this or that' – this or that political party, this or that gender, this or that orientation, this or that demarcation. Protest, resistance and contestation in this system have tended to be framed as: 'if you don't want to tick box A, then feel free to tick box B' and collectivize yourselves in yet another collective. Freedom is reduced to *choice*, and we tend not to notice that the choices are already configured by the exact-self-same social field. In such a situation resistance is encouraged as a matter of cynicism (gay choirs in church halls). The desire for choice and the habitual mistaking of choice for freedom is an operational part of what Foucault calls 'the fascism that causes us to love power, to desire the very thing that dominates and exploits us'.[27] And yet the most radical, revolutionary, political move is likely not to tick *this* or *that* box, but rather to *escape* the system itself. To leave it. To choose like the eponymous character of Herman Melville's *Bartelby* (1853) to 'prefer not to'.[28] And in choosing to *not to*, we escape the macropolitics of social investment. For Deleuze and Guattari this is the most revolutionary of acts: '*lines of escape* of desire; breaches the wall that causes flows to move; assembles its machines and its groups-in-fusion in the enclaves or at the periphery – proceeding in an inverse fashion from that of the other pole: I am not your kind'.[29] And thus a micropolitics operates not as a subset or part of a macropolitics, but as a politics of alternacy, where the assertions of 'I am' become 'I prefer not to'. I prefer not to write a manifesto; I'll just escape yours.

Cruising Labyrinth

Just as the *Cruising Pavilion* withdraws from the organization of the Biennale, the pavilion excites organs that pay little respect to the organization of the organism. This was no clearer than in Andreas Angelidakis's 'Cruising Labyrinth' installation (Figure 10.2).

It is perhaps here that the macrofixations of architecture and the microassemblage of pleasure come into the most intense of proximities. Angelidakis's contribution to the *Cruising Pavilion* was a self-assembling labyrinth of plywood painted black that can be configured to suit a suite of desires. Originally commissioned for a *BUTT Magazine* party in London, Angelidakis explores architecture's long-standing obsession with the walls of labyrinths and more importantly breaches them. The labyrinth panels are full of holes, glory holes, that might allow all manner of anonymous sex act to occur. The 'I am' of one side of the wall all but vanishes on the other. And this reminds us that the relation between the macro and micro is a complex one. Jameson would note, 'The value of the molecular in Deleuze [...] depends structurally on the preexisting molar or unifying impulse against which its truth is read.'[30] It is true. In part. But I tend to think that the reliance is more like the way Angelidakis's 'Cruising Labyrinth' operates at the edge of an exhibition outside the Bienale. The traditional manner by which a labyrinth is thought – as a type of goal-oriented journey of formal manipulation or control – is not how anyone approaches Angelidakis's labyrinth. The labyrinth fails to operate as a labyrinth might, once it is drilled with glory holes. Its key functioning is now micropolitical. It is negotiated in intensity – in the intensities of encounter and connection. One negotiates such a labyrinth not by the axiomatic logic of an architect's plan but rather as a 'magical chain' of seduction, glimpses, grunts, openings, the smell of sweat, organs, pursed lips and rattled piercings. It is partialized (*partiaux*) and operates as Deleuze and Guattari describe of the molecular assemblage: 'inducing – always at a distance – transverse connections, inclusive disjunctions, and polyvocal conjunctions, thereby producing selections, detachments, and remainders, with a transference of individuality'.[31]

The glory hole enacts a type of fragmentation of the body, a 'transference of individuality', a de-individualization, a disavowal of identity, an escape from the 'I am'. It is liberating in the sense that the whole (the unity and totality we habitually associate with selves) might pass through a hole for a while. That which is so often contained, delayed, put to use elsewhere is, for a time, dominant, singular. I had promised above to return to the idea of the micropolitical independence of the organ from the organization of the organism. The point is important because *the independence of organs from the organism reminds us of the independencies of selves from society, of thoughts from axioms and logics, and of architecture from the socio-politico construction of the city*. In summary, the independence of the micropolitical. 'It has often been said and demonstrated', Deleuze and Guattari suggest, 'that an institution cannot be explained by its use, any more than an organ can.'[32] It was a thought that had occupied the philosopher and psychoanalyst for some time. Deleuze would note the operation of the disembodied smile of Louis Carroll's Cheshire Cat in *Difference and Repetition* (1968) and in *The Logic of Sense* (1969), and with Guattari in *Anti-Oedipus* defers to a Gourma story that starts: 'When the mouth was dead, the other parts of the body were consulted to see which of them would take charge of the burial.'[33] In *A Thousand Plateaus*, they return to the idea noting the story of Little Hans, the subject of one of Freud's case studies.[34] Freud told us that when Hans's mother found him at three and a half touching his penis that she threatened him by saying 'if you do that, I shall send for doctor A to cut off your widdler. And then what'll you widdle with?' For

Freud the event was the origin of Hans's fear of castration. However, when asked 'And then what'll you widdle with?' Hans himself, being far more creative than his parents and the psychoanalyst simply replied, 'with my bottom'.[35] An organ, it seems, need not abide by the organizational logic of the organism. These instances are of molecular assembly, and they are also micropolitical revolutions, moments of micropolitical thrust beyond habitual organization. And beyond the habits by which an organ is organized as organism.

On an island in Venice, in the Spazio Punch Birrerie, in the *Cruising Pavilion*, and on one side of one wall of Angelidakis's 'Cruising Labyrinth' stands an architect: 32 years old, a man, gay, of a Danish father and English mother, born in London, studied at The Bartlett, living in the south of France, agnostic, left-leaning, an amateur singer. A man, of this nation or that, of this age or that, of this orientation or that. On the other side of that same wall there is a throbbing organ. Poised to explode. Proportionally the difference from one side to another is statistically significant. About 95 per cent of a body mass on one side. About 95 per cent of an identity. About 95 per cent of the time. On the other about 5 per cent. But this is just the accountancy of the macro – macro quantities, macro divisions, macro classifications, macro delegations, macro functions. Deleuze and Guattari note of every assemblage, that one side faces the strata which make it a body, subject, or complete entity of some kind; and the other faces what is referred to as the 'plane of immanence' on which the body tends to break down or is transformed into something else. What matters for the architect at this very moment is that all of the organism and of the social on one side is beside the point, as the self erupts on the other. A micropolitical revolution that bursts selves and worlds into pure multiplicity. The word 'revolution' was repeated in the discourse dedicated to the *Cruising Pavilion*. It is not that the Pavilion overturned Venice, flooded islands or collapsed architecture or the metropolis, but rather that it cut a line of escape and as Deleuze and Guattari note, 'the revolutionary knows that escape is revolutionary – withdrawal. [...] What matters is to break through the wall.'[36] It may be that every wall has two sides and that both sides are equally modes of desire, but it is only in the molecular and micropolitical mode that pure intensities arise or circulate. Daedalus himself would have pinched an earlobe.

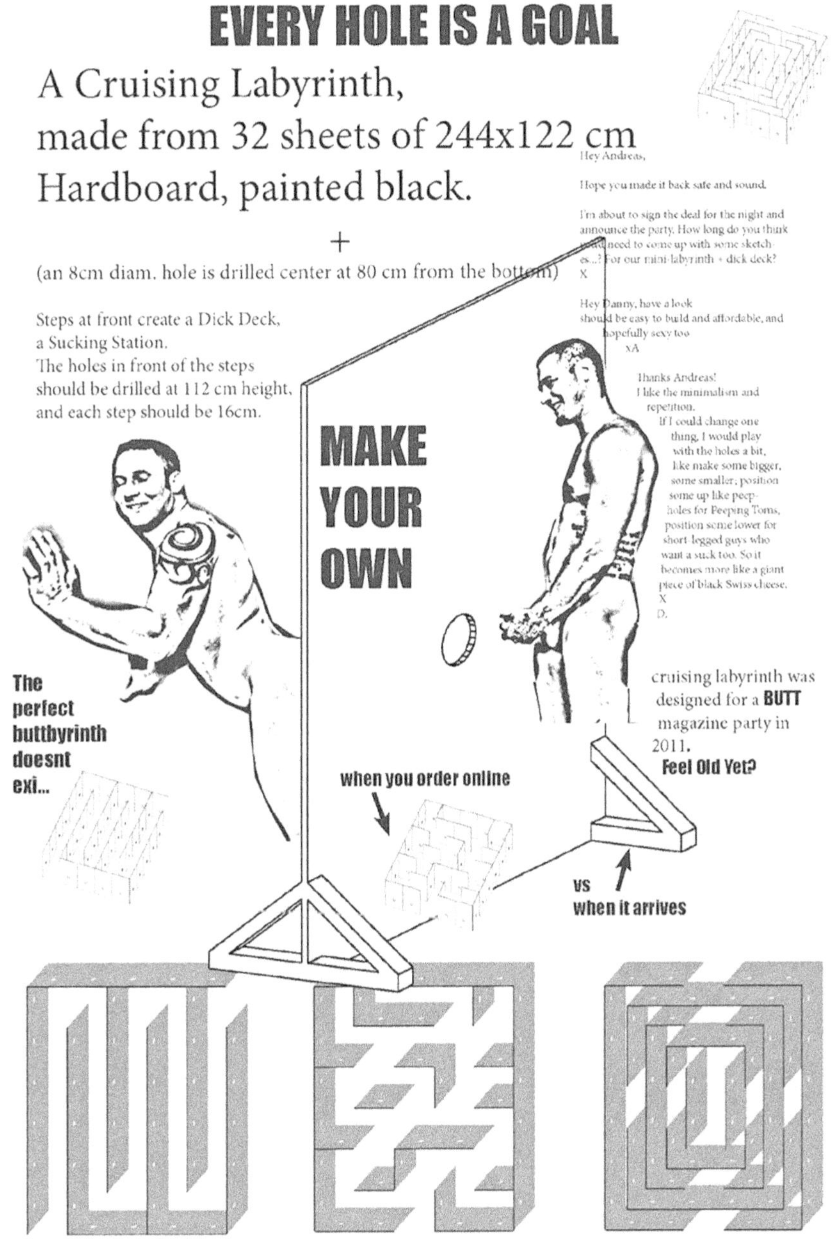

Micropolitics 119

EVERY HOLE IS A GOAL

A Cruising Labyrinth, made from 32 sheets of 244x122 cm Hardboard, painted black.

+

(an 8cm diam. hole is drilled center at 80 cm from the bottom)

Steps at front create a Dick Deck, a Sucking Station.
The holes in front of the steps should be drilled at 112 cm height, and each step should be 16cm.

MAKE YOUR OWN

The perfect buttbyrinth doesnt exi...

when you order online

Hey Andreas,
Hope you made it back safe and sound.
I'm about to sign the deal for the night and announce the party. How long do you think you'd need to come up with some sketches...? For our mini-labyrinth + dick deck?
X

Hey Danny, have a look
should be easy to build and affordable, and hopefully sexy too
xA

Thanks Andreas!
I like the minimalism and repetition.
If I could change one thing, I would play with the holes a bit, like make some bigger, some smaller, position some up like peep-holes for Peeping Toms, position some lower for short-legged guys who want a suck too. So it becomes more like a giant piece of black Swiss cheese.
X
D.

cruising labyrinth was designed for a **BUTT** magazine party in 2011.
Feel Old Yet?

vs
when it arrives

Figure 10.2 Andreas Angelidakis, 'Every Hole Is a Goal', Cruising Labyrinth, *Cruising Pavilion*. Image courtesy of Andreas Angelidakis.

11

War machines

Hangar 12

In a chapter of *A Thousand Plateaus* (1980) dedicated to the *war machine*, Gilles Deleuze and Félix Guattari note the difficulty of differentiating a tool from a weapon.[1] They turn to the work of the military historian and strategist John Frederick Charles 'Boney' Fuller who had noted, 'For ages on end agricultural implements and weapons of war must have remained identical.'[2] It may have been a historian making the point, but it is nevertheless poignantly contemporary. On the evening of 4 August 2020 an immense blast radiated from a storage hangar, Hangar 12, of the Port of Beirut. The Hangar sat on land reclaimed from the sea alongside wharves, amongst other storage hangars, and adjacent to a massive silo of 48 concrete cylinders that held wheat. The explosion that tore through large parts of the city was one of the greatest non-nuclear explosions ever recorded. More than 200 people died, more than 6,500 were wounded, and swaths of the city were blown apart. 77,000 apartments were damaged; 300,000 people were displaced.[3] The source of the blast was 2,750 tonnes of ammonium nitrate, a core ingredient in both agricultural fertilizer and explosives. The plough that might once have been raised in battle 'for ages on end' would that evening become a chemical compound that was at once an agricultural implement and a weapon of war. Deleuze and Guattari defer to Fuller to help make the point that what constitutes a tool or a weapon is not a property intrinsic to something. That is, there is nothing about a plough or a chemical compound that predisposes it to either creation or destruction. It is also the case that what constitutes a tool or a weapon is not fixed by 'the basis of their usage' because there is what Deleuze and Guattari call a 'general convertibility between the two'.[4] A plough that is used to turn soil in autumn might be used to mow down a marauder in Winter.[5] What was in spring an agricultural fertilizer might in summer ignite a city.[6]

What allows something to be a weapon, it seems, is firstly a matter of the relations it enters into. A plough in the hands of a farmer in a field is a tool, where that same plough in the hands of a fighter battling a marauder is a weapon. Though the plough is much the same element, and indeed the farmer may well be the fighter, and the field in which wheat grows may well be the field of battle; the plough-farmer-field assemblage is radically different to the plough-fighter-battlefield assemblage. In this scenario there is an *entraining* of the plough into either the agricultural or the warrior assemblage. The relation between the tool and the weapon thus is more a matter of what something might be capable of doing *in and of* an assemblage than what something intrinsically is. Alongside the 2,750 tonnes of ammonium nitrate that was stored in Hangar 12 were 23 tonnes of fireworks, 50 tonnes of ammonium phosphate (another agricultural fertilizer), 5 tonnes of tea and coffee, 1,000 car tyres, and 5 rolls of slow-burning detonating cord. It is internal traits or what Deleuze and Guattari call 'traits of expression',[7] that are taken up or activated in assemblages, and this particular assemblage, Hangar 12, was poised. The state owned, and operated hangar, may have been a legitimate tool for the storing of agricultural and military supplies; however, it takes little imagination and even less of a spark to convert this tool into a weapon. As Hangar 12 became 'a bomb the size of a warehouse', the large agricultural silos that sat adjacent became both a shield, protecting the western part of the city, but also a tomb.[8] Seven drowned in the grain that was spilt.

Political philosophy

A similar 'general convertibility' was at play in the shift between the two volumes that constitute Deleuze and Guattari's *Capitalism and Schizophrenia* series: *Anti-Oedipus* (1972) and *A Thousand Plateaus* (1980). At its core *Anti-Oedipus* is a tool that resists the role of psychoanalysis in the repression of revolutionary expressions of desire.[9] Most notably it operates to resist oedipal theory ('a grotesque error').[10] But this focus may have been a Trojan horse of a kind harbouring broader concerns. Deleuze and Guattari's alignment of Oedipus with colonization, 'Oedipus is always colonization', suggests as much, and Deleuze does not hesitate in describing *Anti-Oedipus* as 'from the beginning to the end a book of political philosophy'.[11] *A Thousand Plateaus* exists both as a demonstration of notions drawn from *Anti-Oedipus* and also as a series of engagements that exceed the first text. Brian Massumi relates in his 'Translator's Foreword', *A Thousand Plateaus* 'constitutes a very different project. It is less a critique than a positive exercise in the affirmative "nomad" thought called for in *Anti-Oedipus*'.[12] The composition of *A Thousand Plateaus* is more in line with the anti-hierarchical aspect of Deleuze and Guattari's exploration. Rather than a series of chapters building upon each other, the text offers a series of 'plateaux' that allow a multiplicity of connections to be made from a multitude of directions. Jean-Jacques Lecercle in his text *Philosophy through the Looking Glass* (1985) reads the shift from *Anti-Oedipus* to *A Thousand Plateaus* in this way:

> First, politics ... The philosopher becomes militant, fighting for the liberation of desire, both inside and outside his text. The paranoid organisation of *Anti-Oedipus*, with its regular progression (from negative, or critical, to positive tasks) gives way to the schizophrenic maze of *A Thousand Plateaus*, constructed around its own lines of flight, its own flows of desire and délire.[13]

Deleuze and Guattari's early focus on opposition had opened the gates to a series of movements that might serve as escapes from habitual systems of logic, hierarchies and structures of all kinds. This is to suggest the directed tool that *Anti-Oedipus* was, would be detonated in *A Thousand Plateaus*. The book, thus, becomes an example of the *war machine* it is to describe. The concept, the war machine, is a challenging one, not least of all because the object of the war machine is not war. Its core concern, rather, is *creative mutation and change, and the assertion of difference in-and-of-itself*. And this is the complexity of the concept. On the one hand mutation and change suggest the transformation of something, a *déjà là* or a yet to be, that becomes something else. There is here the implication of a pre-existing state or *status quo* that either changes, or from which change is measured. On the other hand, the idea of something asserting or extending a difference in-and-of-itself suggests little respect for a current order or theoretical context. This is why Lecercle talks of *A Thousand Plateaus* as constructing '*its own* lines of flight' and '*its own* flows of desire and délire'.[14] The war machine thus comes to be defined in two key manners. First, by that which it is not: the *status quo* phylum, the striated hierarchies and habits of thought that Deleuze and Guattari call 'the State'. Second, the war machine is of an entirely different order: *altera*, a smooth space that pays no respect to a status quo and that 'exists only in *its own* metamorphoses'.[15]

The State

The war machine might be thought of in terms of its incompatibility with the *State*. For Deleuze and Guattari, the State is the 'inside' of the socius (society and its institutions), entailing the entire system of norms, values, habits, images, or in short, segmentations (molar), that go into ordering the socius and attempting to preserve the order it has realized. Deleuze and Guattari's definition is the 'State apparatus constitutes the form of interiority we habitually take as a model, or according to which we are in the habit of thinking'.[16] Such a definition challenges preconceptions of a necessary conflation of State, governmentality and ideological politics, but it does accord well with the idea of the conflation of the State and colonizations of thought. The State has a gravity that slows the speed of change down, segmenting individuals into standard binary categorizations (women/men, homo/hetero, black/white, immigrant/citizen), and then hierarchizing those categories in order to create more affirmative ways to control those segments: 'Flows of women and children, flows of herds and of seed, sperm flows, flows of shit, menstrual flows: nothing must escape coding'.[17] The State operates to quantify, codify, classify, or as Deleuze and Guattari say 'striate' all.[18] It is why we know exactly how many tonnes of tea and coffee and how many rolls of slow-burning detonation cord were held in Hangar 12 at the Port of Beirut. It is also why ports themselves become so important – as gateways at the border of nation states where the flow of goods, services and bodies might be captured, held and measured, before being deployed elsewhere.[19]

Deleuze and Guattari point to the inherent link between paranoia and the State, suggesting 'the despot is the paranoiac',[20] the subject that internalizes externalities.[21] For the paranoiac everything is focused on them, filtered by them, internalized as part of them. There is nothing that is outside their remit. They are a hollow shell nourished only by what they internalize. Though the binary opposition favouring schizophrenia over paranoia established in *Anti-Oedipus* mellowed as a distinction in *A Thousand Plateaus,* Deleuze and Guattari's sentiment remains clear:[22] If the State is regarded as the paranoiac exercising of interiority, then it requires the construction of borders and boundaries and the demarcation of a 'milieu of interiority' over which it presides.[23] And this interior is fed by appropriation. This is to say, the State operates as a machine of appropriation, swallowing up, consuming all that it can whilst simultaneously giving the impression that it has been and will always be just this way. For Deleuze and Guattari 'if we call this interior essence or this unity of the State "capture," we must say that the words "magic capture" describe the situation well because it always appears as preaccomplished and self-presupposing'.[24] *The State is thus the status quo, the empty interior, 'the habit of thinking', and the self-fulfilling prophecy we tend to call 'history'.*

The war machine

Though it is possible to consider the war machine as the *status quo ante* or as the *Other* of the State, it is inappropriate to understand the two assemblages as opposites or as intrinsically oppositional. This is because much like the weapon and the tool, the war machine and State have no defined relation or a common denominator. It is likely for this reason that Deleuze and Guattari affirm the war machine not through studies of government and power, but rather through literature, ethnology, noology, spatio-geography, epistemology and science, music, metalworking and architecture. The architecture that is specifically referred to in *A Thousand Plateaus* is 'the construction of Gothic cathedrals in the twelfth century'.[25] The art and architectural historian Wilhelm Worringer and the sociologist and urbanist Anne Querrien's accounts are cited. Deleuze and Guattari are specific on the point that 'an "ideological", scientific or artistic movement can be a potential war machine, to the precise extent to which it draws, in relation to a *phylum* a plane of consistency, a creative line of flight, a smooth space of displacement'.[26] The 'smooth space' of the war machine is a spatio-temporality that is radically different to the striations, the *phylum* of State assemblages. Smooth space is the space of intensities and events. It is haptic, not optic. Experienced, not measured. Smooth space is the space of flows, of packs and of nomads. For Deleuze and Guattari, '[s]edentary space is striated, by walls, enclosures, and roads between enclosures, while nomad space is smooth, marked only by "traits" that are effaced and displaced with the trajectory'.[27] Despite the name of the concept, war as such results only when the 'striated space' of the State runs up against the 'smooth space' of the war machine. The wolf pack only hunts sheep when the fields of the farmer intrude upon *its* trajectories.

Defining war machines as abstract machines of mutation and change and as generators of smooth space means that they might be, as the Deleuze scholar Paul Patton notes, 'actualised in a variety of different material domains: they can appear in thought as well as in material practices of resistance to capture'.[28] But resistance is not enough. The war machine is far more about departure and escape than resistance. The distinction is a necessary one. For Deleuze and Guattari:

> The State-form, as a form of interiority, has a tendency to reproduce itself, remaining identical to itself across its variations and easily recognizable within the

limits of its poles, always seeking public recognition (there is no masked State). But the war machine's form of exteriority is such that it exists only in its own metamorphoses; it exists in an industrial innovation as well as in a technological invention, in a commercial circuit as well as in a religious creation, in all flows and currents that only secondarily allow themselves to be appropriated by the State.[29]

There is thus a *radical exteriority* to the war machine that pays no respect to the interior of the State. No respect to habits of thought. Nothing at all to do with what we call history. In this sense 'the war machine is seen to be of another species, of another nature, of another origin'[30] and 'irreducible to the State apparatus, to be outside its sovereignty and prior to its law: it comes from elsewhere'.[31] The point of a radical exteriority, or indeed what might more pointedly be called 'the outside' character of the war machine, can be made with simple reference to the *interior*, *exterior* and *outside* of architecture. If we consider a simple building (let's say a silo) in a city (let's say Beirut): The silo has an interior which functions in certain defined ways: Grain comes in; grain goes out. The city that is exterior to the silo also has its rules and regulations. The city is the *polis* that, as Paul Virilio reminds us, is also the *polis* of the police and the law.[32] The silo, because it is *in* the city, is subject to the city's laws. It thus has both internal and external functions. It is possible to think of the interior of the silo and its exterior as oppositional. One side of a wall faces inwards to the interior and the other outwards to the exterior. The interior generates forces that push out; the exterior resists these forces in holding-in. The interior resists the exterior as the exterior resists the interior. This is the status quo of architecture. But even though this interior and exterior face in different directions and have very different functions, they are not radically different. This is because when we speak of an interior we are already speaking too of an exterior (and vice versa): The two coincide *in* the one wall. Another way of saying this is that the one wall is taken up in (at least) two different assemblages: the interior and the exterior. There is thus a concurrency, an intimacy, between an interior and an exterior. One pays respect to the other, even when they might be thought of as being in a relation of *resistance*.[33] But the war machine relation with the State is not like this. The war machine is not just exterior to the State, not just resisting the State, but instead *outside*. It is more like we might describe a plume of smoke or lightning that might bellow in the sky or flash above a silo. The war machine pays no respect to the interior at all. It operates in-and-of-itself, with its own law and custom, a *nomos*. For Deleuze and Guattari the war machine is not only '*nomos* against *polis*',[34] but more fundamentally '[i]t is a nomos very different from the "law."'[35] Thus:

> It is not enough to affirm that the war machine is external to the apparatus. It is necessary to reach the point of conceiving the war machine as itself a *pure form of exteriority*, whereas the State apparatus constitutes the form of interiority we habitually take as a model, or according to which we are in the habit of thinking.[36]

This is a defining political move for Deleuze and Guattari. It is also the radical move from *Anti-Oedipus* to *A Thousand Plateaus*. The early work starts to look like critique as resistance, a critique that continues to assert the power of that which it resists.

Where critique is brought to bear on the interior, it remains bound to it. An exterior, as it were. The outside, on the other hand, thunders to its own beat. In *A Thousand Plateaus* the philosopher and the psychoanalyst decouple the *anti* from anti-Oedipus, the *de* from decolonization and the *geo* from the geo-historic.[37] They deploy an *anti-de-geo* movement that pays no respect to the norms of Oedipus, colonization and history. In place of acts of resistance against habits of thought, we get a war machine that strikes *lines of flight* and escape. And far better to escape, than to resist. To leave behind. To drift like smoke. To strike like lightning.

Zeitz Museum of Contemporary Art Africa

The Zeitz Museum of Contemporary Art Africa (MOCAA) (2017) occupies a silo in the Port of Cape Town.[38] It is the largest museum dedicated to African art and its diaspora. But we should be careful to note, here the term 'African art' denotes origins rather than ownership. Zeitz MOCAA may be registered as a public, not-for-profit institution and a 'Public Benefit Organisation' in South Africa, but it is very much a private museum.[39] The name Zeitz comes from the German businessman, Jochen Zeitz, whose permanent collection the museum houses. Zeitz started collecting African Art in 2008, or at least he had a curator collect it for him, Mark Coetzee, who would become Zeitz MOCAA's first chief executive officer and director.[40] The Zeitz MOCAA site was developed by a corporation called Victoria and Alfred (V&A) Waterfront, a wholly owned subsidiary of Transnet, a state-owned, rail port and pipeline company. Zeitz would give his collection of art as a lifetime loan and contribute to the initial costs of museum staffing and offices. The V&A Waterfront would provide the building and pay for the renovation and the fees of the designer.

The London-based Heatherwick Studio was entrained to convert the massive 1921 silo into Zeitz MOCAA.[41] The abandoned silo structure was composed of two parts: a block of forty-two concrete cylinders where grain was once held and a much higher grading tower dedicated to the necessary mechanical operations. The renovation of the structure generated 9,500 square metres of space for contemporary African art over six floors: 6,000 square metres for display of the permanent collection and space for rotating exhibitions. Eighty white cube galleries, eighteen education rooms, project spaces for emerging artists, a rooftop sculpture garden, conservation areas, along with the obligatory café (tea and coffee), a restaurant, and a gift and bookstore. A breathtaking six-storey atrium carved from the forty-two concrete cylinders as a billowing void connects the public spaces (Figure 11.1). The grading tower section is dedicated to a 'Silo hotel', occupying six floors above the Zeitz MOCAA. Self-described as a 'magical hotel', the walls were cut away to house impressive windows.[42] Each has fifty-six panels of geodesic glazing, bulging out like diamonds from a pewter ring. From the rooftop, hotel guests can sip cocktails, with an unimpeded view of Robben Island, where Nelson Mandela was imprisoned for 18 years. The habits by which we might conceive of contemporary African art, of colonial and postcolonial cultures, capitalisms, and architectural incursions, are thrown into a palpable tension here. This is a building at war.

When the State is defined in terms of interiority, paranoia, and as a habit of thought, it is to suggest a strange emptiness to it. It's a shell, an empty shell, that wants only to pull the outside in, 'always seeking public recognition', as Deleuze and Guattari note.[43] But to do this it needs to harness forces from the outside. In *A Thousand Plateaus* Deleuze and Guattari draw upon the work of Querrien and her explorations of architecture to make the point. They knew Querrien from their (largely Guattari's) involvement with CERFI, the Centre d'Études de Recherché et de Formation Institutionnelle, a transdisciplinary research cooperative of philosophers, sociologists, economists, artists, writers, cinematographers, urbanists and architects. Querrien had co-founded the organization whose remit was to rethink the relation between the city and the State, by transforming institutional practices into mechanisms that might empower the people that were subjected to these practices. Querrien's work suggests a line of escape from the State operation and an alternate to the bourgeois accommodation upon which so much architecture is focused. Deleuze and Guattari quote from Querrien's text *Devenir fonctionnaire ou le travail d'Etat* in a footnote that strikes like lightning above architecture:[44]

> Is the State founded upon the collapse of experimentation? ... The State is not under construction, its construction sites must be short-lived. An installation is made to function, not to be socially constructed: from this point of view, the State involves in the construction only those who are paid to implement or command, and who are obliged to follow the model of a preestablished experimentation.[45]

Deleuze and Guattari engage Querrien specifically in relation to their assertion that the State has no war machine of its own. It must be captured from its outside and then entrained (and paid) to serve. The war machine of the State is thus like a Colonel Kurtz, a Nikita or a Rambo. A force of mutation and change interned into the military apparatus in order that it might fight for the State. Picked up by the State like a plough might be wielded in a field. But such a relation is always risky. It comes with the potential for revolt. As when Kurtz unfolds into the heart of Africa, Nikita explodes in Europe, and Rambo goes rogue in Asia. The reason that Deleuze and Guattari's reference to Querrien strikes a possible escape for architecture is the identification of *construction and experimentation as being at once at the heart of the State project and yet entirely alternate to it*. In Querrien's account the State cannot construct and experiment itself and must thus harness the force from elsewhere. Construction and experimentation must be interred, controlled and contained. But as with the State's appropriation of the war machine, architecture too might go rogue.

What is most notable about Heatherwick's Zeitz MOCAA is the construction and experimentation at stake. A constructing in existing tectonics, a Euclidean gathering of extruded concrete cylinders that once held grain, and an experimentation in stereotomy: a hodological tunnelling that operates in spite of its context. It is the vortical atrium space that pulses with these forces most palpably. Perhaps on the verge of rupture. 'We felt strongly that we needed to give the space a heart,' Heatherwick suggests. The aim was to inspire 'the same kind of awe that medieval cathedral-goers must have felt centuries ago'.[46] The construction was a serious affair. A succession of concrete sleeves was inserted into the existing concrete silo tubes, which were bound at the top to form an arch to buttress all the forces out and down. The original structure might not have withstood the hollowing that was coming and reinforcing it at the outset was necessary.[47] 'It was part deconstruction, part archaeology,' says Mat Cash, the project lead. 'We were kind of seeing what the existing building wanted to happen and working with that.'[48] The *traits of expression*, of the extant silo structure were taken up, reinforced, before being activated in an entirely new assemblage. And this new assemblage makes it clear that nothing about architecture predisposes it to either creation or destruction. 'Our role was destructing rather than constructing,' Heatherwick notes, 'trying to destruct with a confidence and an energy, and not treating the building as a shrine.'[49] The process commenced with a 20-tonne wrecking ball. 'We had grand plans of thermal lances or waterjet cutting – all sorts of methodologies for doing the final cuts,' Cash suggests.[50] In the end, however, the atrium 'took between two and three million man-hours to complete,'[51] and construction workers used double-blade handsaws and handheld disc grinders to painstakingly carve the curvaceous inner sanctum.[52] Where a tool ends and a hand begins is a line incidental to the constructions of the State, for an 'installation is made to function, not to be socially constructed', as Querrien notes.

The experimentation was both serious and joyous. The outcome is a rounded, morphologically vague, emptiness. This is not a formal deficiency but rather a richness. A voluminous, full, topological emptiness. What was extracted from the concrete cylinder structure operates as public access and circulation space. The atrium draws a crowd – 300,000 in its inaugural year.[53] A spiral stair and two circular glass lifts occupy cylinders that have been partially cut away. People come in; people go out and move up and down as the grain once did. It is cathedral-like in proportion, but more like occupying a magnificent piece of jewellery. It's less form-making, than drawing attention to the empty space entwined, like a necklace might draw attention to a silhouette. This is a smooth space, a place where 'the static relation, form-matter, tends to fade into the background in favor of a dynamic relation, material-forces', as Deleuze and Guattari note of the Gothic vault.[54] The cut edges of the cylinders become demarcation points to a volume that has little to do with them, except that they come to contest the empty space. 'What we really wanted to do was to reveal the structure,' says Heatherwick.[55] He's not referring here to the social structure, or the political structure, but the structure of the silo building. Other reveals might have been collateral – but they are revelations, nevertheless. The Zeitz MOCAA atrium is a hodology into the very striations of structure, the vertical concrete cylinders of agriculture, containment and control. 'The State is perpetually producing and reproducing ideal circles,' Deleuze and Guattari note, 'but a war machine is necessary to make something round.'[56]

On the one hand, it is possible to conceive of Zeitz MOCAA in paranoic colonial terms and likewise just as simple to *post*-the-colonial or *de*-the-colonization. Heatherwick describes the building as 'a beginning', and the museum's first exhibition was called 'All Things Being Equal'.[57] On the other hand, there's something that has gone rogue here. An explosion. No, it's more like the suspended pressure of a slow-burning detonation cord. A pressure that threatens to blow from the inside out. The force that finds itself pulsing inside this silo originates from elsewhere: the outside. There is a radical experimentation here that pays no respect to the interior. No respect to habits of thought. No respect to identity politics as fixed formulation, and no heed to the ideological politics that is our contemporary habit of thought. This might be read as a gross neglect and ignorance. On the other hand, it's an escape route. To not. To not reinforce that which is resisted. This non-ideological politics is itself a force that's hard to pin down. It is far more *anti-de-geo* than it is oppositional. Far more construction and experimentation than building and representation. The architect, in this case the designer, might have been entrained to construct and to experiment for the status quo of capital accumulating entrepreneurs, developers and a self-propelling conga line of wealthy white men, but the architecture fails to oppose and instead threatens to erupt. It involves what Deleuze and Guattari refer to as 'absolute movements of another nature into the common space – those effectuated in the Void, not in nothingness, but in the smooth of the void where there is no longer any goal: attacks, counterattacks, and headlong plunges'.[58] This silo is poised to blow.

Figure 11.1 Heatherwick Studio, *Zeitz MOCAA*, (2017). Image © Iwan Baan.

12

Ethico-aesthetics

Lesbos and London

'Cities are socio-architectural machines that can produce identity,' Paul B. Preciado wrote from the island of Lesbos in 2016.¹ It's a recent iteration of a much-repeated aphorism. Preciado, the philosopher of gender, sexuality and occasionally architecture, falls into a long line of figures who have inverted the habitual adage: 'We build cities,' into the aphorism: 'Cities build us.' It's an inversion that works at both urban and architectural scales. A geographic and temporal world away at the English Architectural Association in London in 1924 Winston Churchill, the then Chancellor of the Exchequer, had captured both adage and aphorism in the epigram: 'We make our buildings and afterwards they make us.'² He repeated the phrase in the House of Lords in 1943, albeit mildly modified, 'We shape our buildings, thereafter they shape us.'³ In the intervening years Churchill had transformed into the lauded wartime prime minister, and he used the epigram to argue that the recently bombed House of Commons should be reconstructed as it had been (*à la* Charles Barry and Augustus Pugin), as a cloistered oblong of dark wood and green leather to be occupied by 427 honourable members.⁴ Preciado's use of the aphorism was not so conservative. In the book *An Apartment on Uranus: Chronicles of the Crossing* (2019), Preciado engages the idea to suggest the island of Lesbos had operated in the 1980s and 1990s as a 'political spatialization of sexuality,'⁵ and 'an impossible reality: a kilometer of sand and sea occupied by 500 naked lesbians'.⁶

Even as it swings like a pendulum from conservative to radical politics, the dialectical switch from 'We build cities' to 'Cities build us' carries the same oversimplified unidirectional causality. The two statements – x produces y, and y produces x – share the problem of reducing the complexity of issues and elements involved in any production, any shaping, any building, to generalized (over)statements of cause and effect. This problem leaves us dangling in the realms of polemic. Churchill used the aphorism 'they shape us' to revive a continental style of architecture, arguing the 'whole character of the British parliamentary institutions depends upon the fact that the House of Commons is an oblong and not a semi-circular structure'.⁷ And Preciado engages in near-tautological twists to assert the aphorism. He convincingly casts the island not only as 'part of a veritable process of politico-sexual initiation',⁸ but also as if it were a person replete with dietary requirements: 'Lesbos was queer, radical, precarious, vegetarian, collectivist'.[9] The deconsecrated chapel that became the House of Commons and 'a kilometre of sand and sea' may well be socio-architectural machines, but just as the singular suggestion we produce them is problematic, so too is the proposition, they produce us. Simple inversions of causality are too often imprinted with the same fault as the original formation. Determinism is determinism, irrespective of the direction in which it swings.

Cities, architectures, populations and bodies are prone to capricious transformation as one abuts the other. Preciado hints as much in describing the Greek Lesbos as an 'island closer to the Turkish coast',[10] and in noting, 'the border is a space where identity is destroyed and produced'.[11] Preciado's Lesbos, that was once sexually liberating, 20 years later is the site of refugee camps and detention centres, 'the criminalization of immigration and forced imprisonment of migrants'.[12] And what Churchill had once called the 'citadel of British liberty' became a space of Brexit-era isolationism and the politics of xenophobia.[13] The hallowed hall became a site to incite harassment. To suggest this wouldn't have happened in a semi-circular structure makes as little sense as imagining its *impossibility* in oblong form. Identity is too fluid a thing to ever find itself produced, shaped or built into any final or fixed form. As simply as a pendulum might become a wrecking ball, a European can become British, a citizen a refugee, an illegal immigrant or a prisoner; the heteronormative become queer, or a philosopher an activist. 'As for me,' Preciado notes in the letter from Lesbos, 'I have stopped constructing my identity as a lesbian, and today I am fabricating myself, with the help of other techniques (hormonal, legal, linguistic ...) as trans'.[14]

Strange contraptions

The terms 'technique' and the prefix-cum-noun 'trans' are particularly productive terms for thinking about the operations of socio-architectural machines. In his book *Chaosmosis: An Ethico-aesthetic Paradigm* (1992), Félix Guattari had spoken of the necessity for 'strictly aesthetic techniques of rupture and suture' as a type of dexterous assembly and artisanal intervention wherein one simultaneously fabricates as one is fabricated, and the relation between the two, between fabricator and fabrication, is what Guattari calls a 'transversal conception of subjectivity'.[15] The relations of cities, architectures societies and selves are always fluid, queer and transversal. Relations that accord far more with the nuances of ethics and the arts of aesthetics than with clunky dialectics, the proverbs of morality, the epigrams of an ideological politics, or the adages of causality. *Every architectural act may be, in this sense, less as a producer of identity than an incursion that continues its ever-disruption*. Our cities and buildings are less constructors of selves and technologies of production than they are complex objects and ramifying techniques of transformation. In *Chaosmosis* Guattari refers to such objects as 'strange contraptions':

> Strange contraptions [...] these machines of virtuality, these blocks of mutant percepts and affects, half-object half-subject, already here in sensation and outside themselves in fields of the possible. They are not usually found at the usual

marketplace for subjectivity and maybe even less at that for art; yet they haunt everything concerned with creation, the desire for becoming-other, as well as mental disorder or the passion for power.[16]

In *Chaosmosis* Guattari turns not to the developmental production of subjectivity (the 'usual marketplace for subjectivity') but instead towards pervasive subjectivities that are themselves productive. That is to say, as Guattari does in the opening paragraphs of the book, the focus is 'subjectivity from the point of view of its production'.[17] The distinction is noteworthy. This book would not be an examination of the manner by which we produce subjectivity but rather an exploration of the complexity of relations that might come to be thought in terms of subjectivity. In such an account, it would be a mistake to imagine subjectivity was the preserve of the human subject, the animal or even delimited to that which might be thought of as organic, and Guattari commences with what he refers to as 'the most encompassing' definition of subjectivity: 'The ensemble of conditions which render possible the emergence of individual and/or collective instances as self-referential existential Territories, adjacent, or in a delimiting relation, to *an alterity that is itself subjective.*'[18] The aim is to see subjectivity not as an outcome of processes of construction but rather as the processes themselves – the 'ensemble of conditions' – by which something or someone might emerge as *subject* or what Guattari collectively calls 'self-referential existential Territories'. And one of the defining features of any subject is that it remains intimately bound ('adjacent, or in a delimiting relation') to those subjects which are beyond it. And that which is beyond, what Guattari often refers to as a 'Universe of reference', itself has subjectivity.[19] It is '*an alterity that is itself subjective*'. When Churchill spoke of the politics of an oblong or when Preciado spoke of the vegetarianism of an island what is being invoked in such phrases is exactly this. The subjectivities of cities, architectures and landscapes that are at once alterior to our own, and in this regard strange, but are also shared because they are contraptions of which we too are a part. Hence, strange contraptions.

Chaosmosis

Chaosmosis extends Guattari's work at the psychiatric clinic, La Borde, which had focused on widening the definitions of subjectivity, aimed at challenging both the (self) fixations of clinical subjects and the role of psychiatric institutions in the 'conservative reterritorializations of subjectivity'.[20] In *Chaosmosis*, when it comes to questions of how a subject might be constituted or how a psychiatric patient might be treated, Guattari directs our attention to art rather than the habitual techniques of the *psy*-institutions, but he bridges the two worlds in deferring to one of the least institutionalized and most artistic of psychoanalysts, Gisela Pankow. Pankow would use modelling plaster and clay and swathe and bathe schizophrenics for therapeutic purpose. The idea was to introduce externalizations, matters beyond a clinical subject, over which they had some control, and which likewise would assert spatial and material parameters of their own. Space for Pankow is at once part of being human and at the same time faces the human from the outside, perceived as stimulating or inhibiting, familiar or hostile.[21] In the book *L'Homme et sa psychose* (1983) she describes the psychotic universe as 'a house' which was one 'whose walls, inhabitants, objects, are foreign and, even moreso, full of threats'.[22] The psychotic patient was introduced to plaster and clay in order to construct, inhabit and think the concreteness of their being and refamiliarize themselves with their bodies. Guattari extends this work in suggesting the relation between the patient and that which was beyond them; the clay and modelling plaster of art therapy was not only about developing an autonomy for the human subject. It was also about recognizing the subjectivity which haunts 'everything concerned with creation' and Guattari would reference Pankow in speaking of 'forms of art [...] constituting the seeds of the production of subjectivity'.[23] Working with clay is to learn its capacities, possibilities and temperaments. Clay and plaster are in an intimate relation with those that work with the material because of the subjectivities that pulse through both. This stance allows Guattari to speak of the work of art as a 'partial object', but not in the way Sigmund Freud, Melanie Klein or Jacques Lacan had used the term.[24] Art for Guattari is partial in the sense that it is 'half-object half-subject', part of your body and partly not (your fingertips, its imprint, your push, its pull), and for Guattari the creator is as much the created, involved in the 'production of subjectivity (machinic, ecological, architectural [sic], religious, etc.)'.[25] Art is also partial in the sense that there is what Guattari calls 'a dimension of autonomy of an aesthetic order' that exerts subjectivity.[26] A work of art is expressive of itself and its makers, audiences, other works of art, the space in which it is found, and the cultures of its production; and the psychoanalyst refers to the artwork as a 'partial enunciator' speaking with many tongues and in tones and gestures that defy singular authoritative (over)statement.[27] For Guattari 'the work of art detaches itself' and asserts its autonomy as 'a certain type of fragment of content that "takes possession of the author" to engender a certain mode of aesthetic enunciation'.[28]

We can think of moments in architectural design where the drawing takes possession of the drawer, as an example of aesthetic autonomy. Moments when a line falls to the page of a sketch pad and then gestures to the next and the next after that. When a design unfolds, and it doesn't feel like you're involved. It's summed up by odd phrases that seed in architectural studios, phrases like: 'It was coming to me.' And it was. An alterior subjectivity. A type of movement, a slide of a site under a sheet of paper under a pencil that corresponds or rhymes with a conceptual intent tucked away – partly yours and partly its. We're not talking about a generalized or complete autonomy of the pencil but a 'partial' autonomy of a 'certain type', operating in a 'certain mode', that Guattari associates with the 'non-human pre-personal part of subjectivity'.[29] We find ourselves joyously lost or suspended in these moments of artistic technique and often say: 'I lost myself in it.' For Pankow this is not just a process of losing the body (*du corps perdu*) but of the body found, afresh.[30] *In those moments when the subjectivity that haunts our art becomes palpable, we learn something of the subjectivity we share with it.* Guattari too finds something latent or nascent in such moments, noting the 'incorporeal domains of entities we detect at the same time that we produce them, and which appear to have been always there, from the moment we engender them'.[31]

Grafting

The *ethico-aesthetic* that is the concern of *Chaosmosis* is also an extension of Guattari's work with Gilles Deleuze. *Chaosmosis* was published shortly after Deleuze and Guattari's *What Is Philosophy?* (1991), where the role of art in the proximities and discontinuities that might come to constitute subjectivities was a point of focus. What Deleuze and Guattari speak of as the 'heterogeneous components' of subjectivity becomes the wheels and cogs – 'half-object half-subject' – of Guattari's strange contraptions. And the idea upon which Deleuze and Guattari conclude their collaborative work, the idea of 'thought as heterogenesis',[32] becomes a departure point for *Chaosmosis* as the queer residue of subjectivities that 'haunt' or likewise, as Guattari says, that constitute a 'nascent subjectivity, which we will continually find in dreams, délire, creative exaltation, or the feeling of love'.[33]

Guattari's account of heterogenesis is anathema to the codified processes of Freud's psychogenesis. What matters is not the unfolding of a predetermined narrative, the cause-and-effect Jacob's ladder of psycho-sexual development, but instead an experimentation and exploration in subjectivity itself. In place of the oedipal narrative, Guattari offers 'the constitution of complexes of subjectivation: multiple exchanges between individual-group-machine'.[34] 'Graft' is a term Guattari borrows from Pankow to describe the recurring hyphen of the 'individual-group-machine'. Pankow had spoken of the '*greffe de transfert*' as connections made between otherwise homogeneous elements. Guattari and Deleuze deployed the term in *Anti-Oedipus* (1972) to describe the machinic 'coupling that takes place within the partial object-flow connective synthesis', noting, 'Production is always something "grafted onto" the product'.[35] So when Preciado suggests that '[c]ities are socio-architectural machines that can produce identity', we might note the impossibility of ever completely differentiating that which is produced from that which produces. In *A Thousand Plateaus* (1980) the term 'graft' came to express rhizomatic connections between heterogeneous elements. Such connections are pre-personal but come with capacities, malleabilities and mobilities that extend the life of the subject in 'an immediate, indefinite multiplicity of secondary roots [that] grafts onto it and undergoes a flourishing development'.[36] That which we may have thought of as isolated instances of 'self' quickly unfold into a complexity of relations with that which is beyond. I imagine this may be why Preciado comes to describe Lesbos as 'an impossible reality'.

In *Chaosmosis* Guattari at once reinforces the transferential graft deployed across his collaborations with Deleuze and emphasizes the aesthetic and political dimension of the notion. He writes, 'Grafts of transference operate in this way, not issuing from ready-made dimensions of subjectivity crystallised into structural complexes, but from a creation which itself indicates a kind of aesthetic paradigm. One creates new modalities of subjectivity in the same way that an artist creates new forms from the palette'.[37] *Guattari thus associates art not only with the capacity for subjectivity but also with the generation of new subjectivities.* Such subjectivities would not operate at the level of the individual, nor be the preserve of that which is corporeal. The 'incorporeal Universes of reference such as those relative to music and the plastic arts' are a core part of the 'non-human pre-personal part of subjectivity [...] crucial since it is from this that its heterogenesis can develop'.[38] The new forms of subjectivity that are the outcome of artistic techniques and the movements constituted by the grafting of the individual-group-machine are political matters. They come with force and have the capacity to either build or destroy.

In those moments in architecture studios where decisions are being made by a pencil, where a design 'was coming', there's not only an odd transversal relation at stake, the you-architecture-pencil, but also an ethics. The right and the wrong of something. This ethics is often summed up in phrases such as 'That's it!' or 'It's not quite right' – phrases we mutter as we draw a line that might become a wall. This ethics, this positioning on a right and a wrong, seeps from the hyphens of the pencil-architecture-you. When things are going well, we submit to the movements of the paper, the hand and the pencil, and the wall that corresponds to the line sweeping as it should. And when things are not going right, the assemblage dismantles: Paper is abandoned, and we torture a pencil in a sharpener. This *right* and *wrong* of a drawing is not about a tut-tutting deferral to moral codes, laws or rules, but rather an impersonal aesthetic impulse towards x rather than y. It is an impulse that emerges amongst the concepts, criteria, paraphernalia, extraneous circumstance, studios and landscapes which operate as the complex contexts of architecture. What we are involved in at such moments is what Guattari calls 'an ethics and politics of the virtual that decorporealises and deterritorialises contingency, linear causality and the pressure of circumstances and significations which besiege us'.[39] This is the ethics of *an 'ethico-aesthetics', a term that comes to stand for all manner of decision-making and creative process that is driven by the liminal qualities of encounters, aesthetic moves, and material parameters.* To be taken up here, rather than there. To act or to retreat.

For Guattari the graft of art was not only therapeutic in a clinical sense for an individual but also political for a population. It was a sense he shared with Deleuze who had turned not to the plastic arts but to literature in his *critical and clinical* project to suggest, 'The ultimate aim of literature is to set free, in the delirium, this creation of a health or this invention of a people, that is, a possibility of life. To write for this people who are missing ... ("for" means less "in the place of" than "for the benefit of")'.[40] Guattari was clearer in demarcating enemies, and for him art operates as a key mode of resistance to the 'great capitalistic machines'[41] and the 'steam roller of capitalistic subjectivity' that produces singular and one-dimensional subjects.[42] And Guattari would identify in art 'a whole subjective creativity which traverses the generations and oppressed peoples, ghettoes, minorities'.[43] The philosopher Eric Alliez notes that '[t]he first effect of *Chaosmosis* is the deterritorialization of the aesthetic towards a radical below/beyond of art, enabling the question left in suspense at the end of *What Is Philosophy?* – "thought as heterogenesis" – to be reformulated and grappled with in a renewed ontologico-political mode'.[44] In order to operate this ontologico-political mode, the politics of ethico-aesthetics involves the capacity to perceive that which 'haunts' a work of art or the capacity to be affected by that which is 'nascent'. Guattari calls such capacities 'pathic subjectivation'.[45] This is at once an aesthetic appreciation and an appreciation of subjectivities beyond ourselves. Indeed, it is founded on *an empathy for alterity. Loving an alterity that is itself subjective.* To love alterity is to appreciate the complexities and the particularities that are not entirely our own. A capacity for compersion or pathos, for that which is beyond: other people, communities and cultures, and, on a slightly different register, other animals, objects and geographies, the earth and the cosmos itself. Written into the very definition of art as a 'strange contraption' is a politics that is operative at individual, social, institutional and ecological scales.[46] This idea is as necessary to the graft of architecture as it is to the paradigm of *Chaosmosis*. 'I simply want to stress,' writes Guattari, 'that the aesthetic paradigm – the creation and composition of mutant percepts and affects – has become the paradigm for every possible form of liberation.'[47]

Killing Architects

When we speak of the liberatory capacities of architecture there is often a deferral to the idea of 'activism in architecture', but this is problematic; it's a little like activism *in* parliament, activism *in* prisons or activism *in* court. It's 'in', in the sense of being held within, but also in the sense that it is an activism that is managed, contained and controlled, operating more often than not as an apologist for the whole of which it is part. Indeed, it is a welcome part because the profession, the prison, the parliament and court will continue to defer to a list of 'activisms' of its members as an excuse for avoiding wholesale change or revolution. There are however architects that have chosen 'not to construct', in order that they take their architectural skills, techniques and understandings, and take their ethico-aesthetic and act outside architecture. I am speaking of groups such as *Forensic Architecture* based at Goldsmith's University in the UK, INDEX in France, *WEAK!* which unfolds from Taiwan to Finland, and the provocatively named *Killing Architects* based in the Netherlands. What such groups invoke is the graft of architecture as a means to enunciate for those who otherwise have no voice '(where "for" means less "in the place of" than "for the benefit of")'. Such groups have made it clear that so much of architecture's power comes from its capacity for *aberrant communication*.[48] That is, to communicate with our disciplinary *outside* – parliaments, prisons and courts, nations, institutions, war, policing – rather than muttering away *inside* the discipline.

Alison Killing established *Killing Architects* studio in 2010 and became well known in 2021 when taking out the Pulitzer Prize for International Reporting alongside her colleagues Megha Rajagopalan and Christo Buschek of BuzzFeed News. Architecture's most prestigious award, the Pritzker prize, that year went to Lacaton and Vassal. The citation for these two awards makes the paternal and colonial character of disciplinary constraints patently clear. The Pritzker citation starts: 'The work of Anne Lacaton and Jean-Philippe Vassal reflects architecture's democratic spirit.'[49] The Pulitzer, on the other hand, was '[f]or a series of clear and compelling stories that used satellite imagery and architectural expertise, as well as interviews with two dozen former prisoners, to identify a vast new infrastructure built by the Chinese government for the mass detention of Muslims.'[50] The pendulum of politics pulses in both, but the true liberatory power of architecture rests firmly in its alterity.

Killing worked on the five key articles published between August and December 2020 that exposed the mass infrastructure and architecture that the Chinese state produced to imprison the Kazakh and Uyghur population, native to the Xinjiang Uyghur Autonomous Region.[51] This was 'the largest-scale detention of ethnic and religious minorities since World War II.[52] The architecture of these detention camps was one technique of state-enforced transformation amongst many, that included forced sterilization, forced labour, perpetual surveillance via facial recognition technology, house and town arrest, thuggish policing and 're-education'. What is particularly horrifying about the architectural techniques involved in the destruction of the population is that these 'purpose-built, high-security camps – some capable of housing tens of thousands of people' were successfully hidden from view.[53] Whilst hiding a CCTV camera might be a simple matter, considerable effort must be expended to hide a network of massive buildings. These structures were 'masked' in maps, silenced by laws that curtail free speech and journalistic enquiry and never the subject of disciplinary discourse despite the scale of investment. The architects of these structures of incarceration are not named, but it's likely that they are all appropriately licensed under the Chinese Architects Act, via registration with the National Administration Board of Architectural Registration (NABAR) and might choose to be members of the Architectural Society of China that runs its own annual design awards programme. The engineers too are hidden behind computer screens and disciplinary niceties.

The tens of thousands of Kazakhs and Uyghurs who are routinely removed from their homes and families and detained were efficiently silenced until Killing engaged architectural techniques to allow the horror to be perceived.[54] That is to say, Killing brought techniques of architecture to bare upon architecture itself, in this case the architecture of mass incarceration. In the first of the six Buzzfeed articles Killing identified 268 structures built since 2017 in Xinjiang province. The process involved identifying 'blanked-out' areas on Baidu Maps (a commonly used Chinese mapping application) cross-referenced with images from external satellite providers: Google Earth, Planet Labs and the European Space Agency's Sentinel Hub (Figure 12.1). The architecture of the new incarceration sites is on par with prison architecture internationally which has an identifiable relation with the services and infrastructure of towns and cities, a recognizable typology, and a consistently denuded style. The only decorative flourish here is a rococo fringe of barbed wire. These architectural qualities often go unnoticed but were key to the process of finding the camps. The aerial architecture of other prisons in China was an easy comparison for Killing to make and makes the official Chinese line seem like gallows humour. Following the Buzzfeed investigation, the Chinese consulate in New York released the statement: 'Xinjiang has set up vocational education and training centers in order to root out extreme thoughts, enhance the rule of law awareness through education, improve vocational skills and create employment opportunities.'[55] Was it Xi Jinping who said 'We shape our buildings, thereafter they shape us'?

The terrifying homogenization sought by the Chinese Communist Party was not just achieved in construction. As the bland architecture of the camps rose, so too was Killing able to map the erasure of cultural landmarks: The domes and minarets of mosques that disappeared from the maps. The Buzzfeed articles make constructions and erasures visible. Text and image and architectural modelling are thrust into compelling aesthetic resonance. BuzzFeed and Killing produced headlines, and standfirsts, text and quotes from interviewees, alongside, adjacent to and overlaid with maps. It was a polyphonic production that allowed readers to scroll and zoom in to see the fortifications, entrance gates, guard towers and perimeter walls of the prisons and camps. And scroll and zoom out to see the geographic scale of the horror. This interactive art operates as what the geographer and urbanist Hagit Keysar calls 'spatial testimony',[56] but this is not just a construction of truths; it also involves a liberation of subjects. When the architecture is made visible, the state is clearly culpable, and the prisoner is audible. And the reader also transforms. The capacity of a readership to activate the technologies and assert spatial and material parameters (much like an architect does) has them inculcated in what Guattari called 'the creation and composition of mutant percepts and affects' necessary 'for every possible form of liberation'.[57]

When we slide the cursor over the Buzzfeed articles and zoom into an image, a map, an architectural model, we as reader become something else. It is a type of aesthetic we enter, an ethic of access we operate. What Killing and Buzzfeed achieved is the re-spatializing of data, giving dimension, voluptuosity, architecture, and flesh back to that which has strategically been reduced to less than two dimensions, 'in the same way that an artist creates new forms from the palette'. The Kazakh and Uyghur people and the audience of Killing's work were all *brought into being* by this stepping away from the discipline, with its techniques in tow.[58] Killing's work is a long way from an image of architecture as either the secretions of the human (we make it) or a secretor of humans (it makes us). Instead Killing takes what Guattari refers to as 'the specificity of the architect's art' in order 'to become an intercessor' speaking for all manner of alterity.[59] To be polyglotte of the polyphonic. To be a tracer of transversality. To be an artist of alterity. This is the graft of an architect today.

Figure 12.1 Megha Rajagopalan, Alison Killing, and Christo Buschek, Compound in the County of Shufu (25 August 2019), 'China Secretly Built a Vast New Infrastructure to Imprison Muslims', *BuzzFeed* news investigation part 1, 27 August 2020. Google Maps, 25 August 2019. Google Maps [online]. Accessed 27 May 2021.

Part Four

'Minor architectures'

Part Four looks to the edges of architecture, its wondrous frayed edges. Jennifer Bloomer suggests that '[t]he concept of minor architecture is both properly deduced from [Manfredo] Tafuri's concept of "major architecture" and illegitimately appropriated from Gilles Deleuze and Félix Guattari's concept of minor literature'.[1] In his text *Theories and History of Architecture* (1980), Tafuri defines 'major architecture' as being that which is complicit with the process of rationalizing the senses, normalizing the course of civilisation and stabilizing semantic structures.[2] Bloomer proposes that one of the tasks of minor architecture is to operate critically upon the dominance of this image. In the chapters that follow, I turn to the illegitimate architectural offspring of Deleuze and Guattari's philosophy. The aim is to chart some of the piquant and poignant zones where architecture's engagements have extended or exceeded the very definitions of architecture itself. In many ways these chapters explore the *afterimage* of Deleuze and Guattari in twenty-first-century architecture and consider the philosophy a 'dark precursor' of an architecture to come.

13

Syntheses

Sub-representational

In the early pages of *Anti-Oedipus* (1972), Gilles Deleuze and Félix Guattari turn to the work of the Swiss artist Adolf Wölfli. Wölfli was known for vast fields of drawing where all manner of god and sacred figure and animal and geometry and pattern and fenestration and musical notation came to fall into unstable orders. Not equilibriums, but vibrant orders, vibrating, pulsing orders that Wölfli would play through pencil on a thin newsprint paper and via a long paper trumpet through the corridors of the Waldau psychiatric clinic in which he resided.[1] This raw art [*art brut*] might remind an architect of the works of Antoni Gaudi or of Friedensreich Hundertwasser. The work of Wölfli connected all manner of element in a type of discord that nevertheless accorded:

> Sunbeams, birds, voices, nerves enter into changeable and genealogically complex relationships with God and forms of God derived from the godhead by division. But all this happens and is all recorded on the surface of the body without organs: even the copulations of the agents, even the divisions of God, even the genealogies marking it off into squares like a grid, and their permutations. The surface of this uncreated body swarms with them, as a lion's mane swarms with fleas.[2]

The drawing surface is a site upon which discordant elements fall and might swarm, migrate and vibrate, but it too has a life of its own. It is a 'lion's mane'. What Deleuze and Guattari are confronting in these early pages of *Anti-Oedipus* is an idea that had been circulating in art for some time and would find sonority in artists such as Wölfli. It is the idea that the planes upon which acts of representation were occurring pre-exist and have a texture and a life of their own. It was a point that the philosopher of aesthetics and art history Hubert Damisch had made in his theoretical excavations of the 'underside' of painting.[3] Damisch identifies a 'thickness' (*épaisseur*) to the surface that can be inscribed in order to bring what is below to the fore. In this scenario lines don't sit on an empty sheet but rather 'plow the canvas through and through'.[4] Georges Seurat had given voice to the same thick compact of canvas and earth, defining painting as 'the art of ploughing a surface',[5] and Paul Cézanne found himself swallowed in this thickness noting 'landscape is invisible because the more we conquer it, the more we lose ourselves in it'.[6] The very surfaces on which we draw are not empty planes on which to represent *this* or *that* – this bird, that sunbeam – but rather are the ground of production, a landscape of furrows and ridges. It was not that the world of Wölfli, Seurat or Cezanne for that matter, was not without the figures of figuration or the configurations of landscape; it was that such elements were complot with the means by which they came to be represented. Plotting with the drawing surface, the plot of land, on which they resided. Deleuze and Guattari would refer to this compote of elements represented and surfaces of representation as a 'subrepresentative field' or the 'sub-representational'.[7] The point for them was philosophical and the implication was that consciousness itself is much like a drawing surface: a site upon which discordant elements fall and might swarm that also has a life of its own. Thoughts swarm in and along the dynamic flows of consciousness or fall from that lion's mane and find themselves in very different fields.

Three syntheses

There are a thousand manners by which a flea, a sunbeam or a bird might fall onto a field, onto the surface of a drawing, or onto an Alessi kettle. And in each scenario, we face the oddity of transformed capacities and resistant characteristics. On the one hand the capacities of a flea, sunbeam or bird are radically altered by the surfaces onto which they fall. A bird will sing in a field very differently to how it might sing into the holes of a Wölfli drawing and differently to how it might sing on a kettle. On the other hand, a flea, a sunbeam or a bird retains characteristics despite their contexts. And we have already noted that though it would sing differently on different surfaces, the bird continued to sing wherever it fell. Unlike Fredrich Engels, Karl Marx was not a lover of birds, but he did nevertheless identify this particular oddity of transformed capacities and resistant characteristics. In an early section of *Capital* (1867) Marx notes that anything, any 'product', that falls into a field becomes a 'commodity' of that field and enters relations with other commodities of the field.[8] But he had also noted, a product was never completely subsumed by the field into which it fell, and for Marx even a commodity is 'a very strange thing, abounding in metaphysical subtleties and theological niceties'.[9] He called this discordant bind of product, the fields of production and metaphysical subtlety: 'commodity fetishism'. The term 'fetishism' would be one that Marx imported from theology or what he called 'the misty realm of religion'.[10] Whilst Marx migrated ideas from a theological field onto the surfaces of economics in critique of capitalism, in *Anti-Oedipus* Deleuze and Guattari shake Marx's ideas onto the field of philosophy and deploy them in critique of psychoanalysis.[11] This shake of fleas from Marx's mane would lead to concepts such as 'economic and social machineries', 'desiring-machines', 'desiring-production' and at least one 'miraculating fetishistic machine'.[12]

This mode of operation – of shaking concepts from one field to another – was productive at multiple scales for Deleuze and Guattari. In *Anti-Oedipus* this process spilled over the ridges of disciplinarity and into the furrows of the brain itself, becoming a model for the machinic operations of the unconscious. This would be a radically different model to the one it supplanted. For Jacques Lacan the unconscious was structured like a language and driven by lack. For Deleuze and Guattari the unconscious was not structural at all, but machinic and driven by desire. In *Anti-Oedipus*, desire is the synthesizing function of the unconscious that brings together the discordant elements (products) and surfaces (the 'fertile domains' of production) that are no less characterful and queer. Deleuze and Guattari would invoke three 'syntheses' to describe the manner by which the elements and surfaces of the unconscious come to accord and how such syntheses might at times erupt, as when a kettle sings.

The first syntheses are referred to as *connective syntheses*. These syntheses are a type of purposeful activity of collecting and collating 'raw material' into a common frame.[13] Deleuze and Guattari would refer to the process as 'inherently connective' and summarize the mode of operation as '"and ..." "and then ..."'.[14] In the connective synthesis, '[t]here is no need to distinguish between producing and its product. [...] the pure "thisness" of the object produced is carried over into a new act of producing'.[15] It might be thought of in terms of singing. The connective synthesis is the pulling together of tunes and lyrics, sound-recording devices, voices, throats, fingers and instruments. Each element is productive. And what they produce when connected is itself not an endpoint but just another element that will be 'carried over' and invite new connections, 'and then ...'. The connective syntheses are thus described by Deleuze and Guattari as something like *presubjective* or *transubjective* relations. There is as yet no singular or finalized song; it is as yet an 'uncreated body'.

The second are called *disjunctive syntheses*. Here products or elements are taken out of contexts, separated from the productive process with which they were once associated. Examples might be either a headphone no longer plugged into an ear, or a bird no longer in flight, or a word no longer in a lyric. Deleuze and Guattari would summarize the mode of operation as 'either ... or ... or'.[16] A disjunctive synthesis is a synthesis of divergent series that do not converge yet somehow manage to communicate by virtue of the difference that passes between them. Thus, a disjunctive synthesis is a 'relation of non-relation' or a relation 'beyond the predicative relation'.[17] A disjunctive synthesis might be plugging a headphone into a bird, and Deleuze and Guattari align such syntheses with what they call the surface of 'recording'. And though this example sounds perverse, it is perhaps no less perverse than the recording process of vinyl albums. Here one series – of song, lyric, voice and instrument – is disembodied (removed from a musician and instrument) and comes to connect to a second series – of plasticized and pressed discs of petroleum and salt – disconnected (removed from an oil field). When we 'press' a vinyl album we amalgamate elements, despite their disconnection. The disjunctive syntheses are thus described by Deleuze and Guattari as *estranged* or *asubjective* relations. There is little that connects song and the furrows and ridges of vinyl but nevertheless it constitutes a recording.

The third are called *conjunctive syntheses*. It is here that the elements brought together – disconnected and disjointed – swarm across a threshold are consumed and consummate (*consommation*). Deleuze and Guattari would refer to the process as 'the production of consumption' and summarize the mode of operation as '"so it's ...,"'.[18] The surface upon which such syntheses occur is a type of catatonic stupor on the verge of overspill. It is the sheer joy of lowering a stylus onto vinyl knowing that all that oddity and unfathomable difference might erupt in just that one album, and for Deleuze and Guattari it is only in this third synthesis that 'the subject is produced'.[19] This subject is neither the habitual one we might think of nor the traditional philosophical one. It is insubstantial, fleeting, transitory. It emerges abruptly and unexpectedly; and it dissolves just as quickly. In *Anti-Oedipus* conjunctive syntheses are cast as the tremor and cut through 'of sensual pleasures, of anxiety, and of pain'.[20] So a conjunctive synthesis is the jouissance of fleas fucking in a leaping lion's mane or the roar of the Pixies album *Doolittle* (1989).

Graphic arts

The Boston band, the Pixies, intended to call their second album *Whore*, but when the London-based graphic artist Vaughan Oliver presented them with an image of the cover, they decided on the title *Doolittle*[21] (Figure 13.1). The cover Oliver had proposed was a grainy black-and-white image of a monkey with a halo. It fell onto the surface along with a cartography of geometric figures, lines, rectangular and triangular, and circles, and three-dimensional numerals 5, 6 and 7, and the names of songs in a cursive font prefixed with small circles indicating direction, like labels marking section lines on an architectural plan. This album cover was as if formed on an oxidizing iron surface or, likewise, recovered from oxidization, as if there were things already on this surface that were removed to reveal others. The overall effect is of a communication of layers without any necessary hierarchy or immediately obvious connection. Like grinding chatter or grating whispers, the album cover was a strange interplay of the organic and industrial. Oliver regarded cover art as 'another music tool' and this tool was the product of one machine in particular:[22] the photomechanical transfer (PMT). The point of the PMT is not to represent this or that but rather to hold multiple images *in impression*. The process involves exposing what is called an 'original copy' to a photosensitive paper, which is then 'mated' with a receiver paper. The two are processed together, which results in an image on one surface being taken up directly by another. Penetrability is one of the most important factors of the PMT process – a capacity to absorb black dots – and even the blandest of technical documents make its disjunctive character clear: 'The offset printing process is an either/or proposition. It either lays ink down on the paper or it doesn't.'[23] It's not a process of originals and of copies, but endless copies, mated, surface to surface. It's a process more akin to consummation than representation. No negative is needed in this process. Far better to call it *Doolittle*.

Post-coital, PMTs hang from a clothesline to dry. Just as the process involved is a play of the organic and machinic, so too is it a play between signification and the arbitrary but nevertheless expressive nature of signs. Oliver had been given the hand-written lyrics of this album prior to working on the cover.[24] In this sense the surface was indeed a ploughing of the vinyl it held. The brooding, grainy, black-and-white monkey of the cover is a reference to the song 'Monkey Gone to Heaven' and the numerals are a reference to its lyrics: 'If man is 5/ Then the devil is 6 [...] If the devil is 6/ Then God is 7'. Whilst the monkey and the numerals of the cover reference lyrics, to what the lyrics reference becomes a murkier affair, of the 'misty realm' as Marx would say, 'subrepresentative' as Deleuze and Guattari would say. The title of the album 'Doolittle' was also an illusory reference. It comes from the song 'Mr. Grieves' and the lyric 'Pray for a man in the middle / One that talks like Doolittle'. This lyric is most likely a misspelled reference to the fictional Welsh veterinarian, Dr Dolittle, who talked to animals. But it might also be a reference to Alfred Doolittle, Eliza's father, who rose to the middle classes in Bernard Shaw's play *Pygmalion* (1912). Or both. And more, this title also speaks to the processes involved in the multifaceted production of this magnificent album: a Dr Doolittle communication between disjunctive music tools. Communication as accord. Making love of discord.

Figure 13.1 Vaughan Oliver's cover for Pixies, *Doolittle* (1989). Image © 4AD.

Communicating Vessels

Oliver and the architect Neil Spiller occupied the same street and spoke the same language. There was something shared in the manner by which things came together for them. An audacious, serendipitous manner that finds in minutiae – this coffee stain, that marigold glove – the possibilities for connection, expression and elaboration. Oliver was already famous for his 4AD album covers when he handled the graphic design of Spiller's first monograph: *Maverick Deviations* (1999), and though there's no collective noun for *mavericks*, the graphic artist and the architect would continue to conspire in friendship.[25] When Oliver passed late in 2019 Spiller was keen that the parts of Oliver that outlived him might not be scattered, but rather held. These parts would come to be, like their shared processes of production, aberrantly transmuted onto a surface – in this case a set of drawings for a memorial 'Longhouse Roof Garden' in Spiller's long-standing *Communicating Vessels* project. The project is based on an island in Shoreditch, Kent, an island that is a necessarily nebulous site, poised between land and the landscapes of memory.[26] The drawings that constitute this project are a cacophony of organs, the organic, inorganic, architectural fragments, memories, machines, desires and sequestered events. It is why this island has both the sense of *déjà vu* and *déjà là* about it. A rousing sense of the already seen and the already there. Through this 'life work' Spiller negotiates the intensity of extant things *in their immediacy,* but he also ruminates on them and lets them rot, ferment or bloom on this island where 'conscious and the subconscious worlds are dallied with to create a psychosexual landscape'.[27] A land ripe for the ploughing.

Longhouse Roof Garden

The Roof Garden that Spiller raises for his friend Oliver would be the second walled garden that he would construct. Both were triggered by the death of friends. The first was a memorial to the architect Lebbeus Woods. The vectors that storm through Woods's garden are constructed with Woods's frenzy and the force of the storm that was surging when Woods died. Oliver's garden too would bear the paraphernalia of his passing alongside the characteristics of Oliver's own production processes. In the Roof Garden drawings there is a swirl of lines that might be clotheslines from which PMTs hang, the orange of discarded negatives, fragments of Oliver's record covers, an eel belt, sharp knives, an architect's 'barnet' that becomes 'a type of surrealist furry crucifix',[28] and an '*x*' marking the love that lingers when a friend has passed (Figure 13.2). It's a procession of 'and, and, and' that partializes the elements. In part they retain their own characteristics and in part adopt capacities afforded by the surface onto which they have fallen. Spiller's drawings extract a residual share of each element's content as a sort of recompense for their perpetual dispossession.

These drawings are a splicing of shared sensibilities. The transfer of elements onto the drawing surface is done with a modus operandi that is as much Oliver's as Spiller's.[29] You can spot in these drawings the Hejduk cathedral with a sword-like snout and wings: the inverted angel of the Longhouse (2015) on which the Roof Garden sits, but it occurs here as a migration of black-and-white dots like those of Oliver's PMTs. Spiller refers to this shared production process as an 'experiment in the husbanding of flesh'.[30] This processual complexity makes the island less Dr Dolittle and more Alfred Jarry's Dr Faustroll or H.G. Wells's Dr Moreau. This drawing practice, that is the product of friends' eyes, does not yield any singular or finalized structure; it is as yet an 'uncreated body'. Simplistic spatial assignations are dangerous here. To have suggested the garden is *on* the Longhouse is either inaccurate or premature. The garden exceeds it, augments it, in dimensions longer than the Longhouse itself. And here 'long' doesn't necessarily refer to length but might be a temporal quality, like rumination. Elements represented, production processes, dimensionality and temporality are inextricable in Spiller's drawings. And inextricable from the island. This thick compact of drawing fields and plots of land is radically different to what Spiller calls the 'well-trodden furrows of other contemporaries [...] using drawing and writing as scrying devices'.[31] He is not interested in the clear empty space of visual acuity or in the instrumental function of drawing that merely inscribes lines on blank sheets or that aligns lines with fixed translatable meanings. Instead, Spiller describes his process as that of a 'cyborgian geomorphological archaeologist' that comes 'armed with many machines – some vintage, some state of the art – who can reveal their depths of spaces to us, as well as their fluctuating nature'.[32] Deleuze and Guattari speak of such a machine as a 'miraculating fetishistic machine', which attracts all the disjunctive elements into a non-organized arrangement 'as so many points of disjunction, between which an entire network of new syntheses is now woven, marking the surface off into co-ordinates, like a grid'.[33]

Damisch refers to moments where from the thickness of the surface, art 'ascends'.[34] Deleuze and Guattari harness the idea and write of a moment where 'the figures of art free themselves from an apparent transcendence or paradigmatic model and avow their innocent atheism, their paganism'.[35] In the Roof Garden drawings we note this ascent and avowal when a scanner, which only scans at certain dimensions, generates a gridded patchwork to the images, like fields we might recognize from flights. Or when squiggles of washing line fold into forms. Or when knives once adrift congregate as 'a gnawing thing', hollowing out memorial structures.[36] And when they emerge, bloom, like wild grass from the towers that house Oliver's artefacts. These sharp forms themselves forming shadows that now look far more like wings than knives. This moment is where Spiller's drawings are at their most *architectural*. Architectural, yes, albeit as what Spiller refers to as 'a system of chance choreography'.[37] A dance of perhaps perspectives, perhaps plans or perhaps sections. This is neither drawing as representation or demarcation, nor drawing as an either/or scenario, but instead the constant extension of an 'either or ... or ... or'. These drawings are mappings that slide into three dimensions and start to unfold instances of the Roof Garden but they equally might slide out of architectural space and back into the drawing surface. A figure-ground of the Longhouse is discernible in such drawings, though not nearly with the fixity of either an architectural plan or the oppositionality of a figure ground. More like a migration of densities or excavations. This drawing process involves 'confronting the blank sheet' as Spiller says, but in such a manner that is estranged from architectural conventions and 'dislocates the trained architectural self'.[38] There's nothing totalized or strictly sensible to this edge. Each disjunctive series is responding to others in their own way with their own languages and sensibilities. That's why the project is called *Communicating Vessels*.

This moment is fleeting, fluctuating. At the instant the Roof Garden seems to take depth, the drawing surface itself saturates and '"the underneath" comes through'.[39] Even Spiller's drawing board asserts thickness over depth at such a moment. Its marks, old shopping lists and coffee stains, its 'scratchings and scrapings', become flooded furrows. This is a moment of overspill or the drawing surface as catatonic stupor. 'So it's ...,' the heaving of a lion's mane or the roar of the Pixies album *Doolittle*. Notwithstanding the 'many machines' involved in the *Communicating Vessels* project and the scanners and PMTs of the Roof Garden, the work of Spiller is quintessentially *drawing*. These are drawings because they *draw forth*, and the architecture elicited is but a shifting residuum of the process. A residue from the ground and the drawing surface, up. Spiller, a cyborgian geomorphological archaeologist, would excavate the sky itself for this Longhouse Roof Garden, a mausoleum for Oliver, the son of a mine surveyor. *x*.

Figure 13.2 Neil Spiller, Longhouse Roof Garden, *Communicating Vessels* (2021). Image courtesy of Neil Spiller.

14

Cosmic artisans

Lightning Ridge

My mother coveted an opal that was somewhere between stone and cloud. It was secured in a match box in the upper right-hand drawer of a bedside table in her room. When I was a child, on special occasions she would retrieve the box and slowly slide the lid open to reveal the contents. Inside the matchbox, the opal lay on a bed of cotton wool. We'd peer from above at the stone nestled in the box in much the same way that others might peer into a nativity scene and focus on the baby Jesus in his manger. These occasions incited reverence. The opal was polished and rounded. Not circular but ovoid. The back, which lay on the cotton wool, was less convex than the front which faced us. It was small – no more than 8 millimetres in length, about 7 at its widest point, and 6 thick – but this opal had an intensity and a depth that exceeded its dimensions. An intensity of mobile colour and a depth that inspired fixation. Overall, it was a milky white. Not a bleached blank white like the cotton wool on which it lay, but a cloudy luminescent wash of whites. More Turner than Constable. For within this cloud was a constellation of other luminescent colours. Pinks and greens, golden glows, and waves of blue. As my mother tilted the matchbox a colour that was not at first obvious would become perceptible, and as the box was moved towards the sunlight of the window, still other colours emerged from the depths and the milky whiteness itself sang.

The special occasions on which the opal would shine from the bedroom, the bedside drawer and the match box would come with the short story of when it was found. My late father had discovered it on my parents' honeymoon in outback Australia. They spent the week following their wedding in a desert place called Lightning Ridge. As a child, this place – that I have never seen for myself – sounded like another world entirely. To avoid the scorching heat some lived underground there, in spaces carved out of the same stone in which the opals were found. My father, however, found my mother's opal on the ground rather than within it. It was in its natural, rough, rocky state and he had it polished into the smooth ovoid jewel it now was. His plan was to one day – a day that never came – set it in a piece of jewellery for my mother. Love, lightning and honeyed moons find themselves in this opal, somewhere between stone and cloud.

Crystals

In *A Thousand Plateaus* (1980), Gilles Deleuze and Félix Guattari write of 'a pure crystal that harnesses cosmic forces'.[1] This image of the crystal sits alongside numerous deferrals to geological phenomena in the book: the earth, stones, stratum, stratification, mining and metallurgy. The *geo* of Deleuze and Guattari's *geophilosophy* was both the geo of geography and geology. This is made clear by the title of an early chapter, '10,000 B.C.: The Geology of Morals (Who Does the Earth Think It Is?)'. Along with this title, the page which marks the commencement of the chapter carries a grainy black-and-white photograph of a lobster, pictured as if it were on its back, and oriented on the page much like a crucifix. Together, the title and the image suggest an exploration poised between crusts, crustaceans and christs. The title 'The Geology of Morals' is a deferral to Fredrich Nietzsche's *On the Genealogy of Morals* of 1887. In his *Genealogy* Nietzsche explores the political and ethical construction of moral concepts and gestures to new social forms that might emerge in the wake of god. Nietzsche had used the image of a crystal and processes of crystallization to describe how the many disparate and oft incompatible features that might define a society 'crystallises eventually into a kind of unity, which is difficult to analyse into its parts, and which, it is necessary to emphasise, absolutely defies definition'.[2] Deleuze and Guattari find in processes of crystallization a similar propensity towards a type of unity, a *univocity*, that pays little heed to traditional or habitual demarcations and definitions. It is possible to speak of a 'geology of morals' when the habits of thought that might have demarcated geology, theology, biology and sociology as separate realms are shelved in favour of the more fluid sensibilities the philosopher and psychoanalyst summarize as 'pluralism = monism'.[3] The crystal becomes an image for the manner by which a plurality of matter hardens into something singularly distinct and identifiable.

Though the phrase 'a pure crystal that harnesses cosmic forces' may sound a little like the rantings of one of Lightning Ridge's crystal shop owners, Deleuze and Guattari's idea is more philosophically than spiritually informed. The idea is informed by Deleuze's early work on Nietzsche and Immanuel Kant, and Deleuze and Guattari's shared interest in the contemporary work of Gilbert Simondon. For Nietzsche, 'the object itself is force, expression of a force'.[4] In such an account all objects – crystals, lobsters, matchboxes, rooms, etcetera – are expressions of the forces that bring them into being. Every object, no matter how polished, bares the mark of the forces of its construction. And in Deleuze's account of Nietzsche, all objects are also registers of the forces by which they are apprehended, for '[e]ven perception [...] is the expression of forces'.[5] Thus to gaze at an object with reverence is to buff the polish. There are (at least) three key forces at play in the expression of the crystal in *A Thousand Plateaus*.

First, Deleuze and Guattari find in crystals *an image for the as-yet-unformed*. Like the 'tantric egg', the 'seed' or the *Body without Organs* of which they speak, the crystal expresses the sense of that which is as yet undetermined.[6] An egg is perhaps the simplest example. An egg is undetermined in the sense that it might become this or that – this lobster, that bird. The crystal has the same liberty. It may be this gemstone, that snowflake, or that salt we sprinkle on lobster. This sense of the unformed was also an aesthetic feature of a kind. A feature of which Kant had spoken of in his

Critique of Judgment (1790) as 'free' and 'vague' beauty (*pulchritudo vaga*) and which Deleuze refers to in his early exploration of Kant as 'a genesis of the feeling of the beautiful itself'.⁷ This may be thought of as a beauty that is prior to its articulation in any particular (art)form. Kant found in seashells, flowers, crystals and bird song a type of a priori beauty, prior to human appreciation, art-theoretical formulations, and distinctions that might have treated content and expression as separate categories.⁸ For Deleuze and Guattari the crystal operates as matter a priori to formal categorization. This stance resonates with that of Simondon who uses crystallization as an image for *individuation*, a type of latent potential that might take one form or another.⁹ But whilst Simondon's crystals emerge in more or less homogenous solutions, Deleuze and Guattari's are of heterogeneous components. All manner of matter (thought, organism, organic and inorganic matter) might crystallize. And they push this idea even further in work that follows *A Thousand Plateaus*. Deleuze would develop the idea of the 'crystal-image' in the second of his two books dedicated to cinema to describe how past and present might be suspended in matter, in this case matters of film.¹⁰ And in a footnote to their last collaborative work, *What Is Philosophy?* (1991), Deleuze and Guattari invoke the studies of Isabelle Stengers and Ilya Prigogene on 'germs of crystals' which are a little like the a proiri of the a priori – germs of crystals may or may not take even crystalline form.¹¹

Second, the crystal of *A Thousand Plateaus* is a dismissal of the *all-too-human logic* that we all too often apply to objects that are beyond us. Deleuze and Guattari share with Nietzsche a sense of the bind involved in being human. For Nietzsche the human was a 'wretched glass capsule' that at once delimited access to the world whilst creating the sense that access was replete.¹² The human was bound to the limits of human perceptions, but the transparency of this capsule is as such that the human rarely notices the constraint. Nietzsche sums up his wariness of this bind in the title of his work *Human, All-Too-Human* (1878), and in *Thus Spoke Zarathustra* (1883) gestures to that which is beyond the wretched capsule, suggesting, 'Man and man's earth are unexhausted and undiscovered.'¹³ Deleuze and Guattari concur and engage the eighteenth-century French naturalist Étienne Geoffroy Saint-Hilaire in noting 'the human in them [in us] is only a straightjacket for inhuman forms and substances'.¹⁴ We note such a straightjacketing in the manner by which we habitually speak about objects, personifying them, humanizing them, subjugating them into human phenomenology and preoccupation. We consistently speak of the earth, other animals, inorganic and cosmic objects as if the human were central to their expression, as if a crystal was not expressing itself for countless millennia before a father *discovers* it and as if it failed to shine as bright after his passing.

Third, Deleuze and Guattari find in the crystal *an escape route*. This is an escape route in much the same sense that microscopes and telescopes might be escape routes, allowing courses to be charted beyond what our senses afford us. In *A Thousand Plateaus*, the escape from the traps of the all-too-human is an escape to the cosmic, but the cosmic of which they speak is a 'virtual cosmic continuum' that runs across all scales of existence, from microscopic to telescopic.¹⁵ From the massing of protons and the orbit of electrons to the stars of the Milky Way, Deleuze and Guattari are concerned with the molecularity shared by all – and all at once. Everything, including ourselves, is of the 'cosmic continuum of which even holes, silences, ruptures, and breaks are a part'.[16] Sounds and silences, planets and people, and opals and eggs are all connected. The crystal is special only because its particular molecularity renders the cosmic perceptible. Every salt crystal operates as a type of micro-macro-scope amplifying the forces that are at once *exterior to* it and *formative of* it, in this case as matters of taste. A quicker way of saying this is to suggest, as Deleuze and Guattari do, that 'the crystal is the macroscopic expression of a microscopic structure'.[17] The crystal thus provides an image of the dynamic relation between molecularity, objects and the cosmos and, in doing so, marks an escape route, a *line of flight* from the all-too-human.

In a footnote to *A Thousand Plateaus*, reference is made to Jacques Cousteau's research on lobsters. Deleuze and Guattari use the footnote to remind readers that it may be difficult to find anything that is not a crystallization of the cosmic continuum, for even the social assemblage of the lobster 'is connected to cosmic forces, or, as Cousteau says, "pulsations of the earth."'[18] For Nietzsche, order may have been a conceit and god may be dead, but for Deleuze and Guattari there are orders plural in the monism of the 'cosmic continua', the shared molecularity of it all. We escape the all-too-human when we give ourselves over to that which is at once beyond us and of which we too are composed, the *uni* of univocity. And this logic allows the philosopher and psychoanalyst to conclude quite reasonably, 'God is a Lobster.'[19]

Cosmic artisans

When Deleuze and Guattari refer to 'a pure crystal that harnesses cosmic forces', it occurs in the context of a discussion of processes by which an artist might harness, tap, consolidate or crystallize forces and phenomena that are beyond them. That is, forces that are not pinned down by well-trodden repetitions, shackled by styles, given to habitual forms, constituted by movements, or articulated in manifestoes, and not yet embedded in repertoires or oeuvres. The artist of which Deleuze and Guattari speak is one that is unencumbered by such things. Their prompt is for an artist to overspill the all-too-human glass capsule and shed the straitjacket, escaping the codes and classifications that are the territories of the earth, and instead 'to become cosmic, to leave the milieus and the earth behind'.[20]

The output of this artist, the 'pure crystal', involves consolidations of '[a]ll kinds of heterogeneous elements' drawn from the cosmos.[21] The artwork in this account is an object of plurality, and its connections are multiplicitous. That is, it doesn't add or subtract from the world (eat or be eaten) but rather multiplies the relations it has with the world beyond. Even when crystallized into an identifiable object – a painting, a piece of music or a singular work of architecture – the object never stratifies into any one symbolic, representational or totalizable order but rather preserves the heterogeneity of the elements of which it is composed. The artwork in this sense is composed of the incompossible, and because elements are not fully consumed (made homogeneous) the object pulses with the cosmos from which it is drawn. For Deleuze and Guattari such a work constitutes '*a destratifying transversality*, moved through elements, orders, forms and substances, the molar and the molecular, freeing a matter and tapping forces.'[22] One might think briefly of the case of Salvador Dalí's 'Lobster Telephone'

(1938), where homogeneous elements were brought together in such a manner that taps into the shared life of technological objects and convoluted organisms, multiplies effects in that shared interaction and, in doing so, frees the sound of the sea.

Consistent with Deleuze and Guattari's broader philosophical thrust, heterogeneous elements are not only those things we might think of as objects but include concepts, regimes of signs, languages and statements, images, sensations and senses, spatial and social formations, people, populations, concrete, contents and expressions. These elements too might be fused in works of art. In his *Schizoanalytic Cartographies* (1989) Guattari would note architecture's explicit role in 'the macroscopic expression of a microscopic structure': the making visible, audible, sense-able or sensational of that which was otherwise formless, intangible, imperceptible.[23] Guattari suggests, 'Architectural space is one concrete operator among many of the metabolism between the objects of the outside and the intensities of the inside'.[24] We can work through this idea of architecture as a metabolizer of outsides and insides, macro and micro characters, in reference to Bruno Taut's Mozart guest room at Kyu Huga Bettei (1936). This room is a component of a cellar space suspended below an existing house and over a steep hillside. It is a cellar, but one with a sea view. In one sense the Mozart room is a simple set of macro-organizational strategies incorporated into an interior milieu. In the room there are timber floors, four wide timber steps of alternating types of wood, a stage of a kind, walls of framed red silk and an inclined ceiling. In another sense, the Mozart room is a set of affirmations, an amplification of intensities that were without form. The *redness* of the silk that lines the walls would be an example. What starts as digested mulberry tree leaves, the cocoon of the Bombyx silkworm, becomes thread woven into fabric sheets. The colour that once was the pigments of the madder plant, the flowers of safflower, the thorns of sorghum or cinnabar becomes the intense cadmium red of a synthetic dye that finds itself pulsing through the silk screens of the room. The music of this space too operates as an intensity that is at once indistinct and deeply impressive. Even in silence the Mozart room has the velvety undercurrent of a bassoon. Taut makes the imperceptible audible here. It is 'no longer the songbird, but the sound molecule', as Deleuze and Guattari note of the a priori 'properly musical content of music'.[25] Together these heterogenous elements – cocoon and colour and silence – become the sonorous thread that ties the Mozart room to the pulse of the sea beyond.

To be attentive to the molecularity of the cosmos is, for Deleuze and Guattari, to be an 'artisan' or better still to be what they call a 'cosmic artisan'. The relation such an artisan establishes with the outside and all that is beyond, the cosmos, is a particular one. This is why the word 'harnesses' in the phrase 'a pure crystal that harnesses cosmic forces' is important.[26] The original French was *capte* and the English translator, Brian Massumi, arrived at the word 'harnesses'.[27] It's an understandable decision. A crystal doesn't capture or control or trap but rather taps into cosmic forces like a composer might connect to birdsong or a translator to an author. It is not that we now have a composer consuming a bird or a translator tweeting from the mouth of an author, but rather a new formation: a composer-bird block, an author-translator block, that involves one giving over to the other in order to become otherwise, to become a piece of music or a book. The architect, Taut, would not mime architectural convention and habit in the Mozart room. He did not mimic the music of Mozart (as Mozart did not mimic the tune of his pet starling), nor did the architect mime the sounds of the sea. There was no direct transference here. Instead, Taut is involved in a 'destratifying transversality', following the contours that constitute the rhythmic character or melodic landscape, unfolding a compact with the world about him. Taut was clear in his desire 'to get to know the foreignness in one's nature', and this cosmic artisan was across the earth, crossing borders, sliding through cultures and throwing out only the smallest of anchors: a few pieces of architecture, watercolours and what he referred to as a 'crystal chain' (*glaserne kette*) of letters.[28]

Palacio de Congressos

The architects José Selgas and Lucia Cano are the love children of Taut. Their work is a migration of colour and matter that forms blocks with landscapes beyond. Selgas and Cano fold one into another as SelgasCano and unfold a shared desire 'to disappear more and more on behalf of nature'.[29] Indeed, SelgasCano are currently based in a tube-like studio that seems to be sinking into a forest floor on the edge of Madrid.[30] The work of SelgasCano over recent decades spans from community centres in Kenya and schools in Nairobi, to the bourgeois gentility of the 2015 Serpentine pavilion and a shared work space in London. These projects barely constitute an oeuvre in the sense that there is little stylistic consistency traceable from one work to the next. What binds the work instead is a freshness, a type of blossoming of heterogeneous investments bound loosely in intensities of colour and expressions of joy. This may well be because at the core of SelgasCano's work is an anti-disciplinary stance that has them more focused on pleasure than precedent. They 'avoid the use of games and mechanisms that lead to disciplinary issues' and instead occupy the dreams, images, animals, games and pleasures of childhood.[31] For them, each project is an opportunity to connect with that which is beyond architecture, with the 'aim of making architecture lose ground to nature once again, minimizing its presence and minimizing its role to the creation of opportunities for new types of nature'.[32] And the route taken is impulsive. A video to explain the logic of their design process for their Serpentine pavilion was called 'The Hungry Pavilion' and took cues from *The Very Hungry Caterpillar* (1969) children's story. Cartoon versions of the architects pose the process in the simplest terms possible: 'One day we had a dream … Next day someone wanted to build it!'[33] SelgasCano's practice reminds me of what is perhaps the most engaging definition of the crystal given in *A Thousand Plateaus*:

> Childhood scenes, children's games: the starting point is a childlike refrain, but the child has wings already, he [sic] becomes celestial. The becoming-child of the musician is coupled with a becoming-aerial of the child, in a nondecomposable block. The memory of an angel, or rather the becoming of a cosmos. Crystal: the becoming-bird of Mozart is inseparable from a becoming-initiate of the bird, and forms a block with it.[34]

SelgasCano describe their boulder-shaped yet cloud-like building, the Palacio de Congressos (2017) in Plasencia, Spain, as being 'like a rock that is poised over the landscape but could fly away at any moment'[35] (Figure 14.1). This concert, conference and convention hall sits at the edge of Plasencia, a town of medieval origins that lies on the Jerte River in the Plasencia valley. The town itself is largely constructed from the stone of the valley, a cream-coloured stone with veins of brown and ochre. The town centre is held tight within the remains of a fortified wall, and beyond apartment buildings mark the fraying of the urban edge as it meets the harsh rocky land that falls to the west. SelgasCano's Palacio de Congressos sits on a 17-metre-high embankment at the edge of this edge. This huge building has a crystalline type of geometry, but not consistently so, its surface ripples in gentle pleats and there are notable Euclidean volumes punched through the boulder shape that mark moments of access and circulation. Despite the solidity and seeming mass of the overall, the envelope of the Palacio de Congressos is composed of sheets of a light, translucent, fluorine-based polymer (ETFE) supported by a framing of circular tubes that hold the envelope at some distance from the concrete core of the building.[36] The exoskeleton here is as porous as that of a lobster and appears similarly discardable were the internal pressures to exceed it. The mass and siting of the structure along with the odd lightness of its material envelope gives the sense that the Palacio is poised between a fall down the hillside and an ascension into the sky. It is a boulder in shape and a paper lantern in aspiration.

An orange ramp slides alongside the structure and opens to a massive orange orthogonal slice cut through the boulder shape and is oriented towards the Sierra de Gata mountains in the distance. The opening has little to do with human scale; it's about 8 metres tall and within it one doesn't feel like being inside anything at all. The building is open and air surges through. Circulation weaves around the perimeter between the outside skin and the central concrete shell of the auditoria that fall below the entrance level and into the landscape. There's a small surreal yellow auditorium with circular doors and a main auditorium in which an orchestras will perform, set deep in the site. This larger space is red halfway up the rounded walls and entering makes you feel as if you're being swallowed. There is a complexity to the creative relation the building establishes with its elements, its volumes, internal spaces, surfaces and circulation. It's a little boulder-like, a little alien, a little odd. There is a series of what might be regarded as inconsistencies: orthogonal and crystalline forms, 1960s sci-fi interiors, blocks of monotone colour, hulking volumes defined by a light and translucent material. The oddity or foreignness of this architecture however is not that these elements are inconsistent, but that they are consistently so. Nietzsche's description of 'a kind of unity, which is difficult to analyse into its parts, and which [...] defies definition' is apt for such an architecture. The forces that might homogenize a building into this or that singular simply defined object are not dominant here. The heterogenous elements are allowed their life.

In text provided to accompany the entry of the Palacio de Congressos for the 2019 European Union Prize for Contemporary Architecture (Mies Van Der Rohe Award), SelgasCano write: '[T]ell me if its final aspect triggers in you the same reminder as G.Sand's for Flaubert, "Don't define the form, don't bother"'.[37] Reference is to the correspondence between George Sand and Gustave Flaubert on the topic of literary form and its relation to content or 'substance'. Sand accused the younger writer of a 'cult for form' and suggested, 'THE FORM to which you attach so much importance, will issue by itself from your digestion. You consider it as an end, it is only an effect.'[38] Sand uses the word 'digestion' for the same purpose that Guattari had spoken of architectures 'of the metabolism' and for the same reason SelgasCano defer to *The Very*

Hungry Caterpillar. All involve a composing with the incompossible in order that one might 'fly away at any moment'.

Deleuze and Guattari find in crystallization an opportunity not only to harden but to harness the cosmic and in doing so liberate molecularity, a *'freeing of the molecular'*[39] that might set even 'love adrift'.[40] Of a night the exterior of Palacio de Congressos takes lights and stairs and ramps and balustrades and people and music and makes of them fluctuations and pulses and shifting luminescence. Amongst cloud, the building looks to have suspended lightning itself on this ridge. This is a destratifying transversality, a becoming cosmos of architecture. Our own engagement with such architecture also involves giving over something of the self and entering a type of child-like awe that connects us with that which is beyond. It's an inherently creative act. No. It is less inherent than *exherent* because it involves giving over the inside to that which is beyond and working to connect rather than conserve. Harness rather than mimic. Become rather than be. It's hard not to be swept up by it all. The Orchestra of Extremadura were playing Mozart's seventeenth piano concerto, K453, that night at SelgasCano's Palacio de Congressos. I was swept up and away, with thoughts of stones and clouds, crystals and crustaceans, birdsong, love, and lighting, and an opal in a matchbox that pulsed with it all.

Figure 14.1 SelgasCano, *Palacio de Congressos*, Plasencia (2017). Image © Hiseo Suzuki.

15

New materialism

Meat

One of the most poignant photographs of the English painter Francis Bacon is a work of butchery. In the monochrome image the artist is seated, not far off the ground but neither his lower body nor the ground is discernible (Figure 15.1). What is visible are bare muscular arms, rounded shoulder blades and the artist's protruding clavicles, otherwise known as collarbones. The high contrast of the image emphasizes these limbs and the concavity of the skin that drapes between them. The inverse effect of the contrast darkens Bacon's face and makes sockets of his eyes. Behind and above the artist, two halves of a pig, spliced open along its spine, are hanging as they might in the window of a butcher's shop. But hanging isn't the only sense one has of this meat. The image is cropped in such a way that the halves of this pig also seem to be rising. Rising from Bacon's shoulder blades like wings of a bat or an archangel. In an interview with the art historian David Sylvester, Bacon suggested he had always 'been very moved by pictures about slaughterhouses and meat, […] they belong very much to the whole thing of the Crucifixion'.[1] Meat that hung but nevertheless rose.

This macabre photograph was part of a series taken by John Deakin in 1952 and published in *Vogue* a decade later.[2] Despite intermittent employment at *Vogue*, Deakin was a Soho street photographer, and his images were raw, hard and harsh. He was also a Colony Club drinking partner of Bacon and would take many of the photographs his friend had used to paint from.[3] These photographs came to be paint-splattered, pinned to the walls and strewn across the floor of Bacon's studio, alongside photographs of the paintings of other artists and pages from books of anatomy. The painter told Sylvester that the 'injury' he inflicted on the subjects of his paintings were the reason he preferred to work from photographs rather than having them sit in his studio, in the flesh.[4] The photographer however had no such qualms. Deakin had noted 'sitters turn into my victims. But […] it is only those with a daemon, however small and of whatever kind, whose faces lend themselves to being victimised at all'.[5] The grating edge of Deakin's disposition was also an aesthetic inclination that accorded with that of Bacon. The art critic, John Russell, wrote that Deakin 'rivalled Bacon in his ability to make a likeness in which truth came unwrapped and unpackaged. His portraits, like Bacon's, had a dead-centered, unrhetorical quality. A complete human being was set before us, without additives'.[6] In this sense the meat that hung in Deakin's photograph of Bacon was less a *vanitas* prop than the rise of limbs.

Just as the meat might have risen from Bacon, so too may Bacon have fallen from the meat. The meat that preoccupied the artist had a life that both predated and exceeded him. The meat is habitually traced to Rembrandt's *The Slaughtered Ox* (1655) via Chaïm Soutine's butcher shop-cum-studio and particularly his *Carcass of Beef* (1925). In the earliest of Bacon's paintings, *Crucifixion* (1933), this meat enters less viscerally and more as a spectral form draped about a skeletal frame. Here the meat was a ghostly figure, black and white, dark like a shadow and yet glowing like a Christ. In his *Crucifixion with Skull* (1933) of that same year the flesh of a Christ figure merged with the meat, now Soutine-red. Over a decade later Bacon's *Painting 1946* (1946) was riddled with the meat, and the bodies of his human subjects too, from this time on, become more bony, fleshy and scrubbed open. In his 1950 *Fragment for a Crucifixion* the meat hung again, but the Christ figure is more the pale pink plumpness of chicken than the deep beef of ox or cow or the taut pork of pig. It is at this point that Deakin takes up the more robust meat and photographs Bacon between the wings of flailed sow. A few years later, the meat rose in this winged arrangement and occupied Bacon's *Figure with Meat* (1954). In this painting the oft-screaming Pope Innocent X is seated, amongst the meat, and the painting repeats the cropping of Deakin's photograph. The Pope, who died the year Rembrandt painted the flayed ox, had already passed into the oils of Diego Velázquez's *Portrait of Innocent X* (c.1650), a few centuries before the portrait passed into Bacon's work. Velázquez's Pope came to occupy a series of more than thirty of Bacon's paintings between 1946 and 1971, but Bacon never saw Velázquez's painting, just as he never saw the Pope concerned. He didn't have to. Instead, he obsessively collected photographs through which Velázquez's Pope had passed. Bacon's *Figure with Meat* thus becomes a strange conjunction point of photographs, figures and flesh. This meat would continue its slow rot in *Pope No. 2* and *Pope No. 3* of 1960 and can be found under the faces and curled with bodies on beds in many of Bacon's portraits of that decade and beyond. But it becomes an entanglement. The flesh of all Bacon's bodies started to slide about the bone. In one of Bacon's last works, *Study of a Bull* (1991), the meat returns to the animal from which it came and steps from Bacon's art much as it had arrived – as a ghostly figure, black and white, dark like a shadow and now glowing like a beast.

'Flesh and meat are life!' Bacon told the last photographer that he would sit for.[7] Francis Giacobetti photographed Bacon late in 1991 and early into the following year, the year of the artist's death. Giacobetti filmed the events and transcribed the recordings. The meat entered the conversation just as it had the photographs, slaughterhouses, paintings and figures. It wasn't there in any symbolic or rhetorical sense. It wasn't cut and pasted like a collage but rather operates as a *machinic phylum*. A migrating from here to there. Entering and departing. Falling and rising. It can be traced as one might follow a vein of quartz through stone, but it's a particularly guttural, visceral topology that makes the connection between all that is of flesh poignantly, violently, erotically, clear. 'We are all meat.' Bacon told the photographer. 'All the inhabitants of this planet are made of meat. And most of them are carnivores. And when you fuck, it's a piece of meat penetrating another piece of meat. There is no difference between our meat and the meat of an ox or an elephant.'[8]

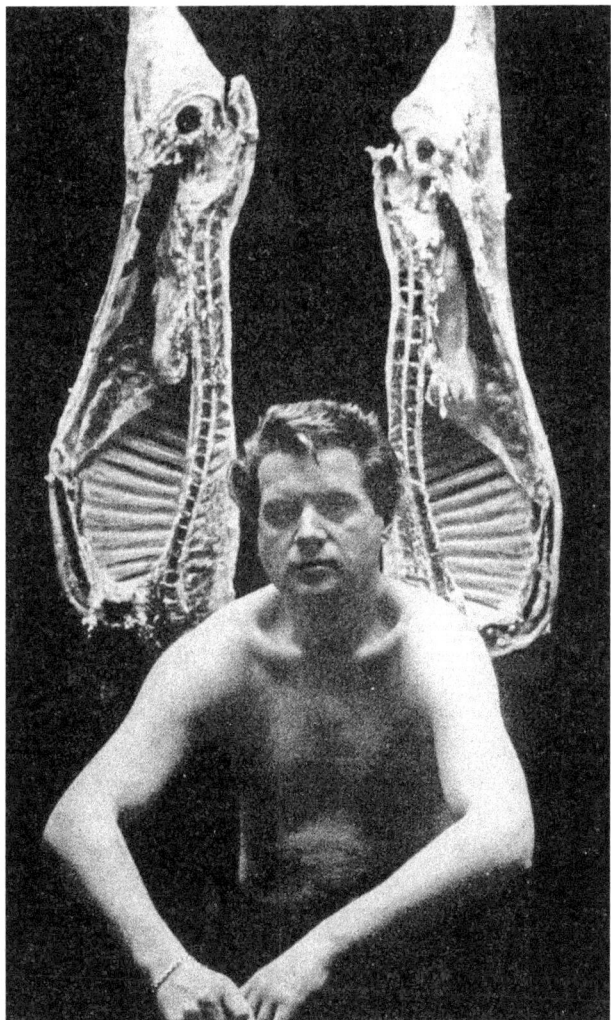

Figure 15.1 John Deakin, 'Portrait of Francis Bacon' (1952).

Matters of fact

In the book *Francis Bacon: The Logic of Sensation* (1981), Gilles Deleuze suggests, 'Bacon is a painter of heads, not faces.'[9] His point is that Bacon is less interested in the structuring of identity than the meat of life. That is, he is not uncovering a sitter's inner essence or exterior form but instead is traversing the life that surges in the very material of the body: the meat that grips the bone, the skin that envelopes the meat. In a chapter titled 'Body, Meat and Spirit, Becoming-Animal', Deleuze negotiates Bacon's work as a materialism towards what today is known as *new materialism*. The focus is odd in some ways, engaging an artist known for portraiture to talk of the non-representational, to speak of materiality and materialism rather than form or identity. But this is the point. The material of oil paint and canvas, the stroke of a brush and the rub of a rag are all material, just as meat, photographs, photographers and artists, fragments of text, and the imprint of a thought might be. Such diverse materials are brought into 'new relationships' in the work of Bacon such that they constitute what Deleuze calls *'matters of fact'*.[10] Deleuze suggests such matters are 'opposed to intelligible relations (of objects or ideas)'[11] and involve the coupling of sensations and Figures 'that are nonillustrative and nonnarrative (and not even logical)'.[12] If we are to negotiate the materiality of it all, as a *matter of fact*, then where better to start than with a painter of portraits, involved in a process that exhausts the habits of narration and rubs away at illustrative representation?

Deleuze's *Francis Bacon* book emerged shortly after *A Thousand Plateaus* (1980) wherein the idea of *faciality* was introduced to challenge 'the sovereign organization of the face'.[13] 'Dismantling the face', Deleuze and Félix Guattari note, 'is the same as breaking through the wall of the signifier and getting out of the black hole of subjectivity'.[14] The work of Bacon, as a compact of backgrounds and foregrounds in a 'shallow depth' was an opportunity to scale such a wall and elide such a hole.[15] Though shallow, Bacon's canvas remains a very full surface, 'so full that the painter must enter into the canvas',[16] and Deleuze suggests that when the artist rubs away at a face to reveal a head it is not that the flesh and bone were not already there; they were just quieter when under the skin. For Deleuze the painter operates to '*dismantle the face, to rediscover the head or make it emerge from beneath*'.[17] A butchering, an autopsy or a self-mutilating cut, like much of Bacon's portraiture, is a making visible of the invisible. A making exterior of insides and intensities. *If interiority is constituted by the form of what one thinks they are, then there is a necessary violence against that form in order for one to be otherwise.* And such an act can be of paint, flesh or thought, and all are exhausted in Bacon's process. He told Sylvester, '[I]t really comes out of an absolute feeling of it's impossible to do these things, so I might as well just do anything. And out of anything, one sees what happens.'[18] When Deleuze turns to the paintings of Bacon and speaks of 'heads, not faces', the phrase stands as a proxy for a set of novel relations that denote a new materialism: Meat, not flesh. Sensations, not significations. Bodies, not subjectivities. Matters of fact, not forms of representation.

Hylomorphism

Deleuze's exploration of the body, meat and spirit of Bacon's art not only reinforces the vitality of matter but also does serious damage to an enduring philosophical axiom that had perpetually subjugated it. The axiom is known as *hylomorphism*. Hylomorphism is the doctrine that any substance is constituted by relations of form and matter. The term is a compound of the Greek words for matter (*hulê*) and shape or form (*morphê*). Aristotle engages the hylomorphic schema in *De Anima* [On the Soul] (c. 350 BC) and uses the relation of souls, bodies and organs as a prime example. He declares that 'matter is potentiality and form is actuality',[19] and that a soul constitutes a 'first actuality'[20] of a body and is the 'substance as form of a natural body which has life in potentiality'.[21] For Aristotle the body has the potential to be this or that, but the soul is necessary for it to actually be something particular. Indeed, a body that is without a soul is, in *De Anima*, considered to be not a body at all, 'except homonymously'.[22] The hylomorphic schema is patently clear: The soul is the *form* of the body, and the body is the *matter* of the soul, and as is true for the body, so too for the organ. Aristotle notes, '[I]f the eye were an animal, eyesight would be its soul, this being the substance as notion or form of the eye'.[23] The idea is simple enough: form and matter are dissociable and that a material must be organ-ized by form in order for it to *perform*.

The Deleuzean philosopher John Protevi offers a simple definition of hylomorphism that makes the privileging of form over matter unambiguous. For him, hylomorphism is 'the doctrine that production is the result of an (architectural) imposition of a transcendent form on a chaotic and or passive matter'.[24] Protevi is explicit about the political implication of the notion and hints (parenthetically) at the architectural association. In this regard he is following the explications of the philosopher Gilbert Simondon that were themselves taken up by Deleuze in his collaborative work with Guattari. For Simondon, 'the hylomorphic perspective correlates to the practice of a person who stays outside of the workshop and only sees what enters and what exits it',[25] and for Deleuze and Guattari to be numb to a material's 'traits', 'latent potentials' and 'variable intensive affects' leads one to operate as a god, a master (or an architect) all too willing to 'submit' matter to *this or that* form.[26] By way of example, Deleuze and Guattari note the hylomorphism of 'the metric plane of the architect, which is on paper and off site'.[27] Whilst the imposition of form *at distance* from a material might sound problematic when we are speaking of the matters of paint and the workshops of architectural production, it's entirely horrific when we think of matters of societies and matters of human and animal flesh. For Simondon, '[w]hat hylomorphism primarily reflects is a social representation of labor … in essence the labor commanded by the free man and conducted by the slave'.[28] In the terminology of Deleuze and Guattari, the matter of a society, its assemblages and performances, becomes the material for the striations (the ordering and appropriation) of the State, and the form–matter division of hylomorphism expressed by Simondon as the slave–master relation is also translated in *A Thousand Plateaus* (1980) as the rout of molecular qualities by macropolitical forces.[29] In this regard, Protevi correlates hylomorphism with 'fascism conceived as the fatal desire for the forceful imposition of complete organ-ization in a body politic'.[30]

Despite Protevi's parenthetical use of the term 'architectural' in his definition of hylomorphism and Deleuze and Guattari's account of 'the metric plane of the architect', for those of us working with matters of concrete as much as matters of thought the differentiation of form and matter occurs as an impossible operation. It may well be that an architect draws 'on paper and off site', but the weight of the pencil will be that of a fabric, metal sheet, brick or concrete, and the paper itself comes to fold and fall in the known and yet invisible contours of landscape. *Any architect who is not negotiating materiality in a pencil or a digital file is likely not negotiating an architecture at all. Form is never absolute and never simply imposed from the outside as an 'external act' since it can only operate in material.* And every material has traits of its own: weights, textures, malleabilities, luminescences, parameters that allow it to be formed in certain ways and not in others, even as such material parameters pass through fleshy fingers and the soft graphite of a pencil tip.

It is the inextricability of matter and form in such *expressions of matter* that Deleuze explores in the work of Bacon. Deleuze suggests that for Bacon far from the head being the matter of the soul, it is instead 'a spirit in bodily form, a corporeal and vital breath, an animal spirit. It is the animal spirit of man: a pig-spirit, a buffalo-spirit, a dog-spirit, a bat-spirit …'.[31] The soul, here is both actuality and potentiality, a breath itself. And it's not a breath that merely resurrects the human, but rather one that screams of animality. In lieu of a habitual organization of form and matter – spirit and meat, human and animal, *de anima* and body – and the fascist imposition of one upon the other, Deleuze suggests that Bacon's work in oil paint and on canvas delivers 'the coupling of sensations: there is one and the same *matter of fact* for two Figures, or even a single coupled Figure for two bodies'.[32]

Becoming-animal

For Deleuze, in Bacon's work 'the marks or traits of animality are not animal forms, but rather the spirits that haunt the wiped off parts, that pull at the head, individualizing and qualifying the head without a face'.[33] He repeats the idea in simpler terms: '[I]t is not the animal as a form, but rather the animal as a *trait*'.[34] The translator of the English edition of Deleuze's *Francis Bacon*, Daniel W. Smith, joins the translator of *A Thousand Plateaus*, Brian Massumi, in noting, the word 'trait' in its original French has a range of meanings. Smith suggests the word means 'to draw' and relates it to 'a graphic line' and 'drawing a line or a set of lines', and notes the term is used 'to designate a distinguishing quality or characteristic mark, a feature that allows one to identify or recognize a thing'.[35] Massumi had noted, '[I]t refers to a graphic drawing, and to the act of drawing a line', 'the purely graphic element', 'an identifying mark', or 'any act constituting a mark or sign', 'the elementary units of language that combine to form a phoneme', and 'a projectile, especially an arrow, and to the act of throwing a projectile'.[36] The multiplicitous denotations of the word suggest what Deleuze is identifying in Bacon's paintings are heterogenous qualities of animality that operate as lines of material relation that he had referred to elsewhere as 'machinic phylum'.[37] These lines are at once graphic, semiotic, aesthetic, of oil paint and canvas; resist simple totalization or summation; and come with a capacity to strike. The *trait* becomes particularly pronounced in the por*trait*ure of Bacon, where animal traits are not structural demarcations (framed in analogy or metaphor) and rest not in formal correspondences (as symbolic transferences) but rather operate in the very meat of the matter itself. 'In place of formal correspondences', Deleuze notes, 'what Bacon's painting constitutes is a zone of indiscernibility or undecidability between man and animal',[38] and the philosopher qualifies the idea in noting, this 'zone of indiscernibility is the entire body, but the body insofar as it is flesh or meat'.[39] Whilst meat operates as 'the common zone of man and the beast', there is nothing stable in the relation constituted by the trait.[40] Meat is far too dynamic to settle so easily. For, '[i]n meat, the flesh seems to descend from the bones, while the bones rise up from the flesh'[41] and Bacon's coupling of the human and the animal is what Deleuze calls 'a latent bullfight'.[42]

Bacon had told Sylvester, 'If I go into a butcher's shop, I always think it's surprising that I wasn't there instead of the animal.'[43] This affection of a human for an animal is oft described as the *momento mori* of Bacon's work, but for Deleuze, this affection does not sit quietly behind the oeuvre in any essentialized form, nor does it transcend as a logos-motif. It is instead articulated in material expression, in matters of fact. In Deleuze's account, meat 'is a "fact," a state where the painter identifies with the objects of his horror and his compassion'.[44] This 'identification' has little to do with identity itself but rather refers to the violent and erotic performance of art in which the artist and audience too are implicated in the act. Identifying the shared meat of it and them all. In mangling, rubbing and scratching away at the face Bacon finds a shared and mobile thread head, which screams from the paintings with the pained sound of a bull, an ox or an elephant. The art of new materialism relies on techniques that *externalize traits* that liberate them from this or that.[45] What in his *Francis Bacon* book Deleuze had called the 'latent bullfight' of the artist's struggle would be spoken of as 'wresting' in his last collaborative text with Guattari, *What Is Philosophy?* (1991). Here, the philosopher and psychoanalyst turn their attention to the aim of art itself: 'By means of the material, the aim of art is to wrest the percept from perceptions of objects and the states of a perceiving subject, to wrest the affect from affections as the transition from one state to another: to extract a bloc of sensations, a pure being of sensations.'[46] What is suggested is that art, '[b]y means of the material', liberates ideas (percepts) from habitual codifications, and liberates affect from habitual relations (affections) in order that something new screams into being, 'a pig-spirit, a buffalo-spirit, a dog-spirit, a bat-spirit ...'. In the mangling, rubbing and scratching of the artist, meat becomes a 'bloc of sensation', that is, an impulse liberated from this or that fixed relation. Anthropocentric and the hylomorphic schemas are butchered in the oils of Bacon's canvases as percept and affect are liberated, as in Bacon's bullfight paintings where 'we hear the noise of the beast's hooves' and find ourselves engorged.[47]

Becoming-architecture

There is one painting where Bacon deals with meat in and of itself. That is, where the meat hangs alone, strangely removed from any figure, human or animal. In *Side of Beef* (1979) the meat may be without human or animal trait, but it is not without traits. In this painting there is something more mechanical, more geometric, more architectural, about the meat. Dissected bone and spinal cords become circles like the holes of plumbing and washbasins, ribs sit like rows of apartment blocks, and the whole concavity of the torso looks a little like a constructivist image of a city from above. As Bacon's human figures took on the meat, the meat in this painting seemed to take on the material traits of human landscapes. The same type of inversion is at play in the work of the graphic artist JR in the Morro da Providência, Porto Maravilha area in Rio de Janeiro (Figure 15.2). But here the inversion sweeps in the other direction. Here an urban landscape and architecture themselves are hollowed out to expose more visceral *matters of fact*. In 2008 JR entered Morro da Providência, the oldest *favela* in Rio. Though entering and exiting are a complex matter here: the favela's borders are ever shifting, negotiated between drug traffickers and police one horrific crime at a time. Murder, rape, torture and kidnappings are common. Such violence has become synonymous with the favela, and to the rest of Rio this habitation encrusted hillside is cast as chaos and horror. Raquel Rolnik, the Brazilian urbanist, however refers to favelas as both 'the territories of disorder' and 'landscapes for life',[48] and it is towards this life that JR turns and turns us all.[49]

For JR the repulsion to the chaotic organization of the hillside, its ramshackle structures and the horror of violence seemed to supersede any form of understanding or compassion for the victims and survivors thereof. He had honed his affection for the compact of strained people and places in the Les Bosquet banlieue on the outskirts of Paris, where '[d]oing graffiti meant that I had to have eyes in the back of my head'.[50] He converted that affection into *affect* in the Kabira slum in Kenya, on the wall between Israeli and Palestinian territories, across the wall between Mexico and the United States, and in the old neighbourhoods of Shanghai and Havana. In the Morro da Providência favela JR would advance his 'Women are Heroes' project, where *who we are* and *where we are* find stark expression. The artist engaged the hillside of the favela that looks out towards the port of Rio. He traced its complex network of laneways and buildings jostling for air and plumbing, entangled with electrical wiring that might be traced as one traces a vein of quartz through stone or meat through an artist's oeuvre. The social networks were no less complex and fraught. The stated aim of JR's project was to 'give voice' to the victims of crime within the area and in doing so allow them to speak their pain in their place.[51] The artist would meet the residents: grandmothers who had lost children and then grandchildren to gang violence. Rape survivors and victims of the drug gangs and the police alike. JR heard their stories and photographed their faces. The images were cropped about the sitter's eyes and upscaled to the size of the structures in which the people lived and were glued to the surfaces of residences.

Though accounts of the project often defer to the idea of 'storytelling', in this work the voice of the artist was absent. 'In Brazil, I left the country and let the people speak for it', JR notes, '[m]y whole world has been how can I keep a distance from it.'[52] The artist was at once 'on paper and offsite', and those whose eyes came to rest on walls and stairs too were hauntingly silent. No, that's not entirely true. They were silent only in the sense that their stories did not constitute narrative accounts. The scaling of figures and organs in excess of human and architectural scales may have been 'nonillustrative and nonnarrative (and not even logical)'[53] and may be 'opposed to intelligible relations'[54] but this did not constitute any type of logical deficiency, nor does it constitute silence. The coupling of sensations and figures here is intense. The eyes of women who were grieving loss, who had survived attack and who had seen all manner of horror inflicted are loud at this monumental scale.

In *A Thousand Plateaus* Deleuze and Guattari negotiate architecture and landscape to speak of faciality as where '[a]rchitecture positions its ensembles – houses, towns or cities, monuments or factories – to function like faces in the landscape they transform', and the philosopher and psychoanalyst invert the relation to ask: 'What face has not called upon the landscapes it amalgamated, sea and hill; what landscape has not evoked the face that would have completed it, providing an unexpected complement for its lines and traits?'[55] The phrasing is a tad romantic. It's like looking at Rembrandt's *The Slaughtered Ox* on a postcard after a Bacon exhibition. There is a bite to meat that is far more violent and erotic, far more pained and animal than picturesque landscapes evoke or visiting a gallery might suggest. When the work of JR falls onto a street, a building, a land, there's something more visceral happening. This is not the imposition of forms of representation over matters of architecture but rather a layering of matters of facades and faces. The layers of brick and steel sheet and orange tile were layered further with wheat glue and the paper, and matters of society, of women's lives, of eyes. Where Bacon had rubbed at the face to get to the head, JR layers the facade to get to the face in a type of exteriorization of inhabitants. Metal rooves fall like eyelids and corrugated iron wrinkles. Tarpaulins become iris, tin sheets squint. Again, there's nothing rhetorical here. Expressive yes, but rhetorical no. The eyes of survivors that shine out of the favela are just that. If hyomorphism is the 'complete organ-ization in a body politic'[56] then there is something radically different occurring here, in Morro da Providência where organs themselves displace the facade and excavate sensation. 'I'm in a faultline. I'm at risk,' JR stated.[57] The quake exteriorizes those things we too often relegate to the inside. Inhabitants kept quiet in inhabitation. If, as Deleuze and Guattari suggest, '[d]ismantling the face is the same as breaking through the wall of the signifier and getting out of the black hole of subjectivity', then dismantling a facade is a register of the force of the asignifying gesture and a resurrection of the organ over the politic to which it had been subjected. The outcome is a single coupled figure, a woman-home, a hillside-people, but the interplay is fraught. It's a material tussle, a bullfight, a wresting. The images of eyes and fragments of faces tear and weather along with the surfaces on which they are placed. What is liberated here in Morro da Providência is a percept related to those silenced in cities. And this evacuation of affect occurs as a pained cry. The type of cry only eyes might make.

Figure 15.2 JR, '28 Millimeters: Women Are Heroes', Action in Favela Morro da Providência, Rio de Janeiro, Brazil, 2008. Image courtesy of JR.

16

Affect

Dark precursors

'There is always a dark precursor that no one sees, and then the lightning bolt that illuminates, and there is the world,' Gilles Deleuze remarks in the final segment of his *Abécédaire*.¹ The *Abécédaire* was an 8-hour long interview with the journalist Claire Parnet filmed for a television series produced by Pierre-André Boutang for channel Arte in 1988–9. It was filmed in Deleuze's third-floor apartment on Avenue Niel, Paris, and was originally intended to be aired after the death of the philosopher. The interview was organized around an alphabet of concepts. It started with 'A is for animal' and addressed Deleuze's preference for spiders, ticks and fleas, over the more domesticated of creatures. In the final segment, having leapt over 'X Unknown, Y Unpronounceable', the journalist turns finally to the letter 'Z', as anyone engaging an alphabet should. 'Z as in Zigzag' and 'the Zed of bifurcation, of lightning', Parnet suggests. '[T]he zed of the fly, the zigging movement of the fly', Deleuze intimates. He smiles broadly and though his breathing is heavy, Deleuze appears joyous to be commencing this final segment. This end was a beginning of a kind. It was a return to the 'A' of animal and the bestiary of Deleuze's oeuvre, a return to the 'dark precursor' [*le précurseur sombre*] he had introduced in his early work *Difference and Repetition* (1968) and a return to the 'zigzag' he had spoken of with Parnet in their book of 1977, *Dialogues*.

The dark precursor was a concept that remained tantalizingly embryonic and yet resonates with so many of Deleuze's ideas and those developed and deployed in his collaborations with Félix Guattari. The concept was introduced as the precondition of a relationship between any two things. A sort of prelude, preamble or pretext that had little to do with the lude of an interlude, the amble of strolling friends or the text of communication. Deleuze's example in *Difference and Repetition* of that which pre-empts a relation was when '[t]hunderbolts explode between different intensities, but they are preceded by an invisible, imperceptible dark precursor, which determines their path in advance but in reverse as though intagliated'.² Too often homogenous elements are described as having a common denominator of resemblance or a shared identity, as the precondition for interacting in a heterogenous series. The relation between philosophy and television, or indeed between architecture and philosophy, would be cases in point. Deleuze asks instead, 'Are identity and resemblance here the preconditions of the functioning of this dark precursor, or are they, on the contrary, its effects?'[3] When lightning strikes it is not that clouds, earth and air have conspired in electrostatic communications to generate a spark; nor is it the case that clouds, earth and air are generated by the lightning. It is that the different electrical charges and material dynamisms of all these elements – their differences – are already operative and merely thrust into perception by lightning. In this way effects *precede*, and resemblance and identity are the outcomes of difference itself, wherein 'the precursor plays the part of the differenciator of these differences'.[4] The example of the zigzag of the thunderbolt became in *Dialogues* with Parnet the circuitousness path of a wasp about an orchid as 'each encounters the other'.[5] Instead of conceiving of the interaction as that of two things, Deleuze considers the singularity at stake. The wasp/orchid is 'a single becoming which is not common to the two, since they have nothing to do with one another, but which is between the two, which has its own direction, a bloc of becoming, an aparallel evolution. This is it, the double capture, the wasp AND the orchid'.[6] For Deleuze both are forming in the wake of the 'zigzag which glides "between"'.[7]

In the *Abécédaire* the 'route of the fly' prompts the question of how it is that two things might be brought together by a third that cares for neither; 'the dark precursor is not a friend', Deleuze notes.[8] From the blackness of the sky, the waves of air pressure and the imperceptible pivots of the planet care not for thunder or lightning. Just as the lightning cares not for the molecules it liberates into the soil of the earth upon which vegetation feeds, and in which worms themselves turn. He tells Parnet the dark precursor is 'about no universals, but rather the aggregates of singularities'.[9] And though this force was neither fixed, totalizable, nor universal, for Deleuze the Z of elementary movement 'presided over the creation of the world'.[10] It was of the curvature of the Big Bang, the folding calculus of Leibniz, and the clinamen that gives life to matter. Deleuze gives Parnet and a television audience beyond a camera and beyond the apartment an origin story that was molecular rather than meta. 'This dark precursor', he suggests, 'is what places different potentials into relation, and once the journey [*trajet*] of the dark precursor takes place, the potentials enter into a state of reaction, and between the two, the visible event flashes, the bolt of lightning.'[11] The final segment of the *Abécédaire* ends with Deleuze's voice, 'Posthumous! Posthumous!'; and then Parnet: 'PostZumous!'

Affect

One of the most challenging and yet compelling aspects of the philosophy of Deleuze and Guattari is the enfolding of concepts and methodologies. The impulse is not towards a scientism that seeks to insulate the object of study from the method of exploration, but rather an acknowledgement that the two are already interwoven as a 'bloc of becoming'. In every thought is already a mode of operation, and in every mode of operation a regime of thoughts. It is this interweaving that makes the collaborations of Deleuze and Guattari artful, and it is this characteristic that entices and enthrals those engaged in creative practices. Architects and architectural theorists find in the work of Deleuze and Guattari a mode of operation that resonates with their own. The processes of architecture are never remote from architectural productions. We come to think of processes and products as being involved in a type of dance where one pulses in the wake of the other. There is in every drawing a sense of the matters at stake, and there is an intimacy between the construction of a drawing and the constructions of earth, steel and concrete. Processes, procedures, outcomes and affects are intagliated. In his book on the affective turn, Nigel Thrift speaks of such an 'avowedly experimental' theoretical weaving in architecture as a 'reenchantment'.[12] An example of this type of experimental weaving in the philosophy of Deleuze and Guattari is how the dark precursor that zigzags in and out of Deleuze's thoughts also weaves through the operations of *affect* integral to Deleuze and Guattari's collaborative work. Though the former is framed as a concept and the latter now a theory or a methodology, there is much that connects the zigzagging dark precursor and the turns of affect – the affect towards which so much contemporary philosophy, art and architectural theory of this century turns.

First, the two precede. The dark precursor is *not an effect but rather that which precedes effects*, preceding identity and resemblance. Affect too precedes, as a 'prepersonal' and 'impersonal' intensity.[13] That is to say, affect is not something a person or a thing has or holds, but rather that which precedes them and traverses them. As Deleuze writes in his early explorations of Baruch Spinoza (another philosopher with a 'z' in his name), affect 'is a sign that registers on the body'.[14] It is not defined as we might define products or things, and it is not the perception that we are then conscious of. It is neither organized nor codified. In its simplest terms affect might be defined as *what the body does*, and we should note here the breadth of definition that Deleuze and Guattari would apply to the word 'body' itself. A body might be a body of thought, a book, an organism, an organ, an architecture, a discipline, a social movement, etcetera; and Deleuze and Guattari repeat Spinoza's statement: 'We do not even know of what a body is capable',[15] in suggesting, 'We know nothing about a body until we know what it can do, in other words, what its affects are.'[16] Even the acts we think of in all-too-human terms tend to involve a multiplicity of bodies and affects that precede. Sexual expression is an example. Against the oedipal codification of sexuality, in *A Thousand Plateaus* (1980) Deleuze and Guattari invoke affect: in sex 'there is a circulation of impersonal affects, an alternate current that disrupts signifying projects as well as subjective feelings, and constitutes a nonhuman sexuality'.[17] We recognize this alternacy in moments of eros and violence and artistic creation, when we forget to assert the 'I am' of signification, and feelings themselves seem to be afterthoughts. In such moments we are lost *in* the moment, swept up and away. When one is 'rolling like thunder, under the covers' it is not that thunder (or Elton John) is there; the affect precedes and bangs through us in a roar, the quaking of intensities, the clap of a thrust. It is the thunder that passes through us and not vice versa.

Second, both the dark precursor and affect chart *an unmediated between*. Deleuze suggests to Parnet that the dark precursor is a space 'between the two' that is 'not common to the two',[18] and for Deleuze and Guattari affect is 'an exteriority that is always external to itself'.[19] Both the dark precursor and affect are distinct from the two bodies which are in relation and the affection that one might have for the other. Deleuze and Guattari note, '[A]ffect is not a personal feeling, nor is it a characteristic; it is the effectuation of a power of the pack that throws the self into upheaval and makes it reel.'[20] The philosopher and psychoanalyst are at pains to note, an affect is not a feeling.[21] It is a point of distinction that Deleuze drew from Spinoza. Spinoza had differentiated between affection [*affectio*] as being from one body to another,[22] and affect [*affectus*] as the capacity 'to affect and be affected' and 'the passage from one experiential state of the body to another'.[23] Like the dark precursor, *affect is not owned by a body (nor a common element shared by bodies) but rather an experiential state that processes a body at a particular moment and relates to either an increase or decrease in a body's capacity.*[24] By way of example, affection might be felt for a voluptuous storm cloud that surges on a horizon, whereas affect is the jolt of the ferro-electric switch and muscular contraction we experience when thunder booms overhead. In one case we ruminate and mediate the relation between a cloud and ourselves; in the other we are banged immediately, directly.

The James-Lange theory of emotion is helpful in differentiating the mediated relation of affection and feeling from the unmediated impact of affect. William James and Carl Lange independently arrived at the psychological theory that emotions follow bodily states, but it is James's example of a bear in the forest that is memorable. 'Common sense', he suggests, 'says [...] we meet a bear, are frightened and run', but James goes on to propose that common sense is not always sensible, especially when it comes to accounts of sensations.[25] For James, the person (let's imagine an architect) walking through a forest who meets a bear (let's imagine something huge) does not then fear the bear (dropping their moleskin notebook) and then run (in their expensive shoes). Instead, the architect in the forest, confronted by a bear, runs and is fearful because they run. The outcome is that a feeling is but an afterthought or rumination on physiological impact or action. A feeling takes the *tone* of a reflection upon the bodily response ('I guess that's why they call it the Blues'). Affect, on the other hand, is what the body does, and it comes first. The implications for art and architecture are fundamental. *For the architect to concern themselves with the 'feeling' they wish a building to instil is to concern themselves with after-the-fact reflection, and this should always be secondary to the raw and roar of unmediated affect.*

Third, both the dark precursor and affect are becomings. Of the zigzag Deleuze tells Parnet, 'We said the same thing about becomings,' and of affect Deleuze and Guattari are equally explicit: 'Affects are becomings.'[26] In the transformation of an architect wandering a forest, into a fleeing victim of bear attack, into a survivor and raconteur, there is significant change or what Deleuze and Guattari call 'incorporeal transformation'.[27] Affects are becomings in that they transform, and any transformation *of this to that* involves a deterritorialization, a return to a more embryonic or fluid state where a body is *neither this nor that*. The body in flight from a bear cares not for the architect but for flight itself. The body is deterritorialized from all the codifications that one might have previously considered to be important – professions, sexualities, genders and agendas – and instead becomes a line of escape. This is what Deleuze and

Guattari call '[t]he deterritorialization velocity of affect'.[28] In art too we find ourselves transformed as the work of art processes us. Deleuze notes, 'For me, it's entirely obvious that someone can take in a painting like a thunderbolt and know nothing about the painting itself.'[29] Such encounters are like bifurcation points, where one tips into something new. At the edges of a forest or a bed or an art gallery or a book, we are transformed from one state, one person, one animal, one sense, to another. *Affect is a becoming-other, where the warrior roars and becomes bear.* Where we lose a sense of one's boundaries in the bang of love and the squall of art. Deleuze and Guattari note of the literature of Heinrich von Kleist, '"The power of this affect sweeps me away," so that the Self (Moi) is now nothing more than a character whose actions and emotions are desubjectified, perhaps even to the point of death.'[30] The becoming *mort* of every *petit mort*.

Fourth, both the dark precursor and affect *strike*. In the *Abécédaire* Deleuze gestures the 'z' in the air with the flick of a wrist. He gestures the *z* of the nose [*nez*], the zigzagged flight of the fly, the striking 'blow of the stick' of the Zen master, and he punctuates in action 'then a lightning bolt, that's how the world was born'.[31] And just as such things might arrive from the outside as the banging residue of a dark precursor, so too might they hurl from an interior, as affect. In *A Thousand Plateaus* Deleuze and Guattari note, 'To the relations composing, decomposing, or modifying an individual there correspond intensities that affect it, augmenting or diminishing its power to act; these intensities come from external parts or from the individual's own parts.'[32] The jump of shock, the perspiration of anxiety, the throbbing heartbeat of love that threatens the security of the ribcage. Crying on a street. Bleeding on a field. Screaming in a forest. There is in such moments a type of thrusting or flying outwards into the world, of that which we too often hold tight inside. An overflow. An excess. A lightning bolt. Such things are at once exterior to habitual senses of self and the systems of signification that we've come to rely upon, to an extent that allows Deleuze and Guattari to suggest an affect 'represents nothing'.[33] In a lecture on Spinoza's concept of affect Deleuze proposes, 'hope as such or love as such represents nothing, strictly nothing'.[34] Such things as love and hate, shock and awe, don't have meaning; they have force, intensity and impact. They strike. Here too, the implications for art and architecture are fundamental. *For the architect to concern themselves with the 'meaning' of a building is to concern themselves with after-the-event rumination, and this should always be secondary to the claw and soar of unmediated affect.*

Where the dark precursor was 'in advance but in reverse' in the sense that those things that we previously took to be the precondition for an interaction – identity and resemblance – were but the outcome or effect of the relation, affect is *in advance and in escape* in the sense that transformation itself is the outcome, and identity and resemblance are not in reverse but rather liberated from a relation that is now a 'pure exteriority'.[35] Deleuze and Guattari note, '[F]eelings become uprooted from the interiority of a "subject," to be projected violently outward into a milieu of pure exteriority that lends them an incredible velocity, a catapulting force: love or hate, they are no longer feelings, but affects … Affects transpierce the body like arrows, they are weapons of war.'[36]

Lightning Farm

In their last collaborative text, *What Is Philosophy?* (1991), Deleuze and Guattari suggest philosophy takes as its object *concepts*; science takes as its focus *functives*, and art is concerned with *affect*; and in the wake of Deleuze and Guattari, architecture, 'the first of the arts', itself seizes up, perspires, fights and throbs to the pulse of the planet.[37] Farah Aliza Badaruddin's *Lightning Farm* (2013) is one such weapon of war (Figure 16.1). The project is a series of divining rods set to tap the spasms of the atmosphere above southern Florida, USA, but this landscape architecture project is also an exploration of the phenomenology of lightening and jolts our sense of architecture itself, reminding us (in a rephrasing of Spinoza) that we do not yet know what an architecture is capable of.

In a simple sense, Badaruddin's *Lightning Farm* is an attempt to address the chemical contamination of the soil and groundwater around Cape Canaveral through the science of *pyrolysis*. Lightning would be harnessed to break down toxic material within the earth into inert forms. It's a creative intervention in anthropogenic devastation. The project centres on the infrastructure necessary for the 'rocket-triggered lightning technology' and a series of airships that 'serve as the observatory platform for a proposed lightning visitor centre and the weather research center'.[38] This molar functionality of the *Lightning Farm* project involves a pragmatic fixation on technologies and their deployment. Badaruddin invents a militarization of the earth in order to compel forces of the cosmos, inventing a machine that might channel a lightning strike, viewed from helicopters and reinforced blimps, planes and cranes, that can but observe at a distance. All manner of a priori material is deployed – metal hulls and hulking forms we half-recognize from machines of war and the heavy-handed mechanics of engineered structures. Badaruddin constructs pyrolysis plants, telescopic apparatus, solar arrays, an observatory airship deck, inflatable balloon suits, Faraday cages, retractable launch pads and 'earth crawlers', *from* parts and assembles them *as* parts, that together might function to farm lightning. However, this architecture does not pose as merely an outcome (an effect) to a well-stated problem (a cause). When Badaruddin turns to the functioning of this architecture, it is not only the macro-function of pyrolysis that matters; this is a project that is equally attuned to the micro-qualities, forces and fluxes that surge and strike as unmediated affect. All of the elements Badaruddin constructs, and the helicopters, blimps, cranes and planes are assembled in order to incite 'a catapulting force'.

In *What Is Philosophy?*, Deleuze and Guattari turn to the animal origins of art and note the 'spider's web contains "a very subtle portrait of the fly," which serves as its counterpoint'.[39] They suggest that the construction of territory, the organization and pragmatic assembly of content (a web, for example) yields more nuanced expressions and more liminal sensations. They note, '[T]erritory implies the emergence of pure sensory qualities, of sensibilia that cease to be merely functional and become expressive features, making possible a transformation of functions.'[40] This is the case of the *Lightning Farm*, where the attention to territory and the assembling of extant technologies cannot help but pre-empt micro-qualities, expressive features and transformations, much as a web awaits 'the zigzag of the fly'. The point is that *this is an architecture that precedes*. Not architecture *as* an event or spectacle, but rather the preconditioning of a place, a material, a people for that which might (or might not) burst forth. Badaruddin is engaging tools, as objects in and of themselves, and assembling them as a precondition to what might come. And there is nothing in this project that pins down the outcome to the architecture.[41] Badaruddin doesn't mimic lightning and there is nothing about the forms of the metal hulls and launch pads that *represent* thunderbolts. The architecture is instead a type of prompt or enchantment of cosmic forces and exists in a contrapuntal relation to the lightning it draws.

And just as this architecture fails to fix outcomes in aesthetic deferral, so too does it fail to finalize itself in form. The drawings of the *Lightning farm* project fly about their object in a manner similar to the northern or Gothic line, a 'line of variable direction that describes no contour and delimits no form', as Deleuze and Guattari note.[42] Badaruddin's drawings are of an architecture in flight and in construction. Pieces are still being lifted into place; people in inflatable balloon suits are still preparing the earth. This process yields a rich complexity of potential actualities. Even Badaruddin's images are still under construction and held in a moleskin notebook, more often used for sketching. The seam that binds the notebook, the folds of the pages, and the edge of the covers are visible. This is not the auto-reflexivity that characterizes modern art and architectural expression, but an unapologetic interweaving of method and outcome. One image of the *Lightning Farm* project is from the cockpit of a helicopter. It is a flyover of what is itself an aerial architecture and a magnificent slipstreaming of process and product in preparation for an affective burst. The drawing style is something we recognize and for which we feel affection. A line work that reminds one of the vectors of Lebbeus Woods, a tonality that recalls the mobile images of Peter Salter, and a perspectival shift that evokes the early flights of Zaha Hadid. The lines are fast, and at times whiplash, and collectively occur as an excitation of perspective in passing. There is in these drawings no singular or fixed point of view or reference; they fall from a cockpit as much as a pencil.[43] The *Lighting Farm* is an architecture being pulled together in flight by a population of machines: 'a power of the pack'.

Wakes

In the wake of Deleuze and Guattari, much architecture is the wresting of an event from the earth itself. A setting into tension. A type of conditioning of clouds, earth and air, a charging of an assemblage. There is a generosity to this architecture, which is not about being *the* spectacle, not about structuring or reinforcing *the* habits, nor concerned with asserting what the earth is or what we ourselves should be. Rather this architecture operates as a rod for intensities that threaten to blow all these things sky high. This is architecture's rich capacity to decolonize: to unstitch territories and territorializations and to operate as a conductor for a new earth and a new people, a larval subject. There is no final form to the *Lightning Farm* project and there is no lightning as yet. Helicopters are still hurriedly lifting parts into place and we too are situated at an intense edge of an architectural event, 'in advance but in reverse as though intagliated'. This sense of anticipation is palpable in the architecture after Deleuze and Guattari. We are poised for 'the lightning bolt that illuminates, and there is the world'.

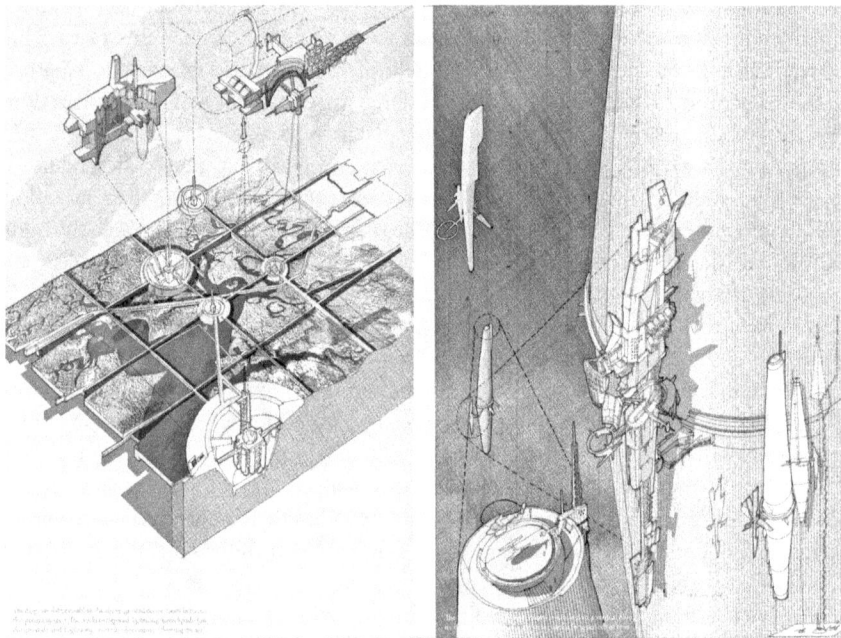

Figure 16.1 Farah Aliza Badaruddin, *Lightning Farm* (2013). Image courtesy of Farah Aliza Badaruddin.

Notes

Preamble

1. Alain Beaulieu and Douglas Ord, 'The Death of Gilles Deleuze as Composition of a Concept', *Deleuze Studies*, (11: 1, 2017): 121–38; André Pierre Colombat, '4 November 1995: Deleuze's Death as an Event', *Man and World*, (29, 1996): 235–49; and Alphonso Lingis, 'Defenestration', Deleuze Conference 2006, University of California, Berkeley, 3 November 2006. Available at https://www.scribd.com/document/41375612/Defenestration-by-Alphonso-Lingis-Deleuze-conference-2006. Accessed 27 November 2019.
2. Gilles Deleuze, 'For Félix', in David Lapoujade ed., *Two Regimes of Madness: Texts and Interviews 1975–1995*, (New York: Semiotext(e), 2006), 383.
3. In 1987 the architectural theorist Catherine Ingraham would describe the relation between post-structural philosophy and architecture as 'slow-dancing'. Catherine Ingraham, 'Slow-Dancing: Architecture in the Embrace of Poststructuralism', *Inland Architect*, (September–October 1987): 44–7.
4. Gilles Deleuze and Félix Guattari, *What Is Philosophy?*, (New York and Chichester: Columbia University Press, 1994), 186. Translation of *Qu'est-ce que la philosophie?*, (Paris: Les Editions de Minuit, 1991), by Hugh Tomlinson and Graham Burchell.
5. Deleuze speaks of his travels in Gilles Deleuze, *Negotiations: 1972–1990*, (New York: Columbia University Press, 1995), 11–12. Translated by Martin Joughin from *Pourparlers: 1972–1990*, (Paris: Minuit, 1990).
6. Félix Guattari and Suely Rolnik, *Molecular Revolution in Brazil*, (New York: Semiotext(e), 2007). Translation of *Micropolítica: Cartografias do desejo*, (Petrópolis: Vozes, 1986) by Karel Clapshow and Brian Holmes, and Félix Guattari, *Machinic Eros: Writings on Japan*, Gary Genosko and Jay Hetrick eds., (Minneapolis, MN: Univocal, 2015). Refer also to Gary Genosko, 'Japanese Singularity', in *Felix Guattari: An Aberrant Introduction*, (Transversals: New Directions in Philosophy), (London and New York: Continuum, 2002), 122–54.
7. Gilles Deleuze and Claire Parnet, *Dialogues*, (New York: Columbia University Press, 1987), 37. Translation of *Dialogues*, (Paris: Flammarion, 1977), by Hugh Tomlinson and Barbara Habberjam.
8. Gilles Deleuze, Vincennes, Cours du 1978/01/24, (4/22). The note is made in reference to the work of Spinoza.
9. Gillian Beer, *Darwin's Plots; Evolutionary Narrative in Darwin, George Eliot and Nineteenth-Century Fiction*, (London: Ark Paperbacks, 1985), 6.
10. Sanford Kwinter, cited in Simone Brott, 'Deleuze and "The Intercessors"', *Log*, (18, Winter 2010): 145.
11. Brott, 'Deleuze and "The Intercessors"', 135–51.
12. John Rajchman, Interview by Simone Brott, 2003. Available at http://eprints.qut.edu.au/67949/2/67949.pdf. Accessed 3 January 2019. For analysis of Rajchman's role as an 'intercesseur' between Deleuze's philosophy and architecture, refer to Frederike

Lausch, 'Changing the Architectonic of Philosophy: John Rajchman's Interest in Folded Architecture', in Tomás N. Castro and Maribel Mendes Sobreira eds., *philosophy@Lisbon*, (Lisbon: CFUL, no. 5, 2016), 39–51.
13   Sylvère Lotringer, 'My '80s: Better than Life', *Artforum*, (14: 8, April 2003): 2.
14   *Semiotext(e)* sponsored the colloquium on 'Schizo-Culture' at Columbia University, 13–16 November 1975. Refer to Sylvère Lotringer, John Rajchman et al., eds., *Semiotext(e): Anti-Oedipus: From Psychoanalysis to Schizopolitics*, (2: 3, 1977), and Sylvère Lotringer, John Rajchman et al., eds., *Semiotext(e): SchizoCulture*, (3: 2, 1978).
15   'Cache followed Deleuze's seminar at the University of Paris for many years, finding in Deleuze a major philosophical inspiration for his own work. Deleuze in turn recognized the originality of Cache, who took up concepts like image, frame, and territory and made them live and move in new ways.' Anne Boyman, 'Translator's Preface', in Bernard Cache ed., *Earth Moves: The Furnishing of Territories*, (Cambridge, MA: The MIT Press, 1995). Translation of *Terre meuble*, (1983, unpublished manuscript) by Anne Boyman.
16   Deleuze notes: 'Bernard Cache, L'ameublement du territoire (forthcoming). Inspired by geography, architecture, and the decorative arts, in my view this book seems essential for any theory of the fold.' Gilles Deleuze, *The Fold: Leibniz and the Baroque*, (New York: Continuum, 2006), note 3, 166. Translation of *Le Pli: Leibniz et le Baroque*, (Paris: Minuit, 1988), by Tom Conley.
17   Deleuze, *The Fold*, 15.
18   Deleuze, *The Fold*, 20.
19   Deleuze, *The Fold*, 41.
20   Michel Feher and Sanford Kwinter eds., *Zone 1/2: The Contemporary City*, (New York: Urzone Inc., 1986), 11.
21   Feher and Kwinter, *Zone 1/2*, 11–13.
22   Feher and Kwinter, *Zone 1/2*, 11.
23   Gilles Deleuze and Félix Guattari, *Anti-Oedipus*, (Minneapolis: University of Minnesota Press, 1983), 39, 285 and 323. Translation of *L'Anti-Oedipe*, (Paris: Les Editions de Minuit, 1972), volume 1 of *Capitalisme et schizophrénie*, by Robert Hurley, Mark Seem and Helen R. Lane.
24   Constantin V. Boundas and Anne Querrien, 'Anne Querrien, La Borde, Guattari and Left Movements in France, 1965–81', *Deleuze Studies*, (10: 3, 2016): 395–416.
25   Gilles Deleuze and Félix Guattari, *A Thousand Plateaus*, (Minneapolis: University of Minnesota Press, 1987). Translation of *Mille plateaux*, volume 2 of *Capitalisme et schizophrénie*, Paris: Les Editions de Minuit, 1980, by Brian Massumi.
26   Feher and Kwinter, *Zone 1/2*, 423–65.
27   Félix Guattari, 'Questionnaire', in Feher and Kwinter eds., *Zone 1/2*, 460.
28   Kenneth Frampton, 'Questionnaire', in Feher and Kwinter eds., *Zone 1/2*, 425.
29   Peter Eisenman, 'Questionnaire', in Feher and Kwinter eds., *Zone 1/2*, 440.
30   Rem Koolhaas, 'Questionnaire', in Feher and Kwinter eds., *Zone 1/2*, 451.
31   Jean-Jacques Lecercle, 'The Pedagogy of Philosophy', review of Gilles Deleuze and Félix Guattari's *What Is Philosophy?*, *Radical Philosophy*, (75, January–February 1996): 44.
32   Hraztan Zeitlian, *Semiotext(e)/ Architecture*, (New York: Semiotext(e), 1992), 3M1.
33   Brott, 'Deleuze and "The Intercessors"', 147.
34   Greg Lynn, *Folding in Architecture, AD*, (Profile 102, 1993): 8.
35   Paul Virilio, 'Critical Reflections', *Art Forum*, (34: 3, November 1995): 83.

36 Michael Speaks, 'It's Out There … The Formal Limits of the American Avantgarde', *Architectural Design*, (68: 5/6, May–June 1998): 26–31.
37 The image is credited as 'Sylvia Kolbowski, New York City, 1/9 subway line, 20 July, 12:55 P.M.' 'Front Matter', *Assemblage*, (41, April 2000): 3.
38 Deleuze and Guattari, *What Is Philosophy?*, 185.
39 Andrew Ballantyne, *Deleuze and Guattari for Architects*, (London: Routledge, 2007), 103.
40 Hélène Frichot and Stephen Loo, *Deleuze and Architecture*, (Edinburgh: Edinburgh University Press, 2013), 6.
41 Deleuze and Guattari, *What Is Philosophy?*, 122.

Part 1

1 Gilles Deleuze and Claire Parnet, *Dialogues II*, (New York: Columbia University Press, 2007), 52. Translated by Hugh Tomlinson and Barbara Habberjam. Refer also to Gilles Deleuze and Félix Guattari, *What Is Philosophy?*, (New York and Chichester: Columbia University Press, 1994), 220. Translation of *Qu'est-ce que la philosophie?*, (Paris: Les Editions de Minuit, 1991), by Hugh Tomlinson and Graham Burchell.

Chapter 1

1 Gilles Deleuze, 'Letter to a Harsh Critic', in Gilles Deleuze, *Negotiations. 1972–1990*, (New York: Columbia University Press, 1995), 6. Translated by Martin Joughin.
2 Tom Conley, 'Translators Forward', in Gilles Deleuze, *The Fold: Leibniz and the Baroque*, (Minneapolis: University of Minnesota Press, 1993), xiii. Translation of *Le Pli: Leibniz et le baroque*, (Paris: Les Editions de Minuit, 1988) by Tom Conley.
3 Deleuze, *The Fold*, 78.
4 Deleuze, *The Fold*, 78.
5 Gottfried Wilhelm Leibniz, *Monadology*, §61. Translation by Robert Latta, 1898.
6 Leibniz, *Monadology*, §61.
7 Leibniz, *Monadology*, §61.
8 Voltaire, 'Elémens de la philosophie de Newton', in *Oeuvres complètes*, vol. 22, (Garnier: Paris, 1877), 434. 'Pouvez-vous bien avancer qu'une goutte d'urine soit une infinité de *monades,* et que chacune d'elles ait les idées, quoique obscures, de l'univers entier'.
9 Deleuze, *The Fold*, 78.
10 Bertrand Russell, *A Critical Exposition of the Philosophy of Leibniz: With an Appendix of Leading Passages*, (Cambridge: Cambridge University Press, 1900), xi.
11 Deleuze, *The Fold,* 9.
12 Alfred North Whitehead, *Process and Reality: An Essay in Cosmology*, David Ray Griffin and Donald W. Sherburne eds., corrected edition, (New York: The Free Press, 1978), 19.
13 Gilles Deleuze and Claire Parnet, *Dialogues II*, (New York: Columbia University Press, 2007), 52. Translated by Hugh Tomlinson and Barbara Habberjam.
14 Deleuze, *The Fold*, 9.
15 Deleuze, *The Fold*, 8–9.

16 Arnauld refers to the account of the death of a ram by immolation, noting that Leibniz imagines a 'ram's soul withdrawing into a part of the incinerated ram that isn't organic'. Reference is to note 19, 143: Letter to Antoine Arnauld, April 1687(GPh, II, 99) (Mason, 125). Leibniz to Arnauld, 30.iv.1687 and Arnauld to Leibniz, 28, viii, (1687). Cited at https://www.earlymoderntexts.com/assets/pdfs/leibniz1686a_3.pdf. Accessed 21 May 2021.
17 Simon O'Sullivan, *Deleuze Dictionary*, 'The Fold'. Available at https://www.simonosullivan.net/articles/deleuze-dictionary.pdf. Accessed 27 November 2020.
18 Deleuze, *The Fold*, 5. The original image can be found: Gilles Deleuze, *Le Pli: Leibniz et le Baroque*, (Paris: Minuit, 1988), 7.
19 Deleuze, *The Fold*, 4.
20 Vidler would use Bernini's sculpture of Santa Teresa as an example. Anthony Vidler, *Warped Space. Art, Architecture, and Anxiety in Modern Culture*, (Cambridge: The MIT Press, 2001), 219.
21 Deleuze, *The Fold*, 3.
22 Conley, 'Translators Forward', x.
23 Deleuze, *The Fold*, 3.
24 Deleuze, *The Fold*, 20.
25 Deleuze, *The Fold*, 20.
26 Deleuze, *The Fold*, 4.
27 Deleuze, *The Fold*, 11.
28 Whitehead would describe the Leibnizian idea of 'the "best of possible worlds" as an audacious fudge produced in order to save the face of a Creator'. Whitehead, *Process and Reality*, 47.
29 This is consistent with the definition given by Whitehead. Whitehead, *Process and Reality*, 23.
30 Deleuze, *The Fold*, 78.
31 Whitehead, *Process and Reality*, 25, 28, 55, 63, 77, 89, 230, 232, 257, 265–6, 287, 302, 318, and Deleuze, *The Fold*, 78.
32 Michel Feher and Sanford Kwinter eds., *Zone 1/2: The Contemporary City*, (New York: Urzone Inc., 1986), 11.
33 Feher and Kwinter, *Zone 1/2*: 11. My italicization.
34 Frank Gehry, interview by Greg Lynn, 'Archaeology of the Digital: Greg Lynn and Frank Gehry on the Computer in Architecture', *Frame*, (13 February). Available at https://www.frameweb.com/article/greg-lynn-frank-gehry-legacy. Accessed 16 February 2021.
35 Greg Lynn, 'Embryologic Houses', in Ali Rahim (guest editor), *Contemporary Processes in Architecture, AD,* (Profile 145, 2000): 31. Reprinted in *AD The Digital Turn in Architecture 1992–2012*, (2013): 126–30.
36 Greg Lynn, 'Architectural Curvilinearity: The Folded, the Pliant and the Supple', in Andreas Papadakis ed., *Folding in Architecture, AD,* (Profile 102, 1993): 8.
37 Lynn, 'Embryologic Houses', 30.
38 Lynn, 'Embryologic Houses', 30.
39 Deleuze, *The Fold*, 78.
40 Lynn, 'Architectural Curvilinearity', 9.
41 Deleuze, *The Fold*, 35.
42 Lynn, 'Architectural Curvilinearity', 12.
43 Lynn, 'Architectural Curvilinearity', 9.

44 Lynn, 'Architectural Curvilinearity', 11. The term 'intensive whole' comes from Helen Castle, the editor of the revised edition of *AD Folding in Architecture*, revised issue (2004): 7.
45 Lynn, 'Architectural Curvilinearity', 12.
46 Lynn wasn't the first to do so. Substantial groundwork was done by Christopher Alexander. Alexander's paper of 1966, 'From a Set of Forces to a Form', asserts that form must yield to, acknowledge and reconcile 'force', which might be either a physical force, a social force such as convention or taste, an economic or technological force or it might correspond to some supposed universal psychological or behavioural tendency. Christopher Alexander, 'From a Set of Forces to a Form', in Gyorgy Kepes ed., *The Man-Made Object*, (New York: Studio Vista, 1966), 96–107.
47 Lynn, 'Architectural Curvilinearity', 12.
48 Deleuzean scholars alongside architects took notice. Brian Massumi writes of Lynn's 'blob-space': 'The self-activity and heterogeneity of this space is in stark contrast to the inertness and homogeneity of the Euclidean matrix, whose invariant axes act as a container for whole figures that are the sum of their parts and are varied, as wholes, through the intervention of a force that enters its space from outside and projects transformations into it. The forces of the blob space are endogenous; those of Euclidean space are exogenous.' Brian Massumi, 'Interface and Active Space: Human-Machine Design'; published in the *Proceedings of the Sixth International Symposium on Electronic Art*, Montreal, 1995.
49 D'Arcy Wentworth Thompson, *On Growth and Form*, (Cambridge: Cambridge University Press, 1942), 16.
50 John Rajchman cited in Simone Brott, 'An Interview with John Rajchman, Department of Art History, Columbia University, on Architecture, Deleuze and Foucault' for *Subjectivizations: Deleuze and Architecture* (Master's Thesis), 10 February 2003. Available at https://eprints.qut.edu.au/67949/. Accessed 21 May 2020.
51 Deleuze, *The Fold*, 9.
52 Deleuze, *The Fold*, 9.

Chapter 2

1 Beatriz Colomina, 'At Home with His Parents', *Assemblage* (30 August 1996): 108–11. Colomina served on the advisory and editorial board of *Assemblage* across volumes 14–41.
2 Colomina, 'At Home with His Parents', 108.
3 The term 'role models' was Colomina's description. Colomina, 'At Home with His Parents', 111.
4 Colomina, 'At Home with His Parents', 111.
5 The term 'pseudoreview' was Colomina's. Colomina, 'At Home with His Parents', 109.
6 Greg Lynn, 'In the Wake of the Avant-garde', *Assemblage* (29 April 1996): 116–25. The 'Origins of the Avant-garde in America: The Philip Johnson Colloquium' organized by the Canadian Centre for Architecture in conjunction with the Museum of Modern Art, New York, and the Columbia University Graduate School of Architecture, Planning and Preservation. Held 1–3 February 1996. The 'Light Construction' exhibition was organized by Terence Riley, Department of Architecture and Design, MoMA. Held 21 September 1995–2 January 1996.

7   Lynn, 'In the Wake of the Avant-garde', 117.
8   Lynn, 'In the Wake of the Avant-garde', 117–18.
9   Lynn, 'In the Wake of the Avant-garde', 125 and 117–18.
10 Lynn, 'In the Wake of the Avant-garde', 117.
11 Lynn, 'In the Wake of the Avant-garde', 121.
12 Gilles Deleuze and Félix Guattari, *Anti-Oedipus*, (Minneapolis: University of Minnesota Press, 1983), 2. Translation of *L'Anti-Oedipe*, (Paris: Les Editions de Minuit, 1972), volume 1 of *Capitalisme et schizophrénie*, by Robert Hurley, Mark Seem and Helen R. Lane.
13 Deleuze and Guattari, *Anti-Oedipus*, 96. Refer also to Chris L. Smith, *Bare Architecture: A Schizoanalysis*, (London: Bloomsbury, 2017), 45–6.
14 Sigmund Freud, 'The Interpretation of Dreams', (1900), in *The Standard Edition of the Complete Psychological Works of Sigmund Freud*, vol. 4, (London: Hogarth Press, 1953), 262–3. Translated and edited by James Stratchey.
15 Deleuze and Guattari, *Anti-Oedipus*, 170 and xx and 4 (respectively).
16 Deleuze and Guattari, *Anti-Oedipus*, 2 and 35. One should note however that there is a difference between the clinical schizophrenia which we might first think of, and this mode of thought to which Deleuze and Guattari refer. 'It is not a question of opposing to the dogmatic image of thought another image borrowed, for example, from schizophrenia, but rather of remembering that schizophrenia is not only a human fact but also a possibility for thought – one, moreover, which can only be revealed as such can through the abolition of that image.' Gilles Deleuze, *Difference and Repetition*, (London: Continuum, 2004), 148. Translation of *Différence et rèpètition*, (Paris: PUF, 1968), by Paul Patton.
17 Vitruvius would repeatedly describe his thesis as 'writing the body of architecture'. Vitruvius, *De Architectura*, (Cambridge, MA: Harvard University Press, 1931), 9.8.15; refer also to 6.pref.7. Translated by Frank Granger.
18 Gilles Deleuze and Félix Guattari, *What Is Philosophy?*, (New York and Chichester: Columbia University Press, 1994), 58. Translation of *Qu'est-ce que la philosophie?*, (Paris: Les Editions de Minuit, 1991), by Hugh Tomlinson and Graham Burchell.
19 Andrew Ballantyne and Chris L. Smith, 'Fluxions', in Ballantyne and Smith eds., *Architecture in the Space of Flows*, (London: Routledge, 2012), 1–39.
20 Deleuze and Guattari, *What Is Philosophy?*, 85.
21 Michel Serres, *Hermes: Literature, Science, Philosophy*, (Baltimore, MD: Johns Hopkins University Press, 1982), 83. Translation by Josué V. Harari and David F. Bell.
22 Deleuze and Guattari, *What Is Philosophy*, 85.
23 Gilles Deleuze and Félix Guattari, *A Thousand Plateaus*, (Minneapolis: University of Minnesota Press, 1987), 3. Translation of *Mille plateaux*, volume 2 of *Capitalisme et schizophrénie*, (Paris: Les Editions de Minuit, 1980), by Brian Massumi.
24 The Nile flowed with water and people long before the Egyptians and their solar deities came to occupy its shifting banks and millennia before Napoleon's soldiers crossed it. Just as the Jordan flowed well before the Philistines, Baal, Astarte and Dagon, or any sense of god-given right to left or right banks. The land was there well before human history came to demarcate, divide and conquer it and well before such places were claimed as promised lands, holy lands, homelands.
25 British reports on Hong Kong described the Hoklo people living about Hong Kong as being there 'since time unknown', Great Britain Colonial Office, Hong Kong, Government Information Services (1970). 'The Hoklo people, like the Tanka,

have been in the area since time unknown. They too are boat-dwellers but are less numerous than the Tanka and are mostly found in eastern waters.' Govt. Press, 219.
26 Deleuze and Guattari, *Anti-Oedipus*, 190.
27 Jacques Lacan, 'The Object Relation and the Intersubjective Relation', in *The Seminars of Jacques Lacan*, Book I, (Cambridge: University of Cambridge Press, 1988). Translation of *Le Séminaire I,* (Paris: Les Editions du Seuil, 1975), by John Forrester. Refer also to Jacques Lacan, 'The Mirror Stage as Formative of the Function of the I as Revealed in Psychoanalytic Experience', 4, in *Écrits*, (New York: W. W. Norton, 1977). This talk was delivered at the 16th International Congress of Psychoanalysis, Zurich, 17 July 1949.
28 Eugène Holland, 'Deterritorializing "Deterritorialization": From the Anti-Oedipus to a Thousand Plateaus', *SubStance*, (20: 3, 66, 1991): 57.
29 Holland, 'Deterritorializing "Deterritorialisation"', 57.
30 Karl Marx, *Capital*, vol. 1, chapter 26, (Harmondsworth: Penguin, 1976). Translation by Ben Fowkes.
31 David Harvey, 'Accumulation by Dispossession', in *The New Imperialism*, (Oxford: Oxford University Press, 2005), 149.
32 Deleuze and Guattari, *Anti-Oedipus*, 138.
33 Deleuze and Guattari, *Anti-Oedipus*, 9.
34 Deleuze and Guattari, *Anti-Oedipus*, 140.
35 Deleuze and Guattari, *What Is Philosophy?*, 96.
36 Deleuze and Guattari, *What Is Philosophy?*, 96.
37 Deleuze and Guattari, *Anti-Oedipus*, 131.
38 Zaha Hadid, 'Zaha Hadid RA on the Influence of Malevich in Her Work: Plane Sailing' in *RA Magazine* (Summer 2014). Available at https://www.royalacademy.org.uk/article/zaha-hadid-ra-on-the-influence-of. Accessed 10 June 2020.
39 Elain Elkann, 'Zaha Hadid at the Royal Academy of Arts' Interview of 8 March 2015. Available at https://www.alainelkanninterviews.com/zaha-hadid-ra/. Accessed 27 November 2020.
40 Zaha Hadid, *Zaha Hadid: The Complete Buildings and Projects*, (New York: Rizzoli, 1998), 19 and 20.
41 Zaha Hadid in *AD* Editorial Team, 'Video: Zaha Hadid Discusses the Influence of Kazımir Malevich on Her Work', 1 September 2016. Available at https://www.archdaily.com/794495/video-zaha-hadid-discusses-the-influence-of-kazimir-malevich-on-her-work. Accessed 12 September 2020.
42 Patrik Schumacher, *Digital Hadid: Landscapes in Motion*, (Basel: Birkhäuser, 2004), 20.
43 Mary McLeod, 'Architecture and Politics in the Reagan Era: From Postmodernism to Deconstructivism', *Assemblage*, (no. 8, February 1989): 44.
44 Javier Pes, 'How a Design for Hong Kong launched Zaha Hadid's Career', in *The Art Newspaper*, 1 February 2017. Available at https://www.theartnewspaper.com/news/how-a-design-for-hong-kong-launched-zaha-hadids-career. Accessed 16 July 2020.
45 Aaron Betsky, 'Beyond 89 Degrees' in *Zaha Hadid: The Complete Buildings and Projects*, 9.
46 Harry Mount, 'Zaha Hadid Was One of Architecture's Greatest Narcissists', *The Spectator*, 4 April 2016. Not recommended, but available at https://www.spectator.co.uk/article/zaha-hadid-was-one-of-architecture-s-greatest-narcissists. Accessed 13 June 2020.
47 Schumacher, *Digital Hadid*, 28.

48 Deleuze and Guattari, *Anti-Oedipus*, 351.
49 Hal Foster, 'New Fields of Architecture: Zaha Hadid', *Artforum* (September 2006). Available at https://www.artforum.com/print/200607/new-fields-of-architecture-zaha-hadid-11491. Accessed 13 June 2020.
50 Deleuze and Guattari, *What Is Philosophy?*, 88.
51 Frank Gehry, 'Passages: Zaha Hadid', *Artforum* (Summer 2016). Available at https://www.artforum.com/print/201606/zaha-hadid-60078. Accessed 14 June 2020.
52 Hadid, 'Zaha Hadid RA on the Influence of Malevich in Her Work'.
53 Gehry, 'Passages: Zaha Hadid'.

Chapter 3

1 I have contemporized the phrasing from 'When you are designing a window, imagine your girlfriend sitting inside looking out'. Alvar Aalto cited in Richard Weston, *100 Ideas That Changed Architecture*, (London: Lawrence King, 2011), 19.
2 Gilles Deleuze and Félix Guattari, *A Thousand Plateaus*, (Minneapolis: University of Minnesota Press, 1987), 311. Translation of *Mille plateaux*, volume 2 of *Capitalisme et schizophrénie*, (Paris: Les Editions de Minuit, 1980), by Brian Massumi.
3 Sigmund Freud, 'The Interpretation of Dreams', (1900), *The Standard Edition of the Complete Psychological Works of Sigmund Freud*, vol. 4, (London: Hogarth Press, 1953), footnote 18. Translated and edited by James Stratchey.
4 Sigmund Freud, 'Two Principles of Mental Functioning', (1911), *The Standard Edition of the Complete Psychological Works of Sigmund Freud*, vol. 12, (London: Hogarth Press, 1953), 222.
5 Freud, 'Two Principles of Mental Functioning', 224.
6 Gilles Deleuze and Félix Guattari, *What Is Philosophy?*, (New York and Chichester: Columbia University Press, 1994), 204–5. Translation of *Qu'est-ce que la philosophie?*, (Paris: Les Editions de Minuit, 1991), by Hugh Tomlinson and Graham Burchell.
7 James Joyce, *Finnegans Wake*, (London: Faber and Faber, 1975), 118. Joyce would also use the term 'chaosfoedted'. Joyce, *Finnegans Wake*, 137.
8 Gilles Deleuze, *The Logic of Sense*, Constantin V. Boundas ed., (New York: Columbia University Press, 1990), 264. Translation of *Logique du sens*, (Paris: Les Editions de Minuit, 1969), by Mark Lester and Charles Stivale.
9 Gilles Deleuze, *Nietzsche and Philosophy*, (London: Althone Press, 1983), 37. Translation of *Nietzsche et la philosophie*, (Paris: PUF, 1962), by Hugh Tomlinson.
10 Gilles Deleuze, *Difference and Repetition*, (New York: Columbia University Press, 1994), 148–9, 157–9 and 167. Translation of *Différence et repetition*, (Paris: Presse Universitaires de France, 1968), by Paul Patton.
11 Gilles Deleuze, *Negotiations. 1972–1990*, (New York: Columbia University Press, 1995), 5. Translated by Martin Joughin.
12 Deleuze, *Difference and Repetition*, 30–2.
13 Deleuze, *Difference and Repetition*, 158.
14 Sigmund Freud, 'Female Sexuality', (1931), *The Standard Edition of the Complete Psychological Works of Sigmund Freud*, vol. 21, (London: Hogarth Press, 1956), 241–58. Translated and edited by James Stratchey.
15 Deleuze, *Difference and Repetition*, 265.
16 Deleuze, *Difference and Repetition*, xix.

17 Deleuze, *Difference and Repetition*, 33–4.
18 Deleuze, *The Logic of Sense*, 147.
19 Deleuze, *Difference and Repetition*, 57, and Deleuze, *The Logic of Sense*, 264.
20 Deleuze, *The Logic of Sense*, 111.
21 Joyce, *Finnegans Wake*, 327.
22 Deleuze, *The Logic of Sense*, 22. This is what Daniela Voss calls a 'genetic productivity'. Daniela Voss, 'Deleuze's Rethinking of the Notion of Sense', *Deleuze Studies*, (7: 1, 2013): 1–25.
23 Deleuze, *Nietzsche and Philosophy*, 58; Fredrich Nietzsche, 'On Truth and Falsity in Their Extramoral Sense', (1873), in Reinhold Grimm and Caroline Molina Y. Vedia eds., *Friedrich Nietzsche: Philosophical Writings*, (New York: Continuum, 1997), 92.
24 Deleuze, *Nietzsche and Philosophy*, 3.
25 Deleuze, *Nietzsche and Philosophy*, 3–4.
26 Deleuze, *The Logic of Sense*, 248.
27 Deleuze, *The Logic of Sense*, 22. See also Phillip Goodchild, *Deleuze and Guattari: An Introduction to the Politics of Desire*, (London: Sage Publications, 1996), 34–5.
28 Deleuze, *The Logic of Sense*, 25.
29 Deleuze, *The Logic of Sense*, 71.
30 Deleuze, *The Logic of Sense*, 240–1.
31 Sigfried Giedion, *Space, Time and Architecture: The Birth of a New Tradition*, (Cambridge, MA: Harvard University Press, 1949), 566.
32 Giedion, *Space, Time and Architecture*, 618. Refer also to Eeva-Liisa Pelkonen, 'Reading Aalto through the Baroque', *AA Files*, (No. 65, 2012): 72–5.
33 Giedion, *Space, Time and Architecture*, 565.
34 Deleuze, *The Logic of Sense*, 304.
35 Deleuze, *The Logic of Sense*, 125.
36 Deleuze, *Logique du sens*, 151.
37 Deleuze, *The Logic of Sense*, 133.
38 Deleuze, *The Logic of Sense*, 133.
39 Bernard Cache, *Earth Moves: The Furnishing of Territories*, (Cambridge, MA: The MIT Press, 1995), 141–2. Translation of *Terre meuble* (1983, unpublished manuscript) by Anne Boyman.
40 According to the translator Anne Boyman, 'What Cache calls "images" are analyzed in terms of framing and territories rather than in terms of model and imitation, figuration and abstraction'. Anne Boyman, 'Translators Preface' in Cache, *Earth Moves*, viii.
41 Cache, *Earth Moves*, 139.
42 Cache, *Earth Moves*, 140.
43 Cache, *Earth Moves*, 1.
44 Cache, *Earth Moves*, 2.
45 Cache, *Earth Moves*, 29.
46 Cache, *Earth Moves*, 117.
47 Deleuze, *The Logic of Sense*, 262.
48 Cache, *Earth Moves*, 116.
49 Cache, *Earth Moves*, 140.
50 Cache, *Earth Moves*, 117.
51 Deleuze, *The Logic of Sense*, 125.
52 Cache, *Earth Moves*, 97.

53 Cache, interviewed by Lynn for, 'Bernard Cache and Greg Lynn Discuss Objectile', *Archaeology of the Digital 09*, (Montréal: Canadian Centre for Architecture, 2015), 5–6.
54 Cache was pulled into the Eisenman/Lynn frame through the AD special edition 'Folding in Architecture'. Andreas Papadakis ed., *Folding in Architecture, AD* (Profile 102, 1993).
55 Mario Carpo, *The Alphabet and the Algorithm*, (Cambridge, MA: The MIT Press, 2011), x.
56 Cache, *Earth Moves*, 88.
57 Deleuze, *The Logic of Sense*, 304.
58 Cache, *Earth Moves*, 109.

Chapter 4

1 Michel Foucault, 'Of Other Spaces', *Diacritics*, (16: 1, Spring 1986): 22. Translation by Jay Miskowiec. Foucault originally delivered 'Des espaces autres' to the conférence au Cercle d'Études architecturales, 14 March 1967. The paper was first published in *Architecture, Mouvement, Continuité*, (5 October 1984): 46–9. Although not part of the official corpus of his work, the manuscript was released into the public domain for an exhibition in Berlin before Foucault's death.
2 Foucault, 'Of Other Spaces', 22.
3 Foucault, 'Of Other Spaces', 22.
4 Foucault, 'Of Other Spaces', 22.
5 Foucault, 'Of Other Spaces', 23.
6 Foucault, 'Of Other Spaces', 23.
7 Foucault, 'Of Other Spaces', 23.
8 Foucault, 'Of Other Spaces', 23.
9 Foucault, 'Of Other Spaces', 23–4.
10 Foucault, 'Of Other Spaces', 24.
11 Foucault, 'Of Other Spaces', 24.
12 Michel Cressole, *Deleuze (Psychothèque)*, (Paris: Editions Universitaires, 1973). Cited in Gilles Deleuze, 'I Have Nothing to Admit', in Sylvère Lotringer ed., *Semiotexte: Anti-Oedipus*, edition, (II/3, 1977), 110.
13 Gilles Deleuze and Félix Guattari, *Anti-Oedipus*, (Minneapolis: University of Minnesota Press, 1983). Translation of *L'Anti-Oedipe*, volume 1 of *Capitalisme et schizophrénie*, (Paris: Les Editions de Minuit, 1972), by Robert Hurley, Mark Seem and Helen R. Lane.
14 Gilles Deleuze and Claire Parnet, *Dialogues II*, (New York: Columbia University Press, 2007), 51. Translated by Hugh Tomlinson and Barbara Habberjam.
15 Deleuze and Parnet, *Dialogues II*, 52.
16 Deleuze and Parnet, *Dialogues II*, 51.
17 Deleuze and Parnet, *Dialogues II*, 52.
18 Deleuze and Parnet, *Dialogues II*, 52. Refer also to Gilles Deleuze and Félix Guattari, *What Is Philosophy?*, (New York and Chichester: Columbia University Press, 1994), 220. Translation of *Qu'est-ce que la philosophie?*, (Paris: Les Editions de Minuit, 1991), by Hugh Tomlinson and Graham Burchell.
19 Deleuze and Parnet, *Dialogues II*, 52.

20 Michel Foucault, 'Maurice Blanchot: The Thought from Outside', in *Foucault/Blanchot*, (New York: Zone Books, 1990), 24. Translation of *La pensee du dehors*, (Paris, Éditions Fata Margana, 1986), by Jeffrey Mehlman and Brian Massumi.
21 Deleuze and Parnet, *Dialogues II*, 71.
22 Deleuze and Parnet, *Dialogues II*, 53–4.
23 Gilles Deleuze, and Félix Guattari, *Kafka: Toward a Minor Literature*, (Minnesota: University of Minnesota Press, 1986), 29 and 31. Translation of *Kafka: pour une littérature mineure*, (Paris: Minuit, 1975), by Dana Polan.
24 The idea of passion would come to be aligned more with subjectivity in conversation with Parnet than it would in Deleuze's work with Guattari. Deleuze writes: 'A person suffering from a passionate or subjective delirium starts a process, indicated by a point of subjectivation: "He loves me"'. Deleuze and Parnet, *Dialogues II*, 109.
25 Deleuze and Guattari, *Anti-Oedipus*, 27.
26 Gilles Deleuze and Félix Guattari, *A Thousand Plateaus*, (Minneapolis: University of Minnesota Press, 1987), 399. Translation of *Mille plateaux*, volume 2 of *Capitalisme et schizophrénie*, (Paris: Les Editions de Minuit, 1980), by Brian Massumi.
27 Rem Koolhaas, *Delirious New York: A Retroactive Manifesto for Manhattan*, first edition, (Oxford: Oxford University Press, 1978). Koolhaas ends the book with his 'Acknowledgments', and his last sentence is 'Above all, *Delirious New York* owes a special debt of inspiration and reinforcement to Madelon Vriesendorp.' Koolhaas, *Delirious New York*, 317. For a fuller explication of the intersections of Vriesendorp and Koolhaas, it is worth reading Nicholas Parr's dissertation 'The Fabrication of Evidence in Rem Koolhaas's Delirious New York', (University of Brighton, 2014).
28 Deleuze and Guattari, *A Thousand Plateaus*, 399.
29 Madelon Vriesendorp in Shumon Basar, 'Couple Format: The Identity between Love and Work', *e-flux architecture*, 2 November 2016. The piece was generated for *Superhumanity*, a project by *e-flux Architecture* at the 3rd Istanbul Design Biennial, produced in cooperation with the Istanbul Design Biennial, the National Museum of Modern and Contemporary Art, Korea, the Govett-Brewster Art Gallery, New Zealand and the Ernst Schering Foundation.
30 FRAC, Centre-Val de Loire, 'Madelon Vriesendorp, Flagrant délit, 1975', collection entry. My italicization. Available at https://www.frac-centre.fr/_en/art-and-architecture-collection/vriesendorp-madelon/flagrant-delit-317.html?authID=207&ensembleID=310#:~:text=Flagrant%20d%C3%A9lit%2C%20drawn%20in%201975,loss%20of%20the%20original%20object. Accessed 3 April 2020.
31 Foucault, 'Of Other Spaces', 22.
32 Beatriz Colomina, 'Disaster Follows Ecstasy Like Form Follows Function', in Shumon Basar and Stephan Trüby eds., *The World of Madelon Vriesendorp: Paintings/Postcards/Objects/Games*, (London: AA Publications, 2008), 40.
33 Colomina is not the only one to want to frame the image in this discourse. Neil Leach writes: 'The corollary to reading the self as a building is the potential to read buildings as the self. In the context of New York, Salvador Dali's famous "paranoid" interpretation of the skyscrapers as representations of Jean-Francois Millet's Angelus, as animated creatures coming alive at sunset "ready to perform the sexual act" speaks of this opposite moment. It is this image, surely, that inspired the highly anthropomorphized illustration … *Flagrant Délit*.' Neil Leach, '9/11', *Diacritics*, (33: 3–4, Fall/Winter 2003): 82.
34 Albeit in the Monicelli Press edition the image that falls immediately within is an image of the Oxford University Press cover rather than the painting itself. The image

finds itself on page 160 either at the conclusion to the chapter on 'The Downtown Athletic Club' or at the commencement of the chapter 'How Perfect Perfection Can Be: The Creation of Rockefeller Center'.
35 Charles Jencks, 'Madelon Seeing through Objects', *The World of Madelon Vriesendorp*, 16.
36 Jencks, 'Madelon Seeing through Objects', 22.
37 Deleuze and Félix Guattari, *Anti-Oedipus*, 18.
38 Deleuze and Félix Guattari, *Anti-Oedipus*, 20.
39 Jencks, 'Madelon Seeing through Objects', 17.

Chapter 5

1 Marcel Proust, *In Search of Lost Time*, vol. 1-7, (London: Centaur Editions, 2016). Translation of *À la Recherché du Temps Perdu* (1913-1927) by C.K. Scott Moncrieff (vols. 1 to 6) and Sydney Schiff (vol. 7).
2 Proust, *The Search*, 1143.
3 Proust, *The Search*, 1143.
4 Proust, *The Search*, 1142.
5 Albert Wolff, in *Le Figaro*, 3 April 1876. Reference was to Renoir's 'Torso, Sunlight Effect (Torse de jeune fille au soleil)' (1875).
6 From Zola's 1880 Salon, *Le Voltaire*, (No. 19, 22 June 1880): 'Quand on se satisfait trop aisément, quand on livre une esquisse à peine sèche, on perd le goût des morceaux longuement étudiés'. The actual target of the critique is contested. Refer to F.W.J Hemmings, 'Zola, Manet, and the Impressionists (1875-80)', *PMLA*, (73: 4, September 1958): 414-15.
7 Proust, *The Search*, 1143.
8 Gilles Deleuze, *Proust and Signs*, (New York: George Braziller, 1972), 145. Translation of *Marcel Proust et les signes*, (Paris: PUF, 1964) by Richard Howard.
9 Deleuze, *Proust and Signs*, 143.
10 Proust cited in Deleuze, *Proust and Signs*, 143. (III, 1041).
11 Deleuze, *Proust and Signs*, 146.
12 The term 'machinic' is used throughout. Gilles Deleuze and Félix Guattari, *Anti-Oedipus*, (Minneapolis: University of Minnesota Press, 1983). Translation of *L'Anti-Oedipe*, (Paris: Les Editions de Minuit, 1972), volume 1 of *Capitalisme et schizophrénie*, by Robert Hurley, Mark Seem and Helen R. Lane.
13 Deleuze, *Proust and Signs*, 145.
14 Deleuze, *Proust and Signs*, 128-9.
15 Deleuze, *Proust and Signs*, 138.
16 Deleuze, *Proust and Signs*, 154.
17 Deleuze, *Proust and Signs*, 153.
18 Deleuze, *Proust and Signs*, 111.
19 Deleuze, *Proust and Signs*, 111.
20 Gilles Deleuze and Félix Guattari, *What Is Philosophy?*, (New York and Chichester: Columbia University Press, 1994), 2. Translation of *Qu'est-ce que la philosophie?*, (Paris: Les Editions de Minuit, 1991), by Hugh Tomlinson and Graham Burchell.
21 Le Corbusier, *Towards a New Architecture*, (New York: Dover Publications, 1986), 4. Translation of *Vers une architecture*, (Paris: Éditions Crès, Collection de L'Esprit Nouveau*, 1923), by Frederick Etchells.

22 *Beijing House II* is a thesis project completed at the Southern California Institute of Architecture (SCI-Arc). Wang would go on to form the Preliminary Research Office based in Los Angeles.
23 Each system might be thought of as 'fragments of disparate universes', as Deleuze had referred to the elements that swarmed in Proust's work. Deleuze, *Proust and Signs*, 144.
24 Deleuze, *Proust and Signs*, 150.
25 Yaohua Wang, 'Under 35-Wang Yoohua', *gooood interview* of 13 July 2018. Accessed at https://www.gooood.cn/under-35-wang-yaohua.htm. Accessed 13 September 2020.
26 Pierre-Auguste Renoir cited in Jean Renoir, *Renoir: My Father*, (New York: New York Review Books, 2001), 69. Translation of *Pierre-Auguste Renoir, mon père* by Randolph T. Weacer and Dorothy Weaver.
27 Jean-Jacques Lecercle, *Philosophy through the Looking Glass*, (La Salle, IL: Open Court, 1985), 173.
28 In *The Fold* Deleuze considered artworks as being composed of elements that had neither a logical nor an organic relation 'neither based on pieces as a long unity or a fragmented totality; nor formed or prefigured by those units in the course of a logical development or of an organic evolution'. Gilles Deleuze, *The Fold: Leibniz and the Baroque*, (Minneapolis: University of Minnesota Press, 1993), 191. Translation of *Le Pli: Leibniz et le baroque*, (Paris: Les Editions de Minuit, 1988) by Tom Conley.
29 'The death cries of the animals whose jugular veins have been opened are confused with the rumbling of the great drum, the whirring of gears, and the shrilling sound of steam. Death cries and mechanical noises are almost impossible to disentangle.' Sigfried Giedion, *Mechanization Takes Command: A Contribution to Anonymous History*, (New York: Oxford University Press, 1948), 246.
30 Proust, *The Search*, 396.
31 Proust, *The Search*, 724.
32 Lewis Mumford, *The Myth of the Machine: Technics and Human Development*, (New York: Harcourt Brace Jovanovich, 1967).

Chapter 6

1 John Ruskin, letter to his father dated 2 June 1852, in E.T. Cook and A. Wedderburn eds., *The Works of John Ruskin*, vol. XX, (London: George Allen, 1904), xxv.
2 Reference is to Alice's coronation dinner in Gilles Deleuze, *The Logic of Sense*, Constantin V. Boundas ed., (New York: Columbia University Press, 1990), 23. Translation of *Logique du sens*, (Paris: Les Editions de Minuit, 1969), by Mark Lester and Charles Stivale.
3 Johann Wolfgang Goethe, 'Another (Coptic Song)', in *The Poems of Goethe*, (London: J.W.Parker, 1853). Translation of 'Ein Andres' (1787) by Edgar Alfred Bowring.
4 Ruskin, *Works* IX, 57.
5 Ruskin, *Works* XIX, 435–6.
6 This characteristic of appropriation is identified in Charles Comte's early definition of appropriation in *Traité de la propriété* [*Treatise on Property*] (1834) where he suggests, '[B]y this action (of connecting) he appropriates (things) to himself. He transforms them into a part of himself, in a way that one could not detach them from him without destroying him.' Charles Comte, *Traité de la propriété*, 2 vols., (Paris: Chamerot, Ducollet, 1834), 51.

7   The sense of Ruskin that flows gently through this chapter owes a debt to three papers: Stephen Kite, 'Building Texts + Reading Fabrics: Metaphor, Memory, and Material in John Ruskin's *Stones of Venice*', in Wouter Van Acker and Peter Uyttenhove eds., *Library Trends: Information and Space: Analogies and Metaphors* (61: 2, Fall 2012): 418–39. Anuradha Chatterjee, *John Ruskin and the Fabric of Architecture*, (London and New York: Routledge, 2018), particularly chapter 2. George L. Hersey, *High Victorian Gothic: A Study in Associationism*, (Baltimore and London: The Johns Hopkins University Press, 1972), 48–60.
8   Ruskin, *Works* XX, xxv.
9   Pierre Guattari, 'La transversalité', *Revue de Psychothérapie institutionnelle*, n°1, 1965. The paper would come to be printed in English in Félix Guattari, *Molecular Revolution: Psychiatry and Politics*, (Harmondsworth and New York: Penguin, 1984 [1977]). Translation by Rosemary Sheed. This is a collection of essays that were published previously in *Psychoanalyse et transversalité* (Paris: Maspero, 1972) and *La Révolution moléculaire* (Paris: Éditions *Recherchés* Séries 'Encre', 1977).
10 Sigmund Freud, 'Introductory Lectures on Psychoanalysis', (1915–6), *The Standard Edition of the Complete Psychological Works of Sigmund Freud*, vol. 15, (London: Hogarth Press, 1953). Translated and edited by James Stratchey.
11 Ruskin, *Works* XXXVI, 454.
12 Guattari, *Molecular Revolution*, 11.
13 Guattari, *Molecular Revolution*, 12–13 and 21.
14 Félix Guattari, *Schizoanalytic Cartographies*, (London: Bloomsbury, 2013), 38. Translation of *Cartographies Schizoanalytiques*, (Paris: Éditions Galilée, 1989), by Andrew Goffey.
15 Guattari, *Molecular Revolution*, 22.
16 Guattari, *Molecular Revolution*, 17.
17 Guattari, *Molecular Revolution*, 11.
18 Camille Robcis, 'The Politics of the Psyche', lecture at the Center for 21st Century Studies, 10 March 2017. Refer also to Camille Robcis, 'Politics and the Psyche', *Humanities magazine* (Spring 2022), a publication of the National Endowment for the Humanities. Available at https://www.neh.gov/article/politics-and-psyche. Accessed 12 May 2022.
19 Guattari, *Molecular Revolution*, 16.
20 What Guattari calls 'institutional therapeutics' is also referred to as 'institutional psychotherapy' (despite Guattari's protestation).
21 Guattari, *Molecular Revolution*, 12.
22 Guattari, *Molecular Revolution*, 17.
23 Guattari, *Molecular Revolution*, 22.
24 Lest they be alienated 'as a distant personage'. Guattari, *Molecular Revolution*, 21.
25 Guattari, *Molecular Revolution*, 16.
26 Gary Genosko, 'Introduction', in *The Guattari Reader*, (Oxford: Blackwell, 1996), 14.
27 Gilles Deleuze, *Proust and Signs*, (New York: George Braziller, 1972), 126–8. Translation of *Marcel Proust et les signes,* (Paris: PUF, 1964) by Richard Howard.
28 Gilles Deleuze and Félix Guattari, *Anti-Oedipus*, (Minneapolis: University of Minnesota Press, 1983), 179. Translation of *L'Anti-Oedipe*, (Paris: Les Editions de Minuit, 1972), volume 1 of *Capitalisme et schizophrénie*, by Robert Hurley, Mark Seem and Helen R. Lane.
29 Ruskin, *Works* XXXVI, 454.
30 Deleuze and Guattari, *Anti-Oedipus*, 179.

31 Foucault, 'Preface', *Anti-Oedipus*, xii.
32 Deleuze and Guattari, *Anti-Oedipus*, 276.
33 Deleuze and Guattari, *Anti-Oedipus*, 293.
34 Guattari, *Schizoanalytic Cartographies*, 38.
35 Architecture has a long history of building the monuments of global capitalism and alongside them the institutions of repression and subjugation (churches, prisons, asylums, schools and shopping malls). The perpetual fixation on the individual built object is for architecture as fraught as the individual psyche was for the *psy* sciences. Architecture has also long been complicit in reinforcing the borders of private property (far too many of us are designing extensions to already extensive private homes or designing weekend destinations for the grossly over-remunerated). And sometimes it can seem that all our heroes of the 1970s and 1980s are now detailing outlets for Prada, operating as surrogates for accountants. And our best educational institutions are producing designers who are 'falling over each other to kiss corporate ass' (as Phillippe Starck so politely said).
36 Ruskin wrote, '[I]f I should succeed, as I hope, in making the *Stones of Venice* touch-stones, and detecting, by the mouldering of her marble, poison more subtle than ever was betrayed by the rending of her crystal; and if thus I am enabled to show the baseness of the schools of architecture and nearly every other art, which have for three centuries been predominant in Europe.' Ruskin, *Works* IX, 57.
37 Ruskin, *Works* Appendix 20, 549. Ruskin also writes: 'the building which at once consummates and embodies the entire system of the Gothic architecture of Venice – the DUCAL PALACE'. Ruskin *Works* X, 327.
38 Ruskin, *Works* XIX, 434.
39 Ruskin, *Works* XIX, 432.
40 Ruskin, *Works* XIX, 432.
41 Ruskin, *Works* XIX, 446.
42 Stephen Kite notes that '[s]ome commentators, such as Kristine Garrigan, accuse Ruskin of a disregard "for the major architectural qualities of plan, mass, and proportion,"' Kite, 'Building Texts + Reading Fabric', 431.
43 Ruskin, *Works* XIX, 432.
44 Ruskin, *Works* XIX, 435–6.
45 In 2016 a competition was held to enclose the amphitheatre. The German firms GMP and SBP won the competition to roof this site of battles and performance, but the competition remains contentious and says much about architecture's cannibalistic appetite. The architects and engineers proposed a rational retractable roof that would cover the space. They describe it in apparently rational descriptions, as a 'scallop shell' that would extend 'in the shape of a star'. The architects GNP are quoted in *Dezeen*. Available at https://www.dezeen.com/2017/02/09/gmp-sbp-verona-arena-retractable-scallop-shell-roof-roman-amphitheatre-italy/. Accessed 13 September 2019. This roof was only a shell or a star by transference – a simplistic metaphoric imposition – a fawning one-liner that sought to tame a place.
46 Marcel Proust, *In Search of Lost Time*, vol. 1–7, (London: Centaur Editions, 2016), 598. Translation of *À la Recherché du Temps Perdu* (1913–1927) by C.K. Scott Moncrieff (vols. 1 to 6) and Sydney Schiff (vol. 7).
47 Deleuze and Guattari, *Anti-Oedipus*, 43.
48 Deleuze and Guattari, *Anti-Oedipus*, 43. It is perhaps not coincidental that Anuradha Chatterjee engages the concept of weaving in *John Ruskin and the Fabric of Architecture*, chapter 2.

49 Later in *Anti-Oedipus*, Deleuze and Guattari return to Proust to expand the definition. They explore a moment in Proust where 'everything comes apart, but this time in a *molecular* and pure multiplicity, where the partial objects, the "boxes," the "vessels" all have their positive determinations, and enter into aberrant communication following a transversal that runs through the whole work; an immense flow that each partial object produces and cuts again, reproduces and cuts at the same time'. Deleuze and Guattari, *Anti-Oedipus*, 88.
50 Ruskin, *Works* XIX, 436.

Chapter 7

1   Diller + Scofidio eds., *Back to the Front: Tourisms of War*, (France: F.R.A.C. Basse Normandie, 1994).
2   Frederic Migayrou, 'The Extended Body: Chronicle of a Day with No History', in Diller + Scofidio eds., *Back to the Front: Tourisms of War*, (France: F.R.A.C. Basse Normandie, 1994), 167.
3   Migarou, 'The Extended Body', 167.
4   Migarou, 'The Extended Body', 67.
5   Migarou, 'The Extended Body', 190-1.
6   Migarou, 'The Extended Body', 167.
7   Sarah Whiting, 'Tactical Histories: Diller + Scofidio's "Back to the Front: Tourisms of War"', *Assemblage*, (28, December 1995): 77.
8   Migarou, 'The Extended Body', 166.
9   Migarou, 'The Extended Body', 191.
10 Deleuze had suggested similarly in *The Logic of Sense*: 'What would be the purpose of rising from the domain of truth to the domain of sense, if it were only to find between sense and nonsense a relation analogous to that of the true and the false?' Gilles Deleuze, *The Logic of Sense*, Constantin V. Boundas eds., (New York: Columbia University Press, 1990), 68. Translation of *Logique du sens*, (Paris: Les Editions de Minuit, 1969), by Mark Lester and Charles Stivale.
11 The descriptor 'delirium' stands in place of all histories and theories that are at once rational *and* irrational. Deleuze and Guattari would use the example of capitalism itself as 'a very particular delirium', but it is hard to imagine anything or any thought that would not fit this descriptor. Gilles Deleuze, 'Capitalism: A Very Special Delirium', in Félix Guattari, *Chaosophy: Texts and Interviews 1972-1977*, Sylvère Lotringer ed., (Los Angeles: Semiotext(e), 2009). Translated by David L. Sweet.
12 Deleuze, 'Capitalism: A Very Special Delirium', 35.
13 An inherency of difference would accord with Deleuze's understanding of a 'difference in itself': a difference liberated from identity. Gilles Deleuze, *Difference and Repetition*, (London: Continuum, 2004), Chapter 1. Translation of *Différence et rèpètition*, (Paris: PUF, 1968), by Paul Patton. Deleuze earlier had suggested, 'duration' is 'what differs in nature', that is, with itself. Gilles Deleuze, *Bergsonism*, (New York: Zone Books, 1988), 113. Translation of *Le Bergsonisme* (Paris: Presses Universitaires de France, 1966), by Hugh Tomlinson and Barbara Habberjam.
14 Deleuze, *The Logic of Sense*, 82-93.
15 Gilles Deleuze and Félix Guattari, *Anti-Oedipus*, (Minneapolis: University of Minnesota Press, 1983), 2. Translation of *L'Anti-Oedipe*, (Paris: Les Editions de

Minuit, 1972), volume 1 of *Capitalisme et schizophrénie*, by Robert Hurley, Mark Seem and Helen R. Lane.
16 Deleuze and Guattari, *Anti-Oedipus*, 23.
17 Guattari, *Chaosophy*, 61.
18 Deleuze and Guattari, *Anti-Oedipus*, 283.
19 Deleuze and Guattari, *Anti-Oedipus*, 338.
20 Deleuze and Guattari, *Anti-Oedipus*, 375–401.
21 Deleuze and Guattari, *Anti-Oedipus*, 105.
22 Deleuze and Guattari, *Anti-Oedipus*, 384.
23 Deleuze and Guattari, *Anti-Oedipus*, 342.
24 Deleuze and Guattari, *Anti-Oedipus*, 324.
25 Félix Guattari, *Schizoanalytic Cartographies*, (London: Bloomsbury, 2013), 36. Translation of *Cartographies Schizoanalytiques*, (Paris: Éditions Galilée, 1989), by Andrew Goffey.
26 Deleuze and Guattari, *Anti-Oedipus*, 321.
27 Michel Foucault, 'Preface' to Deleuze and Guattari, *Anti-Oedipus*, xii.
28 Foucault, 'Preface', xii.
29 Foucault, 'Preface', xi.
30 Foucault, 'Preface', xiii.
31 William Shakespeare, *The Tragedy of Hamlet, Prince of Denmark*, (1859–1601).
32 Michel Foucault, *The History of Sexuality*, vol. I: An Introduction, (New York: Pantheon Books, 1978), 12. Translation of *Histoire de la sexualité*, (Paris: Editions Gallimard, 1976), by Robert Hurley.
33 Deleuze and Guattari, *Anti-Oedipus*, 15; refer also to note 23, 394. Gisela Pankow, *L'homme et sa psychose*, (Paris: Aubier, 1969), 68–72.
34 Deleuze and Guattari, *Anti-Oedipus*, 96–7.
35 Deleuze and Guattari, *Anti-Oedipus*, 235.
36 Félix Guattari, 'Schizoanalysis', *The Yale Journal of Criticism*, (11: 2, 1998): 433.
37 Félix Guattari, *The Guattari Reader*, ed., Gary Genosko, (Oxford, UK: Blackwell, 1996), 133.
38 Gilles Deleuze, 'Five Propositions on Psychoanalysis', in David Laboujade ed., *Desert Islands and Other Texts 1953–1974*, (Paris: Semiotext(e), 2004), 280. Translation of Gilles Deleuze, *L'Îles déserte et autres textes: Textes et entretiens 1953–1974*, (Paris: Minuit, 2002), by Christopher Bush, Charles Stivale, Melissa McMahon, Alexander Hickox and Teal Eich. Originally published in Italian, 'Relazione di Gilles Deleuze' in Armando Verdiglione, ed., *Psicanalisi e Politica; Atti del Convegno di studi tenuto a Milano l'8–9 Maggio 1973*, (Milan: Feltrinelli, 1973).
39 Ian Buchanan, 'Architecture and Control Society', *Interstices*, (20, 2020): 13.
40 Elizabeth Diller cited in Georges Teysott, 'The Mutant Body of Architecture' in Elizabeth Diller and Ricardo Scofidio eds., *Flesh: Architectural Probes*, (New York: Princeton Architectural Press,1994), 9.
41 Teysott, 'The Mutant Body of Architecture', 11.
42 Migarou, 'The Extended Body', 169–70.
43 Diller + Scofidio, *Blur: The Making of Nothing*, (New York: Harry N. Abrams, Inc., 2002), 44.
44 Gilles Deleuze, *Pure Immanence: Essays on a Life*, (New York: Zone Books, 2001), 43. Translated by Anne Boyman.
45 Diller + Scofidio, *Blur: The Making of Nothing*, 162.

46 Diller Scofidio + Renfro, 'Blur Building: Swiss Expo 2002, Yverdon-Les-Bains, Switzerland' at the office website. Available at https://dsrny.com/project/blur-building. Accessed 25 March 2021.
47 Teysott, 'The Mutant Body of Architecture', 35.
48 Diller + Scofidio, *Blur: The Making of Nothing*, 162.
49 Elizabeth Diller and Anthony Vidler, 'Architecture Is a Technology That Has Not yet Discovered Its Agency', in Peter Eisenman and Anthony Vidler eds., *Log 28, Stocktaking*, (28, Summer 2013), 21 and 22.
50 Teysott, 'The Mutant Body of Architecture', 16.
51 Migarou, 'The Extended Body', 168.

Chapter 8

1 'Si vous êtes pris dans le rêve de l'autre, vous êtes foutu.' Gilles Deleuze at La Fémis, 'Qu'est-ce que l'acte de creation?' Conférence donnée dans le cadre de 'Mardis de la Fondation'- le 17 March 1987. Available at https://www.ina.fr/ina-eclaire-actu/video/i06321444/gilles-deleuze-a-la-femis. Accessed 13 September 2021. Refer also to Eugénie Cottet, *Le palais de Tokyo, 1984–2002: l'échec du Palais de l'Image*. Histoire. 2019. Dumas-02464323. Archives nationales: 1989 0353/7. Article de presse du 03/04/1987 dans *Le Film français* (n° 2135) par P.R.: 'Les Chantiers du palais de Tokyo'. The event is also noted in the Archives Nationale, 'Intellectuels, discours enregistrés, allocutions' 1908–2014, Cote: 3AV/141-3AV/147, 5AV/56-5AV/64, 6AV/1-6AV/1, 8AV/816-8AV/817. In Eleanor Kaufman's book, *Deleuze & Guattari: New Mappings in Politics, Philosophy, and Culture*, (Minneapolis: University of Minnesota Press, 1998), the talk would be titled 'Having an Idea in Cinema' and dated 17 May 1987, and the section of the talk where Deleuze cautions about the dreams of others would be removed (and not marked with an ellipsis). The entirety has been transcribed in Gilles Deleuze, 'What Is the Creative Act?' in David Lapoujade ed., *Two Regimes of Madness, Texts and Interviews 1975–1995* (2006), 312–24. Translated by Ames Hodges and Mike Taormina. Page references are to this text.
2 La Fémis takes its name from Fondation Européenne pour les Métiers de l'Image et du Son. La Fémis is the École Nationale Supérieure des Métiers de l'Image et du Son, formerly known as the Institut des hautes études cinématographiques, IDHEC. It was inaugurated on 18 November 1986.
3 Deleuze, 'What Is the Creative Act?', 312.
4 Deleuze, 'What Is the Creative Act?', 312.
5 Deleuze, 'What Is the Creative Act?', 316.
6 Deleuze, 'What Is the Creative Act?', 317.
7 Deleuze, 'What Is the Creative Act?', 318.
8 'la Finlande n'eut qu'à construire, rien à détruir' in 'Finlande', *Architecture d'Aujourd'hui*, (10 October 1937): 66–8. Refer also to Fabienne Chevallier, 'Finland through French Eyes: Alvar Aalto's Pavilion at the Paris International Exhibition of 1937', *Studies in the Decorative Arts*, (7: 1, Fall–Winter, 1999–2000): 65–105. Translated by Richard Wittman.
9 Jean-Marc Larbordière, *L'architecture des années 30 à Paris*, (Paris: Éditions Massin, 2009).

10 '1937 ne doit tout de même pas assurer le triomphe de la médiocrité.' André Bloc, 'En vue de l'exposition de 1937. Le concours des musées d'art moderne', *L'Architecture d'Aujourd'hui*, (10, décembre 1934–janvier 1935): 12–13.
11 Andrew Ayers, *The Architecture of Paris: An Architectural Guide*, (Fellbach: Edition Axel Menges, 2004), 238.
12 See, for example, Pierre Vago, 'Le concours des musées d'art moderne et l'exposition internationale de 1937', *L'Architecture d'Aujourd'hui*, (10, décembre 1934–janvier 1935): i–iv. David Cascaro and Claire Staebler, 'Interview with Lacaton & Vassal: Comme Un Paysage Sans Limite / Like an Endless Landscape', *Palais 15*, (Numéro spécial histoire du Palais de Tokyo, 2012): 97–109.
13 Deleuze, 'What Is the Creative Act?', 318.
14 Simone Brott, 'The Le Corbusier Scandal, or, Was Le Corbusier a Fascist?', *Fascism*, (6: 2, 2017): 196–227.
15 Gilles Deleuze and Félix Guattari, *A Thousand Plateaus*, (Minneapolis: University of Minnesota Press, 1987), 399–507. Translation of *Mille plateaux*, volume 2 of *Capitalisme et schizophrénie*, (Paris: Les Editions de Minuit, 1980) by Brian Massumi.
16 Deleuze refers to the history of philosophy as 'philosophy's own version of the Oedipus complex'. Gilles Deleuze, *Negotiations. 1972–1990*, (New York: Columbia University Press, 1995), 5. Translated by Martin Joughin.
17 Gilles Deleuze, *Difference and Repetition*, (New York: Columbia University Press, 1994), 146. Translation of *Différence et repetition*, (Paris: Presse Universitaires de France, 1968), by Paul Patton.
18 Deleuze, 'What Is the Creative Act?', 313.
19 Deleuze, 'What Is the Creative Act?', 314.
20 Gilles Deleuze and Claire Parnet, *Dialogues II*, (New York: Columbia University Press, 1987), vii. Translation of *Dialogues*, (Paris: Flammarion, 1977), by Hugh Tomlinson and Barbara Habberjam. Refer also to Gilles Deleuze, *Nietzsche and Philosophy*, (London: Althone Press, 1983), 88. Translation of *Nietzsche et la philosophie*, (Paris: PUF, 1962) by Hugh Tomlinson. A similar sentiment is expressed in *What Is Philosophy?*: 'When immanence is no longer immanent to something other than itself it is possible to speak of a plane of immanence. Such a plane is, perhaps, a radical empiricism.' Gilles Deleuze and Félix Guattari, *What Is Philosophy?*, (New York and Chichester: Columbia University Press, 1994), 47. Translation of *Qu'est-ce que la philosophie?*, (Paris: Les Editions de Minuit, 1991), by Hugh Tomlinson and Graham Burchell.
21 Deleuze and Félix Guattari, *What Is Philosophy?*, 38.
22 David Lapoujade, 'From Transcendental Empiricism to Worker Nomadism: William James', *Pli 9*, (2000): 194. Translated by Alberto Toscano.
23 William James, 'Preface', in *The Meaning of Truth*, (New York: Longman Green and Co., 1911), xvii.
24 Friedrich Engels, 'Herr Eugen Dühring's Revolution in Science', in *Karl Mark Frederick Engels Collected Works*, (New York: International Publishers, 1976), vol. 25, 125.
25 Lapoujade, 'From Transcendental Empiricism to Worker Nomadism', 194.
26 Deleuze, 'What Is the Creative Act?', 312.
27 Deleuze, *Difference and Repetition*, 139.
28 Andrew Ayers, 'Palais de Tokyo rejuvenated in Paris by Lacaton & Vassal', in *The Architectural Review*, 28 May 2012. Available at https://www.architectural-review.com/today/palais-de-tokyo-rejuvenated-in-paris-by-lacaton-vassal. Accessed 13 September 2020.

29 Ayers, 'Palais de Tokyo rejuvenated in Paris by Lacaton & Vassal'.
30 Anne Lacaton and Jean-Philippe Vassal in conversation with Mathieu Wellner, 'Surplus', in Muck Petzet and Florian Hellmeyer eds., *Reduce, Reuse, Recycle*, catalogue for the German Pavilion, 13th International Architecture Exhibition, (La Biennale di Venezia, 2012), 13. Refer also Maria José Marcos and Gonzalo Herrero Delicado, 'Trebamo li doista (nove) gradevine u svojim gradovima? / Do we really need (new) buildings in our cities?', *Oris* (75, 2012), 116.
31 Ayers, 'Palais de Tokyo Rejuvenated in Paris by Lacaton & Vassal'.
32 Edwin Heathcote, 'Palace of Darkness', in *Apollo*, (176: 601, September 2012): 42.
33 Jean-Phillippe Vassal, cited in Gonzalo Herrero Delicado and Maria José Marcos, 'Demolizioni espositive: Exhibition after Demolition', *Domus*, (959, June 2012): 48.
34 Lacaton and Vassal, 'Surplus', 14.
35 Lacaton and Vassal cited in Andrew Ayers, 'Fun Palace', *The Architectural Review AR*, (1384, June 2012): 51.
36 Jean-Phillippe Vassal, cited in Coen de Vries & Thais Cshunderlick, *Palais de Tokyo: Interiors, Buildings, Cities – Fundamentals*, TU Delft (1 July 2019), 9. Available at https://issuu.com/thais9324/docs/coen_thais_-_palais_de_tokyo__booklet_. Accessed 13 September 2020.
37 Deleuze, *Difference and Repetition*, xx.
38 'Erewhon', in this reading, is 'at once the originary "nowhere" and the displaced, disguised, modified and always re-created "here-and-now"'. Deleuze, *Difference and Repetition*, note 7, 333.
39 Deleuze, *Difference and Repetition*, 285.

Part 3

1 Gilles Deleuze and Félix Guattari, *A Thousand Plateaus*, (Minneapolis: University of Minnesota Press, 1987), 153. Translation of *Mille plateaux*, volume 2 of *Capitalisme et schizophrénie*, (Paris: Les Editions de Minuit, 1980), by Brian Massumi.

Chapter 9

1 Rosalind Krauss, 'Two Moments from the Post-Medium Condition', *October*, (116, Spring, 2006): 59.
2 Le Corbusier, *The Modulor: A Harmonious Measure to the Human Scale Universally Applicable to Architecture and Mechanics*, second edition, (Basel: Birkhäuser, 2004), 55. Translation of *Le modulor* (1954) by Peter de Francia and Anna Bostock. Le Corbusier acknowledges a connection to Renaissance exemplars, listing the work of Durer, Leonardo and Francesco di Giorgio, among others, as precursors. Le Corbusier, *The Modulor*, 5. Refer also to Le Corbusier, *Modulor 2, 1955, (Let the User Speak Next)*, Continuation of 'The Modulor' 1948, (Basel: Birkhäuser, 2004), 296. Translation of *Le modulor 2* (1955) by Peter de Francia and Anna Bostock.
3 Le Corbusier, *The Modulor*, 60–1.
4 Le Corbusier, *Towards a New Architecture*, (New York: Dover Publications, 1986), 4. Translation of *Vers une architecture*, (Paris: Éditions Crès, Collection de L'Esprit Nouveau, 1923,) by Frederick Etchells.

5   Le Corbusier, *The Modulor*, 34.
6   While working in the United States, Le Corbusier devised a second version of the system, in which the original height of 1.75 meters (approximately 5 feet, 8 inches) became 6 feet. The height seemed to have epic connotations: 'Have you never noticed that in English detective novels, the good-looking men, such as the policemen, are always six feet tall?'. Le Corbusier, *The Modulor*, 56. Refer also to Lance Hosey, 'Hidden Lines: Gender, Race, and the Body in "Graphic Standards"', *Journal of Architectural Education*, (55: 2, November 2001), note 27, 110.
7   Alexander Tzonis and Liane Lefaivre, 'The Mechanical Body versus the Divine Body: The Rise of Modern Design Theory', *JAE*, (29: 1, Humanist Issues in Architecture, September 1975): 4.
8   Le Corbusier, *Modulor 2*, 44.
9   Le Corbusier, *Modulor 2*, 20.
10 Le Corbusier, *Modulor 2*, 20.
11 Maurice Merleau-Ponty, 'The Intertwining-The Chiasm', in *The Visible and the Invisible*, (Evanston: Northwest University Press, 1968). Translation of *Le visible et l'invisible*, (Paris: Gallimard, 1964), by Alphonso Lingis.
12 Jacques Derrida, *Resistances of Psychoanalysis*, (Stanford: Stanford University Press, 1998), 30. Translation by Peggy Kamuf, Pascale-Anne Brault and Michael Naas.
13 Le Corbusier, *Modulor 2*, 52.
14 Gilles Deleuze, 'Desert Islands', in David Laboujade ed., *Desert Islands and Other Texts 1953-1974*, (Paris: Semiotext(e), 2004), 10. Translation of Gilles Deleuze, *L'Îles déserte et autres textes: Textes et entretiens 1953-1974*, (Paris: Minuit, 2002), by Christopher Bush, Charles Stivale, Melissa McMahon, Alexander Hickox and Teal Eich.
15 Gilles Deleuze, *Nietzsche and Philosophy*, (London: Althone Press, 1983), 26-30. Translation of *Nietzsche et la philosophie*, (Paris: PUF, 1962) by Hugh Tomlinson.
16 The term 'double bind' was coined by Gregory Bateson but was core to the work of Nietzsche (and Deleuze's study of Nietzsche).
17 Deleuze, 'Desert Islands', 10.
18 David Laboujade, *Desert Islands and Other Texts 1953-1974*, [editor's note] 11.
19 Rachel Mesch, *Having It All in the Belle Epoque: How French Women's Magazines Invented the Modern Woman*, (Stanford, CA: Stanford University Press, 2017), 205-7.
20 'La ville Le Corbusier', *Le nouveau femina* (20, Bureau de la revue, Décembre 1955).
21 Deleuze, 'Desert Islands', 14.
22 David Laboujade notes that the essay appears on a bibliography sketched by Deleuze in 1989 under the section titled 'Difference and Repetition', Laboujade, *L'Îles déserte et autres textes*, [editor's note] 11.
23 Deleuze, 'Desert Islands', 9.
24 Deleuze, 'Desert Islands', 9.
25 Deleuze, 'Desert Islands', 9.
26 Deleuze, 'Desert Islands', 10.
27 Deleuze, 'Desert Islands', 10.
28 Krauss, 'Two Moments from the Post-Medium Condition', 59.
29 Deleuze, 'Desert Islands', 10.
30 Deleuze, 'Desert Islands', 10.
31 Deleuze, 'Desert Islands', 10.

32 Modulorbeat, 'One Man Sauna', *Arch Daily*. Available at https://www.archdaily.com/513739/one-man-sauna-modulorbeat. Accessed 27 November 2019.
33 Kulurstiftung des Bundes, 'Das Detrout Projekt'. Available at https://www.kulturstiftung-des-bundes.de/de/projekte/buehne_und_bewegung/detail/das_detroit_projekt.html. Accessed 27 November 2020.
34 Modulorbeat, 'im Spannungsfeld von Stadt und Landschaft', Available at https://www.modulorbeat.de/office. Accessed 27 November 2020.
35 Deleuze, 'Desert Islands', 10.
36 Alyn Griffiths, 'Modulorbeat Creates One Man Sauna Inside a Stacked Concrete Tower', *Dezeen* (5 June 2014). Available at https://www.dezeen.com/2014/06/05/modulorbeat-one-man-sauna-stacked-concrete-tower/. Accessed 13 September 2020.
37 Elizabeth Grosz, 'Women, Chora, Dwelling', in Jane Rendell, Barbara Penner, Iain Borden eds., *Gender Space Architecture: An Interdisciplinary Introduction*, (London: Routledge, 2000), 38.
38 Gilles Deleuze, *Foucault*, (Minneapolis, MN, and London: University of Minnesota Press, 1988). Translation of *Foucault* (Paris: Minuit, 1986) by Sean Hand. Foucault's own definition relates to where power relations turn back upon the self: the 'power that one brought to bear on oneself'. Michel Foucault, *The History of Sexuality, Vol. 2: The Use of Pleasure*, (New York: Pantheon, 1990), 80. Translation of *L'usage des plaisirs*, (Paris: Gallimard, 1978) by Robert Hurley.
39 Deleuze, *Foucault*, 10.
40 Refer to Réda Bensmaïa's 'Foreword' in Gilles Deleuze and Félix Guattari, *Kafka: Toward a Minor Literature*, (Minnesota: University of Minnesota Press, 1986), xx. Translation of *Kafka: pour une littérature mineure*, (Paris: Minuit, 1975), by Dana Polan. Refer also to Gilles Deleuze and Claire Parnet, *Dialogues*, (New York: Columbia University Press, 1987), 25. Translation of *Dialogues*, (Paris: Flammarion, 1977), by Hugh Tomlinson and Barbara Habberjam.
41 Deleuze and Parnet, *Dialogues*, 25; and Gilles Deleuze and Félix Guattari, *A Thousand Plateaus*, (Minneapolis: University of Minnesota Press, 1987), 399–400. Translation of *Mille plateaux*, volume 2 of *Capitalisme et schizophrénie*, (Paris: Les Editions de Minuit, 1980), by Brian Massumi.
42 Isabelle Stengers, *Cosmopolitics I*, (Minneapolis: University of Minnesota Press, 2010). Translation of *Cosmopolitiques*, vol. 1, *La guerre des sciences*, (Paris: La Découverte; Les Empêcheurs de penser en rond, 1996), by Robert Bononno.
43 Adrian Forty, *Concrete and Culture: A Material History*, (London: Reaktion Books, 2012), 197.
44 Walter Smerling and Ferdinand Ulrich eds., on behalf of the RuhrKunstMuseen, Public Art Ruhr, *Die Metropole Ruhr und die Kunst im öffentlichen Raum*, (Cologne 2012), 170.
45 Deleuze, 'Desert Islands', 10.
46 The concept is introduced in Gregory Bateson, 'Toward a Theory of Schizophrenia', *Steps to an Ecology of Mind: Collected Essays in Anthropology, Psychiatry, Evolution, and Epistemology*, (New Jersey: Jason Aronson Inc., 1987 [1972]), 205–32. Refer also to Jeffrey A. Bell, *Philosophy at the Edge of Chaos: Gilles Deleuze and the Philosophy of Difference*, (Toronto: University of Toronto Press, 2006), 84–106.
47 Gilles Deleuze and Félix Guattari, *Anti-Oedipus*, (Minneapolis: University of Minnesota Press, 1983), 113–21. Translation of *L'Anti-Oedipe*, (Paris: Les Editions de Minuit, 1972), volume 1 of *Capitalisme et schizophrénie*, by Robert Hurley, Mark Seem and Helen R. Lane.

48 Deleuze and Guattari, *Anti-Oedipus*, 114–15.
49 Deleuze and Guattari, *Anti-Oedipus*, 115.
50 Griffiths, 'Modulorbeat Creates One Man Sauna Inside a Stacked Concrete Tower'.
51 Griffiths, 'Modulorbeat Creates One Man Sauna Inside a Stacked Concrete Tower'.
52 Kulurstiftung des Bundes, 'Das Detroit Projekt'.
53 Cited in Sybul Fuchs, 'The "Detoit Project" in Bochum' (12 December 2013). Available at https://www.wsws.org/en/articles/2013/12/12/boch-d12.html. Accessed 13 September 2020.

Chapter 10

1   Gilles Deleuze and Félix Guattari, *A Thousand Plateaus*, (Minneapolis: University of Minnesota Press, 1987), 213. Translation of *Mille plateaux*, volume 2 of *Capitalisme et schizophrénie*, (Paris: Les Editions de Minuit, 1980), by Brian Massumi.
2   Deleuze and Guattari, *A Thousand Plateaus*, 439.
3   Gilles Deleuze and Félix Guattari, *Anti-Oedipus*, (Minneapolis: University of Minnesota Press, 1983), 247. Translation of *L'Anti-Oedipe*, (Paris: Les Editions de Minuit, 1972), volume 1 of *Capitalisme et schizophrénie*, by Robert Hurley, Mark Seem and Helen R. Lane.
4   Deleuze and Guattari, *A Thousand Plateaus*, 276.
5   Deleuze and Guattari, *A Thousand Plateaus*, 276.
6   Fredric Jameson, *The Political Unconscious: Narrative as a Socially Symbolic Act*, (New York: Cornell University Press, 1981), 10.
7   Mark Roseman, 'National Socialism and the End of Modernity', *The American Historical Review*, (116: 3, June 2011): 688–701. Simone Brott, 'The Le Corbusier Scandal, or, Was Le Corbusier a Fascist?', *Fascism*, (6: 2, December 2017): 196–227.
8   Beatriz Colomina and Mark Wigley, 'Toilet Architecture: An Essay about the Most Psychosexually Charged Room in a Building', *PIN-UP*, (23, Fall Winter 2017/18): 231.
9   Deleuze and Guattari, *Anti-Oedipus*, 88.
10 Deleuze and Guattari, *Anti-Oedipus*, 42.
11 One tooth the architect had was removed as a teenager – coincidentally it was a molar.
12 Deleuze and Guattari, *Anti-Oedipus*, 88, 324 and 326.
13 Deleuze and Guattari, *Anti-Oedipus*, 309.
14 Deleuze and Guattari, *Anti-Oedipus*, 181.
15 Press release, 'Cruising Pavilion 16th Venice Architecture Biennale 24 May–1 July 2018', 2. Available at https://cruisingpavilion.com/. Accessed 13 September 2021. The Cruising Pavilion went on to have two more incarnations: Cruising Pavilion, New York, at *Ludlow 38*, 22 February–7 April 2019; and, Cruising Pavilion, Stockholm, at *ArkDes*, 20 September–10 November 2019.
16 Spazio Punch homepage. Available at https://www.spaziopunch.com/about. Accessed 13 September 2021.
17 I should note, my understanding of the architecture of such spaces has been helpfully informed by Charles Drozynski, 'Folds of Desire', in Drozynski and Diana Beljaars eds., *Civic Spaces and Desire*, (London and New York: Routledge, 2020): 132–45; and Laurence Kimmel, 'Stygian Dark: What the Presence and Architecture of Sex Clubs

Reveal about the Politics of Public and Private Space in a City', in Drozynski and Beljaars eds., *Civic Spaces and Desire,* 121–31.

18 Cited in Alison Hugill, 'Cruising for Sex in the Garden of Eden: Architecture and Desire in Venice', *Momus – A Return to Art Criticism,* (23 June 2018). Available at https://momus.ca/cruising-for-sex-in-the-garden-of-eden-architecture-and-desire-in-venice/. Accessed 27 November 2021.

19 Michel Foucault, *The History of Sexuality,* vol. I: An Introduction, (New York: Pantheon Books, 1978), 12. Translation of *Histoire de la sexualité,* (Paris: Editions Gallimard, 1976), by Robert Hurley.

20 Cruising Pavilion 16th Venice Architecture Biennale 24 May–1 July 2018, press release 2.

21 This construct is also Foucauldian in the sense that *resistance* to the hegemonic pressures of the social field and the metropolis are framed as the only possibilities for liberation.

22 This story also highlights the complexity of the macropolitical as a politics based on predefined, preconfigured, structures, axioms and logics. The press release operates in the political mode of stamping child. It's a type of Freudian configuring that establishes a group as an 'illegitimate child' whilst continuing to pay too much respect to a fatherly figure: a 'proper metropolis' and its 'structuring disciplinary features'. The best one can do in such a political construct is to *resist.* To shout: 'I am not x … at least not in some regards!' But such shouts don't tend to excite the masses. And the architecture, the 'public sites' and 'dedicated establishments' of cruising come to be spaces of *resistance* that have also been already pre-figured into the same metropolis and its social fabric. Foucault's notion of 'other spaces' might have heralded a new fascination for those spaces that operate as 'counter-sites' to social habit, but such spaces remain spaces of resistance only – often sanctioned, minor protests, that do little other than reinforce the dominance of the social field to which they are bound. Resistance comes to be like neighbours sharing sugar whilst musing on the base structure of Marx or quietly masturbating under the quilt of Freud's superego.

23 Deleuze and Guattari, *Anti-Oedipus,* 276.

24 Deleuze and Guattari, *Anti-Oedipus,* 277.

25 Manifesto by Yvonne Farrell and Shelley McNamara, Freespace, *La Bienale di Venezia.* Cited at https://www.labiennale.org/en/architecture/2018/introduction-yvonne-farrell-and-shelley-mcnamara. Accessed 13 November 2021.

26 Cruising Pavilion Manifesto, in 'Press Release', Cruising Pavilion 16th Venice Architecture Biennale 24 May–1 July 2018. Press release at https://cruisingpavilion.com/. Accessed 13 November 2021.

27 Michel Foucault, 'Preface', *Anti-Oedipus,* xiii.

28 Herman Melville, *Bartleby, the Scrivener: A Story of Wall Street,* (New York: Melville House, 2011).

29 Deleuze and Guattari, *Anti-Oedipus,* 277.

30 Jameson, *The Political Unconscious,* 38.

31 Deleuze and Guattari, *Anti-Oedipus,* 286–7.

32 Deleuze and Guattari, *Anti-Oedipus,* 180–1.

33 Gilles Deleuze, *Difference and Repetition,* (New York: Columbia University Press, 1994), 195. Translation of *Différence et repetition,* (Paris: Presse Universitaires de France, 1968), by Paul Patton. Gilles Deleuze, *The Logic of Sense,* Constantin V. Boundas ed., (New York: Columbia University Press, 1990), 38. Translation of

Logique du sens, (Paris: Les Editions de Minuit, 1969), by Mark Lester and Charles Stivale. Refer also to Deleuze and Guattari, *Anti-Oedipus*, 142.
34 Deleuze and Guattari, *A Thousand Plateaus*, 4 and 256.
35 Sigmund Freud, 'Two Case Histories ("Little Hans" and the "Rat Man"), Analysis of a Phobia in a Five-Year-Old Boy (1909)', *Standard Edition of the Complete Psychological Works of Sigmund Freud*, vol. 10, (London: The Hogarth Press, 1955).
36 Deleuze and Guattari, *Anti-Oedipus*, 277.

Chapter 11

1 The concept of the war machine is developed extensively in *A Thousand Plateaus* and particularly in the twelfth plateau: '1227: Treatise on Nomadology – The War Machine'. Gilles Deleuze and Félix Guattari, *A Thousand Plateaus*, (Minneapolis: University of Minnesota Press, 1987), 351–423. Translation of *Mille plateaux*, volume 2 of *Capitalisme et schizophrénie*, (Paris: Les Editions de Minuit, 1980), by Brian Massumi.
2 Deleuze and Guattari, *A Thousand Plateaus*, 395. Reference is to J.F.C. Fuller, *Armament and History*, (New York: Charles Scribner's Sons, 1945), 5.
3 Legal Action Worldwide (LAW), '4 August 2020 Beirut Port Explosion: The Legal System Continues to Fail Victims a Year Later', Report published 3 August 2021. Available at https://www.legalactionworldwide.org/accountability-rule-of-law/new-report-4-august-beirut-port-explosion-the-lebanese-legal-system-continues-to-fail-victims-one-year-on/. Accessed 12 November 2021.
4 Deleuze and Guattari, *A Thousand Plateaus*, 395.
5 Deleuze and Guattari, *A Thousand Plateaus*, 395.
6 Deleuze and Guattari would suggest of such relations 'the same *machinic phylum* traverses both'. Deleuze and Guattari, *A Thousand Plateaus*, 395.
7 Deleuze and Guattari, *A Thousand Plateaus*, 405–9.
8 Gareth Collett, cited in Forensic Architecture and Mada Masr, 'Beirut Port Explosion' investigation. Available at https://forensic-architecture.org/investigation/beirut-port-explosion. Accessed at 27 November 2021. Collett is an explosives expert.
9 Gilles Deleuze and Félix Guattari, *Anti-Oedipus*, (Minneapolis: University of Minnesota Press, 1983), 170. Translation of *L'Anti-Oedipe*, volume 1 of *Capitalisme et schizophrénie*, (Paris: Les Editions de Minuit, 1972), by Robert Hurley, Mark Seem and Helen R. Lane.
10 Deleuze and Guattari, *Anti-Oedipus*, 97.
11 Gilles Deleuze, *Negotiations; 1972–1990*, (New York: Columbia University Press, 1995), 170. Translation of *Pourparlers: 1972–1990*, (Paris: Minuit, 1990), by Martin Joughin.
12 Brian Massumi, 'Translator's Introduction', *A Thousand Plateaus*, xi. Deleuze and Guattari endow politics as their ultimate metaphysic; '[f]or politics precedes being'. Deleuze and Guattari, *A Thousand Plateaus*, 203. For a thorough introduction to the political philosophy of Deleuze and Guattari refer to Paul Patton, *Deleuze and the Political*, (London and New York: Routledge, 2000).
13 Jean-Jacques Leclercle, *Philosophy through the Looking Glass*, (La Salle, IL: Open Court, 1985), 190–1.

14 Deleuze and Guattari, *A Thousand Plateaus*, 422. Refer also to Daniel W. Smith, 'Deleuze and the Liberal Tradition: Normativity, Freedom and Judgement', *Economy and Society*, (32: 2, May 2003): 299–321.
15 Deleuze and Guattari, *A Thousand Plateaus*, 360. My italicization.
16 Deleuze and Guattari, *A Thousand Plateaus*, 354.
17 Deleuze and Guattari, *Anti-Oedipus*, 112.
18 Deleuze and Guattari, '1440: The Smooth and the Straited', *A Thousand Plateaus*, 474–500.
19 Laleh Khalili describes ports as 'the clearest distillation of how global capitalism operates today'. Laleh Khalili, *Sinews of War and Trade: Shipping and Capitalism in the Arabian Peninsula*, (New York: Verso, 2020), 3.
20 The full sentence reads, 'The despot is the paranoiac: there is no longer any reason to forego such a statement, once one has freed oneself from the characteristic familialism of the concept of paranoia in psychoanalysis and psychiatry, and provided one sees in paranoia a type of investment of a social formation.' Deleuze and Guattari, *Anti-Oedipus*, 193.
21 Deleuze and Guattari, *Anti-Oedipus*, 193.
22 I make this point in difference to Eugène Holland. Holland asserts; 'The binary opposition privileging schizophrenia over paranoia in *Anti-Oedipus* no longer holds in *A Thousand Plateaus*.' Eugène W. Holland, 'Deterritorializing "Deterritorialization": From Anti-Oedipus to a Thousand Plateaus', *SubStance,* (20: 3, Iss. 66, 1991): 55–65.
23 Deleuze and Guattari, *A Thousand Plateaus*, 427.
24 Deleuze and Guattari, *A Thousand Plateaus*, 427.
25 Deleuze and Guattari, *A Thousand Plateaus*, 364. They also refer to 'the construction of bridges in the eighteenth and nineteenth centuries' but do not elaborate further. Deleuze and Guattari, *A Thousand Plateaus*, 364.
26 The term 'phylum' is one that Deleuze and Guattari borrow from biology where it denotes a specious category ('below' kingdom). The notion that Deleuze and Guattari often refer to is that of a 'machinic phylum', that is to suggest in addition to biological lineages there is a connection between organics and non-organics with comparable self-organizing processes. Deleuze and Guattari, *A Thousand Plateaus*, 422–3.
27 Deleuze and Guattari, *A Thousand Plateaus*, 381.
28 Patton, *Deleuze and the Political*, 110.
29 Deleuze and Guattari, *A Thousand Plateaus*, 360.
30 Deleuze and Guattari, *A Thousand Plateaus*, 354.
31 Deleuze and Guattari, *A Thousand Plateaus*, 352.
32 Paul Virilio, *Speed and Politics*, (New York: Semiotext(e), 2006), 39. Translation of *Vitesse et Politique*, (Paris: Édition Galilée, 1977), by Marc Polizzotti.
33 Or as Deleuze notes in his book on Foucault: 'The outside is not a fixed limit but a moving matter animated by peristaltic movements, folds and foldings that together make up an inside: they are not something other than the outside, but precisely the inside of the outside.' Gilles Deleuze, *Foucault*, (Minneapolis, MN, and London: University of Minnesota Press, 1988), 96–7. Translation of *Foucault* (Paris: Minuit, 1986), by Sean Hand.
34 Deleuze and Guattari, *A Thousand Plateaus*, 353.
35 Deleuze and Guattari, *A Thousand Plateaus*, 360.
36 Deleuze and Guattari, *A Thousand Plateaus*, 354. My italicization.
37 Deleuze and Guattari, *A Thousand Plateaus*, 293.

38 Cape Town is colloquially named the 'Mother City' and it claims to be the first metropolis in Africa. The word 'metropolis' is derived from the Greek *metros* meaning mother and *polis* meaning city.
39 Zeitz MOCAA, 'Zeitz MOCAA Vision'. Available at https://zeitzmocaa.museum/wp-content/uploads/2020/03/ZM-Vision.pdf https://zeitzmocaa.museum/about-us/. Accessed 27 November 2021.
40 'Our mission,' explains Zeitz MOCAA CEO Mark Coetzee, 'is securing seminal artifacts from the African continent and making sure they stay on the African continent. As an institution, it's important for us to empower not only the voices here but the youth, so they can see the art and voices coming out of their community and develop a sense of pride in the art of their country.' Mark Coetzee, cited in Hadley Keller, 'Thomas Heatherwick Gives *AD* a Tour of the Zeitz MOCAA', 15 September 2017. Available at https://www.architecturaldigest.com/story/thomas-heatherwick-cape-town-zeitz-mocaa-south-africa. Accessed 27 November 2021.
41 Roslyn Sulcas, 'A Provocative Museum Places African Art on the Global Stage', *The New York Times,* 27 October 2017. Available at https://www.nytimes.com/2017/10/27/arts/design/zeitz-museum-contemporary-art-cape-town.html. Accessed 13 September 2021.
42 'Heatherwick Studio's Historic Grain Silo Complex Set to Open in September in Cape Town', *South Africa Architecture News,* 20 July 2017. Available at https://worldarchitecture.org/articles/cvfhc/heatherwick_studio_s_historic_grain_silo_complex_set_to_open_in_september_in_cape_town.html. Accessed 13 September 2021.
43 Deleuze and Guattari, *A Thousand Plateaus*, 360.
44 Deleuze and Guattari, *A Thousand Plateaus*, note 29, 554–5.
45 Anne Querrien, *Devenir fonctionnaire ou le travail d'Etat,* (Paris: CERFI), 26–7.
46 Johnny Tucker, 'We Wanted It to Feel Like a Carved Thing': Zeitz MOCAA by Heatherwick Studio', *Desingcurial,* 27 November 2017. Available at https://www.designcurial.com/news/zeitz-mocaa-by-heatherwick-studio-5984484/. Accessed 27 November 2021.
47 Arup was the engineer on the project.
48 Mat Cash cited in Keller, 'Thomas Heatherwick Gives *AD* a Tour of the Zeitz MOCAA'.
49 Thomas Heatherwick cited in Amy Frearson, 'Thomas Heatherwick: 'There was a real worry about whether we could get people to come inside', *Dezeen* (22 September 2017). Available at https://www.dezeen.com/2017/09/22/thomas-heatherwick-interview-zeitz-mocaa-art-museum-cape-town/. Accessed 13 September 2021.
50 Mat Cash, cited in Tucker, 'We Wanted It to Feel Like a Carved Thing'.
51 Cash, 'We Wanted It to Feel Like a Carved Thing'.
52 Keller, 'Thomas Heatherwick Gives *AD* a Tour of the Zeitz MOCAA'.
53 Zeitz MOCAA, 'An Icon Opens Its Doors: In Review: First Year of Operation September 2017–August 2018', Annual Report, 8.
54 Deleuze and Guattari, *A Thousand Plateaus*, 364.
55 Thomas Heatherwick cited in Keller, 'Thomas Heatherwick Gives *AD* a Tour of the Zeitz MOCAA'.
56 Deleuze and Guattari, *A Thousand Plateaus*, 367.
57 Heatherwick cited in Frearson, 'Thomas Heatherwick: "There was a real worry about whether we could get people to come inside"'.
58 Deleuze and Guattari, *A Thousand Plateaus*, 400.

Chapter 12

1. Paul B. Peciado, 'Journey to Lesbos', in *An Apartment on Uranus: Chronicles of the Crossing*, (New York: Semiotext(e), 2020), 178. Translation of *Un appartement sur Uranus,* (Paris: Éditions Grasset, 2019), by Charlotte Mandell.
2. Winston Churchill, cited in Adrian Gilbert Scott, 'Rebuilding the House of Commons', a lecture before the Town and Country Planning Association (London), 24 November 1943. Published in *Building and Engineering* (11/24, 24 November 1945): 67.
3. Winston Churchill, 'Speech on Rebuilding the House of Commons', speech to the meeting in the House of Lords, in Hansard, vol. 393 (C Deb, 28 October 1943), §403.
4. Though there were 646 members at the time, the proposal was for 427 seats.
5. Preciado, 'Journey to Lesbos', 178.
6. Preciado, 'Journey to Lesbos', 179.
7. Churchill cited in Scott, 'Rebuilding the House of Commons', 67. Refer also to Churchill, 'Speech on Rebuilding the House of Commons', §405; wherein Churchill notes, 'The semi-circular assembly, which appeals to political theorists, enables every individual or every group to move round the centre, adopting various shades of pink according as the weather changes.'
8. Preciado, 'Journey to Lesbos', 178.
9. Preciado, 'Journey to Lesbos', 179.
10. Preciado, 'Journey to Lesbos', 178.
11. Preciado, 'Journey to Lesbos', 180.
12. Preciado, 'Journey to Lesbos', 180.
13. Churchill, 'Speech on Rebuilding the House of Commons', §405.
14. Preciado, 'Journey to Lesbos', 179–80.
15. Félix Guattari, *Chaosmosis: An Ethico-aesthetic Paradigm*, (Bloomington: Indiana University Press, 1995), 4. Translation of *Chaosmose,* (Paris: Editions Galilée, 1992), by Paul Bains and Julian Pefanis. The relation between the two is transversal, 'since social symbolism can become a sexual material, and sexuality, a ritual of social aggregation', as Gilles Deleuze and Guattari had noted 20 years earlier. Gilles Deleuze and Félix Guattari, *Anti-Oedipus*, (Minneapolis: University of Minnesota Press, 1983), 179. Translation of *L'Anti-Oedipe*, volume 1 of *Capitalisme et schizophrénie*, (Paris: Les Editions de Minuit, 1972), by Robert Hurley, Mark Seem and Helen R. Lane.
16. Guattari, *Chaosmosis*, 92.
17. Guattari, *Chaosmosis*, 1.
18. Guattari, *Chaosmosis*, 9. My italicization.
19. Guattari, *Chaosmosis*, 63, 95 and 82.
20. Guattari, *Chaosmosis*, 3.
21. Gisela Pankow, *L'homme et son espace vécu: Abord analytique de la parile poétique*, (Paris: Aubier, 1986).
22. Gisela Pankow, *L'Homme et sa psychose*, (Paris: Aubier Montaigne, 1983), 269. My translation.
23. Guattari, *Chaosmosis*, 25.
24. Guattari, *Chaosmosis*, 14.
25. Guattari, *Chaosmosis*, 14.
26. Guattari, *Chaosmosis*,13.

27 Guattari, *Chaosmosis*, 14.
28 Guattari, *Chaosmosis*, 14.
29 Guattari, *Chaosmosis*, 9.
30 Pankow, *L'homme et son espace vécu*, 131–3.
31 Guattari, *Chaosmosis*, 16.
32 Gilles Deleuze and Félix Guattari, *What Is Philosophy?*, (New York and Chichester: Columbia University Press, 1994), 199. Translation of *Qu'est-ce que la philosophie?*, (Paris: Les Editions de Minuit, 1991), by Hugh Tomlinson and Graham Burchell.
33 Guattari, *Chaosmosis*, 6.
34 Guattari, *Chaosmosis*, 7.
35 Deleuze and Félix Guattari, *Anti-Oedipus*, 6.
36 Gilles Deleuze and Félix Guattari, *A Thousand Plateaus*, (Minneapolis: University of Minnesota Press, 1987), 5. Translation of *Mille plateaux,* volume 2 of *Capitalisme et schizophrénie*, (Paris: Les Editions de Minuit, 1980), by Brian Massumi.
37 Guattari, *Chaosmosis*, 7.
38 Guattari, *Chaosmosis*, 9.
39 Guattari, *Chaosmosis*, 29.
40 Gilles Deleuze, *Essays Critical and Clinical*, (Minneapolis: University of Minnesota Press, 1997), 4. Translation of *Critique et Clinique*, (Paris: Les Éditions de Minuit, 1993) by Daniel W. Smith and Michael A. Greco.
41 Guattari, *Chaosmosis*, 41.
42 Guattari, *Chaosmosis*, 26.
43 Guattari, *Chaosmosis*, 91.
44 Eric Alliez in Alliez and Brian Massumi, 'Performing the Ethico-aesthetic Paradigm', *Performance Research,* (19: 3, 2014): 15.
45 Guattari, *Chaosmosis*, 26.
46 Guattari, *Chaosmosis*, 9.
47 Guattari, *Chaosmosis*, 91.
48 When Deleuze and Guattari turn to the transversality of communications, they refer to the 'aberrant communication' between sexes, they note, the sexes communicate 'with each other in a transverse mode where each subject possesses both of them, but with the two of them partitioned off, and where each subject communicates with one sex or the other in another subject'. Deleuze and Guattari, *Anti-Oedipus*, 60. Refer also to 43 and 88.
49 Jury citation, The Pritzker Architecture Prize (2021). Available at https://www.pritzkerprize.com/laureates/anne-lacaton-and-jean-philippe-vassal. Accessed 25 March 2022.
50 Pulitzer Prize citation (2021) for 'a distinguished example of reporting on international affairs, using any available journalistic tool'. Available at https://www.pulitzer.org/winners/megha-rajagopalan-alison-killing-and-christo-buschek-buzzfeed-news. Accessed 25 March 2022.
51 Megha Rajagopalan, Alison Killing and Christo Buschek of *BuzzFeed News* produced the following articles: 'China Secretly Built a Vast New Infrastructure to Imprison Muslims', 26 August 2020; 'A Uighur Woman Who Was at Risk of Being Forcibly Sent Back to China and Detained Has Arrived Safely in the US', 25 September 2020; 'What They Saw: Ex-Prisoners Detail the Horrors of China's Detention Camps', 26 August 2020; 'Blanked-Out Spots on China's Maps Helped Us Uncover Xinjiang's Camps', 26 August 2020; 'Inside a Xinjiang Detention Camp', 2 December 2020, and 'We Found the Factories Inside China's Mass Internment Camps', 27 December 2020.

52 Rajagopalan, Killing and Buschek, 'China Secretly Built a Vast New Infrastructure to Imprison Muslims'. Available at https://www.buzzfeednews.com/article/meghara/china-new-internment-camps-xinjiang-uighurs-muslims. Accessed 12 June 2021.
53 Rajagopalan, Killing and Buschek, 'China Secretly Built a Vast New Infrastructure to Imprison Muslims'.
54 Rajagopalan, Killing and Buschek, 'China Secretly Built a Vast New Infrastructure to Imprison Muslims'.
55 Rajagopalan, Killing and Buschek, 'China Secretly Built a Vast New Infrastructure to Imprison Muslims'.
56 Hagit Keysar, 'A Spatial Testimony: The Politics of Do-It-Yourself Aerial Photography in East Jerusalem', *Environment and Planning D: Society and Space*, (37: 3, 28 September 2018): 523–41.
57 Guattari, *Chaosmosis*, 91.
58 A 'people yet to come' as Deleuze and Guattari say. Deleuze and Guattari, *A Thousand Plateaus*, 378.
59 Félix Guattari, *Schizoanalytic Cartographies*, (London: Bloomsbury, 2013), 237. Translation of *Cartographies Schizoanalytiques*, (Paris: Éditions Galilée, 1989), by Andrew Goffey.

Part 4

1 Jennifer Bloomer, *Architecture and the Text: The (S)crypts of Joyce and Piranesi*, (New Haven: Yale University Press, 1993). Refer also to John Paul Ricco, 'Jacking Off: A Minor Architecture', *Steam*, (1: 4, Winter 1994): 236–42.
2 Manfredo Tafuri, *Theories and History of Architecture*, (London: Granada Publishing, 1980), 82. Translation of *Teorie e storia dell'architettura*, (Rome and Bari: Laterza, 1968), by Georgio Verrecchia.

Chapter 13

1 Walter Morgenthaler, *Ein Geisteskranker als Künstler*, (Bern and Leipzig: E. Bircher, 1921).
2 Gilles Deleuze and Félix Guattari, *Anti-Oedipus*, (Minneapolis: University of Minnesota Press, 1983), 17–18. Translation of *L'Anti-Oedipe*, volume 1 of *Capitalisme et schizophrénie*, (Paris: Les Editions de Minuit, 1972), by Robert Hurley, Mark Seem and Helen R. Lane.
3 Hubert Damisch, *Fenêtre jaune cadmium, ou les dessous de la peinture*, (Paris: Seuil, 1984), 99–120. In *What Is Philosophy?* Deleuze and Guattari refer to the 'thickness' (*épaisseur*) that Damisch identifies, suggesting that such thickness is 'at the level of the architectural plane when Scarpa, for example, suppresses the movement of projection and the mechanisms of perspective so as to inscribe volumes in the thickness of the plane itself'. Gilles Deleuze and Félix Guattari, *What Is Philosophy?*, (New York and Chichester: Columbia University Press, 1994), 195. Translation of *Qu'est-ce que la philosophie?*, (Paris: Les Editions de Minuit, 1991), by Hugh Tomlinson and Graham Burchell. Damisch, *Fenêtre jaune cadmium*, 80.
4 Damisch, *Fenêtre jaune cadmium*, 80.

5   Georges Seurat, cited in Deleuze and Guattari, *What Is Philosophy?*, 194.
6   Joachim Gasquet, *Cézanne: A Memoir with Conversations*, (London: Thames and Hudson, 1991), 154. Translation by Christopher Pemberton.
7   Deleuze and Guattari, *Anti-Oedipus*, 300.
8   Marx demarcated the 'natural form' and the 'value form' of a commodity as elements in and of themselves (natural) and elements in the context of exterior systems (value). Karl Marx, *Capital: A Critique of Political Economy*, vol. 1, (Harmondsworth: Penguin, 1976), 138–9. Translation of *Das Kapital: Kritik der politischen Oekonomie* (Hamburg: Verlag von Otto Meissner, 1867), by Ben Fowkes.
9   Marx, *Capital*, 163.
10 Marx, *Capital*, 165.
11 In this case to demonstrate that 'all sexuality is a matter of economy'. Deleuze and Guattari, *Anti-Oedipus*, 12.
12 Deleuze and Guattari, *Anti-Oedipus*, 183 and 326.
13 Deleuze and Guattari, *Anti-Oedipus*, 33.
14 Deleuze and Guattari, *Anti-Oedipus*, 5.
15 Deleuze and Guattari, *Anti-Oedipus*, 7.
16 Deleuze and Guattari, *Anti-Oedipus*, 12.
17 Deleuze and Guattari, *Anti-Oedipus*, 42.
18 Deleuze and Guattari, *Anti-Oedipus*, 17.
19 Deleuze and Guattari, *Anti-Oedipus*, 17.
20 Deleuze and Guattari, *Anti-Oedipus*, 4.
21 Pixies, *Doolittle*, (London, 4AD, released 17 April 1989).
22 Vaughan Oliver cited in Daniel E. Slotnik, 'Vaughan Oliver, 62, Dies; His Designs Gave Indie Rock "Physical Dimension"', *New York Times*, 3 January 2020.
23 J.D. Corey, *Making PMT Halftone Prints*, (May 1977), 6. A report prepared for the United States Energy Research and Development Administration under contract number EY-76-C-04-0613 USERDA.
24 Simon Larbalestier, 'Cover Story Interview – the Pixies – *Doolittle* – with photography by Simon Larbalestier', *Rockpop Gallery*, (30 April 2009). Larbalestier took the base photograph of the monkey, halo and the numerals.
25 Neil Spiller, *Maverick Deviations: Architectural Works (1986–1998)*, (New York: Wiley, 1999).
26 Neil Spiller, 'Drawing as Communicating Vessels: An Apologia (or Not)', in *Drawing Futures – Speculations in Contemporary Drawing for Art and Architecture*, (London: UCL Press, 2016), 37.
27 Neil Spiller, 'The Geomorphology of Cyborgian Geography', in Simone Ferracina ed., *Organs Everywhere (OE)*, (no. 2, 2011): 16.
28 Neil Spiller, personal correspondence, 17 September 2021.
29 Spiller had noted of the Longhouse below this garden that 'desire and love provide the engines that power this maelstrom of objects and vectors'. Neil Spiller, 'Feverish Delirium: Surrealism, Deconstruction and Numinous Presences', *AD*, (89: 4, 2019): 89.
30 Neil Spiller, 'Ethics, Architecture and Little Soft Machinery', *AD*, (78: 6, 2008): 96.
31 Spiller, 'Feverish Delirium', 89. Spiller had noted of the Longhouse below this garden that 'desire and love provide the engines that power this maelstrom of objects and vectors'. Neil Spiller 'Feverish Delirium: Surrealism, Deconstruction and Numinous Presences', *AD*, (89: 4, 2019): 89.
32 Spiller, 'The Geomorphology of Cyborgian Geography', 9.

33 Deleuze and Guattari, *Anti-Oedipus*, 13.
34 Hubert Damisch, preface to Jean Dubuffet, *Prospectus et taus écrits suivants*, vol. I, (Paris: Gallimard, 1967), 18–19. Refer also to Hubert Damisch, 'The Inventor of Painting', *Oxford Art Journal*, (33: 3, 2010): 304. Translation of 'L'inventeur de la peinture' (2001) by K. Minturn & E. Trudel.
35 Deleuze and Guattari, *What Is Philosophy?*, 194.
36 Spiller, personal correspondence, 17 September 2021.
37 Spiller, personal correspondence, 17 September 2021.
38 Spiller, 'Landscape Drift', 78.
39 Deleuze and Guattari, *What Is Philosophy?*, 194.

Chapter 14

1 Gilles Deleuze and Félix Guattari, *A Thousand Plateaus*, (Minneapolis: University of Minnesota Press, 1987), 349. Translation of *Mille plateaux,* volume 2 of *Capitalisme et schizophrénie,* (Paris: Les Editions de Minuit, 1980), by Brian Massumi.
2 Friedrich Nietzsche, *The Genealogy of Morals: A Polemic*, vol. 8, (Edinburgh and London: T.N.Foulis, 1913), 93. Translation of *Zur Genealogie der Moral: Eine Streitschriftl,* (Leipzig: Verlag von C.G.Neuman, 1887), by Horace B. Samuel.
3 Deleuze and Guattari, *A Thousand Plateaus,* 20.
4 Gilles Deleuze, *Nietzsche and Philosophy,* (London: Althone Press, 1983), 6. Translation of *Nietzsche et la philosophie,* (Paris: PUF, 1962), by Hugh Tomlinson.
5 Deleuze, *Nietzsche and Philosophy,* 3.
6 Chris L. Smith, 'Bodies without Organs and Cities without Architecture', in Constantin Boundas and Vana Tentokali eds., *Architectural and Urban Reflections after Deleuze and Guattari,* (London and New York: Rowman and Littlefield, 2018), 83–102.
7 Immanuel Kant, *Critique of Judgement,* (Indianapolis: Hackett, 1987), 229–32. Translation of *Kritik der Urteilskraft* (Berlin and Libau: Lagarde and Friederich, 1790), by Werner S. Pluhar. Gilles Deleuze, *Kant's Critical Philosophy: The Doctrine of the Faculties,* (London: The Althone Press, 1984), 53. Translation of *La Philosophic Critique de Kant,* (Paris: Presses Universitaires de France, 1963), by Hugh Tomlinson and Barbara Habberjam.
8 Kant, *Critique of Judgement,* 217 and 222–3.
9 Simondon presents '*physical individuation as a case of the resolution of a metastable system*, starting from a system state like that of supercooling or supersaturation, which governs the genesis of crystals'. Gilbert Simondon, 'The Position of the Problem of Ontogenesis', *Parrhesia,* (7: 1, 2009): 6.
10 Gilles Deleuze, *Cinema 2: The Time-Image,* (Minneapolis: University of Minnesota Press, 2007), chapter 4 'Crystals of Time', 68–97. Translation of *Cinéma 2: L'Image-Temps,* (Paris: Les editions de Minuit, 1985), by Hugh Tomlinson and Robert Galeta. Deleuze's first book dedicated to cinema was Gilles Deleuze, *Cinema 1: The Movement-Image,* (Minneapolis: University of Minnesota Press, 2007). Translation of *Cinéma 2: L'Image-Mouvement,* (Paris: Les editions de Minuit, 1983), by Hugh Tomlinson and Barbara Habberjam.
11 Gilles Deleuze and Félix Guattari, *What Is Philosophy?*, (New York and Chichester: Columbia University Press, 1994), note 1, 225. Translation of *Qu'est-ce que la*

philosophie?, (Paris: Les Editions de Minuit, 1991), by Hugh Tomlinson and Graham Burchell. Reference is to lIya Prigogine and Isabelle Stengers, *Entre le temps et l'éternité*, (Paris: Fayard, 1988), 162–3.

12 Friedrich Nietzsche, 'The Birth of Tragedy', in *Basic Writings of Nietzsche*, (New York: Modern Library, 2000), 127. Translation of *Die Geburt der Tragödie* (1872) by Walter Kaufmann. Nietzsche refers to 'a kind of magic glass by means of which the see straight into one's "being"'. Friedrich Nietzsche, *Human All-Too-Human: A Book for Free Spirits*, (Edinburgh and London: T.N.Foulis, 1910), 166. Translation of *Menschliches, Allzumenschliches: Ein Buch für freie Geister*, (Chemnitz: Schmeitzner, 1878), by Helen Zimmern. In *Human, All-Too-Human* Nietzsche had also spoken of artists and authors as those who might break the capsule, giving their humanity over to the materials with which they work and in giving voice to that which was beyond the human. In a chapter 'Concerning the Soul of Artists and Authors', Nietzsche introduces the idea of the 'inspired unrest' of the Greek temple 'as if his [god's] spirit had suddenly entered a stone and now desired to speak through it'. Nietzsche, *Human All-Too-Human*, 153.

13 Friedrich Nietzsche, *Thus Spoke Zarathustra: A Book for All and None*, (Cambridge: Cambridge University Press, 2006), 58. Translation of *Also sprach Zarathustra: Ein Buch für Alle und Keinen*, (Leipzig: Verlag von E.W. Fritzsch, 1883–1892), by Adrian Del Caro.

14 Deleuze and Guattari, *A Thousand Plateaus*, 46.
15 Deleuze and Guattari, *A Thousand Plateaus*, 95. Refer also to 240.
16 Deleuze and Guattari, *A Thousand Plateaus*, 95.
17 Deleuze and Guattari, *A Thousand Plateaus*, 57.
18 Deleuze and Guattari, *A Thousand Plateaus*, note 26, 549.
19 Deleuze and Guattari, *A Thousand Plateaus*, 40.
20 Deleuze and Guattari, *A Thousand Plateaus*, 345.
21 Deleuze and Guattari, *A Thousand Plateaus*, 323 and 335.
22 Deleuze and Guattari, *A Thousand Plateaus*, 335.
23 Deleuze and Guattari, *A Thousand Plateaus*, 57.
24 Félix Guattari, *Schizoanalytic Cartographies*, (London: Bloomsbury, 2013), 236. Translation of *Cartographies Schizoanalytiques,* (Paris: Éditions Galilée, 1989), by Andrew Goffey.
25 Deleuze and Guattari, *A Thousand Plateaus*, 248.
26 Deleuze and Guattari, *A Thousand Plateaus*, 349.
27 The original phrase was 'au lieu du pur cristal qui capte des forces cosmiques'. Gilles Deleuze and Félix Guattari, *Mille plateaux*, vol. 2 of *Capitalisme et schizophrénie*, (Paris: Les Editions de Minuit, 1980), 431.
28 Bruno Taut, 'Japans Kunst', cited in Esra Akcan, 'Toward a Cosmopolitan Ethics in Architecture: Bruno Taut's Translations out of Germany', *New German Critique*, (99, 33: 3, Fall 2006): 7.
29 José Selgas, 'SelgasCano Believes in Architecture That Is Lightweight, Transparent, Open and Respectful of Nature', *Forbes* (7 July 2019). Available at https://www.forbes.com/sites/yjeanmundelsalle/2019/07/07/selgascano-believes-in-architecture-that-is-lightweight-transparent-open-and-respectful-of-nature/?sh=20a1030f24cd. Accessed 13 September 2020.
30 Nils Ballhausen, *Wo Architekten arbeiten / Where Architects Work*, (Basel: Birkhäuser, 2013), 44–6.
31 SelgasCano, *ElCroquis* (171, SelgasCano, 2014): 5.

32 SelgasCano, *ElCroquis*, 5.
33 Serpentine Galleries, 'The Hungry Pavilion'. Available at https://www.youtube.com/watch?v=Abx6UFt21yQ. Accessed 13 September 2020.
34 Deleuze and Guattari, *A Thousand Plateaus*, 350.
35 Lucia Cano cited in David Cohn, 'SelgasCano's Surreal Auditorium in Western Spain', *Architectural Record* (1 August 2017). Available at https://www.architecturalrecord.com/articles/12870-selgascanos-surreal-auditorium-in-western-spain. Accessed 13 September 2020.
36 SelgasCano's commitment to disappear on behalf of nature is not merely a rhetorical inversion of an oft-repeated aphorism but part of 'an intense search for new outlets for nature using artificial means, [and] applying technologies borrowed from other fields'. SelgasCano, *ElCroquis*, 5.
37 SelgasCano submission to the European Union Prize for Contemporary Architecture, Mies Van Der Rohe Award, 2019. Available at https://miesarch.com/work/3992. Accessed 13 September 2020.
38 George Sands, 'CCCII. To Gustave Flaubert, in Paris Nohant, 12 January 1876', in *The George Sand-Gustave Flaubert Letters*, (Project Gutenberg, 2004). Translated by A.L.McKenzie.
39 Deleuze and Guattari, *A Thousand Plateaus*, 346.
40 Deleuze and Guattari, *A Thousand Plateaus*, 349.

Chapter 15

1 Francis Bacon cited in David Sylvester, *Interviews with Francis Bacon*, (London: Thames and Hudson, 1980), 23.
2 *Vogue* UK, July 1962.
3 Bacon only painted four sitters from life; the remainder were from photographs. He would suggest, 'Even in the case of friends who will come and pose, I've had photographs taken for portraits because I very much prefer working from the photographs than from them […] if I both know them and have photographs of them, I find it easier to work than actually having their presence in the room. […] if I have the presence of the image there, I am not able to drift so freely as I am able to through the photographic image.' Bacon cited in Sylvester, *Interviews with Francis Bacon*, 38.
4 Deakin photographed Henrietta Moreas, George Dyer, Isabel Rawsthorne, Lucian Freud and Muriel Belcher for Bacon.
5 John Deakin cited in Robin Muir, *Under the Influence: John Deakin, Photography and the Lure of Soho*, (London: Art/Books, 2014), 12.
6 John Russell, *Francis Bacon*, (London: Thames and Hudson, 1979), 172.
7 Bacon interviewed by Francis Giacobetti in February 1992, published as 'Francis Giacobetti interviews Francis Bacon: "I Painted to Be Loved"', *The Art Newspaper*, (no. 137, 1 June 2003): 28.
8 Bacon cited in Giacobetti, 'I Painted to Be Loved', 29.
9 Gilles Deleuze, *Francis Bacon: The Logic of Sensation*, (New York: Continuum, 2003), 20. Translation of *Francis Bacon: Logique de la Sensation*, (Paris: Editions de la Différence, 1981), by Daniel W. Smith.
10 Deleuze, *Francis Bacon*, 4.

11 Deleuze, *Francis Bacon*, 4.
12 Deleuze, *Francis Bacon*, 65.
13 Gilles Deleuze and Félix Guattari, *A Thousand Plateaus*, (Minneapolis: University of Minnesota Press, 1987), 188. Translation of *Mille plateaux,* volume 2 of *Capitalisme et schizophrénie,* (Paris: Les Editions de Minuit, 1980), by Brian Massumi.
14 Deleuze and Guattari, *A Thousand Plateaus,* 188.
15 Deleuze, *Francis Bacon*, 119, 136, 138, 143, 149.
16 Deleuze, *Francis Bacon*, 96.
17 Deleuze, *Francis Bacon*, 20-1.
18 Bacon in Sylvester, *Interviews with Francis Bacon*, 13.
19 Aristotle, *De Anima Books I, II and III*, (Oxford: Clarendon, 1993), 414a14–414b10, page 59. Translation by D.W. Hamlyn.
20 Aristotle, *De Anima,* ii 1, 412b5-6.
21 Aristotle, *De Anima,* ii 1, 412a20-1, and similarly that it 'is a first actuality of a natural body which has life in potentiality'. Aristotle, *De Anima,* ii 1, 412a27-8.
22 Aristotle, *De Anima,* ii 1, 412b10-24.
23 Aristotle, *De Anima*, 412a22–412b21.
24 John Protevi, *Political Physics: Deleuze, Derrida and the Body Politic,* (London: Athlone, 2001), 8.
25 Gilbert Simondon, *L'Individu et sa genèse physicobiologique,* (Paris: Presses Universitaires de France, 1964), 40. My translation.
26 Gothic architecture would be the point of difference for Deleuze and Guattari, where 'the static relation, form-matter, tends to fade into the background in favor of a dynamic relation, material-forces'. Deleuze and Guattari, *A Thousand Plateaus,* 364.
27 Gilles Deleuze and Félix Guattari, *Anti-Oedipus,* (Minneapolis: University of Minnesota Press, 1983), 368. Translation of *L'Anti-Oedipe,* volume 1 of *Capitalisme et schizophrénie,* (Paris: Les Editions de Minuit, 1972), by Robert Hurley, Mark Seem and Helen R. Lane.
28 Simondon, *L'Individu et sa genèse physicobiologique,* 48-9.
29 Deleuze and Guattari, *A Thousand Plateaus,* 196.
30 Protevi, *Political Physics,* 193.
31 Deleuze, *Francis Bacon*, 20.
32 Deleuze, *Francis Bacon*, 65.
33 Deleuze, *Francis Bacon*, 21.
34 Deleuze, *Francis Bacon*, 21.
35 Daniel W. Smith, Translator's note, in Deleuze, *Francis Bacon,* note 6, 173-4.
36 Brian Massumi, 'Notes on the Translation and Acknowledgments', in Deleuze and Guattari, *A Thousand Plateaus,* x.
37 Deleuze and Guattari, *A Thousand Plateaus,* 335 and 406.
38 Deleuze, *Francis Bacon*, 21.
39 Deleuze, *Francis Bacon*, 22.
40 Deleuze, *Francis Bacon*, 22.
41 Deleuze, *Francis Bacon*, 22.
42 Deleuze, *Francis Bacon*, 22.
43 Bacon in Sylvester, *Interviews with Francis Bacon*, 46.
44 Deleuze, *Francis Bacon*, 23.
45 To draw the intensities forth is to invoke the 'nonorganic life' of art, as the art historian Wilhelm Worringer had called it. For Worringer 'the morphological law of inorganic nature still echoes like a dim memory in our human organism' (and

for Deleuze such dim memories that 'haunt the wiped off parts' screech in Bacon's heads). Wilhelm Worringer, *Abstraction and Empathy: A Contribution to the Psychology of Style*, (New York: International Universities Press, 1908 [1953]), 247.
46 Gilles Deleuze and Félix Guattari, *What Is Philosophy?*, (New York and Chichester: Columbia University Press, 1994), 167. Translation of *Qu'est-ce que la philosophie?*, (Paris: Les Editions de Minuit, 1991), by Hugh Tomlinson and Graham Burchell.
47 Deleuze, *Francis Bacon*, 42.
48 Raquel Rolnik, 'Housing, Public Space and the Future of the City', (4 May 2021). Available at https://www.publicspace.org/multimedia/-/post/housing-public-space-and-the-future-of-the-city. Accessed 27 November 2021.
49 The territories of the unconscious and the sites of architecture have much in common. For the psychoanalysts Félix Guattari and Suely Rolnik, the *favelas* of Brazil, often maligned and borne from a complex history, offer a way of understanding the unconscious and subjective systems of enunciation. In their book of 1982, *Molecular Revolution in Brazil*, Rolnik and Guattari suggest an architecture of 'urban systems which are not cities, and rural systems which are not rural' and those which lack formal planning, such as the *favelas*, generate insights into the operations of subjectivity itself. Félix Guattari and Suely Rolnik, *Molecular Revolution in Brazil*, (New York: Semiotext(e), 2007), 411. Translation of *Micropolítica: Cartografias do desejo*, (Petrópolis: Vozes, 1986) by Karel Clapshow and Brian Holmes. Likewise, the famed psychoanalysts suggest the inverse is also true. That is, an understanding of the territories of the unconscious might allow us to better think about the situation of the favelas. Indeed, Guattari goes as far as suggesting, 'an experiment totally restricted to the *favelas* can learn things from the social field that are certainly fundamental'. Guattari, in Rolnik and Guattari, *Molecular Revolution*, 144.
50 JR in Thomas Hobbs, 'Backdrops to a Riot: JR on How His Confrontational Street Art Went Global', *The Guardian* (7 June 2021). Available at https://www.theguardian.com/artanddesign/2021/jun/07/backdrops-to-a-riot-how-jrs-confrontational-street-art-went-global. Accessed 28 March 2022.
51 JR, 'Women Are Heroes: Brazil', *JR-art.net*. Available at https://jr-art.net/projects/rio-de-janeiro. Accessed 28 March 2022.
52 JR, cited in Carole Cadwalladr, 'JR: 'I Realised I Was Giving People a Voice'', *The Guardian*, (11 October 2015). Available at https://www.theguardian.com/artanddesign/2015/oct/11/artist-jr-i-realised-i-was-giving-people-a-voice-les-bosquets-french-banksy. Accessed 8 June 2021.
53 Deleuze, *Francis Bacon*, 65.
54 Deleuze, *Francis Bacon*, 4.
55 Deleuze and Guattari, *A Thousand Plateaus*, 172–3.
56 Protevi, *Political Physics*, 193.
57 JR, cited in Cadwalladr, 'JR: 'I Realised I Was Giving People a Voice''.

Chapter 16

1 Gilles Deleuze and Claire Parnet, *L'Abécédaire*, directed by Pierre-André Boutang (1988–9). The final session of the *L'Abécédaire*, 'Z as in Zigzag' ['Z comme Zig zag'], is available at https://www.youtube.com/watch?v=ywQXi_z_59k. Accessed 27 November 2021. References herein are to the film.

2   Gilles Deleuze, *Difference and Repetition*, (New York: Columbia University Press, 1994), 119. Translation of *Différence et repetition*, (Paris: Presse Universitaires de France, 1968), by Paul Patton.
3   Deleuze, *Difference and Repetition*, 119.
4   Deleuze, *Difference and Repetition*, 119.
5   Gilles Deleuze in Deleuze and Claire Parnet, *Dialogues*, (New York: Columbia University Press, 1987), 32. Translation of *Dialogues*, (Paris: Flammarion, 1977), by Hugh Tomlinson and Barbara Habberjam.
6   Deleuze and Parnet, *Dialogues*, 7.
7   Deleuze and Parnet, *Dialogues*, 32.
8   Deleuze, *Difference and Repetition*, 145.
9   Deleuze and Parnet, 'Z as in Zigzag', *L'Abécédaire*.
10 Deleuze and Parnet, 'Z as in Zigzag', *L'Abécédaire*.
11 Deleuze and Parnet, 'Z as in Zigzag', *L'Abécédaire*.
12 Nigel Thrift, *Non-representational Theory: Space, Politics, Affect*, (London and New York: Routledge, 2008), 2 and 65.
13 Refer to Chris L. Smith, *Bare Architecture: A Schizoanalysis*, (London: Bloomsbury, 2017), chapter 3 'The Impersonal'.
14 Gilles Deleuze, 'Spinoza: Three Ethics', in *Essays Critical and Clinical*, (Minneapolis: University of Minnesota Press, 1997), 138–51. Translation of *Critique et clinique*, (Paris: Minuit, 1993) by Daniel Smith and Michael Greco.
15 Spinoza cited in Gilles Deleuze, 'What Can a Body Do?', in *Expressionism in Philosophy: Spinoza*, (New York: Zone Books, 1992), 226. Translation of *Spinoza et la probleme de l' expression*, (Paris: Les Editions de Minuit, 1968), by Martin Joughin.
16 Gilles Deleuze and Félix Guattari, *A Thousand Plateaus*, (Minneapolis: University of Minnesota Press, 1987), 257. Translation of *Mille plateaux*, volume 2 of *Capitalisme et schizophrénie*, (Paris: Les Editions de Minuit, 1980) by Brian Massumi.
17 Deleuze and Guattari, *A Thousand Plateaus*, 233.
18 Deleuze and Parnet, *Dialogues*, 32.
19 Deleuze and Guattari, *A Thousand Plateaus*, 356.
20 Deleuze and Guattari, *A Thousand Plateaus*, 240.
21 Deleuze and Guattari, *A Thousand Plateaus*, 399–400.
22 Massumi succinctly defines affection as 'an encounter between the affected body and a second, affecting, body'. Brian Massumi, 'Notes on the Translation and Acknowledgments', in Deleuze and Guattari, *A Thousand Plateaus*, xvi.
23 Massumi, 'Notes of the Translation and Acknowledgments', xvi.
24 Chris L. Smith, 'Affection for Aborted Architecture', in Marko Jobst and Hélène Frichot eds., *Architectural Affects after Deleuze and Guattari*, (London: Routledge, 2021), 132–48.
25 William James, 'What Is an Emotion?', *Mind*, (9, 1884): 188.
26 Deleuze and Guattari, *A Thousand Plateaus*, 256.
27 Deleuze and Guattari, *A Thousand Plateaus*, 80–2.
28 Deleuze and Guattari, *A Thousand Plateaus*, 356.
29 Deleuze and Parnet, 'N as in Neurology' [N comme neurologie], *L'Abécédaire*. Available at https://www.youtube.com/watch?v=EP1rhxMkrhk. Accessed 17 January 2022.
30 Deleuze and Guattari, *A Thousand Plateaus*, 356.
31 Deleuze and Parnet, 'Z as in Zigzag', *L'Abécédaire*.
32 Deleuze and Guattari, *A Thousand Plateaus*, 256.

33   Deleuze and Guattari, *A Thousand Plateaus*, 259.
34   Gilles Deleuze, 'Lecture Transcripts on Spinoza's Concept of Affect', delivered at the University of Paris 8, Vincennes 24 January 1978 and was later elaborated in a series of lectures (particularly the lecture of 24 March 1981).
35   Deleuze and Guattari, *A Thousand Plateaus*, 356.
36   Deleuze and Guattari, *A Thousand Plateaus*, 356.
37   Gilles Deleuze and Félix Guattari, *What Is Philosophy?*, (New York and Chichester: Columbia University Press, 1994), 186. Translation of *Qu'est-ce que la philosophie?*, (Paris: Les Editions de Minuit, 1991), by Hugh Tomlinson and Graham Burchell.
38   Geoff Manaugh, BLDGBLOG, (23 August 2013). Available at https://bldgblog.com/2013/08/lightning-farm/. Accessed 13 September 2021.
39   Deleuze and Guattari, *What Is Philosophy?*, 185.
40   Deleuze and Guattari, *What Is Philosophy?*, 183.
41   Deleuze and Guattari, *A Thousand Plateaus*, 400.
42   Deleuze and Guattari, *A Thousand Plateaus*, 499.
43   Deleuze told Parnet regarding the wasp *and* orchid that '[t]o fly is to trace a line, lines, a whole cartography. One only discovers worlds through a long, broken flight'. Deleuze and Parnet, *Dialogues*, 36.

Selected bibliography

Alexander, Christopher, 'From a Set of Forces to a Form', Gyorgy Kepes ed., *The Man-made Object*, New York: Studio Vista, 1966, 96–107.
Alliez, Eric and Massumi, Brian, 'Performing the Ethico-aesthetic Paradigm', *Performance Research*, vol. 19, no. 3, 2014: 15–26.
Aristotle, *The Works of Aristotle*, Oxford: Clarendon Press, 1931. Translation by J.I. Beare.
Aristotle, *De Anima: Books I, II and III*, Oxford: Clarendon, 1993. Translation by D.W. Hamlyn.
Artaud, Antonin, 'To Have Done with the Judgement of God', Susan Sontag ed., *Antonin Artaud: Selected Writings*, New York: Farrar, Straus and Giroux, 1976, 555–75. Translation by Helen Weaver.
Ballantyne, Andrew, *Deleuze and Guattari for Architects*, London: Routledge, 2007.
Ballantyne, Andrew and Smith, Chris L. eds., *Architecture in the Space of Flows*, London: Routledge, 2012.
Basar, Shumon and Trüby, Stephan eds., *The World of Madelon Vriesendorp: Paintings/Postcards/Objects/Games*, London: AA Publications, 2008.
Bateson, Gregory ed., 'Toward a Theory of Schizophrenia', *Steps to an Ecology of Mind: Collected Essays in Anthropology, Psychiatry, Evolution, and Epistemology*, New Jersey: Jason Aronson Inc., 1987, 205–32.
Beaulieu, Alain and Ord, Douglas, 'The Death of Gilles Deleuze as Composition of a Concept', *Deleuze Studies*, vol. 11, no. 1, 2017: 121–38.
Beer, Gillian, *Darwin's Plots; Evolutionary Narrative in Darwin, George Eliot and Nineteenth-Century Fiction*, London: Ark Paperbacks, 1985.
Bell, Jeffrey A., *Philosophy at the Edge of Chaos: Gilles Deleuze and the Philosophy of Difference*, Toronto: University of Toronto Press, 2006.
Bloomer, Jennifer, *Architecture and the Text: The (S)crypts of Joyce and Piranesi*, New Haven: Yale University Press, 1993.
Boundas, Constantin V. and Querrien, Anne, 'Anne Querrien, La Borde, Guattari and Left Movements in France, 1965–81', *Deleuze Studies*, vol. 10, no. 3, 2016: 395–416.
Boundas, Constantin and Tentokali, Vana eds., *Architectural and Urban Reflections after Deleuze and Guattari*, London and New York: Rowman and Littlefield, 2018.
Brott, Simone, 'Deleuze and "The Intercessors"', *Log*, vol. 18, Winter 2010: 131–51.
Brott, Simone, *Architecture for a Free Subjectivity: Deleuze and Guattari at the Horizon of the Real*, London: Routledge, 2011.
Brott, Simone, 'The Le Corbusier Scandal, or, Was Le Corbusier a Fascist?' *Fascism*, vol. 6, no. 2, December 2017: 196–227.
Butler, Samuel, 'Darwin among the Machines', *The Press*, Christchurch, 13 June 1863.
Canguilhem, Georges, 'Machine and Organism', Jonathan Crary and Sanford Kwinter eds., *Incorporations*, New York: Zone, 1992, 45–69.
Cache, Bernard, *Earth Moves: The Furnishing of Territories*, Cambridge, MA: The MIT Press, 1995. Translation of *Terre meuble*, (unpublished manuscript 1983), by Anne Boyman.

Carpo, Mario, *The Alphabet and the Algorithm*, Cambridge, MA: The MIT Press, 2011.
Chatterjee, Anuradha, *John Ruskin and the Fabric of Architecture*, London and New York: Routledge, 2018.
Colombat, André Pierre, 'November 4, 1995: Deleuze's Death as an Event', *Man and World*, vol. 29, 1996: 235–49.
Colomina, Beatriz, 'At Home with His Parents', *Assemblage*, no. 30, August 1996: 108–11.
Colomina, Beatriz and Wigley, Mark, 'Toilet Architecture: An Essay about the Most Psychosexually Charged Room in a Building', *PIN–UP*, no. 23, Fall Winter 2017/18: 229–36.
Damisch, Hubert, *Fenêtre jaune cadmium, ou les dessous de la peinture*, Paris: Seuil, 1984.
Damisch, Hubert, *L'Origine de la perspective*, Paris: Champs Flammarion, 1987.
Deleuze, Gilles, 'De Sacher-Masoch au masochisme', *Arguments*, vol. 5, no. 21, January–April 1961: 40–6.
Deleuze, Gilles, *Nietzsche and Philosophy*, London: Althone Press, 1983. Translation of *Nietzsche et la philosophie*, Paris: PUF, 1962, by Hugh Tomlinson.
Deleuze, Gilles, *Kant's Critical Philosophy: The Doctrine of the Faculties*, London: The Althone Press, 1984. Translation of *La Philosophic Critique de Kant*, Paris: Presses Universitaires de France, 1963, by Hugh Tomlinson and Barbara Habberjam.
Deleuze, Gilles, *Proust and Signs*, New York: George Braziller, 1972. Translation of *Marcel Proust et les signes*, Paris: PUF, 1964, by Richard Howard.
Deleuze, Gilles, 'Coldness and Cruelty', *Masochism*, New York: Zone, 1989, 8–138. Translation of 'Le Froid and le Cruel' in *Presentation de Sacher-Masoch*, Paris: Les Editions de Minuit, 1967, by Jean McNeil.
Deleuze, Gilles, *Difference and Repetition*, New York: Columbia University Press, 1994. Translation of *Différence et repetition*, Paris: Presse Universitaires de France, 1968, by Paul Patton.
Deleuze, Gilles, *The Logic of Sense*, New York: Columbia University Press, 1990, Constantin V. Boundas ed., Translation of *Logique du sens*, Paris: Les Editions de Minuit, 1969, by Mark Lester and Charles Stivale.
Deleuze, Gilles, 'I Have Nothing to Admit', *Semiotext(e) Anti-Oedipus*, vol. 2, no. 3, 1977: 111–16. Translation by Janis Forman.
Deleuze, Gilles, *Francis Bacon: The Logic of Sensation*, New York: Continuum, 2003. Translation of *Francis Bacon: Logique de la Sensation*, Paris: Editions de la Difference, 1981, by Daniel W. Smith.
Deleuze, Gilles, *Cinema 1: The Movement-Image*, Minneapolis: University of Minnesota Press, 2007. Translation of *Cinéma 1: L'Image-Mouvement*, Paris: Les editions de Minuit, 1983, by Hugh Tomlinson and Barbara Habberjam.
Deleuze, Gilles, *Cinema 2: The Time-Image*, Minneapolis: University of Minnesota Press, 2007. Translation of *Cinéma 2: L'Image-Temps*, Paris: Les editions de Minuit, 1985, by Hugh Tomlinson and Robert Galeta.
Deleuze, Gilles, *Foucault*, Minneapolis and London: University of Minnesota Press, 1988. Translation of *Foucault*, Paris: Les Editions de Minuit, 1986, by Sean Hand.
Deleuze, Gilles, *The Fold: Leibniz and the Baroque*, New York: Continuum, 2006. Translation of *Le Pli: Leibniz et le Baroque*, Paris: Les Editions de Minuit, 1988, by Tom Conley.
Deleuze, Gilles, *Negotiations: 1972–1990*, New York: Columbia University Press, 1995. Translation of *Pourparlers; 1972–1990*, Paris: Les Editions de Minuit, 1990, by Martin Joughin.
Deleuze, Gilles, *Essays Critical and Clinical*, Minneapolis: University of Minnesota Press, 1997. Translation of *Critique et Clinique*, Paris: Les Éditions de Minuit, 1993, by Daniel W. Smith and Michael A. Greco.

Deleuze, Gilles, *Pure Immanence: Essays on a Life*, New York: Zone Books, 2001. Translated by Anne Boyman.
Deleuze, Gilles, *Desert Islands and Other Texts 1953–1974*, David Laboujade ed., Paris: Semiotext(e), 2004. Translation of Gilles Deleuze, *L'Îles déserte et autres textes: Textes et entretiens 1953–1974*, Paris: Les Editions de Minuit, 2002, by Christopher Bush, Charles Stivale, Melissa McMahon, Alexander Hickox and Teal Eich.
Deleuze, Gilles, *Two Regimes of Madness: Texts and Interviews 1975–1995*, David Lapoujade ed., New York: Semiotext(e), 2006. Translation by Ames Hodges and Mike Taormina.
Deleuze, Gilles and Guattari, Félix, *Anti-Oedipus*, Minneapolis: University of Minnesota Press, 1983. Translation of *L'Anti-Oedipe*, volume 1 of *Capitalisme et schizophrénie*, Paris: Les Editions de Minuit, 1972, by Robert Hurley, Mark Seem and Helen R. Lane.
Deleuze, Gilles and Guattari, Félix, *Kafka: Toward a Minor Literature*, Minnesota: University of Minnesota Press, 1986. Translation of *Kafka: pour une littérature mineure*, Paris: Les Editions de Minuit, 1975, by Dana Polan.
Deleuze, Gilles and Guattari, Félix, *A Thousand Plateaus*, Minneapolis: University of Minnesota Press, 1987. Translation of *Mille plateaux*, volume 2 of *Capitalisme et schizophrénie*, Paris: Les Editions de Minuit, 1980, by Brian Massumi.
Deleuze, Gilles and Guattari, Félix, *What Is Philosophy?*, New York and Chichester: Columbia University Press, 1994. Translation of *Qu'est-ce que la philosophie?*, Paris: Les Editions de Minuit, 1991, by Hugh Tomlinson and Graham Burchell.
Deleuze, Gilles and Parnet, Claire, *Dialogues*, New York: Columbia University Press, 1987. Translation of *Dialogues*, Paris: Flammarion, 1977, by Hugh Tomlinson and Barbara Habberjam.
Deleuze, Gilles and Parnet, Claire, *Dialogues II*, New York: Columbia University Press, 2007, revised edition. Translated by Hugh Tomlinson and Barbara Habberjam.
Derrida, Jacques, *Resistances of Psychoanalysis*, Stanford: Stanford University Press, 1998. Translation by Peggy Kamuf, Pascale-Anne Brault and Michael Naas.
Derrida, Jacques, *Demuere: Fiction and Testimony*, Stanford: Stanford University Press, 2000. Translation of 'Demeure' by Elizabeth Rottenberg.
Diller, Elizabeth and Scofidio, Ricardo eds., *Back to the Front: Tourisms of War*, France: F.R.A.C. Basse Normandie, 1994.
Diller, Elizabeth and Scofidio, Ricardo eds., *Flesh: Architectural Probes*, New York: Princeton Architectural Press, 1994.
Diller, Elizabeth and Scofidio, Ricardo eds., *Blur: The Making of Nothing*, New York: Harry N. Abrams, Inc., 2002.
Drozynski, Charles and Beljaars, Diana eds., *Civic Spaces and Desire*, London and New York: Routledge, 2020.
Farson, Daniel, *The Gilded Gutter Life of Francis Bacon*, London: Century, 1993.
Feher, Michel and Kwinter, Sanford eds., *Zone 1/2: The Contemporary City*, New York: Urzone Inc., 1986.
Forty, Adrian, *Concrete and Culture: A Material History*, London: Reaktion Books, 2012.
Foucault, Michel, *The History of Sexuality*, Vol. I: *An Introduction*, New York: Pantheon Books, 1978. Translation of *Histoire de la sexualité*, Paris: Editions Gallimard, 1976, by Robert Hurley.
Foucault, Michel, *The History of Sexuality*, Vol. 2: *The Use of Pleasure*, New York: Pantheon, 1990. Translation of *L'usage des plaisirs*, Paris: Gallimard, 1978, by Robert Hurley.

Foucault, Michel, 'Des espaces autres', conférence au Cercle d'Études architecturales, 14th of March 1967, in *Architecture, Mouvement, Continuité*, vol. 5, October 1984: 46–9.

Foucault, Michel and Blanchot, Maurice, *Foucault/Blanchot*, New York: Zone Books, 1990. Translation of *La pensee du dehors*, Paris: Éditions Fata Margana, 1986, by Jeffrey Mehlman and Brian Massumi.

Freud, Sigmund, *The Standard Edition of the Complete Psychological Works of Sigmund Freud*, London: Hogarth, 1953. Translation by James Stratchey.

Frichot, Hélène, *Creative Ecologies: Theorizing the Practice of Architecture*, London: Bloomsbury, 2018.

Frichot, Hélène and Loo, Stephen, *Deleuze and Architecture*, Edinburgh: Edinburgh University Press, 2013.

Genosko, Gary, *Felix Guattari: An Aberrant Introduction*, Transversals: New Directions in Philosophy, London and New York: Continuum, 2002.

Giedion, Sigfried, *Space, Time and Architecture: The Birth of a New Tradition*, Cambridge, MA: Harvard University Press, 1949 [1941].

Giedion, Sigfried, *Mechanization Takes Command: A Contribution to Anonymous History*, New York: Oxford University Press, 1948.

Guattari, Félix, *Molecular Revolution: Psychiatry and Politics*, Harmondsworth and New York: Penguin, 1984. Translation by Rosemary Sheed. This is a collection of essays that were published previously in *Psychoanalyse et transversalité*, Paris: Maspero, 1972, and; *La Révolution moléculaire*, Paris: Éditions *Recherchés* Séries 'Encre', 1977.

Guattari, Félix, *Schizoanalytic Cartographies*, London: Bloomsbury, 2013. Translation of *Cartographies Schizoanalytiques*, Paris: Éditions Galilée, 1989, by Andrew Goffey.

Guattari, Félix, *Chaosmosis: An Ethico-Aesthetic Paradigm*, Bloomington: Indiana University Press, 1995. Translation of *Chaosmose*, Paris: Galilee, 1992, by Paul Bains and Julian Pefanis.

Guattari, Félix, *Chaosophy: Texts and Interviews 1972–1977*, Sylvère Lotringer ed., Los Angeles: Semiotext(e), 2007. Translation by David L. Sweet, Jarred Becker and Taylor Adkins.

Guattari, Félix, *Machinic Eros: Writings on Japan*, Gary Genosko and Jay Hetrick eds., Minneapolis: Univocal, 2015.

Guattari, Félix and Rolnik, Seuly, *Molecular Revolution in Brazil*, New York: Semiotext(e), 2007. Translation of *Micropolítica: Cartografias do desejo*, Petrópolis: Vozes, 1986, by Karel Clapshow and Brian Holmes.

Hadid, Zaha, *Zaha Hadid: The Complete Buildings and Projects*, New York: Rizzoli, 1998.

Harvey, David, *The New Imperialism*, Oxford: Oxford University Press, 2005.

Hersey, George L., *High Victorian Gothic: A Study in Associationism*, Baltimore and London: The Johns Hopkins University Press, 1972.

Holland, Eugène, 'Deterritorializing "Deterritorialization": From the *Anti-Oedipus* to *A Thousand Plateaus*', *SubStance*, vol. 20, no. 3, Iss. 66: Special Issue: Deleuze & Guattari, 1991: 55–65.

Hollier, Denis, *Against Architecture: The Writings of Georges Bataille*, Cambridge, MA: The MIT Press, 1992. Translation of *La Prise de la Concorde*, Paris: Editions Gallimard, 1974, by Betsy Wing.

Ingraham, Catherine, 'Slow-Dancing: Architecture in the Embrace of Poststructuralism', *Inland Architect*, September–October 1987: 44–7.

Irigaray, Luce, *An Ethics of Sexual Difference*, Ithaca, NY: Cornell University Press, 1984. Translation of *Éthique de la différence sexuelle*, Paris: Les Éditions de Minuit, 1984, by Carolyn Burke and Gillian C. Gill.

Irigaray, Luce, *Luce Irigaray: Key Writings*, New York: Continuum, 2004.

James, William, *The Meaning of Truth: A Sequel to Pragmatism*, London: Longmans, Green and Company, 1909.
Jameson, Fredric, *The Political Unconscious: Narrative as a Socially Symbolic Act*, New York: Cornell University Press, 1981.
Jardine, Alice, 'Woman in Limbo; Deleuze and His Br(others)', *SubStance*, vol. 13, no. 3–4, 1984: 46–60.
Jobst, Marko and Frichot, Hélène eds., *Architectural Affects after Deleuze and Guattari*, London: Routledge, 2021.
Joyce, James, *Finnegans Wake*, London: Faber and Faber, 1939.
Kaufman, Eleanor, *Deleuze & Guattari: New Mappings in Politics, Philosophy, and Culture*, Minneapolis: University of Minnesota Press, 1998.
Kimmel, Laurence, 'Stygian Dark: What the Presence and Architecture of Sex Clubs Reveal about the Politics of Public and Private Space in a City', Charles Drozynski and Diana Beljaars eds., *Civic Spaces and Desire*, London and New York: Routledge, 2020, 121–31.
Kite, Stephen, 'Building Texts + Reading Fabrics: Metaphor, Memory, and Material' in John Ruskin's *Stones of Venice*', Wouter Van Acker and Peter Uyttenhove eds., *Library Trends: Information and Space: Analogies and Metaphors*, vol. 61, no. 2, Fall 2012: 418–39.
Koolhaas, Rem, *Delirious New York: A Retroactive Manifesto for Manhattan*, first edition, Oxford: Oxford University Press, 1978.
Krauss, Rosalind, 'Two Moments from the Post-Medium Condition', *October*, vol. 116, Spring 2006: 55–62.
Lacan, Jacques, *Encore, the Seminar of Jacques Lacan*, Book XX (1972–1973), Jacques-Alain Miller ed., New York: Norton, 1998. Translation of *Le Séminaire, Livre XX: Encore*, Paris: Èditions du Seuil, 1975, by Bruce Fink.
Lacan, Jacques, *The Seminars of Jacques Lacan*, Cambridge: University of Cambridge Press, 1988. Translation of *Le Séminaire*, Paris: Les Editions du Seuil, 1975, by John Forrester.
Lacan, Jacques, *Écrits: A Selection*, New York: W. W. Norton, 1977. Translation by Alan Sheridan.
Lapoujade, David, 'From Transcendental Empiricism to Worker Nomadism: William James', *Pli*, no. 9, 2000: 190–9. Translated by Alberto Toscano.
Le Corbusier, *Towards a New Architecture*, London: The Architectural Press, 1927. Translation of *Vers une Architecture*, Paris: Éditions Crès, Collection de 'L'Esprit Nouveau', 1923, by Frederick Etchells.
Le Corbusier, *The Modulor: A Harmonious Measure to the Human Scale Universally Applicable to Architecture and Mechanics*, second edition, Basel: Birkhäuser, 2004. Translation of *Le modulor* (1954), by Peter de Francia and Anna Bostock.
Le Corbusier, *Modulor 2 (Let the User Speak Next)*, Continuation of 'The Modulor' 1948, Basel: Birkhäuser, 2004. Translation of *Le modulor 2* (1955) by Peter de Francia and Anna Bostock.
Leclercle, Jean-Jacques, *Philosophy through the Looking Glass*, La Salle, IL: Open Court, 1985.
Leclercle, Jean-Jacques, 'The Pedagogy of Philosophy', *Radical Philosophy*, vol. 75, January–February 1996: 44–6.
Leroi-Gourhan, André, *Gesture and Speech*, Cambridge, MA: The MIT Press, 1993. Translation of *Le Geste et la parole*, Paris: Albin Michel, 1964, by Anna Bostock Berger.
Lotringer, Sylvère and Rajchman, John et al., eds., 'Semiotext(e)', *Anti-Oedipus: From Psychoanalysis to Schizopolitics*, vol. 2, no. 3, 1977.

Lotringer, Sylvère and Rajchman, John et al., eds., 'Semiotext(e)', *SchizoCulture*, vol. 3, no. 2, 1978.
Lotringer, Sylvère, 'My '80s: Better than Life', *Artforum*, vol. 14, no. 8, April 2003: 2.
Lynn, Greg, 'Architectural Curvilinearity: The Folded, the Pliant and the Supple', Andreas Papadakis ed., *Folding in Architecture, AD*, Profile 102, 1993: 8-15.
Lynn, Greg, 'In the Wake of the Avant-garde', *Assemblage*, no. 29, April 1996: 116-25.
Lynn, Greg, *Animate Form*, New York: Princeton Architectural Press, 1999.
Lynn, Greg, 'Embryologic Houses', Ali Rahim ed., *Contemporary Processes in Architecture, AD*, Profile 145, 2000: 26-35.
Marcos, Maria José and Delicado, Gonzalo Herrero, 'Trebamo li doista (nove) gradevine u svojim gradovima?/Do We Really Need (New) Buildings in Our Cities?', *Oris*, vol. 75, 2012: 8-17.
Marx, Karl, *Capital: A Critique of Political Economy*, Friedrich Engels ed., Harmondsworth: Penguin,1976. Translation of *Das Kapital: Kritik der politischen Ökonomie*, Hamburg: Verlag von Otto Meissner, 1867, (based on the fourth edition (1890)), by Ben Fowkes.
McAnulty, Robert, 'Body Troubles', John Whiteman, Jeffrey Kipnis and Richard Burdett eds., *Strategies in Architectural Thinking*, Cambridge, MA: The MIT Press, 1992, 180-97.
Muir, Robin, *A Maverick Eye: The Street Photography of John Deakin*, London: Thames and Hudson, 2002.
Muir, Robin, *John Deakin, Photography and the Lure of Soho*, London: Art/Books, 2014.
Merleau-Ponty, Maurice, *Phenomenology of Perception*, London: Routledge and Kegan Paul, 1962. Translation of *Phénoménologie de la perception*, Paris: Gallimard, 1945, by Michael Smith.
Merleau-Ponty, Maurice, *The Visible and the Invisible*, Evanston: Northwest University Press, 1968. Translation of *Le visible et l'invisible*, Paris: Gallimard, 1964, by Alphonso Lingis.
Mumford, Lewis, 'The First Megamachine', *Diogenes*, vol. 55, July-September 1966: 1-15.
Mumford, Lewis, *The Myth of the Machine: Technics and Human Development*, New York: Harcourt Brace Jovanovich, 1967.
Nietzsche, Friedrich, 'The Birth of Tragedy', *Basic Writings of Nietzsche*, New York: Modern Library, 2000, 1-144. Translation of *Die Geburt der Tragödie* [1872] by Walter Kaufmann.
Nietzsche, Friedrich, *The Genealogy of Morals: A Polemic*, vol. 8, Edinburgh and London: T.N.Foulis, 1913. Translation of *Zur Genealogie der Moral: Eine Streitschriftl*, Leipzig: Verlag von C.G.Neuman, 1887, by Horace B. Samuel.
Nietzsche, Friedrich, *Human All-Too-Human: A Book for Free Spirits*, Edinburgh and London: T.N.Foulis, 1910. Translation of *Menschliches, Allzumenschliches: Ein Buch für freie Geister*, Chemnitz: Schmeitzner, 1878, by Helen Zimmern.
Nietzsche, Friedrich, *Thus Spoke Zarathustra: A Book for All and None*, Cambridge: Cambridge University Press, 2006. Edited by Adrian Del Caro and Robert B. Pippin. Translation of *Also sprach Zarathustra: Ein Buch für Alle und Keinen*, Chemnitz: Ernst Schmeitzner, 1883-91, by Adrian Del Caro.
Pankow, Gisela, *L'homme et sa psychose*, Paris: Aubier, 1969.
Pankow, Gisela, *L'homme et son espace vécu: Abord analytique de la parile poétique*, Paris: Aubier, 1986.
Pelkonen, Eeva-Liisa, 'Reading Aalto through the Baroque', *AA Files*, no. 65, 2012: 72-5.

Preciado, Paul B., *An Apartment on Uranus: Chronicles of the Crossing*, New York: Semiotext(e), 2020. Translation of *Un appartement sur Uranus*, Paris: Éditions Grasset, 2019, by Charlotte Mandell.
Proust, Marcel, *In Search of Lost Time*, vol. 1-7, London: Centaur Editions, 2016. Translation of *À la Recherché du Temps Perdu* (1913-1927) by C. K. Scott Moncrieff (vols. 1 to 6) and Sydney Schiff (vol. 7).
Rajchman, John, *Constructions*, Cambridge, MA: The MIT Press, 1998.
Rajchman, John, *The Deleuze Connections*, Cambridge, MA: The MIT Press, 2000.
Ruskin, John, *The Works of John Ruskin*, E. T. Cook and A. Wedderburn. eds., London: George Allen, 1904.
Schumacher, Patrik, *Digital Hadid: Landscapes in Motion*, Basel: Birkhäuser, 2004.
Serres, Michel, *Hermes: Literature, Science, Philosophy*, Baltimore, MD: Johns Hopkins University Press, 1982. Translation by Josué V. Harari and David F. Bell.
Simondon, Gilbert, *L'individu et sa genese physico-biologique*, Paris: Presses Universitaires de France, 1964.
Simondon, Gilbert, 'The Position of the Problem of Ontogenesis', *Parrhesia*, vol. 7, no. 1, 2009: 4-16.
Smith, Chris L., 'Text and the Deployment of the Masochist', *Angelaki: Journal of Theoretical Humanities*, 'Shadows of Cruelty: Sadism, Masochism and the Philosophical Muse - Part One', vol. 14, no. 3, 2009: 45-57.
Smith, Chris L., *Bare Architecture: A Schizoanalysis*, London: Bloomsbury, 2017.
Smith, Chris L. and Ballantyne, Andrew, 'Flow: Architecture, Object, Relation', *Architectural Research Quarterly (ARQ)*, Cambridge University Press, vol. 14, no. 1, 2010: 21-7.
Speaks, Michael, 'It's Out There … The Formal Limits of the American Avantgarde', *Architectural Design*, vol. 68, no. 5/6, May-June 1998: 26-31.
Spiller, Neil, *Maverick Deviations: Architectural Works (1986-1998)*, New York: Wiley, 1999.
Stengers, Isabelle, *Cosmopolitics I*, Minneapolis: University of Minnesota Press, 2010. Translation of *Cosmopolitiques*, vol. 1, *La guerre des sciences*, Paris: La Découverte; Les Empêcheurs de penser en rond, 1996, by Robert Bononno.
Stivale, Charles ed., *Gilles Deleuze: Key Concepts*, Chesham: Acumen, 2005.
Stoner, Jill, *Toward a Minor Architecture*, Cambridge, MA: The MIT Press, 2012.
Sylvester, David, *Francis Bacon: Interviews by David Sylvester*, New York: Pantheon Books, 1975.
Sylvester, David, *Interviews with Francis Bacon*, London: Thames and Hudson, 1980.
Sylvester, David, *Looking Back at Francis Bacon*, London: Thames and Hudson, 2000.
Tafuri, Manfredo, *Theories and History of Architecture*, London: Granada Publishing, 1980. Translation of *Teorie e storia dell'architettura*, Rome and Bari: Laterza, 1968, by Giorgio Verrecchia.
Thompson, D'Arcy Wentworth, *On Growth and Form*, Cambridge: Cambridge University Press, 1942.
Thrift, Nigel, *Non-representational Theory: Space, Politics, Affect*, London and New York: Routledge, 2008.
Tzonis, Alexander and Lefaivre, Liane, 'The Mechanical Body versus the Divine Body: The Rise of Modern Design Theory', *JAE*, vol. 29, no. 1, Humanist Issues in Architecture, September 1975: 4-7.
Vidler, Anthony, *The Architectural Uncanny: Essays in the Modern Unhomely*, Cambridge, MA: The MIT Press, 1992.

Vidler, Anthony, *Warped Space: Art, Architecture, and Anxiety in Modern Culture*, Cambridge, MA: The MIT Press, 2001.
Virilio, Paul, *Speed and Politics*, New York: Semiotext(e), 2006. Translation of *Vitesse et Politique*, Paris: Édition Galilée, 1977, by Marc Polizzotti.
Virilio, Paul, 'Critical Reflections', *Art Forum*, vol. 34, no. 3, November 1995: 83.
Vitruvius, *De Architectura*, Cambridge, MA: Harvard University Press, 1931. Translation by Frank Granger.
Weston, Richard, *100 Ideas That Changed Architecture*, London: Lawrence King, 2011.
Whitehead, Alfred North, *Process and Reality: An Essay in Cosmology*, David Ray Griffin and Donald W. Sherburne eds., corrected edition, New York: The Free Press, 1978.
Zeitlian, Hraztan, *Semiotext(e)/Architecture*, New York: Semiotext(e), 1992.

Index

Aalto, Alvar 37–8, 40–2, 88
Abraham, Raimund 4
activism 8, 104, 137
AD (the journal) 6, 8, 13
aesthetics 2, 5, 19–21, 64, 91, 93, 113, 132–5, 138–9, 143, 154, 161, 166, 177
   aesthetic autonomy 134
   aesthetic enunciation 134
   aesthetic paradigm 135, 137
   see also ethico-aesthetics
affect 2, 4, 7, 16–17, 19, 43–4, 132, 136–7, 139, 165–9, 172–7
   affective turn 2, 7, 173
affection 53, 112, 166–8, 174, 177, 215 n22
Agacinski, Sylviane 5
Alexander, Christopher 4
Alliez, Eric 4, 136
alterity 101, 133, 136–7, 139
Angelidakis, Andreas 112, 117–19
animals 15–17, 22, 73, 137, 147, 155, 158, 191 n29
   birds 143–5, 154–5, 157–8, 160
   fish 4, 15, 17–23, 72, 74–5
   flies 7–8, 16, 171–2, 175–7
   lobsters 154, 156, 159
   monkeys 18, 146–7
   other non-human animals 20, 83, 157, 161–2, 166–7, 169, 174–5
   spiders 7–8, 171, 176
   wasps 4, 90, 172, 216 n43
   see also becoming-animal, organism
anthropocentrism 4, 167
anti-logos 61, *see also* logocentrism
Anyone corporation 3–5, 85
Appropriation 13, 41, 124, 127, 165, 191 n6.
Arendt, Hannah 78
Aristotle 39, 164–5
Artaud, Antonin 15, 79
assemblage 2, 48–50, 52, 103, 107, 110, 112–18, 121–2, 124–5, 128, 136, 156, 165, 177, *see also* molar assemblages, molecular assemblages
Assemblage (the journal) 6, 8, 25–6, 33

Bacon, Francis 161–4, 166–9, *see also* Deleuze, Gilles, *Francis Bacon*
Badaruddin, Farah Aliza 176–8
Ballantyne, Andrew 7
Baroque 6, 13–4, 16–23, 42, 57
   Baroque architecture 13–14, 16–17, 19, *see also* San Carlo alle Quattro Fontane; Borromini, Francesco.
   Baroque house 17–18
Bateson, Gregory 199 n16
Beckett, Samuel 70, 80, *see* also stone sucking.
becoming 50, 80, 160, 172, 174–5
   becoming animal 158, 163, 166
   becoming architecture 160, 167
   becoming child 158, 160
   becoming other 133, 175
   double-becoming 4, 172
Beer, Gillian 2
Beijing 29, 31, 33, 63–5
Beijing House II 63–5
Beirut 121, 123, 125
Betsky, Aaron 33–4
Bettelheim, Bruno 81
birds *see* animals
Blanchot, Maurice 50
blobs 13, 22, 183 n48
Bloomer, Jennifer 141
Blue Slabs 31–5
Blur building 83–6, 113
body 14–15, 17, 19, 21–2, 37, 49, 54, 63–4, 68, 84–6, 97–8, 100, 107, 117–18, 134, 143, 145, 149, 161, 163–6, 169, 173–5
   flesh 60, 62, 84, 98, 139, 149, 161–2, 164–6
   meat 161–8

Body without Organs (BwO) 83, 143, 154,
    see also organs
bone see organs
Borromini, Francesco 16–17
Bos, Caroline 5
Boundas, Constantin V. 7
British Houses of Parliament 67, 131
Brott, Simone 3, 5, 7
Butler, Samuel 94
Buzzfeed 138–9

Cache, Bernard 3, 6, 43–5
Cano, Lucia see SelgasCano
Cape Town 127
capitalism 3, 20, 29, 70, 144, 193 n35
capture 123–4, 127, 157, 172
    magic capture 124
Carpo, Mario 44
Carroll, Lewis 42, 79, 117
Cash, Mat 128
castration anxiety 40, 55, 69, 72, 118
causality 19, 111, 131–2, 136
Centre d'Études, de Recherches et de
    Formation Institutionnelles
    (CERFI) 1, 4, 127
chaodyssey 38, 40
chaos 15, 28–9, 37–8, 41, 78, 100, 103, 168
chaosmos 38, 40, see also Guattari, Felix,
    Chaosmosis
Christ 153–4, 162
Chrysler building 52–3
Churchill, Winston 131–3
cinema 1, 87–8, 90–2, 113, 155
codification 27–8, 33, 42–3, 81, 116, 167,
    173–4
    classification 28–31, 79, 81, 93, 107–10,
        118, 156
    demarcation 28–9, 32–3, 37, 47, 49, 51,
        70, 80, 92–3, 107–10, 113–14, 116,
        124, 128, 149, 154, 166
    generalization 15, 28, 78, 90–1, 98, 100,
        104, 108, 110, 131, 134
Colomina, Beatriz 5, 25–6, 55, 109, 113
colonization 2, 8, 29–30, 33, 122–3, 126,
    128, 177
commodity fetishism see fetish
Communicating Vessels 148–51
concept creation 63, 90, 94
conceptual personae 50, 80

concrescence 15–16, 19
concrete 17, 22, 27, 89, 91–4, 102–4, 110,
    112, 121, 126–8, 157, 159, 165, 173
    abstractions of concrete 8, 13, 15, 17,
        91, 103, 165
constructivism 33, 59, 62–3, 65, 167
consummation 54, 55, 145–6
consumption 39, 43, 55, 67–8, 72, 78, 124,
    145, 156–7
continental islands see islands
continua 43–4, see also cosmic continuum
continuous variation of matter 17, 20, 44,
    see also matter
Cook, Peter 4
cosmic 154–8, 160, 177
    cosmic artisans 156–8
    cosmic continuum 155–6
cosmopolitics 103
Crary, Jonathon 4
crucifixion 148, 154, 161–2
cruising 112–14, 116
    Cruising Labyrinth 116–19
    Cruising Pavilion 112–13, 115–18
crystals 154–60
    crystallization 135, 155–6

Daedalus 118
Dalí, Salvador 55, 156
Damisch, Hubert 5, 143, 149, 208 n3
dark precursors 141, 171–5
Davidson, Cynthia 4–6, 13
D-Day 78–9, 82, 86
Deakin, John 161–3
decolonization see colonization
deconstruction 5–6, 13, 19, 21, 25, 33, 39,
    128
defenestration 1
De Landa, Manuel 3–4
Deleuze, Gilles,
    Deleuze, *Cinema 1: The Movement-
        Image*, 87
    Deleuze, *Cinema 2: The Time-Image*, 87
    Deleuze, *Difference and Repetition*
        39–40, 90, 94, 117, 171
    Deleuze, *Essays Critical and Clinical*
        80–1, 84
    Deleuze, *The Fold* 3, 6, 13–14, 16–23,
        45
    Deleuze, *Francis Bacon* 163–4, 166–7

Deleuze, *Kant's Critical Philosophy* 154–5
Deleuze, *The Logic of Sense* 38, 40–2, 44, 67, 79, 117
Deleuze, *Nietzsche and Philosophy* 41–2, 100, 154
Deleuze, *Proust and Signs*, 61–2, 70
Deleuze, Gilles and Guattari, Félix
   Deleuze and Guattari, *Anti-Oedipus* 3, 26–7, 30, 49, 71, 74, 78–83, 103, 107, 110, 117, 122–3, 125–6, 135, 143–6
   Deleuze and Guattari, *Kafka: Toward a Minor Literature* 50, 141
   Deleuze and Guattari, *A Thousand Plateaus* 5, 14, 37, 51, 107, 117, 121–7, 135, 154–6, 158, 164–6, 168, 173, 175
   Deleuze and Guattari, *What Is Philosophy?* 5, 7, 27, 34, 62, 90–1, 135–6, 155, 167, 176
Deleuze, Gilles and Parnet, Claire
   Deleuze and Parnet, *Abécédaire* 171–2, 175
   Deleuze and Parnet, *Dialogues* 49–50, 171–2
   see also Parnet, Claire
delirium 78–9, 85, 103, 136
   neurotic delirium 78, 80–1, 86
   schizophrenic delirium 78
Denari, Neil 5, 64
Derrida, Jacques 4–5, 13, 39, 97–8
desert islands *see* islands
desire 26, 31, 45, 51–2, 55–6, 67–9, 71, 79, 81–2, 100–4, 107–9, 111–14, 116, 118, 122–3, 133, 145, 158, 165
   desiring machines 54, 70, 80, 83, 144
   desiring-production 31, 49, 55, 144
deterritorialization 30–1, 34, 50, 136, 174–5
Detroit-Projekt 101, 104
difference 38, 53, 79, 82–3, 86, 93, 107, 145–6, 172
   'to' or 'from' 39–40
   'in and of itself' 39, 79, 86, 123
digital turn 6, 13, 19–22, 63, *see also* parametricism
disciplinarity 5, 8, 11, 13, 19, 22, 25, 49, 52, 75, 83, 87, 89–90, 93, 109, 112–14, 137–9, 144, 158, *see also* interdisciplinarity

Diller, Elizabeth 5, 7, 84–6, 112–13, *see also* Scofidio, Ricardo
Dogs *see* animals
Dostoyevsky, Fyodor 87–8
double-bind 98, 100–1, 103–4, 128
drawing 16, 31–4, 37–9, 41–4, 67–8, 98, 134, 136, 143–4, 148–50, 166, 173, 177
   drawing as materialism 134, 165, 173
   drawing as representation 38–9, 136
   drawing surface 42, 44, 143–4, 148–50

Earth 16, 27–34, 37–8, 83, 101–2, 137–8, 143, 154–6, 158, 172–3, 176–7
eating 67–8, 70, 72–3, 156, *see also* consumption
ecologies 2, 7–8, 14, 16, 18, 30–1, 69, 72, 100, 134, 137
Eisenman, Peter 4–5, 13, 25
Embryologic Houses 13, 19–23
Empire State building 52–3
empiricism 87, 89–92, *see also* radical empiricism
Engels, Fredrich 91, 144
enunciation 107, 134
Erewhon 94, 198 n38, *see also* Butler, Samuel
eros 1, 38, 173, 177
escape 30, 83, 89–90, 104, 107, 110, 12–14, 116–18, 126–7, 129, 155–6, 174–5
ethics 2, 89, 132, 136
ethico-aesthetics 70, 131, 135–7
extensity 1
exteriority 125, 173, 175, *see also* interiority; outside

faces 88, 125, 161–4, 166–9
faciality 164, 168
fantasy 38, 44, 54–5
Farrell, Yvonne 115–16
fascism 78, 82, 89, 109, 116, 165–6
favela 1, 167–9, 214 n49, *see also* Morro da Providência
feelings 49, 54, 68, 135, 155, 164, 173–5
Feher, Michel 3, 4, 19
La fémis 87–92
fetish 27
   commodity fetishism 144
   miraculating fetishistic machine 144, 149
   religious fetish 144

228 Index

fish *see* animals
Flagrant Délit 51–6
Flaubert, Gustave 159
flesh *see* body
flies *see* animals
flow 7, 21, 26–8, 53, 64, 71, 73, 78, 80, 92, 100, 111, 114, 116, 122–5, 135, 144
fold 3, 5–6, 13–23, 32–3
    folding in architecture 6, 13–14, 17, 19–22
    folded mixtures 22
    perplication 13, 16
    see also Deleuze, *The Fold*
Footprint (the journal) 8
force 21–2, 32–4, 37–8, 41, 44, 49–51, 53, 56, 63–4, 70, 74, 86, 91–2, 100, 108–11, 125, 127–9, 136, 148, 154, 156–7, 159, 165, 169, 172, 175–6
    germinal forces 37
form 2, 6, 14, 17, 21–2, 31–2, 34, 43, 62–4, 72–4, 89, 91, 108, 111, 116, 124–5, 128, 132, 135, 139, 149, 154–7, 159, 163–7, 169, 172, 177, *see* also informe
Forty, Adrian 103
Foster, Hal 3, 34
Foucault, Michel 4, 47–52, 54–5, 71, 74, 81–2, 116
    Foucault, 'Of Other Spaces' 47–50
    Foucault, 'Preface' to *Anti-Oedipus* 71, 81
    see also repressive hypothesis
frame 37–8, 43–5, 55
Frichot, Hélène, 7–8
Freud, Sigmund 26, 30–1, 37–40, 50, 54–5, 68, 70–1, 74, 79–83, 108–9, 114, 117–18, 134–5, *see* also castration anxiety, Oedipal theory, transference
Fuller, John Frederick Charles 'Boney' 121
function 2, 4, 17, 34, 41–2, 61, 63, 80, 109–10, 117–18, 125, 127–8, 172, 176

Gehry, Frank O. 19, 34
Genosko, Gary 70
geography 4, 27, 29, 31, 33, 43, 47, 60, 71, 73, 78, 100–2, 108, 124, 137, 139, 154

geo-historic real 1, 8, 27, 91–2, 126
geology 31–3, 59, 65, 70, 72–3, 100–1, 154
geophilosophy 27, 30–1, 154
germinal forces *see* force
Giacobetti, Francis 162
Giedion, Sigfried 42, 64
glory hole 112, 117, *see* also cruising
Gothic 73–4, 124, 128, 177, 213 n26
Gothic line 177
graft 83, 135–7, 139
Grosz, Elizabeth 5–6, 102
Guattari, Félix
    Guattari, *Chaosmosis* 132–3, 135–7
    Guattari, *Machinic Eros* 1
    Guattari, *Molecular Revolution* 68–70
    Guattari, *Schizoanalytic Cartographies* 81, 157
Guattari, Félix and Rolnik, Seuly, *Molecular Revolution in Brazil* 214 n49

Haag Bletter, Rosemarie 4
Hadid, Zaha 5, 31–5, 177, *see* also Zaha Hadid Architects (ZHA)
hands *see* organs
'Hangar 12' 121–3
Harvey, David 30
Hays, K. Michael 6, 26
heads *see* organs
Heatherwick, Thomas 128
Heatherwick Studio 126–7, 129
Herzog, Jacques 5
heterogeneity 21, 55, 80, 135, 155–8
heterogenesis 135–6
heterotopia *see* other spaces
history 4, 28–31, 47, 54, 77–8, 82, 90, 124–6
    history of architecture 21, 25–6, 57, 64, 71, 103
    history of philosophy 39, 90
Ho, Tao 5
Holl, Steven 5
Holland, Eugene 30, 204 n22
Hong Kong 28, 31–4
House of Lords 131, *see* also British Houses of Parliament
hylomorphism 164–5

identity 20, 29, 38–40, 44, 74, 86, 93, 98, 112, 117–18, 128, 131–2, 135, 163–4, 167, 171–3, 175

informe 17, 21
Ingraham, Catherine 5, 179 n3
inorganic life 15–17, 21–3, 148, 155, 213 n45
interdisciplinarity 22, *see also* disciplinarity
interiority 124–5, 127, 164, 175, *see also* exteriority; outside
intermingling 7, 70-1, 74
intensity 1, 23, 27–31, 37, 50–1, 54–5, 77–8, 110–11, 116–18, 124, 148, 153, 157–8, 164, 172–3, 175, 177, 213 n45
invagination 97–8, 102–3
Ishiyama, Osamu 5
islands 28–9, 31, 33, 41, 100–3, 112, 118, 126, 131–3, 148–9
   continental islands 100
   desert islands 100–3
   oceanic islands 100–2
Isozaki, Arata 5

James-Lange theory of emotion 174
James, William 91, 174
Jameson, Fredric 5, 109, 117
Jencks, Charles 55–6
Jobst, Marko 7
Johnson, Phillip 26, 33
Joyce, James 38, 40–2, 44, 74
JR 167–9

Kant, Immanuel 39, 90, 154–5
Karatani, Kojin 5
Kennedy, Alicia 6
Keysar, Hagit 139
Killing, Alison 137–9
Killing Architects 137
Kipnis, Jeffrey 26
Klein, Melanie 134
Koolhaas, Rem 4–5, 51, 53–5
Krauss, Rosalind 5, 97
Kurosawa, Akira 87–8
Kwinter, Sanford 3–4, 19
Kyu Huga Bettei 157

La Borde, the psychiatric clinic 1, 69, 79, 133
labyrinth 116–9
Lacan, Jacques 29, 134, 144
Lacaton and Vassal 92–4, 137

landscape 2, 21, 27, 31, 33–4, 37–8, 43, 60, 62, 71–2, 74, 102, 104, 133, 136, 143–4, 148, 158–9, 165, 167–8, 176
Lapoujade, David 91
Leclercle, Jean-Jacques 5, 7, 64, 122–3
Le Corbusier 63, 88–9, 97–100, 199 n6
Lefaivre, Liane 98
Leibniz, Gottfried Wilhelm 3, 6, 13–19, 21–3, 57, 172
Lesbos 131–2, 135
Libeskind, Daniel 4–5
libido 29–31
lightning 153, 160, 171–2, 175–8
Lightning Farm 176–8
Lightning Ridge 153–4
line of flight 124, 156, *see also* escape
Livesey, Graham 7
lobsters *see* animals
logic of sense 40–2, 44, *see also* Deleuze, *Logic of Sense*
logocentrism 39, 42, *see also* anti-logos
London 51, 72, 107, 117–18, 126, 132, 146, 158
Longhouse Roof Garden 148–51
Lotringer, Sylvère 3–4, 9
love 25, 29, 40, 49–56, 68, 81–2, 111, 116, 135–6, 147–8, 153, 158, 160, 175, 189 n24
Lynn, Greg 5–6, 13, 19–23, 25–6, 44

machines 2, 31, 54, 60–5, 70–1, 80–1, 83, 85, 94, 111, 116, 122, 131–2, 135–6, 144, 146, 148–50, 176–7
   architecture as machine 62–5, 97–8, 113, 131–2, 176–7
   art as machine 60–2
   see also desiring machines, war machines
machinic 1–2, 61–2, 80, 134–5, 144–6, 162
   machinic phylum 80, 123–4, 166, 204 n26
macropolitics 107–14, 116, 165, 202 n22
magic capture *see* capture
Maisonnier, André 98–9
Massumi, Brian 4–5, 122, 157, 166
Marx, Karl 30–1, 71, 74, 79–82, 108–9, 114, 147
matter 2–3, 13–15, 17, 21–2, 80, 89, 91, 110, 128, 154–6, 158, 164–6, 169, 172

continuous variation of matter 17, 22
matters of fact 163–4, 167
materialism (and new materialism) 2, 7, 91, 162–5
McNamara, Shelley 115–16
meat *see* body
Melville, Herman 116
Merleau-Ponty, Maurice 98, 102
metabolism 157, 159
Migayrou, Frédéric 77–9, 86
milieu 4–6, 90, 124, 157, 175
miraculating fetishistic machine *see* fetish
modernity 26, 53, 92
modernism 26, 33, 42, 52, 64, 89, 92, 97–8, 109
Modulor 97–9, 102
Modulorbeat 101–5
molarity 107–10, 112–14, 117, 123, 156, 176
molecularity 81, 107, 110–11, 116–18, 155–7, 160, 165, 172
monadology 14–17
  monads 14–5, 17, 19–20
Moneo, Rafael 5
monkeys *see* animals
Morro da Providência 167–9
mouth *see* organs
Mozart, Wolfgang Amadeus 157–8, 160
micropolitics 107, 111–12, 115–18
multiplicities 15, 19, 40–1, 43, 61, 63, 69, 73, 91, 110, 118, 122, 135, 156, 166, 173
Mumford, Lewis 65
Muuratsalo Summer House 41

neurosis 26, 28, 50, 77–8, 80–1, 86
New York 3–4, 6, 49, 51–5, 89, 138
Nietzsche, Friedrich 41–2, 100, 154–6
nomadism 17, 122, 124
nonsense 42, 68, 70, 194 n10, *see* also sense
Nouvel, Jean 5

oceanic islands *see* islands
object 3, 17, 22, 28, 41, 43–4, 50, 53–4, 62, 64, 70, 73, 77, 81, 88, 91, 93–4, 98, 107–8, 132, 134–5, 137, 145, 154–7, 159, 164, 167, 177
  epiphoric object 98, 103
  see also partial objects

objectile 3, 44–5, *see* also subjectile
Oedipal theory 25–6, 28, 34, 68–70, 80, 91, 104, 122, 135, 173
Oedipus 25–7, 29, 39–40, 79, 82–3, 104, 122, 126
Office of Metropolitan Architecture (OMA) 51, 55
Oliver, Vaughan 146–50
One Man Sauna 101–5
organic life 157, 21–3, 42, 110, 133, 146, 148, 155, 191 n28, 204 n26
organisms 16, 22, 81, 110, 116–18, 155, 157, 173, 213 n45
organs 29, 61–2, 70, 83–4, 86, 110–11, 116–18, 143, 148, 154, 164–5, 168–9, 173
  anus 83, 98, 110
  bone 161–4, 166–7
  hands 33, 82, 121, 128
  heads 52, 82, 97, 143, 163–4, 166–9
  hearts 1, 68, 73, 101, 127, 175
  mouth 67–68, 70–1, 73, 83, 110, 117, 157
  tongue 20, 29, 98, 100, 110, 134
  other organs 29, 40, 70, 82, 98, 111, 117, 145
O'Sullivan, Simon 16
other spaces 47–8, 50, *see* also Foucault, 'Of Other Spaces'
Oury, Jean 69, *see* also La Borde, transferential constellation
outside 4, 6, 16, 22, 26–7, 34, 37–8, 43, 44, 77, 81, 85, 93, 102–3, 112, 125–8, 132, 134, 137, 157, 165, 175, 204 n33

packs 124, 174, 177, *see* also swarms
Palacio de Congressos 158–60
Palais de Tokyo 87–9, 92–4
Pankow, Gisela 81, 83, 133–5
paralogism of displacement 103–4, *see* also double bind
parametricism 13, 22, 44
Parnet, Claire 49–50, 54, 171–4, *see* also Deleuze, Gilles and Parnet, Claire
Paris 1–2, 60, 68, 87–9, 94, 100, 112, 168, 171
partial objects 63–4, 72, 74, 81, 84, 110, 134–5, 194 n49

passion 50–2, 55, 67–8, 71, 74–5, 111, 133, 167, 189 n24, *see* also sympathies
perplication *see* fold
perversion 38, 40, 42–4, 50, 56, 81, 83, 86, 145
photomechanical transfer (PMT) 146, 148, 150
phyla *see* machinic phylum
Pixies 146–7, 150
political philosophy 30, 70, 79–80, 95, 107, 122–3, 125–6, 154, 165, 169, 203 n12, *see* also macropolitics, micropolitics
politics 2–3, 8, 30, 40, 67, 70, 82, 84, 94–5, 107–18, 123, 128–9, 131–3, 135–7, 165, 169, 202 n22
poststructuralism 5, 39, 64
Preciado, Paul B. 131–3, 135
predication 39–43, 64, 110, 145
prehension 18–19, 21–2, 50
Prigogene, Ilya 155
primitive accumulation 30
Pritzker prize 137
Prix, Wolf 5
Proust, Marcel 59–64, 70, 74
psy sciences, 26, 29, 55, 68, 69–71, 79–83, 104, 114, 118, 122, 133–5, 144, 167, 174
    psychiatry 69–70, 133–4, 143
    psychoanalysis 26, 29, 55, 68, 69–71, 79–83, 104, 114, 118, 122, 133–4, 144
    psychology 39, 48, 55, 91, 174
Pulitzer prize 137

Querrien, Anne 4, 124, 127–8

radical empiricism 91
Radman, Andrej 8
Rajchman, John 3, 6, 22
Rashid, Hani 5
Reich, Wilhelm 15, 80
Reiser, Jesse 5
Renoir, Pierre-Auguste 59–60, 62–3
representation 6, 32, 38–41, 43–5, 55, 60, 62–3, 90, 116, 129, 143–4, 146, 149, 156, 164–5, 169, *see* also sub-representational
repressive hypothesis 82, 113

resistance 4, 80, 82, 102, 104, 114, 116, 124–6, 136, 202 n22
reterritorialization 34, 133
30 Rockefeller Plaza (RCA building) 52–3
Rolnok, Rachel 168
Rolnik, Seuly 214 n49
Ruskin, John 67–8, 71–5
    Ruskin, *Stones of Venice* 67, 72
    Ruskin, 'Verona and Its Rivers' 68, 72–3
Russell, Bertrand 15

San Carlo alle Quattro Fontane 16–18, 22, *see* also Baroque architecture
Sand, George 159
schizo culture 3, 9, 27, 31, 78, 81, 122
schizoanalysis 3, 70, 77–83, 86
Schumacher, Patrik 33
Scofidio, Ricardo 77, 84–6, 112–13
Selgas, José 158
SelgasCano 158–60
semiotext(e) 3, 5, 9
sense 37–8, 40–5, *see* also logic of sense, nonsense
Serpentine pavilion 158
Serralta, Justino 98–9
Serres, Michel 28
sex 26, 38, 43–4, 52, 54–5, 71, 74, 80–2, 107, 112–14, 117, 131–2, 135, 148, 173–4
    sex and the social 71, 74, 80–2
    sexual expression 82, 86, 107, 111–12, 114, 117, 173
    sexual fetish *see* fetish
signification 3, 41, 49, 95, 116, 136, 146, 164, 169, 173–5
silo 122, 125–9
Simondon, Gilbert 154–5, 165, 210 n9
singularity 3, 172
Smith, Daniel W. 166
Sohn, Heidi 7
Solà-Morales, Ignasi de 5
space 17, 20, 22, 33–4, 37–8, 40, 47–53, 55, 68–9, 85–6, 88, 90, 93, 97, 102, 110, 112–13, 115–16, 123–4, 127–8, 132–4, 149, 157, 173
    smooth space 5, 123–4, 128–9
    striated space 5, 123–4
    see also other spaces

spiders *see* animals
smooth space *see* space
striated space *see* space
Speaks, Michael 3, 6
Spencer, Douglas 7
Spiller, Neil 148–51
Spinoza, Baruch 173–6
State (the) 123–5, 127–8
    nation states 60, 83, 89, 122, 126–7
Stengers, Isabelle 103, 155
stone 4, 19, 67–75, 80–1, 83, 89, 92–3,
    153–4, 159–60, 162, 168
    stone sucking 70, 81, 83
    touchstones 67, 72, 193 n36
Stoner, Jill 7
strange contraptions 132–3, 135, 137
structure (architecture) 4, 16–17, 32, 34,
    52, 63–4, 84–5, 89, 92, 102, 112,
    126, 128, 131–2, 138, 149, 159, 168,
    176
structure (philosophy) 7, 26, 43–4, 49, 61,
    64, 70, 80–1, 91, 94–5, 100, 108,
    110, 114, 122, 141, 145, 149, 156–7
style 57, 88–90, 93, 109, 131, 138, 156, 177
schizo culture 3, 9, 27, 31, 78, 81, 122
subjectile 44, *see also* objectile
subjectivity 2, 4, 7, 16, 26–7, 29, 103–4,
    132–6, 145, 164, 169, 173
sub-representational 144, 147
surface 14, 20–2, 32, 42–4, 85, 92, 94,
    112–3, 143–6, 148–50, 159, 164,
    168–9
    'thickness' of the surface 143, 149–50
swarms 15–8, 22–3, 78, 84–5, 143–5, *see
    also* packs
Sylvester, David 161, 164, 166
sympathies 11, 13, 15, 19, 38, 48–56, 89
syntheses 80, 143–6, 149
    conjunctive syntheses 145–6
    connective syntheses 135, 145
    disjunctive syntheses 145–7

Tafuri, Manfredo 141
Taut, Bruno 157–8
territory 27–9, 31–2, 86, 176
Teysott, Georges 84–5
theology 30, 144, 154
thickness of the surface *see* surface

Thompson, D'Arcy Wentworth 21
Thrift, Nigel 173
tools 31, 49, 75, 97–8, 113, 121–2, 124,
    128, 146–7, 177, *see also* weapons
topology 21, 128, 162
touchstones *see* stone
traits 8, 17, 122, 124, 166–8
    animal traits 166–7
    traits of expression 122, 128, 165
transcendental empiricism 89–92
transcendental idealism 90
transference 68–71, 74, 117, 135, 158, 166
transferential constellation 69
transversality 68–75, 132, 136, 139, 156,
    158, 160
typology 48, 109, 138
Tzonis, Alexander 98

universals 37, 90, 97–8, 104, 172
universes 11, 14–15, 28–9, 59–60, 62,
    80–1, 133–5
univocity 154, 156
utopia *see* other spaces
Uyghur 137, 139

Vassal, Jean-Phillippe *see* Lacaton and
    Vassal
van Berkel, Ben 5–6
Venice 64, 67, 72–4, 112, 118
Venice Architecture Biennale 64, 112,
    115–16
Verona 67–8, 72–5
    Verona Arena 73–5
Vidler, Anthony 5, 85
Virilio, Paul 4, 6, 125
virtual cosmic continuum *see* cosmic
Vitruvius 98, 184 n17
Voltaire 15
Vriesendorp, Madelon 51–6

Wang, Yaohua 63–5
war 64, 73, 77–8, 89, 121, 123–4, 126,
    137–8, 175–6
war machines 51, 83, 121–8, 203 n1
wasps *see* animals
weapons 121–2, 124, 175–6, *see also* tools
Whitehead, Alfred North 14–15, 18–19,
    90, 182 n28

Wigley, Mark 109, 113
Wölfli, Adolf 143–4
Worringer, Wilhelm 124, 213–14 n45, *see also* Gothic line
Woods, Lebbeus 5, 64, 148, 177

Xinjiang 137–8, 207 n51

Zaera-Polo, Alejandro 5
Zaha Hadid Architects (ZHA) 33
Zeitlian, Hraztan 5
Zeitz MOCAA 126–9
zigzag 171–2, 174, 177
Zone (publications) 3–6, 19

www.ingramcontent.com/pod-product-compliance
Lightning Source LLC
Chambersburg PA
CBHW071826300426
44116CB00009B/1461